The Life of Richard
Waldo Sibthorp

for Anne

The Life of Richard Waldo Sibthorp

Evangelical, Catholic and Ritual Revivalism
in the Nineteenth-Century Church

Michael Trott

sussex
ACADEMIC
PRESS

BRIGHTON • PORTLAND

2 4 6 8 10 9 7 5 3 1

First published 2005
in Great Britain by
SUSSEX ACADEMIC PRESS
PO Box 2950
Brighton BN2 5SP

and in the United States of America by
SUSSEX ACADEMIC PRESS
5824 N.E. Hassalo St.
Portland, Oregon 97213–3644

British Library Cataloguing in Publication Data
A CIP catalogue record for this book is available from the British Library.

Library of Congress Cataloging-in-Publication Data
Trott, Michael.
    The life of Richard Waldo Sibthorp : evangelical, Catholic, and
    ritual revivalism in the nineteenth-century church / Michael Trott.
    p. cm.
    Includes bibliographical references and index.
    ISBN 1-84519-062-9 (hardcover : alk. paper)
    1. Sibthorp, Richard Waldo, 1792–1879. 2. Catholic Church—
    England—Clergy—Biography. 3. Catholic converts—England—
    Biography. I. Title.
    BX4705.S62T76 2005
    282'.092—dc22
                                                            2004019281
                                                            CIP

Typeset and designed by G&G Editorial, Brighton
Printed by The Cromwell Press, Trowbridge, Wiltshire
This book is printed on acid-free paper.

CONTENTS

PREFACE

Richard Sibthorp* was unfortunate in his relatives. Humphrey, his paternal grandfather, Sherardian professor at Oxford between 1747 and 1784 was, during a period of general academic somnolence, a by-word for indolence. Richard's brother was even more notorious. Charles de Laet Waldo Sibthorp, elected member for Lincoln in 1826 was still its representative in 1855, the year of his death. He was Parliament's licensed jester, an arch reactionary who hated railways, foreigners, and the Crystal Palace. Few issues of *Punch* went by without a reference to his latest eccentricity, and the magazine's cartoonists delighted in his unconventional appearance. And Richard too, has come down to posterity as a figure of fun; a rather charming eccentric, undoubtedly sincere, but weak-minded and of little significance to the history of the Church in the nineteenth century.

For a brief period following his conversion to Catholicism in 1841, Sibthorp's name was rarely out of the newspapers. But it was his fleeing back to the Church of England just two years later, claiming that Rome was the Harlot of Revelation while, at the same time, confiding to Catholic friends 'he loved her still,' that permanently established his reputation as a crackpot. The only full biography, written by his friend and Lincoln curate, John Fowler, was published a year after his death. It took as its theme 'lives of pathetic failure are ofttimes most instructive' and although generally sympathetic its author never denies that his subject's 'judgment was strangely fitful and uncertain'. The last century saw three short studies, which all endorsed this received opinion. R. D. Middleton's 1936 essay (in *Magdalen Studies*) followed much the same lines as Fowler.

---

* Because Sibthorp's name was so often incorrectly written as Sibthorpe no attention is drawn to this in what follows. For those unused to writing the name, the temptation to add an e can be almost irresistible! Sibthorp's frequent underlinings are italicised in the extracts from his letters.

Christopher Sykes's highly readable 1953 monograph (in *Two Studies in Virtue*) – written from a Roman Catholic standpoint, as a counterweight to the Anglican bias of the former works – rather emphasised the theme of eccentricity and Michael Clifton's 1998 study (in *A Victorian Convert Quintet*) was equally unsympathetic.

In what follows it is argued that Richard Sibthorp suffered unfairly, although quite predictably, at the hands of contemporary commentators and that his biographers have too readily reflected their bewilderment. Examined more closely, his life raises important questions regarding the nature of religious authority. Far from being weak-minded, he accepted ridicule as the cost of remaining loyal to dearly held beliefs. Although Sibthorp must remain a minor player in the history of the nineteenth-century Church, his preaching was widely influential and the widespread fascination with his erratic pilgrimage contributed both to challenging and ultimately reinforcing historical prejudices.

In adolescence, Sibthorp started out on a life-long search for sanctity, a quest inspired by the piety of his tutor, an émigré priest. Believing that holiness was to be found only in Roman Catholicism, as an undergraduate at Magdalen College he was narrowly prevented from converting. This is well known. What has been left largely unexplained is how, just four years later, he had become a fervent gospel preacher, a 'second George Whitefield.' This study argues that he found the holiness he sought among the Methodists of Lincolnshire, whose Arminian theology he fully embraced. By the time of his Anglican ordination in 1815, his religious *psyche* was established, founded on a few key beliefs: that true religion must lead to holiness, that the bible alone comprises the supreme source of religious authority, and that the office of the Holy Spirit is to guide each humble believer into the true meaning of the Word. Unfortunately, in the world that Sibthorp undertook to serve, holy men disagreed about the interpretation of Scripture, some who claimed to reverence it led lives of deceit and hypocrisy, and even the humblest and most earnest enquirer could be left unclear as to the path of obedience. The great tragedy of Sibthorp's life was that by upbringing and personality he was unable to bow to any external authority – institution, individual, or system – that might have provided him with a path through these perplexities. He bowed only to God, and waited on the Spirit's voice to lead him into the assurance he sought.

As a young man, Sibthorp conformed despite seeing holiness in Rome, because he believed Scripture condemned her as Antichrist. He became an Evangelical through Methodism, because the Methodists were holy, and because Arminianism seemed more conducive to holiness than theories of imputed righteousness. At length, however, he became disillusioned with Evangelicalism: his standards were high, and he found it hard to reconcile its protestations regarding the bible with the divisions it generated and the hypocrisies he detected in it. For a while, as he tried to integrate his religious yearnings with an adequate explanation of Scripture, he wandered in theological by-paths, until Samuel Wilberforce claimed him for the High Church. It was Sibthorp's need to reconcile sacramental teachings with the Scriptures that led him to typological explanations of the Church, and it was faithfulness to this theory of interpretation that drew him to ritualism and then into the Church of Rome.

Thus, in a strange reversal, the bible made him a Catholic, a path that was smoothed because he recalled so well the quiet holiness of Lincolnshire Catholics thirty years before. Tragically, he soon discovered that either his memory was at fault, or that the world had changed. Expecting devotions that would at last fulfil his spiritual yearnings, he found rather a 'folk religion,' encouraged at the highest level, that he could not reconcile with biblical faith. Struggling with the perplexity this caused he was led to consider afresh those texts that prophesied that the bride of Christ would fall into idolatry. What he had once believed about the imminent judgement coming upon this apostate Church again filled his thoughts. Fearful obedience to Scripture tore him from Rome after only months as her priest. The remainder of his life was touched with sadness as he tried to clarify what the prophecies really meant and as he searched for truth and sanctity in a world of human imperfection. It was deepening unhappiness that carried him back, at the age of seventy-two, into the Roman priesthood, in the hope that she at last might resolve his spiritual perplexity. It was not to be, and long before his death, fourteen years later, he had become a man apart who no longer 'believed in Churches.'

This present study attempts to demonstrate that despite his weaknesses, Sibthorp's life was touched with nobility. He was a man of contradictions; stubborn, but sometimes too easily led; timid, but also at times courageous; short-sighted and erratic, but willing to live for two decades as a humble penitent. Above all, he sought sanctity and his ambition to serve God in accordance with such light as he possessed never wavered. In great old age he worked hard to inspire fellow Catholics with his own love for the bible, and his posthumous offering, a book of daily meditations on the Scriptures, received Bishop Bagshawe's somewhat uncertain *imprimatur*. It was a neglected gift. Perhaps understandably, for those who knew the author best surely wondered if he had himself ever found the rest and spiritual fulfilment that his little studies promised the faithful believer. Some indeed knew that in his last months Sibthorp had struggled desperately to gain an assurance of salvation, still listening for the inner voice that had been such a fitful and uncertain guide.

I would like to thank Professor McClelland for encouraging me to study such a fascinating and comparatively neglected figure and for his unfailing kindness and support. I am particularly grateful for his patience in responding to my questions and willingness to transcribe – sometimes at great length – relevant material that he had come across. I also owe a debt of gratitude to Dr. Dennis Mills, whose father worked on the Sibthorp estate and whose knowledge of the family and its history is unsurpassed. He and his wife were unstinting in sharing with me the information they had gained from their researches. I should not have thought of following-up the fascinating lives of Sibthorp's eccentric relations if it had not been for them.

I would also like to acknowledge the kindness and hospitality of Miss Stephanie Cholmeley, a direct descendant of Richard Sibthorp's paternal aunt, Sarah Sibthorp. At her home on Bodmin Moor she allowed me free access to the large collection of family papers assembled by her father, Guy Hargeaves Cholmeley. Of the Librarians and Archivists who have been so helpful it is perhaps invidious to mention one in particular, but I would especially like to thank Dr. Peter Nockles at the John Rylands Library who encouraged me to believe that there were many Catholics interested in Sibthorp's strange career. To Anthony Cornwell, who spent many hours reading the text and checking references, I am particularly grateful.

'Love never ends.' For my wife who has not only accepted a home littered with lever arch files and musty volumes, but has lived with Richard Sibthorp as well as me, there must be the greatest praise of all.

ILLUSTRATIONS

Jacket illustration: Father Richard Sibthorp aged 80. Portrait in the chapel of St. Anne's Bede Houses, Lincoln.

Illustrations (pages 116 to 127)

The author and publisher acknowledge with thanks permission to reproduce the following:

Lincoln Library, for 3, 6 and 13: From the Local Studies Collection, Lincoln Central Library, by courtesy of Lincolnshire County Council, Education and Cultural Services Directorate.

The Life of Richard Waldo Sibthorp

Evangelical, Catholic and Ritual Revivalism
in the Nineteenth-Century Church

I

THE SIBTHORPS OF CANWICK

In the eighteenth century, identifying responsibility for the cure of souls could be a complicated business. Richard Sibthorp, the seventh and last child of a wealthy landowner, was privately baptised at his home, Canwick Hall, just outside the city of Lincoln, on 4 November 1792, exactly a month after his birth. In the absence of the vicar of Canwick, the ceremony was undertaken by his curate, Francis Swan, a member of a prominent local family of surgeons and clerics.[1] As incumbent of two city churches and two parishes near Boston, Swan had many other pastoral responsibilities. Before his death in 1845, aged ninety-two, he had acquired more livings, but had the misfortune to live on into an age when views on the clerical vocation had changed, even in a backwater like Lincoln. The tide had begun to turn long before. On Sunday, 17 August 1817, the clerk of the city church of St. Peter-at-Arches was forced to dismiss the assembled congregation because Swan had failed to arrange for a celebrant. The next day, one of his flock wrote to the *Lincoln Mercury*, complaining that although the rector had an income of not less than £2,000 a year, he was too selfish to pay a curate.[2]

Not long after this scandal the vicar of Canwick died, and in May 1818 the Mercers' Company, as patrons, met to elect his successor. There were two candidates, both young men, George Quilter and Richard Sibthorp. A letter had been received from the parishioners in favour of Richard, and his widowed mother was anxious for her favourite son's success. The Mercers however, chose Quilter.[3] It was a wise decision. He gave the parish 53 years of conscientious service; a popular and caring pastor, with a large family. Richard himself never married and it is likely that if he had been successful he would not have stayed long, for he never really settled anywhere. Nevertheless, Canwick remained important to him. Throughout a wandering life, birthplace and family gave him a position and an identity. He felt an attachment to Lincoln, and often returned. But he was never comfortable there: perhaps he was too well known, or maybe the familiar scenes re-awakened uneasy thoughts? For it was in this ancient city that his strange personality was shaped, and from here he set out upon the journey of spiritual discovery that was his life.

An Eighteenth-Century Family

According to Christopher Sykes, Richard was born into 'a rich and ancient Lincolnshire family noted for its rigid Protestantism.'[4] This must be qualified; the Sibthorps were not ancient, save in the sense that every family is. Indeed, in 1792 they were almost *arrivistes*. During the latter part of the previous century, Gervase Sibthorp – having migrated to Lincoln from the Nottinghamshire village where his ancestors had been yeoman farmers – married into wealth and set up as a merchant.[5] His affairs prospered, and his son, John, inheriting his father's shrewdness, continued to do well, becoming one of the city's MPs. In 1702, he married Mary Browne, the daughter of a considerable landowner; it was a prudent connection, and there were to be other such marriages that helped to raise the Sibthorps into the ranks of the 'greater gentry.'[6] He died in 1718, but his widow 'managed by skilful contrivance to save sufficient out of her income to buy an estate.'[7] She bought land in north Lincolnshire and in 1730 acquired from a Roman Catholic family the estate of Canwick, situated to the south of the city, across the valley of the Witham, with an impressive view of the Minster.

Mary's only brother died childless leaving the bulk of his considerable property to her eldest son Coningsby. He inherited land in Lincolnshire and Nottinghamshire as well as a house in North Mymms called *Skimpans*, where Richard's sister and five brothers would be born. While Coningsby remained a bachelor, his brother Humphrey married twice: first to Sarah Waldo, the daughter and heiress of a wealthy London livery-man, and four years after her death, in 1753 to Elizabeth Gibbs, who brought with her the estate of Instow in Devon. Her husband, who outlived her, was single-minded in his ambition to establish the wealth and standing of his descendants. He died at Instow, where the tablet his son placed in the parish church neatly summarises the man:

> At the Charterhouse he imbibed with the rudiments of early education a taste for literature, which was afterwards improved with every advantage assiduous application in the University of Oxford could afford. There elected Demy, and successively Fellow, of Magdalen College, he devoted himself with unremitting ardour and attention to the great study of medicine, and more particularly to botanical pursuits . . . He was the favourite pupil of the great Dillenius, the Professor of Botany in the University, whom by a preference to many competitors he succeeded in the honours of the Professorial chair. He was learned, religious, temperate, continually refusing himself the enjoyments which he had discovered a pleasure in extending to others. He had a heart to feel distress, and his frugal habits gave him in the fortune he possessed the power to relieve it, and while with just severity he reproved the idle and profligate, the unfortunate he frequently assisted and always consoled. His learning was extensive, his knowledge of men and manners uncommon, and his many friends enjoyed the

advantage of both. Of his frugality, his descendants feel the benefit. The blessings that attend temperance and religion were his own. Habitual self-denial gave
tone and vigour to a constitution naturally delicate and prolonged his life,
burdened with few infirmities, to an extent of days which is the lot of few.
Accustomed to contemplate death as a refuge from the cares of human life, in
the assurance of a blessed immortality through the mediation of our common
Saviour, he met it with serenity on the seventeenth day of August 1797, in the
86th year of his age . . .[8]

The old man's dynastic ambitions determined his attitude to the
marriage plans of his second son, Richard's father, also named
Humphrey, who in 1768, aged 24, formed a connection with a Miss F.
She possessed a fortune of £3000, but the professor, doubting the standing
of her family, threatened disinheritance if the matter was pursued.[9] Eight
years later Humphrey proposed to Susannah Ellison, whose father had
begun to establish one of the wealthiest families in Lincolnshire. The
grand source of the Ellison riches was their acquisition from Lincoln City
Council in 1740 of the lease of the Fossdyke Navigation, the ancient canal
connecting Lincoln to the Trent. It proved a spectacularly successful
investment as industrialisation began to increase the demand for
Lincolnshire agricultural produce.[10] In 1775, Richard Ellison, 'already a
man of wealth and considerable local influence', went on to found, along
with Abel Smith, Lincoln's first bank.[11] Yet, Professor Sibthorp was
unsure even of Miss Ellison's suitability and on 5 December 1776
Humphrey's half-brother John[12] wrote from Lincoln College to advise him
of their father's reaction. 'I suppose his sentiments concerning Miss
Ellison will reach you before this arrives, happy should I have been to
inform you that they are favourable to your wishes, but then neither
fortune nor family seem adequate to his expectation'.[13] Fortunately for
the finances of future generations, his objections were overcome; the
couple married the following year and went to live at *Skimpans*.[14]

Coningsby Sibthorp became High Sheriff of Lincolnshire, and represented the City in Parliament – with interruptions – from 1733 to 1768.[15]
His nephew, Richard's father, who became heir to the estate following the
premature death of an elder brother in 1766, wished for similar employment, and in the year of his marriage was returned as member for Boston,
and appointed Recorder of Lincoln. In 1782, after considerable local poli-
ticking, he was posted Colonel of the Royal South Lincolnshire Militia.
Thus by the year of Richard's birth, the respectability of his family seemed
secure. There were estates in five counties, and the promise of future
income as the pecuniary implications of dynastic alliances slowly
unwound. If the family could not be described as 'ancient', it was by now
well-established. It also had academic standing. Dr Humphrey Sibthorp
and his son, John, the only child of his second marriage, were in succession Sherardian Professors of Botany at Oxford University. As a scholar,

Humphrey has received a bad press. Professor from 1747 to 1784, Sir James Smith described him as 'an idle nonentity, who neglected his lectures and published nothing.'[16] However, the intellectual distinction of John Sibthorp was universally acknowledged. He travelled extensively in the pursuit of botanical specimens, exhausting his strength. 'No name has a fairer claim to botanical immortality, among the martyrs of the science.'[17] On his death, in 1796, he bequeathed part of an estate that he had purchased at South Leigh, Oxfordshire, to endow the Sibthorpian Chair of Rural Economy.

Colonel Humphrey shared this intellectual curiosity. Richard described him as a scholar, and the award of a DCL Degree (1777), a *penchant* for continental travel, and the eclectic nature of his library would appear to bear this out.[18] He was also a *connoisseur* and J. M. W. Turner painted at least one watercolour for him.[19] Something of his taste descended to his sons; both Richard and his elder brother, Charles, were great collectors.[20] In 1801, his first child, Mary Esther, married John Sibthorp's friend and botanical collaborator, John Hawkins of Trewithen in Cornwall. Hawkins became a fellow of the Royal Society, and his obituary notice in the *Gentleman's Magazine* (September 1841) spoke of him as, 'celebrated throughout Europe for his general knowledge on all subjects, his science, literature and travels.'[21] For Richard's generation, the Hawkins connection was a reminder of a scientific heritage almost entirely absent from nineteenth-century Canwick.[22]

As regards 'rigid Protestantism,' the family was indeed conventionally religious. Yet this too must be qualified, for a travel diary kept by John Sibthorp, Richard's great-grandfather, reveals an intriguing absence of prejudice. On May 6, 1699, visiting Keverin, near Mons, he wrote 'Here I had the honour to see ye Ar. Bishop of Cambray who received me very courteously. In all appearances hee is one of the finest Gentleman (*sic*) a man can see. Author of *Telemachus*.' This was Fénelon, whom Richard much admired. Ten days later he wrote, 'wee went to ye Spellicans an English convent where I saw my Lady Strafford and Mr Compton's daughter as also Mdm. Mildmay, Oxfordshire, Sister Constantine, who were all very civill to me. The Honble. Barbara Boyl Abbess but ill of ye Gout.' More conventionally, from Brussels he was favourably impressed with the Jesuit churches, filled with pictures of 'ye Fathers and ye Saints.'[23]

Colonel Humphrey possessed a similar openness. Relinquishing his parliamentary seat in 1784, he took to the life of a country gentleman, and as his family grew, moved to Canwick. He enjoyed foreign travel and in 1792 was in Germany. There he met an émigré priest whom he invited to become his children's French tutor. According to H. D. Beste, the Abbé Beaumont was 'formerly rector of the University of Caen, and appointed canon of the cathedral of Rouen. He had been about to take possession of his stall, when the order was issued, on account of the approach of the Duke of Brunswick, that every priest who should still refuse to take the oath prescribed by the civil constitution of the clergy should be banished from France within fifteen days.'[24] Brunswick was defeated and the Revolution saved at Valmy on 20 September; six months later England was at war with France, requiring Colonel Sibthorp to be with his regiment.

It is not known how long Beaumont lived at Canwick, but he was unlikely to have been there long after his appointment, in December 1793, as priest to the Lincoln Catholic Mission, following the death of the Jesuit, Fr. Richard Knight. During the War the Colonel was away with his regiment at various locations in the Midlands and on the East Coast, usually accompanied by his wife and youngest son. By 1797 they were at Norman Cross, near Peterborough, a large prisoner-of-war camp and barracks complex. In September the following year the regiment was ordered to Dublin, to assist in suppressing the Irish Rebellion. The Colonel's family remained behind at Colchester, where the Militia had lately been encamped. From there his eldest son Coningsby sent him a letter that hints at the priest's continuing influence. 'We all went to Halstead yesterday ... the country thereabouts is very beautiful. At Gosfield about two miles further is the seat of the Marquis of Buckingham and in a small house by the roadside there are about 20 nuns whom we visited and bought some trifling things of.' He ended with greetings from his mother, sister, and 'Dick.'[25] The nuns, Poor Clares who left France in 1795[26], had links with Beaumont. In 1816, E. J. Willson wrote that the Catholic church in Lincoln contained 'a beautiful painting of the "taking down from the cross" supposed to belong to the flemish school which was presented to the Chapel by the Rev. William Beaumont BD, professor of rhetoric and ex-rector of the University of Caen in Normandy and was brought into this country by the english (*sic*) nuns of Gravelines in France when expelled from thence at the time of the Revolution.'[27]

A Nineteenth-Century Family

If the Sibthorps felt unthreatened by Beaumont's religion, other influences were coming to bear. *The Lincoln Date Book* for 6 September 1798 reads 'Market Harborough, illuminated in honour of the arrival of the South Lincoln Militia, under the command of Col. Sibthorp, *en route* to Ireland.'[28] The regiment arrived after the Rebellion was over and its Colonel found time to sit for a portrait.[29] But although avoiding the conflict, he was unlikely to have been spared accounts of Roman Catholic atrocities: evidence of the deep passions that religion could generate.[30] His offer to extend his regiment's stay in Ireland, although declined, drew from the new viceroy, Lord Cornwallis, an effusive letter of gratitude.[31] Returning to England, the following summer he took his family to Instow, and at the end of the holiday, Richard was sent, just before his seventh birthday, to school at Eltham. In April 1800 the Colonel was returned unopposed as MP for Lincoln. When the war resumed he divided his time between the Militia encamped near Ipswich, and attendance at Parliament as a respected independent member courted by Canning.[32] In 1804, his regiment was ordered to Sandgate, near Folkestone, from where the French invasion preparations could clearly be seen.

For Mrs. Sibthorp, who now remained at Canwick, it was an anxious time. Two of her children were on active service and the delicate health of Coningsby who as heir remained at home, was also a concern. He never married, and died in 1822, at the age of 40. Writing to him after his graduation from Corpus Christi College, Oxford, in 1804, his father's formal style betrays some anxiety:

> 'You are now entering into another Habit of Life, far more active, far more perilous. In introducing you to it, Parental Fears and Hopes succeed by turns, changing in quick succession. May you resist every seduction from that honourable and dignified course, . . . knowing that you possess a sound and strong understanding if you shall chuse to make use of it, and not lean upon the crutch of others weaker than your own.'[33]

His brother next in age, Charles was born – rather appropriately – on 14 February 1783. He matriculated at Brasenose College but soon left, confessing half a century later, that 'he did not like reading at all, and hated it when at Oxford.'[34] In September 1803 he was posted cornet to the Royal Scots Greys stationed at Canterbury, remaining on the South Coast until the invasion threat was lifted; later he saw service in the Peninsular War. When in February 1812, some months after transferring his commission to the fourth Royal Irish Dragoons, he married an Irish heiress, his paternal aunt, Lady Sewell wrote to her sister Mrs Cholmeley: 'Charles I fear will get deeper and deeper into difficulties as it cannot be supposed he will economise with the additional burden of a wife, and the father it is supposed will make good his threat of never giving her a shilling.'[35]

Colonel Sibthorp reposed most confidence in his third son, Henry Walker, who in 1799 at the age of fifteen joined the Royal Navy as a midshipman. Over a hundred of his letters home survive. The judgement of the Lincolnshire archivist accurately describes the impression they create of a 'high-spirited, affectionate, self-disciplined boy, with his ambition centred on his naval career, his frequent frustration, his uncomplaining acceptance of disappointment.'[36] Anxious for his son's promotion Colonel Humphrey enlisted the help of William Wilberforce and even approached the Prime Minister directly.[37] The young man eventually became a lieutenant in 1805, but his parent's hopes were cruelly dashed when *HMS Ajax* exploded in the Dardenelles on 14 February 1807, killing him along with most of the crew.

In Humphrey, the surviving brother closest to Richard in age, there seemed little to cause his mother concern. He spent most of his life in the frustrating task of managing the family's business and political affairs. Elected fellow of Exeter College in 1806 and ordained three years later, in 1817 he was presented to the 'valuable rectory' of Washingborough, close to Canwick. The following year, he married his cousin Mary Esther Ellison, thus further cementing links between the two families. The *Lincoln Date Book* in noting his passing (1865) did not refer to his clerical character, but observed that 'The deceased gentleman was in affluent circumstances, and as he was a most liberal landlord and neighbour, his decease will be greatly regretted.'[38]

As regards Mrs Sibthorp herself, little documentary evidence remains. John Fowler, Richard's friend and first biographer – who must have asked him about her – wrote of her humour, but also a tendency to act as the 'squire's lady.'[39] A brief note she sent to John Hawkins when he was courting her daughter may illustrate the former quality, as well as domestic constraints on her *hauteur*. 'I return to you with my best thanks the Book of Figures, and I am told by the Colonel that I was guilty of an extreme incivility to you last night – for though you politely offered to *throw away* your time in attending us ladies wherever we were pleased to go – I had neither the good manners to say that I felt obliged, or even that I should be glad to see you.'[40]

The Youngest Son

Richard was by six years the youngest of his mother's six children, autumnal compensation for a dead baby four years before. Towards him, during the anxious war years, she was over-protective and over-indulgent and he well appreciated how this upbringing had shaped his character. Writing to Edward Bickersteth in 1821, he was self-critical to the point of brutality: 'I have been brought up in luxury – accustomed from a child to every gratification I could desire. The spoilt child of a most affectionate and tender mother, no hot-house plant was more guarded and nursed and nourished than I have been.'[41]

Richard spent eight happy years at Eltham, recalling, in his eightieth year, the names of school friends, and the 'great game' that they played.[42] He formed life-long friendships and corresponded with the daughter of the Rev. John Smith, the school's owner, until his death. School offered perhaps greater security than the peripatetic life he had led hitherto. Even his home could seem threatening. In April 1800, Colonel Humphrey, celebrating his return to Parliament, invited the local citizenry to dine at Canwick. The outcome was unsettling: 'an illiterate rabble . . . abused the hospitality of the munificent donor. Whole joints of meat were taken from the table and others were torn away from the hands of carvers. The kitchen, the larder and other offices were broken open; and much furniture was destroyed.'[43] The Colonel may have brooded on this incident. In 1811, he undertook substantial rebuilding work, acting as his own architect. Very robust construction methods were employed, with unfortunate consequences for the appearance and comfort of Canwick Hall. Maddison, the family's chronicler, observed that Sibthorp had 'determined to build a house that would survive a siege.'[44]

By the time Richard left Eltham in 1807, a gloom had settled on his family. Henry's tragic death had brought a terrible sadness. An echo of this grief may be detected in the memorial that Richard erected almost half a century later.[45] It is a deep lament: 'Ingenuous, brave, gentle. Alas, my brother!' It was about this time that Colonel Sibthorp suffered a stroke, from which he never recovered. Yet, just the previous year he had begun the posthumous publication of John Sibthorp's *Flora Graeca*. The issue of this great work, which was not completed until 1840, brought lustre to the family name, but also highlighted a fading inheritance. The sadness at Canwick presaged a new mood: a perceptible narrowing of horizons as intellectual confidence and openness seemed to yield before a more introspective, more anxious state of mind.

One sign of the changed atmosphere was a sense of financial insecurity, as though what marriage and the accidents of birth and death had brought, might as easily be lost. The frugality of Professor Sibthorp has been noted. In old age, he sought to enhance the family's prospects by leaving a substantial legacy for any of his grandchildren who decided to set up in commerce.[46] Colonel Humphrey also worried about money, and explained his difficulties to Hawkins, soon to become his son-in law: 'You know that I have come late in life to a considerable estate, but from which there are more considerable deductions than you can know of.' He undertook to provide £4,000 for his daughter, adding that this would require him to relinquish his parliamentary seat: 'to resign an old family interest and resign the partialities of those who flatter me with them to others is a task that will require some management and delicacy.'[47] Thus, he did not stand in the 1806 election, 'making reference to his decline in health and faculties, and to his limited means and numerous family.'[48] He also declined a baronetcy, on the grounds that his means were insufficient to support the dignity.[49]

Born into an entailed and increasingly indebted estate[50] it was not certain that Richard should enjoy a personal wealth sufficient to give him private means. Indeed, the small and rather uncertain income that he drew from charges on the family property[51] would not alone have been sufficient. But he and his siblings were to benefit from substantial legacies. On his mother's death in 1826, he and his brother Humphrey were named residuary legatees and such was the size and complexity of her estate that they were still receiving payments many years later.[52] Among the extended family, the Waldo connection was particularly lucrative. In

1805 Sarah Wollaston, the cousin of his grandfather's first wife, died aged 97. Her twenty children had all died and she left most of her fortune to the Canwick family. Another relative, Peter Waldo, an eminent divine and author of *Commentary on the Liturgy of the Church of England*, died childless in 1804 and bequeathed his considerable property to the younger children of Colonel Humphrey and his sister Sarah Sibthorp who in 1768 had married Montague Cholmeley of Easton. In gratitude, Richard's father took the additional surname and arms of 'Waldo.'[53] The bequest was subject to the life interest of Waldo's wife who was aged sixty-two when widowed. She lived to be a hundred. Not until 1845, following three years litigation in Chancery, was each beneficiary paid £14,323.[54] Richard also benefited from the will of his aunt, Lady Sewell, widow of the Master of the Rolls. She died in 1820, dividing the bulk of her £25,000 estate between Humphrey and himself. This led to some bad feeling. Another nephew, Montague Cholmeley, wrote that he had heard 'by a circuitous route that she had amassed a large fortune . . . I cannot help wishing that *equal* claims of relationship had received equal marks of Recognition.'[55] Richard's mother attempted to pacify the Cholmeleys, 'this I do believe was the reason Lady Sewell gave her bank stock to Humphrey and Richard, they had neither of them even a Curacy or an Home except their Father's house . . . Your dear and good father whom I sincerely loved and respected must have managed well to educate in the way he did so large a family, to keep such an hospitable house, to do so much good and to leave so much property.'[56] Despite this diplomacy, the distribution of Lady Sewell's life interest in her father's stock was litigated, it being argued that his will intended only the Cholmeley children to benefit. The Vice-Chancellor disagreed, commenting, 'The obscurity and ambiguity of the deed seemed to indicate that the testator had been very old.'[57]

Yet despite such fortune, Colonel Sibthorp's sense of financial insecurity proved a self-fulfilling prophecy and his stewardship of the estates has been judged a disappointment.[58] He attempted to consolidate, selling in 1800, the property at North Mymms, and just before his death in 1815, parts of the Instow estate and various lands in Lincolnshire. The funds were used to rebuild the Hall and to buy more Canwick land at premium prices. His descendants settled into the role of a county family of strong Tory opinions reluctant to adapt to a changing society. The Sibthorp finances slowly deteriorated, the male line failed, and with the death of Coningsby Charles Sibthorp in 1932, the family name was extinguished.

A Calamitous Inroad

In 1807, Richard left Eltham, where he had had 'no thought nor care beyond the day.'[59] It was the end of childhood innocence. Returning home to a grieving family, troubles crowded in on him. Not least, the unsettling prospect that in the autumn he would be going to Westminster School. His brothers would have left him in little doubt about the rigours that awaited him there. What is more likely than that it was at this time that he opened his heart to Beaumont, despite knowing that his father had forbidden religious conversation? At the end of his life, reflecting on the dawning of individual religious consciousness, he wrote: 'May not most of us trace back our great fall into sin and guilt by some early, perhaps childish transgression: our doing something that we knew we ought not to do.'[60] Perhaps part of the explanation of his lifelong ambivalence towards Roman Catholicism was that he somehow associated it with his own fall from grace.

The priest had undertaken not to proselytise, but when faced with the spiritual needs of one he had known so long, how could he keep silent?[61] Some insight into his personality can be gained from the memoirs of Henry Digby Beste, who in 1797, on inheriting his father's estates, had resigned a Magdalen fellowship and returned to Lincoln. Long attracted to Roman Catholicism, he contacted Beaumont, who strove for his conversion, which occurred in May the following year.[62] Though Beste had no high opinion of his friend's intellect, he succumbed to the Frenchman's intense sense of divine vocation, quite absent from the Anglican clergy he knew. Such comparisons were not discouraged. Beste recalled him entering 'my house one day, bursting into laughter: "Why do you laugh, M. L'Abbé?" said I. "I have just met the Rev. Mr——, with the first volume of his theological works in his arms." "What is there to laugh at in that?" "He was carrying the eldest of his children."'[63] Under Beaumont's care, the Lincoln Catholic community grew in confidence, and when Bishop Milner came to confirm in October 1809 there were fifteen candidates, compared with just three, four years before.[64]

Richard too, was drawn into the religious certainty and deep spirituality of his tutor. Years later he remembered the Abbé's devotion to the breviary, 'which he called his *wife*.'[65] Perhaps he was introduced to local Catholics: both the country gentry and city families of good standing, such as the Willsons, who numbered the Cholmeleys among their friends.[66] Edward Willson, who assisted in Pugin's conversion, was just twenty in 1807. Not much older was Francis Martyn, the priest at Louth, an attractive personality and fervent for conversions. Gillow said that 'he brought more Protestants into the Church than any of his contemporaries.'[67] In middle age, Richard reflected on what had first attracted him to Roman Catholicism. It was the *holiness* of her adherents. 'I never forgot what had forcibly impressed me . . . the apparent devotedness to religious duties, the supreme place which these seemed to have in their regard, the cheerfulness yet earnestness of piety, which marked some members of her communion, whom I then met with. I had found little of these things among my Protestant acquaintance . . . ' Holiness, and also earnestness: 'Conceiving that religion, if anything, should be the chief thing with every man; knowing it, on divine authority, declared to be "the one thing needful," when I seemed to find it so esteemed by Catholics, and knew it not to be so esteemed by most of my Protestant acquaintance, but holding quite a secondary and accidental place in their regard, I not unreasonably judged these latter wrong and those right. I sought to connect myself with the former in the enjoyment of the privileges they alone seemed to understand and value.'[68]

After a painful year at Westminster, Richard was removed.[69] Anxious that his youngest son should become a Magdalen scholar, Colonel Humphrey sent him to a tutor, Godfrey Fausset, curate of Holton near Oxford, fellow of the College and future Margaret Professor. His pupil failed to achieve a demyship and in December 1809 matriculated at University College. It was a family disappointment; there had been many Sibthorps and Cholmeleys on Magdalen's books. For his part, Martin Routh the president valued these Lincolnshire connections and corresponded with Sibthorp about their shared interests as county landowners. In February 1810, he received a letter from him about a drainage scheme at Wainfleet. The Colonel closed his letter by saying that he intended to present his son 'a second time a candidate for a demyship, secured from the dangers of a public school and under the care of one who has been a member of that Society over which you preside.'[70] This time he was successful and in July was enrolled along with Zachary H. Biddulph and William Mills. The Colonel wrote again: 'Not to rejoice in his success, not to express my gratitude would require a weak head and a bad heart and I am not conscious beyond the ordinary infirmity of decaying nature of either. *Your* demy I hope will fulfill all that in me is lacking . . . the solid foundation is now securely laid, whereon it will be his own fault, if he raise not a goodly superstructure.'[71]

The foundation was in the process of being undermined. Richard wrote in 1871 that it was, 'very early in my college life' that God 'bid me to remember Him and His claims on me.' And, he added, it was the Roman Catholic Church that 'helped to fasten the nail.'[72] At Oxford he attended Mass, making no secret of his interest in Catholicism,[73] and was placed under the spiritual care of Samuel Rock, the priest at Kiddington.[74] This may have been at Martyn's instigation, who was now serving at Walsall, where Rock's relatives were mainstays of the Catholic community. Eventually, after an exchange of letters with Bishop Milner, Richard came to a decision. Early in November 1811, 'he suddenly disappeared from Oxford, neither the College authorities, nor the members of his family knowing for some time the place of his concealment.'[75] Over sixty years later, he recalled the adventure. 'I passed two nights at his (Bishop Milner's) house at Wolverhampton on my first flight from Oxford to join the Catholic Church, from which I was brought back (*vi et armis* I may say), under police surveillance and Chancery Order, by my eldest brother Coningsby . . . Biddulph was my confidant in my first flight to

Birmingham. I do not blame him. My family pressed him so hard, about the possible return of paralysis to my father, if I kept hid longer, that he could hardly but give way.'[76]

On 7 November, Colonel Sibthorp wrote to President Routh, complaining that his son's intentions had been kept from him:

> 'The dread of public examination in the Schools was not the inducement of my son's flight from College. It is founded on a deeper and far more afflictive cause, which makes his return *impossible* and has been kept from my knowledge or suspicion in the kindest motives, until the cause and effect could no longer be concealed. He falls the second victim within your and my knowledge to Catholic cunning and adds another triumph to their unwearied ambition of proselytism. I received last night a long justification of the steps he had taken and means to take, much too artificial to be his own. Of one expression, "If you or my mother wish to see me you shall instantly" I have taken advantage on the moment.[77] I do not impute the letter to Rock, with whom my son has had frequent conferences, who appears from one of his letters I have in my possession, to be an ignorant bigot, but I rather ascribe it to the well known Milner, who has been in the habit of corresponding and fixing the fluctuations of his mind.'[78]

Richard did not convert. He recalled being 'brought back a prisoner, sighing for St. Clement's . . . An interval of two or three hours had (humanly speaking) seen the deed done, and myself a member of the Church of Rome.'[79] He had been away for several days, having stayed with Martyn before going to Milner, but failed to take the decisive step. Some hesitation was hardly surprising, given his age and the gravity of the matter. In 1841, the following statement appeared in an anonymous polemical pamphlet: 'Mr. Sibthorp, when he was about 18 years old, was converted to the Roman Catholic religion by a French priest at Lincoln; the timely interference of his friends, assisted by the police, prevented a retreat to France where the young convert intended, as it is as (*sic*) said to join himself to a monastic order.'[80] Although incorrect and garbled, this does hint at an important consideration. Where would he have gone, what would he have done? After all, he was the youngest son. When Henry Beste converted, Bishop Douglass asked him if he was aware of the civil consequences. 'The penal laws are repealed, but you will lose your *état civil*.'[81] Beste owned substantial property and both his parents were dead. Richard's case was different. To become a Roman Catholic would be to make ashamed those he loved and to move to the margins of society, away from Canwick and its comfortable assumptions. He could never decide to which world he wished to belong.

Colonel Sibthorp, bewildered and angry, wrote to Routh, 'I suspect what I cannot prove that the priest who resides at Lincoln has had a deep and busy hand in the plot . . . his conduct has been evil, mean, and iniquitous. Long has individual liberty contributed to his comfort and private benevolence cherished him. He has broken all the ties of obligation and gratitude which bind man to man, to make a convert, and has endeavoured and may succeed in the tenderest point to wound to death the person who has been his defender and benefactor.'[82] He may well have translated hurt feelings into action. Writing in 1826, Beste said that he went to London to convert, in order to avoid any difficulties that might arise for Beaumont in Lincoln, adding, 'Subsequent machinations against him prove my apprehensions to have been well-founded.'[83] The exile relinquished the mission in 1818; three years earlier he was described in a return of émigré clergy as *'infirme, asthmatique.'*[84]

Atoning for Criminal Misconduct

Richard, at first reluctant to confess the error of his ways, succumbed to strong pressure, not least, the possible damage to his father's health. So that by January the Colonel was able to report: 'My dear Richard, more than half recovered from the errors into which he half betrayed himself and were indissolubly fastening upon him by the subtle Milner, for his sake, for my sake . . . has promised to alleviate the weight of my afflictions.' He submitted to the prescribed régime. 'The conversation of our worthy friend, Mr. F. Swan and the books he has read at home, have had the best effects, and little remains to be done than to overcome the conscious sense of shame and the fear of obloquy, reproach, contempt and ridicule, which predominate in the natural timidity of his disposition.' In order to, 'remove this irrational dread and to strengthen his mind in the *true* Catholic Church' he was sent for counselling to John Smith at Eltham.[85]

It was a sensible decision, and from there Richard wrote to the President a letter that was all that could be wished. He referred to his 'criminal misconduct' and the 'total change' in his opinions. 'My return to my Society, and your kind care, is an object most closely interwoven with the happiness of my father. It could not of this account be of unconcern to me; but when I consider the generous lenity exercised towards me, in permitting me to ensure that happiness by again resuming my demy's gown, I feel it a bounden duty, both in justice to the offended discipline, and in gratitude to the kind generosity, of the College, to accept with eagerness the proffered good.' He promised to demonstrate his sincerity by 'a steady continuance in the doctrines of the Church of England, of that Church in which I was first made a Christian . . . Permit me to hope that my attachment to its worship and doctrine may be strengthened by the experience I have had of the errors of its most ancient and even now most inveterate enemies; tho' that experience has been indeed dearly bought by the misery inflicted on my family and the sacrifice of my character and credit.'[86]

He was as good as his word, and on return to Lincoln sent a note (dated

10 March 1812) to an unnamed correspondent, a copy of which found its way to Magdalen College archives: 'Revd Sir, I received your note this evening . . . thank you for your enquiries after my health. In reply to the principal contents of your note I must beg to state that I desire no further communication on the subject of religion may take place between us. Confirmed by a closer examination and unprejudiced enquiry *in possession* of that faith in which I was born and bred, it is my determination by the aid of the Almighty to live and die a firm tho' unworthy member of the Established Church of this country. I again beg that this my settled decision may stop any further communication on your part. With best wishes for your happiness, temporal and eternal.'[87]

A month later the Colonel acknowledged the President's generosity in allowing his son to return. 'I have detained my son to this last moment, me he has repaid by every act of filial obedience and shewing himself conspicuous in every act of religious conformity to our steady Reformed faith of individual charity . . . I wished to accompany my son and present him before you but lengthening days have but brought to us hard weather and I dare not step out I am so shaken.'[88] He took the advice of his nephew, John Cholmeley, until recently a Magdalen fellow, and assigned Richard to a private tutor, Thomas Collins, 'a Tory and a High Churchman of the old school,' who tutored most of the Gentlemen Commoners.[89] On 27 April, Lady Sewell wrote from her Oxford home, 'Hump (*sic*) and Richard have been here these last three weeks. The latter looking in good health and spirits and I hope doing all he ought.'[90]

In 1816 Richard was presented with £6, 'on account of his conduct during his residence as an undergraduate.' Thanking the President, he wrote that though he was unaware that it deserved any particular approbation, 'it was my general wish and endeavour that it should be such as, for more reasons than one, was called for by my situation in College'.[91] Of his final examination, in May 1813, another Lincolnshire man, Thomas Grantham, wrote a full account. After construing a parable in the Greek Testament and being questioned on it, transition was 'made to other principal points in Divinity and these required to be proved by Texts.' The examiners then turned to the Greek and Latin texts he had prepared, in particular Aristotle's *Rhetoric* and the *Nicomachean Ethics*.[92] Grantham was awarded a first; Richard, never noted for his scholarship, gained a second.

There was much of obedience, and little of enthusiasm in the young man's renewed adherence to the Church of England. It became something more. In the months after returning from Milner, Richard was led to accept that the bible – the authority of which he never doubted – foresaw the emergence of the Papacy as Satan's instrument to corrupt the church. That Rome was prophesied Antichrist was a painful discovery. The Church of England seemed to offer little to a young man in whom there burned an ardent devotional flame, and thus he 'often mourned that truth seemed to have less power than error.'[93] No record remains of what Mr. Swan said to him, or of the reading that so persuaded him, save one stray reference in a letter of Lord Macaulay. In 1827, when Richard was a regular preacher at St. John's Bedford Row, the historian's sisters were among his most enthusiastic hearers, for which offence their brother teased them:

> 'I always thought your hero Sibthorpe a goose. But the excellent story you tell me of him puts the matter out of all doubt. I hope that Miss Edgeworth's Harrington will never fall in his way. If it should, he will infallibly turn Jew, nourish his beard and eat the Passover while his congregation is waiting for a Good Friday sermon . . .
>
> I wish that I knew where my old friend Mrs. Meeke lives, I would certainly send her intelligence of the blessed effects of her writings. I grieve to think how carelessly I have read them and how little I have considered them in a theological light . . . A new edition of Laughton Priory (sic) ought certainly to be published cheap for distribution among the poor Irish. It would aid Lord Farnham in his mighty work.[94] He would be the very person to preside over the British and Foreign Laughton Priory Association. . . .
>
> So the Jesuits kept Sibthorpe in hiding. Alas, my dear Carolina Wilhelmina Amelia, I must . . . pronounce your anecdote in that respect fudge. I suspect that, having experienced the good effects of fictitious narrative in his own case, he intends to try the same experiment on other people and to pass himself off for Juliano Algernon I suppose. If he really were, like Juliano, confined as insane I cannot much blame his keepers.'[95]

The inference is that Richard read *Langhton Priory*, a novel by Gabrielli (Mrs Meeke) which was published by Minerva Press in 1809. It is the story of a well-meaning but weak minded Catholic landowner, the dupe of his chaplain, an evil Italian Jesuit, who to conceal a criminal past keeps a young man (Juliano Algernon) secretly imprisoned. At somewhat tedious length the priest's wrong-doings are uncovered and all ends happily. The novel is not specifically anti-Catholic but pursuing its aim that 'all works of fiction should hold out some moral,' contrasts English reason with Continental superstition. Mr Langhton ends his days with 'Mr. Berrington, the new chaplain, . . . a man of sense, erudition and real piety and a most agreeable companion. He was . . . as a Catholic divine, all that Dr. Murray was as a Protestant Minister . . . Mr. Langhton's devotion under his guidance was become infinitely more rational, his real piety no longer obscured by superstition.'[96]

It may be surmised that Richard was presented with other more substantial volumes. The *Book of Homilies*, for example: 'the Popes and Prelates of Rome, for the most part . . . are worthily accountable among the number of false Prophets and false Christs, which deceived the world a long while.'[97] When the young Ambrose Phillipps de Lisle was near to being converted by an émigré priest, the 'host of controversial works' put into his hands included 'Faber's works upon the prophecies; Bishop Newton's, on the same subject; also Mede's works upon the prophecies.'[98] All agreed that the papacy was self-evidently the Antichrist predicted in the writings of St. Paul and St. John. According to Bishop Newton, 'Such a prophecy as this is at once an illustrious proof of divine revelation and an excellent antidote to the poison of popery. It is like a two-edged sword that will cut both ways, and wound the deist with one side, and the papist with the other.'[99]   Whatever he read, Richard was persuaded, and for the rest of his life carried an unquestioning belief in the inspiration of Scripture that could not be dissevered from a dark suspicion that therein Roman Catholicism stood condemned.

Following Mede, Bishop Newton believed that the Papal Antichrist would reign for 1260 years, after which the events culminating in the *Parousia* would commence.[100] Unclear as to dates, he felt that a close eye should be kept on developments across the Channel: 'as the kings of France have contributed greatly to her (Rome's) advancement, it is not impossible, nor improbable, that some time or other they may also be the principal authors of her destruction.'[101] For Richard Sibthorp's generation, the events inaugurated by the French Revolution, in particular the captivity of the Pope, had a profound impact. Could it be that the prophesied End Times had begun? Among the commentators arguing this was an Artillery Captain, Charles Maitland, a friend (soon to become brother-in-law[102]) of Richard's cousin, Robert Cholmeley, a curate in Leeds. In 1813, Maitland published *The History of the Beast of the Apocalypse*. Although the *Eclectic Review* queried his conclusion that the 1260 years had expired[103] increasing numbers of Evangelical commentators, including Cholmeley, were convinced.[104] The following year Maitland published again, *A Brief and Connected View of Prophecy*, linking the decline of the Papacy with the coming millennial hope.[105] Richard was told that he was living in the Last Days and that Rome was under sentence of condemnation. It was a conclusion he accepted and that shaped his life.

Holiness Regained

Could truth and holiness really be opposed? Could it really be the case that submission to the authority of Scripture led necessarily to a religion of worldliness and superficiality? In the immediate aftermath of the events of November 1811, Richard was subdued and dejected; resolved to be a dutiful son, he found refuge in his Anglican baptism. Yet, four years later he had become a celebrated gospel preacher, 'setting the hinterland of Lincoln aflame.'[106] Of this intervening period, almost nothing is known. The reason for the dramatic change can only be conjectured. But the basis of an explanation is available. In turning from Rome, Richard was introduced to Protestants of undeniable fervour. At Oxford and in Lincolnshire

there were those anxious to convince him of what he afterwards acknowledged: 'that all Catholics are not in earnest, nor all Protestants indifferent
about their salvation: far otherwise.'[107]

John Cholmeley, who had recently left Magdalen to become rector of
Burton Coggles in Lincolnshire, probably recommended that his cousin
Richard should attend the Oxford ministry of John Natt, the popular
Evangelical preacher. This was the advice he gave his sister when she went
to live in the city: 'I should have thought the preacher at St Giles a much
more useful expounder of Scripture than Mr. Yeadon.'[108] Richard's
closest College friend, a distant relative, was the son of T. T. Biddulph,
incumbent of St James's, Bristol, and the acknowledged leader of the West
Country Evangelicals. Zachary wholeheartedly shared his father's beliefs.
He became vicar of Backwell in Somerset, and died in 1842. A published
eulogy set out 'the great doctrines he insisted upon with much earnestness
. . . the total and full apostasy of mankind . . . pardon for the most guilty
in the atoning blood . . . justification by faith through the imputed righteousness of Christ . . . the need for man to be born again.'[109]

The part paid by Zachary Biddulph in his friend's evangelical conversion is not recorded. But it is known that Richard drew close to other
earnest students, including Philip Filleul of Pembroke College, Henry
Baker Tristram of Christ Church and John Hunter who matriculated as
a Gentleman Commoner of Magdalen in May 1814. 'These and other
friends met weekly at each other's rooms for prayer and the study of Holy
Scripture.'[110] Until Hunter died in 1844, Richard wrote to him regularly,
and they exchanged information about other members of the circle,
including William Whitmarsh Phelps, who arrived in Oxford shortly
before Richard's departure in 1815.

Richard however, eschewed the moderate Calvinism of his Oxford
contemporaries and in tracing the roots of his zeal, the significance of
Methodism must be reckoned with. Most accounts of the rise of the
Evangelical party within the Church of England discount much direct debt
to John Wesley.[111] In 1764, for example, of the thirty-four clergymen to
whom he wrote seeking support, only three replied. But there were
Anglican sympathisers, and prominent among them was a little group of
clergy, living close to one another along the Great North Road. In
Leicestershire: Dr. Thomas Ford of Melton Mowbray and Thomas
Davenport of Alexton; and in Lincolnshire, John Pugh, incumbent of
Rauceby and Cranwell, and William Dodwell, rector until 1824, of Welby
and Stoke.[112] There are scattered references to all these men in Wesley's
Journals. For example, in July 1775, Ford, who was converted under
Wesley's open-air preaching,[113] wrote a 'most affectionate letter' to him;
fifteen years later, they were still on close terms.[114] Wesley wrote to
Davenport shortly after the 1782 Conference regretting he had not
attended, but said that one of his local preachers would go to Alexton to
help in the ministry.[115] Both Dodwell and Pugh were at this Conference,

and the previous year's. Wesley preached for them both.[116] At Oxford, Pugh was captivated by the faith of Joseph Benson, a fellow student, and had moved to his Lincolnshire livings as a committed Evangelical. He strongly opposed Calvinist theology and was 'prepared to preach in Methodist meetings outside his own parishes, and risk the wrath of the mob as well as his fellow incumbents.'[117]

However, the key figure in explaining Richard's conversion must be Dodwell. Thomas Cocking, a Wesleyan itinerant in the Grantham area, said that he and Ford were 'principal instruments of planting the seeds of piety in several parts of the circuit.' They were 'bright and shining lights' and 'owed much to Methodism themselves for the grace they had attained, and were not ashamed . . . to acknowledge the people from whom, under God, their spiritual information had been derived.' Of Dodwell he observed:

> 'Many resorted to his ministry, which was attended with many blessed effects, not only in his own church, but also in different parts of the country which he was in the habit of occasionally visiting. There was a strain of persuasive eloquence in his preaching, which was very attractive; and his discourses were strikingly descriptive and deeply spiritual.'[118]

In 1807, the *Methodist Magazine* published Dodwell's sermon on the 'Authenticity and Divinity of the Scriptures.'[119] A convinced Arminian, in a later article, he reproduced extracts from Barrow's sermons, 'asserting and explaining the doctrine of general redemption.'[120] Both causes became dear to Richard Sibthorp. Writing in 1809 to the *Magazine*'s editor, his friend Joseph Benson, Dodwell suggested other possible articles and floated a scheme he had in mind, of founding a religious school, 'something like that at Kingswood' but 'not confined to the children whose parents are of any particular denomination.'[121] By this stage of his life he had amassed a considerable fortune, and was looking for some worthy scheme to support. In 1824, the year of his death, he donated £10,000 to the Wesleyan Missionary Society and an equal sum to the British and Foreign Bible Society.

Dodwell's health was never good, and he employed a series of pious assistants. One was the prominent Methodist, Peard Dickinson. He recalled 'my fixed residence was at Stoke, from whence as soon as I had finished the morning service, I instantly took horse, and reached Welby in sufficient time to go through the afternoon service. As people from the neighbouring parishes often attended at Stoke, I received invitations from several of them to come and preach among them, which I accepted from time to time.'[122] He was in Lincolnshire for only a year, being appointed in 1787, to the City Road Chapel in London, where he remained until his death in 1802.

The Cholmeley seat, Easton Hall, was in the parish of Stoke, and although it cannot be confirmed that it was in the little church there that Richard's Cholmeley cousins experienced spiritual awakening, this seems the most likely explanation of their Evangelical fervour. Both the vicar and his curates were in earnest[123] and Dickinson's 'profound piety bordering on mysticism' and 'holiness of heart'[124] must surely have impressed his young hearers. During the latter's brief Lincolnshire ministry, Montague Cholmeley was 15; he was to become a Vice-President of the Society for Promoting Christianity among the Jews and a patron of other Religious Societies.[125] His brother John was 14. He became rector of Burton Coggles in 1811, but died within four years. A plaque in the parish church proclaims his zeal: 'he will long be remembered with gratitude and affection, as the faithful rector of the flock committed to his care. His ministry was short: like a warning voice it was heard. It is gone. Be ye also ready.'

Robert Cholmeley, who also became a committed Evangelical clergyman, was aged just seven during Dickinson's curacy. If as a child he imbibed Wesleyan theology, in later life he came to distrust the Methodists as unscrupulous rivals. When curate of Knostrop near Leeds he wrote: 'The Wesleyans are far from careful in admitting their members. They are much like the Pharisees of old, and we in the Church are cold or asleep.'[126] In January 1815 he was instituted rector of Wainfleet, where his first task was to build a new church. When it was opened in July 1821, Richard Sibthorp delivered the first sermon.[127]

The Cholmeley connection may explain the Methodist enthusiasm that characterised Richard Sibthorp's early Anglican ministry. Friendship between his family and the Cholmeleys stretched back to the early eighteenth century; both families were rising in status, and both sent their children to Westminster School. The links were sealed in 1764, when Sarah Sibthorp married Montague Cholmeley, heir to Easton Hall. Thereafter visits were frequent, and if reason was required, Sarah obliged by having fourteen children, and grandchildren almost too numerous to count. This network of relations became a constant call upon Richard's epistolary endurance, but it was a burden he never begrudged. With so many mouths to feed, squabbling between the families over the Waldo and Sewell legacies was perhaps inevitable, and the law courts were kept busy. But there was no breach, and as Richard grew into manhood, the bonds of friendship became deeper. In the crisis of 1811 Colonel Humphrey sought John Cholmeley's advice, and would surely have encouraged his son to visit Easton and discuss his religious concerns with these relatives who were fervent, yet secure in their Anglicanism. If he had known of their rector's links with the Methodists, he may have been more circumspect. For it was among them that his son seems to have found the holiness he sought.[128] Perhaps he was taken to Skillington, a few miles from Easton, where the Methodist cause owed its origin to Dodwell?[129] Its Society, 'one of the best and most influential in the circuit', was often visited by the rector or his curate.[130] Richard ever spoke in the highest terms of Methodist piety. In January 1845, he said of his 'old Methodist friend,' Mrs. Allenby, that she 'like many of the Wesleyans is really a very holy and devout woman.'[131]

His early appreciation of Methodist devotion gave him an unshakeable belief in the 'invisible church' which he was later to find hard to square with Catholic orthodoxy. In 1864, he told his friend Bloxam that while his sympathies were with the Church of Rome, this was 'in entire consistency with the unquestioning belief, the most genuine recognition, – I hardly know words strong enough to express my judgement herein – of salvation out of her communion.' He then called into evidence a long list of Evangelical saints ending with 'Wesley and Fletcher of Madeley, whose personal friends were mine.'[132] Perhaps he meant Dodwell. He certainly meant Robert Carr Brackenbury, the squire of Raithby in Lincolnshire, with whom Sibthorp shared the platform when the Lincoln Bible Society was founded in 1816. Born in 1752, Brackenbury undertook pioneering work for Methodism on Jersey, accompanied Wesley on preaching tours to Scotland and Holland, and was at the great man's deathbed in March 1791. Wesley spoke highly of Raithby,[133] where there was an extensive library, much used by the Methodist preachers.[134] When Brackenbury died in August 1818, the *Minutes of Conference* spoke of him as one of 'those exalted saints' whose 'graces would have been highly esteemed in the character of a Christian in the purest age of Christianity.'[135] His widow lived until 1847. Two years before, Richard wrote to Mrs. Allenby, 'I hope whenever you see or write to Mrs. Brackenbury, you make my Christian regards to her. I frequently think of Raithby, and past days.'[136]

A generation after Wesley's death, some of his followers remained committed Churchmen. Richard too remained true to the Church of England, from conviction, as well as in consideration for his father, who by 1813 required constant nursing.[137] But when he became an Anglican minister, his preaching, pastoral care and theology all had a distinctly Wesleyan emphasis. Indeed, in 1818 his election to a Magdalen fellowship was opposed on these grounds. In writing to the President, he tackled the issue head-on:

'I have recently been given to understand that there is probability of my election to a fellowship being opposed and that this opposition, I am also informed is founded (at least avowedly) on my supposed dissent from the doctrines and disciplines of the Established Church . . . it is a charge which in its consequences may not only materially affect my future situation in life but which may (which is of far more consequence) injure at present my character and reputation. That I have endeavoured to subvert, keep out of view or in any way differ from the doctrines of the Church of England, is not, as far as I have learned, attempted to be proved. The general assertion is made, but not one particular point specified . . . on which I am supposed to follow or teach doctrines contrary to those of the Establishment. . . .

You may perhaps readily believe Rev. Sir, that I am not necessitated to continue in the Church of England to obtain a livelihood . . . I have no motive but preference, or conviction of her excellence, to induce me to remain in her ministry . . . I . . . preach her doctrines because I believe them scriptural and true . . . being well satisfied that no one who is desirous of living a godly and Christian life need forsake the communion of the Established Church of our land.'[138]

The Trials of a Gospel Preacher

With his heart absorbed in the reality of the unseen world, Richard remained at Oxford to prepare for the Anglican ministry and on 10 December 1815 was ordained deacon by the Bishop of Lincoln.[139] His father had died in April and wishing to be near his mother, he accepted an appointment as curate to John Rawlins Deacon, rector of Waddington and vicar of Harmston. Both parishes were just a short step from Canwick. Over half a century later John Fowler spoke to some who could still recall his dramatic impact and the power and eloquence of his preaching.

'The youngest, the oldest, the most ignorant, were all held in wrapt attention, and for a long time too. Beginning almost in a whisper, with what fervid eloquence he would close! . . . In this his first charge, he continued barely a year; but the effects of his ministrations there have continued to the present day: for he preached with all the enthusiasm of a Whitefield.'[140]

In its obituary of the preacher, *The Lincolnshire Chronicle* spoke of crowds walking from Lincoln to hear him, and of one old man, still living in Waddington, who could remember the young curate pleading with his people, that the cross of Christ could not be held in one hand.[141]

Richard Sibthorp was a young man, somewhat timid and not particularly robust, and it seems surprising that he should have been able, so early in his ministry, to preach with such effect. Perhaps there was some inherited ability? His brother Charles, although rarely taken seriously, often entertained the House of Commons with forceful, if somewhat incoherent speeches. Friendship with the Methodists would surely have helped him, for among them ordinary men and woman could speak eloquently of the state of their souls, and persuasively press home lessons from Scripture. They would have attributed any spiritual insight or authority in speaking to the Holy Spirit, and so did Richard, leaving no hints of any early training. However, the trust that the Waddington Methodists placed in him is shown in a remarkable concession. When he became curate they discontinued their meetings and committed themselves completely into his care.

This was remarkable because by 1816 – despite Wesley's wish that the

Anglican converts should remain in the Church of England – Methodism was becoming a separate denomination. Chapels had been established even where the Anglican minister was an Evangelical. The one in Welby, for example, dated from 1803, despite the fact that Dodwell had opened his own home for class meetings. Everywhere the Methodist folk were abandoning the parish churches in order to worship and celebrate the Sacraments in their own chapels. But in Waddington the trend was reversed. Writing in 1829, Watmough recalled the unusual circumstances:

'In the year 1802 the leaven of Methodism extended its influence to the village of Waddington, and a little society was formed, which increased and grew for about 12 years, till the Rev. Waldo Sibthorpe B.D. became minister of that parish. It was then given up into his hands, and the cause of Methodism, as to its outwards appearances, though not its fruits and effects, appeared for a season to depart from that place. The case was this. Mr. Sibthorpe was pious; and his zeal to promote piety in others, induced him to tread in our steps, so far as to establish meetings similar to our class meetings for the spiritual improvement of those of his hearers who chose to avail themselves of the privilege of regularly attending them. He even went so far our way, at that time, as to make use of our hymns, both in his class meetings and prayer meetings; so that the difference between himself and us appeared to some so much like a shadow, that it was thought no evil could result to our people, if entirely put under his pastoral direction and care; and therefore our preaching and cause being quite given up, the members of our society became the objects of his care, and the weekly contributions previously made among them for the support of our interest, Mr. Sibthorpe continued to collect among them, and devoted the money to the interest of the Bible Society.'[142]

It is possible that the decision at Waddington owed more to the Anglican sympathies of the local Wesleyan hierarchy, than to wishes of the villagers. Brackenbury, for example, shared Wesley's views in most things and was the patron of two livings. Watmough, in explaining the unfortunate *dénouement*, gives a strong hint of pressure from above:

'Mr Sibthorpe, however, continued but a short time at that place. He was soon banished from that scene of his labours, and his sheep were left without a shepherd – a circumstance which makes it doubtful whether our preaching ought to have been given up, or whether our people ought to have put themselves, or to have been put by others, under his pastoral care in the manner they were.'[143]

In the spring of 1817, after less than eighteen months, Richard left his curacies. It became a standard example of what the separatists kept saying; the Church of England could not be trusted with the cure of souls. Fifty years later another Methodist minister wrote:

'The small Society at Waddington prospered very well till it was placed in the hands of the Rev. Richard Sibthorp, who was then minister of the Parish. It was thought right, as he was a pious and zealous preacher, to leave the cause with him. They found, when he had to leave the place, that they had to begin the work afresh. He had neither kept them that were left with him, nor added any new members. – Our Church parsons don't know how to keep believers alive, somehow. I don't understand how it is. Mr. Sibthorp collected the weekly moneys as we had done, but gave them to the Bible Society.'[144]

It has usually been assumed that Richard left so soon because he incurred the wrath of his bishop.[145] George Pretyman Tomline, appointed to the diocese in 1787, was a shrewd man and a theologian of some note, and determined to combat any influences that might 'weaken attachment to our Protestant Interest, and endanger our Ecclesiastical Establishment.' This meant carefully circumscribing Protestant dissent, and resisting Catholic claims; 'We are beset on every side, we have enemies within as well as without.'[146] One enemy within the camp was Evangelicalism, the dangers of which he dwelt on in a number of Triennial Charges, which were collected in his notorious *Refutation of the Charge of Calvinism Against the Church of England* (1811). Enthusiasm of any kind concerned him. His opposition to Methodism was unbending. Wesley, just months before his death, wrote pleading with him to stop persecuting his followers by refusing them the protection of the Toleration Act.[147] Ten years later Wilberforce was hard put to prevent Pitt presenting a Bill inspired by the bishop, aimed at curtailing the ministrations of Methodists and 'Gospel Clergymen.'[148] The bishop was ruthless in expelling curates whose views displeased him. For example, in June 1802, Dodwell appointed George Bugg to Welby. Three months later Pretyman sent an ultimatum. Bugg's 'doctrine and manner is (*sic*) objectionable to the parishioners in the highest degree, I desire that you will immediately dismiss him from your curacy, and at the same time inform him that I shall not permit him to take another in my diocese.'[149]

At his Triennial Visitation of July 1815, the bishop turned his attack onto another insidious enemy, the Bible Society. He considered its constitution 'to be very dangerous to the established religion and to the orthodox principles of those who attended its meetings, as it admits members of every creed and no creed' and advised his hearers to 'mark them that cause division and offence and avoid them.' Although he refused to have his address published, his words, as reported in the press,[150] drew a vigorous response from Evangelical pamphleteers. One conceded that the bishop had 'obtained among his contemporaries the character of possessing a peculiarly judicious mind' and then observed, 'perhaps the lapse of years may have impaired it.' He characterised the Charge as 'haughty arrogant assertion, combined with a kind of insulting compassion' for his weak-minded clergy who supported the Society.[151]

The attacker remained anonymous. Richard, having no such inhibitions, was at the centre of moves that led to the establishment of a Bible Society Auxiliary in Lincoln. Most of his support came from local laymen of independent mind, such as Edward Charlesworth, the ubiquitous Lincoln physician. None of the Tory gentry wished to be involved, certainly not Richard's brother, Coningsby, the city's MP.[152] In reporting the inaugural meeting held on 20 November 1816, the *Mercury* quoted the Rev. Edward Burns of Birmingham as stressing the legitimacy of clergymen pledging their support. It then noted, 'At this moment an unguarded expression escaped the lips of a gentleman of Lincoln which was thought to reflect on the clergy of the city for not being present at the meeting.' Richard Sibthorp, however, was present. Naturally timid, he was also extremely stubborn. Now that his father was dead, he would bow to no authority but the Highest. He told the audience that he was 'Connected with this ancient city by many ties, born in its immediate neighbourhood, a citizen of no mean city . . . its temporal and spiritual interests must ever be near my heart . . . If to remove prejudice, if to soften down those little differences which it must be regretted exist between Christians of different denominations, if to promote concord and unity, be to advance the interests of a place, then is the Bible Society eminently calculated to produce this effect.'[153]

In his youthful impetuosity, Richard went on to offer further provocation to authority and in January chaired a meeting of the Horncastle Bible Society. Worse followed. Mrs. Bromhead later explained how he was led into clerical irregularity.

'It seems only just to the memory of the Rev. Richard Waldo Sibthorp that the truth should be known about his "preaching in barns." He was too ardent "by all means" to save some, but in those days, preaching in barns was an ecclesiastical offence. He was too strict an observer of the rules to have offended deliberately. Mr. Sibthorp was staying in the country with Mrs. Allenby of Kenwick House near Louth. The small parish church had only one service on Sundays and in country houses it was customary to call in the servants and share a service at home. Mr Sibthorp was asked to preside . . . Mrs. Allenby was so charmed by his exposition that she asked him to prolong his stay to next Sunday . . . During the week the good lady invited many friends to the treat. When the Lord's Day came there were many guests beyond what the drawing room would hold. Mrs. Allenby suggested moving into the barn and the gentle guest yielded.'[154] The offence was repeated at another location, and it was in the immediate wake of these events that in March 1817 Sibthorp left Lincolnshire. But it may not have been simple cause and effect. For it was not until August that he wrote to his bishop of it being, 'Some weeks . . . since it was communicated to me that you had been informed that I was guilty of some irregular proceedings in this diocese.' Richard's attempted exculpation was unlikely to have satisfied Tomline:

'I did on two different occasions expound the Word of God to assemblies of far more than twenty persons, collected for the purpose, in the parishes of other ministers. But . . . on both occasions an exposition of Scripture, intended to be confined nearly to the individuals of the families with whom I was resident at the time, was extended without any interference or consent of mine, to many more. The irregularity was wholly unpremeditated. It was a hasty act to which I was hurried by circumstances I had not the power, or at least not the firmness to control – on both occasions the number of persons attending was the sole cause why the expositions were given in a building adjoining the house . . . In neither case did I make use of any building licensed for the use of dissenters. These circumstances (while not palliating) may be different from what you have previously heard.'[155]

It is likely that quite soon after his curate arrived Deacon decided that the arrangement could not work. The rector was a keen sportsman and freemason, both he and the patron of Harmston, Samuel Thorold, were members of the Witham Lodge.[156] Thorold's domestic arrangements were notorious and the young preacher's fervour could not have been at all to his taste. Deacon would also have been well aware of Tomline's views. In January 1817, the Waddington Methodists licensed a new meeting room indicating that they already anticipated Sibthorp's departure. Soon after he left they began to build a chapel, which in August was registered with the diocesan authorities.[157]

Richard had to go to Oxford to be ordained to the priesthood by Bishop Legge. In Lincolnshire, he never shook off a reputation for being more than half a Wesleyan. And his enemies, the enemies of Evangelicalism in the county, were quite ready to use this ammunition against him. When the Freemen of the Mercers' Company declined to present him to the living of Canwick in 1818, they were probably aware of potential complications with the bishop.[158] The opposition to his fellowship application on the grounds of supposed dissent, already referred to, obliged him to submit a testimonial signed by his clerical brethren in Hull, to which town he migrated after quitting his curacies.[159]

2

THE TENTS OF KEDAR
Hull and Tattershall

With revolution in the air, 1817 was a bad year to be associated with dissenters. In moving to Hull, Richard could start the process of re-building his tattered credibility as a Churchman, for here Evangelical orthodoxy was combined with a fervent attachment to the Established Church. Joseph Milner, who by his powerful personality and forceful preaching had established the religious climate of the town, had been dead for twenty years,[1] but Thomas Dykes, incumbent of the newly consecrated St. John's in the town centre, was a worthy successor. In the aftermath of the War – years 'remarkable for the dissemination of seditious and disloyal opinions' – he stood firm, 'against the evils of anarchy . . . the whole weight of his moral influence was thrown into the scale of order and the British Constitution. As he had resisted the revolutionary projects of 1795, so did he resist the seditious schemes of 1817.'[2] In this he was ably assisted by John Scott, son of the Bible commentator, who became his curate in 1799 and in 1816 was presented by Samuel Thornton to the living of St Mary, Lowgate. In crossing the Humber, Richard Sibthorp became an insider again. The churches were thronged with like-minded worshippers, many of whom were drawn from the professional and merchant classes. He stayed in Hull only fifteen months, but it was long enough to establish some life-long friendships, and in times of difficulty he returned there, seeking perhaps to rekindle the sense of acceptance that he found when fleeing from the displeasure of Bishop Tomline.

Dykes, who was at the inauguration of the Lincoln Bible Society and aware of Sibthorp's eloquence, invited him to preach a charity sermon at St. John's. This he did on 30 March 1817 and over £70 was collected for the Female Penitentiary. Receiving other invitations to preach[3] he took lodgings in the town, and in June accepted a curacy at St. Mary's, which gave him title for ordination to the priesthood. But just a few weeks later his preaching was interrupted by a serious chest complaint. Richard was not emotionally robust, and there would be other examples of illness at times of crisis. In September his College friend Hunter wrote to W. W. Phelps: 'I have also heard from Sibthorp, who I lament to say, has been under the necessity of repairing to a celebrated physician at Leeds to put himself under his care on account of a pulmonary disorder, occasioned I am inclined to think by his over-exertion.'[4] His doctor was probably Dykes's brother-in-law, William Hey junior. By October he had recovered sufficiently to return to Lincoln to address the first Anniversary Meeting of the Bible Society. With him on the platform were his cousin, Robert Cholmeley, and John Scott. Although unable then to speak at length, explaining that while willing in spirit his flesh remained weak, he was soon ministering regularly at St. Mary's. At Canwick for Christmas, he took the opportunity of further provoking the bishop by chairing the Bible Society Anniversary at Horncastle. Five days later, on 7 January, he officiated at his brother's marriage to Mary Ellison in Beverley.[5]

How much Richard gained from his brief time in Hull is difficult to gauge. Although enhancing his Anglican respectability, he did not adopt even the mild Calvinism of the clergy there, who claimed to base their beliefs on the Homilies and Articles rather than the *Institutes* of John Calvin. Dykes said, 'I question whether either Calvinists or Arminians would own *me*.'[6] Scott too was concerned to demonstrate his entire regularity and wrote that 'even Calvin and Beza little thought that they should have any followers so mad (I use their own word) to reject such an Episcopacy as ours which had freed itself from the usurpations of Popery.'[7] But, as the son of one who famously took up arms in the fight for Calvinism against the onslaught of the Bishop of Lincoln,[8] he was more explicit than his colleague. In his commonplace book he wrote, 'Irresistible grace is an unfortunate and obnoxious expression . . . but while we give up the term let us beware that we give up no portion of the truth.'[9]

That Richard disagreed is evident from his first published sermon, preached at St. John's on 19 May 1818 'at the close of a temporary residence.' It provides an insight into his heart as well as his theological understanding, and in its plea for the reality of Christian holiness, set the *leitmotif* for the rest of his life. His theology was eclectic, owing much to the Articles and to John Wesley, something perhaps to John Scott, and undoubtedly something to Beaumont. Much of what he said was negative. He disliked systems, whether the theories of Calvin, or the traditions of the High Churchmen, seeing in both a substitute for heart religion. Instead, he proposed 'certain important truths, and no less important duties,' that he believed essential to the 'present and final well-being' of his hearers.

The first truth was justification by faith, 'the mark of a standing or a falling church.' The basis of the Christian life was 'the meritorious sacrifice and satisfaction of the Redeemer, embraced and appropriated to ourselves by faith.' It was foundational because it acknowledged mankind's sinfulness and thus inability 'of ourselves to think a good thought, much less establish any claim to heaven by our own good deeds . . . ' He acknowledged that some saw it as a doctrine, 'dangerous and licentious, and as leading certainly and ultimately to a disregard of good works,' but could not agree: only on this rock could holiness be built. Those who severed obedience from its origin in faith destroyed the peace of Christians by disconnecting the will of man from the mind of God.

Justification was the foundation of holiness: 'If we would enter into heaven . . . our corrupt natures must be changed, our unruly appetites subdued, our vile affections crucified.' Beaumont would have approved, as he would have when Richard proceeded to attack Calvinism, both in its extreme form ('the licentiousness of antinomianism') and the more moderate view of those who believed that 'Christ is to be imputed to the believer as his only *sanctification.*'[10] Wesley had been suspicious of the term 'imputed righteousness,' it was, he wrote, 'not scriptural . . . not necessary . . . it has done immense hurt.'[11] Richard, on balance, agreed. 'That the perfect righteousness of the Redeemer, to be imputed to his believing people in order to their final acceptance, may appear to many a doctrine of the gospel, I do not deny: but for any one to consider this as his only sanctification; and to hold and to teach that no other is required, and no personal holiness to be sought after in order to salvation; I cannot but account a dangerous deceit.'

The final truth he urged his hearers to strive for was the doctrine of regeneration, 'a doctrine, for the subversion or explaining away of which, powerful but unsuccessful efforts have of late been made . . . ' His allusion was to the continuing controversy surrounding the publication of Mant's Bampton Lectures, strongly upholding the High Church view of baptism. In reply, John Scott had published *An Inquiry into the effect of Baptism.* Despite using Prayer Book imagery, Scott saw the sacrament as symbolic, although conceding that regeneration might accompany it.[12] Richard's intense yearning for holiness led him wholeheartedly to support his vicar. Each Christian, he said, 'must undergo such a thorough and internal change as may fitly be called, in a spiritual sense, "a new birth."' But 'scripture, common sense and daily experience' contradicted any assertion that baptism invariably produced such a change. 'To represent this great and essential change . . . as necessarily produced wherever the sacrament of baptism is rightly administered; and to teach that no other regeneration, than such a baptismal regeneration, is to be looked for, or insisted upon; is to introduce again the darkness of popery . . . ' In 1818, the controversy still smouldered,[13] and Richard was presumably aware of how closely Mant's theological views were identified with those of the Bishop of Lincoln.[14]

Thus the preacher rejected unconditional baptismal regeneration, but neither could he accept the Calvinist view, that regeneration came to the elect alone as God's unmerited and irrevocable gift of faith. In fact, in presenting regeneration as a truth to be fought for, Richard was still pleading for holiness, for a real rather than notional Christianity. But the debate he referred to was rather about the origin of the Christian life, and on this subject the sermon contains no information, either as to how regeneration is originally conferred or who are its fitting recipients. John Wesley, too, had been concerned to stress regeneration as a life's work, of which the new birth was but a beginning, 'a remedy for all our disease, all the corruption of our nature. For "God hath also . . . given us his Holy Spirit," to renew us . . . in his moral image namely righteousness and true holiness.'[15] However, in his understanding of prevenient grace Wesley had shown – at least to his own satisfaction – how those 'dead in trespasses and sins' might progress to the new birth. Richard's religion was ever experimental not speculative, but in an increasingly fractious religious world, a lack of clarity on the important issue of regeneration made him intellectually vulnerable.

After outlining these key doctrines he approached his theme from another direction by urging his hearers to obey *the laws of the gospel*: 'That the moral law. . .hath not yet ceased to be a rule of life, is particularly declared by our church to be the doctrine of the scriptures.' Separation from the world was essential, as was diligent use 'of those means of grace, prayer and the study of the scriptures.' He then launched into an attack on the shallowness of contemporary Evangelicalism, that, in its intensity, foreshadowed aspects of the Tractarian *critique*:

> 'There is an easy religion (if religion it may be called,) which consists in frequent attendance upon public ordinances; in active exertions in support of religious and charitable institutions; and in fluently discoursing on religious topics, and on different distinguished professors or ministers of religion. A *substitute for religion* this, to which we are peculiarly exposed by the present circumstances of the Christian church in this country, and therefore one particularly deserving of notice. It is not the running from one means of grace to another, and from one sermon and one preacher to another; (a practice more amusing than profitable;) nor the being active in the cause of the various benevolent and Christian institutions, now happily abounding in this country – an activity in itself highly laudable: it is not this that constitutes that vital religion, that religion of self-denial, deadness to the world, and devotedness to God and his service, which alone can be availing to eternal salvation. We must daily mortify our corrupt affections, watch against evil tempters, struggle against those sins which do not meet the eye of man; we must carry about with us habits of self-denial, patient endurance of evil, and not less "patient continuance in well doing"; if we would indeed be disciples of the self-denied and lowly Jesus.'

In the coming years he was to encounter not a few having 'the form of godliness' without its power. Sincere faith could arise, he said, only from a 'close and intimate relation to the great and almighty Jehovah,' and 'lamented that real Christians seem generally to enjoy so little of this "spirit of adoption."' Firmly believing that 'as many as are led by the Spirit of God are the sons of God,'[16] Richard was sure that this inner work would serve to prevent, 'those shameful dissentions (*sic*) which prevail among Christians . . . '

Overall, the sermon underlines how influential the Catholic tradition remained in Richard's thinking, acquired directly from the priests he had known, and mediated indirectly through Wesley, whose High Church origins permeated his theology. Nevertheless, the preacher was confident that he simply expounded his Church's understanding of Scripture, and that obedience to these basic truths would ensure that when 'the books are opened . . . we may see each other with joy and exultation, being placed at his right hand, and welcomed with an approving smile.' His parting words were full of affection for those 'of every rank and situation' who had welcomed him to the town.[17] Of the friendships he made there, some were to endure: that, for example, with the physician, William Hulme Bodley and his wife; sixty years later he was still writing to Mrs. Bodley. He also drew close to the Scotts and John Scott addressed one of his last letters to him.[18] The two families, noted for producing celebrated architects, were linked in 1846, when Georgina, daughter of Mr and Mrs Bodley married John Scott's nephew, a Brighton surgeon;[19] twelve years later her sister, Martha, came to Lincoln as the wife of John Fowler.[20]

Hull provided good training in parish administration; both Scott and Dykes were diligent in organising for the care of souls. For example, Joseph Milner had established Friday evening meetings aimed at 'Christian intercourse and mutual edification' among the clergy and invited laymen. Dykes continued these, and Richard introduced the practice in his own churches. Intercourse with the two clergymen could also have helped him to develop his homiletic gift. Most importantly, Hull connected him with 'respectable' Evangelicalism opposed to dissent in any form. In speaking against Catholic Emancipation Dykes stressed, ' the importance, to the permanent well-being of the country, of all those safeguards which the wisdom of our ancestors had thrown around the throne and government of this country.'[21] When Richard left, it was with much clearer Anglican credentials.

The Church Missionary Society

In July 1817, Edward Bickersteth was in Hull to speak at the annual meeting of the Church Missionary Society.[22] Newly appointed as Assistant Secretary he was anxious to form local Associations. Richard was determined there should be one in Lincoln and in February the following year informed Bickersteth that a letter had been sent 'to the Cathedral and parochial clergy inviting them to join.' But, 'should they decline, which I fully expect they will' he would proceed anyway.[23] He was beginning to learn some discretion, saying that his aim was 'to avoid, as much as can be done, without injuring the cause, all publicity and noise.'[24] Among Lincoln's small Evangelical community he was becoming something of a hero, and in 1818, as a mark of their esteem, five guineas was pledged annually for the maintenance and education of an African boy, to be given his name. The subscription was still being paid five years later.[25]

He was also becoming a sought-after preacher. Advertising the inaugural meeting of Doncaster's Church Missionary Association, to be held in May 1818, the organisers hoped that the 'Rev. J. Sibthorpe' might attend.[26] He did not, being for most of the month in London at the annual meetings of the Religious Societies, and attending at the Mercers' Company. For his mother, his failure to secure the Canwick incumbency was a great disappointment, but she was soon reconciled, and in October wrote to her niece, Sarah Cholmeley: 'Oh! How I wish Richard had got this living that I might have him near me . . . (yet) . . . not having Richard we could not have a better man than Mr. Quilter . . . He is very religious and what the world in derision calls an evangelical preacher.'[27]

Richard's own disappointment was lessened because he had already accepted the living of Tattershall, believing it an important acquisition for the Evangelical cause in Lincolnshire. Yet he was unsure whether to settle there or appoint a curate, having, whilst in London, discussed the possibility of his taking up a post with the Church Missionary Society. Returning to Canwick, on 22 May he wrote to Bickersteth explaining that although strongly attracted to missionary work he did not think he could go overseas: 'I candidly own I have not yet felt, not at least permanently or decidedly, what I conclude a missionary call. I have thought of the cost and as yet, I will use no disguise, I shrink from it. For I have an only parent whose happiness here seems closely (from peculiar circumstances) interwoven with mine and whose delicate and tottering frame would I believe, sink under a separation from me under such circumstances as would attend my leaving this country as a missionary.'

He was, however, willing to undertake an administrative role and serve as an itinerant speaker. Precisely what duties were envisaged is unclear, but there was an increasing burden upon the Mission's home staff. With the post-war depression, more candidates were coming forward and those selected were quartered with Bickersteth for training. Pratt, the C.M.S. Secretary, beside his committee work edited the monthly *Missionary Register*. Both men undertook extensive speaking tours, and when in London worked long hours each day. Nevertheless, Bickersteth, anxious for graduates to serve overseas, questioned whether employing one as a clerk was appropriate. Richard had no doubts:

'The labour you say is great, but then I think how good and glorious is the cause. You say it is in great measure mere drudgery and so much so that an individual will hardly undertake it gratuitously. It may be so: but though perhaps I have not that flame of zeal and love to the Redeemer which burns in the Mission, I may through divine grace have a spark or two which may make me willing to freely labour in such a cause. I told you I would enter upon no situation that would prevent my discharging the great duty of preaching the gospel. This will not be prevented and if I cannot have the advantage of a regular congregation; I shall have another, that of speaking the Word of Life in different places, where sometimes the voice of a stranger is acceptable. Some of my friends tell me that what I may have to do is business that any lay clerk may go through, I cannot but think that the cause so consecrates the business that it is no degradation for a minister and no perversion of his calling to undertake it.'

But all this was for the future; having accepted a call to Tattershall, he wished to minister there, at least for a while:

'I am at present fixed in a situation in this county; of course, as being in this county important and which I have obtained without any obstacle. A few months will prove whether I am equal to the duty of two services every Sunday . . . and will enable me I hope to judge in some measure whether I shall be most acting for the glory of God and the good of souls by staying in it or exchanging it for another and that the one I have proposed to fill.'

In the meantime, he agreed to join Bickersteth on deputation following the meeting to inaugurate the Lincoln Church Missionary Association, planned for July 30. 'After accompanying you I can return to my flock here to consider the whole matter, with, as you will observe some little experience of what I may have to do, and between then and Christmas I hope we shall come to a decision.'[28]

Mrs. Sibthorp wrote proudly of his summer exertions: 'Richard has had a delightful tour of nearly 1200 miles for the Church Missionary Society. Highly gratified he has been upon a subject so congenial to his every wish and desire, during the five weeks he was out, he was only five nights at any inn. He was most kindly and handsomely received by different families, meeting with many pious and respectable characters and was much impressed at finding such a general spirit prevailing for the cause of true religion; and making known to all the world the gospel of our Blessed Redeemer.'[29]

It was the first of many such tours. 'The messengers of the Churches seldom failed, wherever they went, to meet with some honourable Gaius; so that if they slept at an inn, it came to be marked as a proof of missionary deadness.'[30] Appealing for funds, candidates and prayer, the ostensible aims, went along with a concern that each hearer should become a 'real Christian.' What was written of Bickersteth, applied equally to Richard Sibthorp: 'His mission was felt to be that of an Evangelist to the British Churches. His direct advocacy of the Society was one of the least of the services he rendered. "He promoted our cause," says a beloved friend at the Missionary House, "chiefly by the way in which, by his exhortations, his example, his influence, he raised the spiritual tone of the places he visited."[31] Half a century before, Wesley had been forced to take his message into the fields, a way had now been found for itinerancy to be combined with respectability.

Returning to Lincolnshire

Sibthorp's appointment to Tattershall was announced in the *Mercury* on 29 May 1818. The patron was a wealthy Devon landowner, the first Earl Fortescue, although estate responsibilities were largely in the hands of his son, Viscount Ebrington, a reformist Whig MP and an Evangelical. Ebrington was married to the daughter of Lord Harrowby – 'an Evangelical of the inner circle'[32] – and thus brother-in-law to Henry Ryder, Bishop of Gloucester. In April 1817 he and his father paid a rare visit to their Lincolnshire estates, spending a weekend at Tattershall, when the forthcoming vacancy was perhaps discussed.[33] As the living was a donative and outside the bishop's jurisdiction, the patron was free to present it to whomsoever he wished. Appointing Sibthorp was a political statement. It also suited family circumstances. Ebrington's brother, a student at Magdalene was intended for the church; the benefice was offered and accepted on the understanding that if necessary it would be vacated when he achieved the canonical age in May 1820.

Tattershall was once an important Lincolnshire town. Its wide market place and gracious Georgian houses speak still of departed glories. During Richard's incumbency it was a bustling place, and even possessed a 'millinery establishment conducted by Miss Wood who journeyed to London twice a year for fashions and novelties therewith to supply the ladies of the neighbourhood.'[34] But improving communications, especially the inauguration in 1824 of a regular steam packet service between Boston and Lincoln, meant an inevitable decline in its importance. Testifying to an even more splendid past is Tattershall Castle, a magnificent brick structure built for Lord Cromwell between 1433 and 1455: 'the prototype of much of the brick architecture of Tudor times.'[35] Later in life the builder's thoughts turned from earthly to heavenly security and he began a new church, along with a secular college, school, and almshouses.[36] Completed in 1485, Holy Trinity is one of the largest parish churches and finest examples of Perpendicular architecture in the county. The college has long vanished[37] but the bede houses survived, and remodelled in the seventeenth century, still fulfil their charitable purpose. The town had a radical reputation.[38] Mid-way through Richard's ministry, there 'were great rejoicings in the town on the acquittal of Queen Caroline ... at night lighted tar barrels were carried round and then thrown into an immense bonfire, the boys decorated with rosettes of ribbons shouting

round it "Long live Queen Caroline!"[39] Coningsby Sibthorp was a strong
supporter of the King, and those who read the newspapers knew that their
pastor had campaigned for his brother in the general election of June
1818.[40] Perhaps this contributed to his sense of isolation, for Richard
never felt 'at home' in Tattershall as he had done at Hull, and frequently
worried whether he had mistaken his ministry.

Nevertheless, he found that he could cope well with parish responsibilities and strove to make Tattershall a model: an island of spirituality in
a sea of formalism and apathy. Thus, during the autumn of 1818, invitations to preach away were declined: 'I really believe it my duty to stay at
home . . . I cannot procure in my absence any one to fill my pulpit whose
doctrines I approve, or who is approved of by my parishioners. I am here
nearly a solitary in a spiritual wilderness.'[41] By the turn of the year he was
clear that he should not move to London, 'my parish claims my first
love.'[42] The numbers attending his ministry were rising rapidly. 'Richard's
whole day is spent in doing good, before he went to Tattershall there were
very few attended the church and now you can scarcely get a seat,' wrote
his mother.[43]

This isolated part of Lindsey presented a sharp contrast to the comfortable religious world of Hull and the new incumbent was under few
illusions about the difficulties he faced. Before taking up the appointment,
he published an address to his future parishioners.[44] Parts of it were sternly
practical, and in referring to defective churchmanship, including lateness
of attendance, neglect of kneeling, the misuse of private baptism and the
'hurried, slovenly and formal manner' with which the occasional offices
were too often performed, he sought to emphasise his own regularity. He
extolled the liturgy, 'the first of uninspired compositions . . . I cannot but
consider those congregations deprived of it, however pious and efficient
their ministers may be, as sustaining a great loss.'[45] Amongst Evangelical
clergymen an emphasis on the decorum of Prayer Book worship and the
'community of worshippers' was seen as a strategy to resist the growth of
Methodism.[46] Thus the separation was being sealed, for there is no reason
to believe that the Tattershall Wesleyans ever considered discontinuing
their meetings during Sibthorp's incumbency.

Announcing his intention to be a faithful pastor, his published address
set out 'the private duties of a minister,' placing first 'the instruction of
children.' In 1815, a National School based on the 'Madras system' had
been established in the south transept, and each week he sought to spend
some hours there. It was the Church's duty: 'To instruct your children,
particularly those of such of you as, from your circumstances in life, may
not be able conveniently to have them educated elsewhere. . . to imbue
their minds with proper and religious principles . . . a duty particularly
incumbent upon ministers of religion, I shall do my utmost to discharge
it, by catechising, explaining the catechism of our church, and occasionally portions of scripture; and using other means of informing the youthful

mind on the most important subjects, as I have time and opportunity.'[47] Throughout his life Sibthorp retained a deep sense of the importance of Christian education. Speaking in 1821, he probed with some insight the motivations and impulses of young people, and the role of religious education in correcting an inherent tendency to self-deception. This education should ' make them good and happy themselves, blessings to their parents, friends and neighbours, ornaments of their church and country . . . '[48] Precept was matched with practice. In 1948, F. M. Yglesias recalled that over fifty years before, as a young curate, he had gone round the church 'with an old man who had left Tattershall for Lincoln in early life, who remarked, when he came to the south transept: "There were never such good scholars came out of Tattershall, like those who were taught here." Asked who the master was, he said, "Schoolmaster had nothing to do with it. It was Mr. Sibthorp – he was parson then, and used to teach them himself, that did it."'[49]

The School Anniversary was an important day in the village calendar. Sympathetic note was taken in the *Mercury* of that held on Thursday 8 August 1822.

'The morning was ushered in by the ringing of bells, which continued with their enlivening peal the whole of the day. At 10.30 the Rev. R. Sibthorp met at the school and placed the children in proper order, they then marched with an excellent band of music and a flag bearing the motto "Train up a child in the way He should go." After the band followed several clergymen, the committee and others of the parishioners who should chose to join them and they paraded through the village of Coningsby . . . On their return they sat down to a dinner of old English fare, roast beef and plum pudding. In the afternoon a sermon was preached by the Rev. J. Jowett rector of Silk Willoughby . . . The children then marched to the market cross where the Rev. Mr. Sibthorp gave the most deserving of them bibles and other useful books and to each of them a large plum cake . . . Too much cannot be said in praise of the minister and committee for their laudable exertions in so worthy a cause as that of promoting the educational welfare of the rising generation.'[50]

Also emphasised in the address was the duty of 'private visiting . . . especially, of such as are sick, and generally of all the flock, entrusted to my care.' Their pastor undertook to provide 'every spiritual and temporal assistance,' and trusted that 'in going from house to house, I may be regarded not as an intruder but as a friend' and prayed 'that our town may become in the highest and spiritual sense, as a "well-watered garden."'[51] To this end, meetings for prayer and bible study were undoubtedly held and attendance encouraged. In January 1819, he wrote to Bickersteth declining an invitation to join a deputation to the Irish churches: 'I have been able by the blessing of God to set on foot some plans for the good of the Parish that makes me particularly loathe to quit my station even for a few weeks.'[52]

Commenting on Sibthorp's farewell sermon at Hull, Fowler noted disapprovingly the absence of any reference to the Holy Communion.[53] There is a similar omission from the Tattershall address, but in the *Advertisement* this is referred to and a surprising reason given: 'the *importance of the subject* appeared to the writer, so great, that he felt it exceedingly difficult to compress . . . all that he would have felt it his duty to say, had he in any degree dwelt upon it.' Parishioners were assured that the subject would be fully explained from the pulpit.[54] There may be here a hint of uncertainty, making the author unwilling to put his thoughts into print. But he should be taken at his word. He looked to John Wesley, who in *The Duty of Constant Communion* spoke of the 'Christian sacrifice' as 'the food of our souls' leading us, 'on to perfection.'[55] Whatever his ecclesiastical allegiance, Richard never denied the surpassing importance of the Eucharist.

Yet for all the writer's pastoral ambitions, it was in the pulpit that he made the greatest impact. Yglesias recollected that he 'often heard the elder people speak of Mr Sibthorp's remarkable ministry and the crowds who came in waggon loads from the waterside and beyond to hear his preaching.' Some 'would point out the bow-windowed house in the Market Place as that which he had occupied . . . and who spoke of the affectionate respect he had inspired and the great work he had done.'[56] The clerical novelist, Erskine Neale, may well have heard him, and in *The Bishop's Daughter* (1842) made a Tattershall sermon on 'remembered sin' the turning point of his novel.[57] His heroine, Lady Montresor, so valued Sibthorp's preaching that she would forsake her own parish, despite the objections of 'her cultured friend' Miss Chevenix to such 'uncanonical, indefensible and vagrant proceedings,' a view perhaps shared by some of Sibthorp's clerical colleagues.

The author described the peculiar quality of the preaching, and its appeal to spiritual and other appetites. 'His voice was singularly musical, and the powers of imagination as well as the results of learning . . . were very captivating. Moreover, he was a *Celibat* (*sic*) – no mean recommendation in the eyes of the many fair who crowded around his pulpit.' When Richard left Tattershall, unmarried, aged thirty-two, some hopes were surely dashed. If he never married it was not for want of female admirers: but there is no evidence of any romantic involvement. During the final years of his mother's life, he grew even closer to her, particularly after the premature death of his brother Coningsby in 1822.[58] Involvement with any other female he seems to have found uncomfortable and avoided as much as possible. He once received 'a letter enclosing a packet of violets from one foolish woman' describing it as an example of 'my old plague of female interference.'[59]

For the modern mind the fact that Sibthorp was to establish a church choir and have several of the boys boarding with him, may raise a question mark. Yet, clergy families were happy to entrust their sons to him.

There was never any hint of scandal; not even at times when many who knew him best felt betrayed by his religious changes. Indeed, such sexual references as can be found are of a far more conventional nature. Neale wrote that his hero had been 'nearly brought within the pale of Romanism' through 'an attachment formed for him by an accomplished lady holding the Romish faith.' And one newspaper, editorialising on the reasons for his rapid exit from the Catholic priesthood in 1843, solemnly maintained that he had so succumbed to hearing female confessions that it was 'thought he was tired of being a bachelor.'[60] These writers did not know him. Those who did, such as the Lincolnshire squire, Sir Charles Anderson, never doubted the purity of his personal life.[61] It must be concluded that as Sibthorp preached so he strove to live. And as a preacher, he was in real earnest about holiness. Neale testified to 'a power, a solemnity and a pathos . . . No man perhaps ever more deeply probed the recesses of the human heart than he did in the searching application with which he generally wound up his pulpit addresses.'[62]

Sermons in print cannot convey the personality of a preacher, but in a *Second Address to the Inhabitants of Tattershall* published on New Year's Day 1819, an echo can be heard of Sibthorp pleading for the souls of his people. A solemn call for reflection, it was aimed particularly at parishioners rarely seen at church, who were asked to remember those who had died during the past year:

'The fond parents, who watched over your infancy with anxious care . . . perhaps the wife of your bosom, who shared your cares and hopes, your joys and sorrows; perhaps your children, to whom you had looked as the prop and support of your old age; and many assuredly of those, who entered with you into life, as full of expectations and anxieties as yourself – are no more. "They are fled away as a dream, and shall not be found: yea they are chased away as a vision of the night." And your time also, my dear Brethren, must ere long arrive. The hour must soon come when each of you will be carried to your long home, "and the mourners go about in the streets:" when you shall live, (and that perhaps but for a very short time,) only in the recollection of a few surviving friends, and the stranger and the way-faring man shall tread the turf that lies over your mortal remains, heedless and ignorant of him whom it covers.'[63]

The subject is conventional enough, the thoughts certainly not original, but the sheer pressure of the imagery, and the directness, in itself eloquent, must have left his hearers in no doubt as to the seriousness of the matters he pressed upon them. The spiritual and the practical were disturbingly combined: 'when we stand around the death-bed of a beloved object, and anxiously watch each fleeting breath, how indescribably solemn is the thought (and yet how just and how true!) that a few minutes will decide the Eternal state of that soul and put it beyond the reach either of any more joy, or any more pain.' Tattershall was not Hull, and the sins he rebuked were not those of hypocritical professors but swearing, Sabbath-breaking, drunkenness, impurity. 'Be not offended at this plainness of speech . . . examine well your consciences . . . you are on the very brink of the bottomless pit. You are suspended over it by a hair; by that thread of life, which God can in a moment cut.' More than formal profession was needed: 'If any man savingly believe in Christ, he will do His Will, and keep his commandments. His faith will work by love, and evidence itself in holiness of heart and life.'[64]

By the time of Neale's novel the preacher had become a Roman Catholic, perhaps explaining why the author detected, 'a mysticism . . . a dash . . . of what bordered on the romantic and speculative in religion', referring to one celebrated sermon on the offices of Satan, as a particular example of this. Yet, 'there was too, *at this period*, a force, vividness and SCRIPTURAL TRUTH about Mr. Sibthorp's ministrations which won for them acceptance even with the fastidious, and the worldly and the indifferent. His preparations for the pulpit were the evident fruits of severe and well-directed study. His sermon was never written. It was delivered from notes. But it was no crude, hasty or immature effort . . . The gem was elaborately set. It came rounded, sparkling, and polished, from the crucible of study, reflection, and prayer.' Neale said that Sibthorp invariably passed Friday and Saturday in privacy, and would tackle his subject with 'earnestness and ardour,' adding, 'Such diligence must tell.'[65]

The sermon featured in *The Bishop's Daughter* was almost certainly delivered at Tattershall. The book explores the impact of its solemn warning that before the 'Supreme, the remembrance of sin never perishes.' 'Mr Sibthorp had left the pulpit long, long before Lady Montresor was sufficiently recovered to leave the church.' Something long forgotten had been re-awakened, and although assured that only 'sin for which no contrition had been expressed and no pardon . . . sought,' was meant, she had not drawn that conclusion.[66] There was something quite characteristic in this. Most Evangelical preachers would have been at pains to stress the certainty of forgiveness, but Richard Sibthorp probed the conscience, ever seeking for contrition and for reality.

Seeking Direction

After becoming established in his parish, Richard found it harder to resist requests that he leave it. Visiting his ageing mother at Canwick was a priority, as was deputation work for the Religious Societies. He enjoyed London and was usually at the May meetings. He also kept up links with Oxford and was scrupulous in attending to College business. Providing for his pulpit during an extended absence was a concern, but the C.M.S. could sometimes supply an ordained man waiting to leave on missionary service. In 1819, John Perowne was his *locum tenens* during a tour of the West Country and Midlands.[67] On returning to Lincolnshire in August,

Sibthorp accompanied Dr Steinkopff of the Bible Society to a number of meetings in the county. Back in Tattershall for the autumn and again immersed in the parochial ministry, he resisted further invitations to preach away. 'I am at this place, not only without any clerical help that I could approve of, but without any help at all, except, as we say, accidentally.'[68] He decided a curate was required and with the arrival of a Mr. Llewellyn in June 1820, was able to undertake his annual tour for the Religious Societies. The following year he was appointed by the C.M.S. 'Honorary Governor for Life, having rendered very essential services', one of the three so honoured, another was the celebrated minister of St Paul's Sheffield, Thomas Cotterill.[69]

In November 1820, Richard wrote to Bickersteth with significant news. 'I have lately been called upon to offer myself for a station of very great importance in this county: a church in its most flourishing town. How it may be determined I cannot tell, "The lot is cast into the lap, but the whole disposing thereof is of the Lord." But I have been urged to offer for it by arguments that seemed the strongest possible, "If you do not come forward no other Evangelical minister is likely."'[70] After a period of reflection, he determined to accept, 'as a more important station than my present.'[71] The town was Boston, where under the incumbency of Bartholomew Goe the parish church had become unable to accommodate the numbers wishing to worship.[72] In April 1818 the *Mercury* reported, 'The opulent and spirited town of Boston is to erect a chapel auxiliary to the Established Church so that the most beautiful parish church in England should not be deformed by galleries.'[73] A Committee was formed, funds solicited, and in December the Corporation promised an endowment yielding £100 per annum. The following May a private Act of Parliament provided that for the first fifteen years the right of patronage would lie with the subscribers.[74] On 23 June 1820, the first stone was laid and later that year Sibthorp was invited to stand for election to the ministry.[75]

This development encouraged Bickersteth to re-open a matter that remained unresolved and in his reply asked his friend whether his true call might not be to the mission field: to India. Richard was troubled and replied on 8 February. 'Your letter reached me on Monday morning and its contents have been a continual subject of my thoughts and meditations ever since – Oh that God might count me worthy to bear this charge and that I might live and die in that blessed and heavenly work to which your letter invites me. I wish much for the advice and opinion of Mr. Pratt and yourself as to my line of duty under present circumstances. It is my first and anxious desire to be employed as a feeble instrument in the hands of God, in promoting the Kingdom of Christ among the heathen. I have again and again during the last two years given myself before God to it, if He should see fit to send me.' He felt convicted by 'the last commandment of the Lord,' which 'is not yet fulfilled and still is binding as ever on those who are called to the ministry of the Gospel.' Indeed, he believed the call was linked to his spiritual health: 'my desires toward this work have been stronger as my views of Divine things have been safe . . . and . . . that keeping this work in view has had, through the grace of God, a salutary effect on my own mind. It has always stirred me up to more watchfulness. Nor can I deny that when I have stood back from it, for I have done so, I have been strongly influenced by the love of ease, by timidity, and by the loss of approbation in my ministry at home. If I know anything of the witness . . . of my own heart it would be the highest blessing . . . to see . . . my way clear to India.'

Painfully aware how his upbringing had shaped his character he doubted his capacity. 'Hardships I have scarcely known and inconvenience but seldom, and pride, sloth and timidity have been produced by the circumstances of my early life.' This led on to the most compelling objection. 'That my own family, who have scarcely I feel any other idea of a missionary than of something, half enthusiast, half knave, will oppose such a step you can easily imagine. I sometimes reflect upon the subject and can hardly conceive what they will think or do. But to one of them I owe a duty, which I do not to the rest: to my dear and aged mother. Particular circumstances have made the tie between her and myself close. Her mind though gradually opening to the excellency of religion is not so far opened to give me up, as Hannah of old to God and his work. Her life hangs upon a thread . . . I would not without the clearest call and her approbation leave England during her lifetime . . . Yet, I should not consider this any obstacle to my immediately giving myself up to missionary work, for the period that God may be pleased to spare her to me would not, I conceive be lost to that work, if employed in studies preparatory to it. I should be ready (when) the last tie was cut that held me to England to go forth into the vanguard.'

As regards Boston, the position was becoming clearer. 'There is another candidate, not, I fear an Evangelical and the votes of the Trustees . . . are nearly even between us, but . . . I think it probable I shall have a small majority in my favour. The opposite party have intimated an intention of applying to the bishop to prevent my election, or not to license me if elected.' He said he would resist any attempt to set limits to his ministry. Indeed, re-awakened to the missionary call, he was no longer sure whether actively to pursue the appointment. 'Am I to persevere for Boston and to look to God to order the issue of that business or am I to put before me from this moment the work you call me to and to seek it henceforth, looking to God to hedge up my way and wall up my path if I am going wrong?'[76]

Within a few days of this letter, there was a dramatic change in his family circumstances. His eldest brother, Coningsby, member for Lincoln since 1814, and an unbending Tory, had antagonised many of the city's inhabitants by refusing to present a widely-supported petition on behalf of Queen Caroline. On the evening of 23 February 1821, the linchpin was maliciously removed from a wheel of the carriage in which he and three relatives were travelling and in the ensuing accident he suffered terrible injuries.[77] Richard, who bore the main burden of his mother's grief,[78] was now sure that he could not leave Lincolnshire and writing to Bickersteth a fortnight later, confirmed that he would accept a call to Boston. 'Considering this and that if I withdraw there is humanly speaking no probability of the gospel now being established there, . . . and above all since I may safely trust my Heavenly Father . . . a sense of duty not inclination leads me.' However, 'There is a pious and valuable minister now residing near Boston who has no less than three times, in his letters to me, intimated that I may, after accepting the post for a short time, resign it; – and has twice added that he may then be ready and willing to take it.' Thus, he would still prepare for India, 'to carry the good news of his love (if he shall see good to send me) to those who have yet to hear it . . . the principal objection to the occupying of Boston for a time is the hindrance it will present to my studies, but I must use greater diligence.'[79] As a pledge of serious intention he asked his friend to contact the celebrated Cambridge orientalist, Professor Samuel Lee, and soon received a formidable reading list, including grammars, dictionaries and texts in Bengalee, Arabic, Hindustanee and Parsee.[80] Above all, Lee recommended the study of Hebrew with a view either to translation or the revision of a translation.[81] Thoughts of India now filled his mind, and if his mother had died in the summer of 1821, rather than five years later, it seems certain he would have sailed. 'I can truly say that the subject is principally uppermost in my mind all the time – I fear I am sometimes impatient . . . I feel at times much cast down and troubled at my delaying at all to enter on this work . . . I am naturally impatient beyond most.'[82]

Leaving the parish to his curate, in May he was at Cambridge speaking for the C.M.S., and there met Lee, as well as other leading Evangelicals, such as Simeon, Farish, and Scholefield. The *Cambridge Chronicle* was impressed. 'The Rev. Sibthorp adverted in a feeling manner to the privilege of living in times like these, as possessing a decided advantage over the envied period of the Reformation; in as much as our Reformers beheld only the first glimmerings of that light which was now approaching to meridian fullness. And as our arms and commerce had been extended almost throughout the world, he claimed the same privilege of extension for our holy religion.'[83] The missionary William Jowett, brother of the rector of Silk Willoughby, was delighted. He advised the Society to send him 'to some of the more intelligent associations, as Bristol, Birmingham, Hull, York and Leeds and that for this purpose he should seriously study everything connected with one or more of the Society's stations.' This, he added, 'would serve greatly to enlarge and confirm and clear his views.'[84]

Richard spent the summer preaching among the churches of north Lincolnshire and the East Riding, and in the autumn gave up his house at

Tattershall and returned to live at Canwick, where both his brother and mother were in poor health. From there he wrote to William Jowett, 'My mother is much as usual, gradually, I think getting thinner and weaker. Yet I hope her mind is fixing on better things and a better world; and, under the blow which has long impended and which I truly shrink from contemplating I trust through God's mercy I shall have the consolation of sorrow not without hope.' He confessed that with his books packed-up his studies had been desultory, but he had profited from 'a work by Mr. Hughes – *Travels in Albania*'; and now wondered whether his call might be to the Mediterranean. He reported that the Boston subscribers had elected him by a large majority, but ominously, the bishop wished to see him. Richard feared that restrictions would be placed on his extra-parochial ministry, and to this he would not agree. Committed to England during the lingering decline of his mother, somewhat disenchanted with Tattershall, where he was expecting that Fortescue would soon replace him, and unsure about Boston, he sighed, 'As to my present prospects I certainly do not walk by sight.' He told Jowett of a recent incident that might be significant: 'About a month since I received the offer of two livings in this county a few miles from this place, with the certainty, if spared, of another, not far off in a few years. Was it God's will 'to fix me in this county and give me two or three stations to fill in it?' Perhaps not: 'I hope I cast the burden on God and I believe he has cleared away the difficulty. Yesterday the patron intimated that as I could not officiate myself at them he must decline to present me; at the same time I got the offer of them for a pious neighbour.'[85] With the death of John Deacon, the livings of Harmston and Rouston had become vacant. The patronage had passed to Benjamin Thorold, the son of Joseph Hart, the hymn writer, who was far more sympathetic to vital religion than his father-in-law, whose name he had taken; indeed, it was about this time that he became a Methodist preacher.[86]

Confirmation that Sibthorp's future was not in Lincolnshire came soon. If the Evangelicals hoped that Tomline's recent translation to Winchester would ease their position, they were soon disappointed, for George Pelham had perhaps even less sympathy with his 'serious' clergy. No record can be traced of the grounds of his refusal to licence the Boston subscribers' choice, but undoubtedly he was quick to seize on any opposition.[87] In the event, the outcome was not the setback to the gospel that Richard had feared. The electors compromised and the Rev. Richard Conington, a recent graduate of Lincoln College, and member of a well-established Horncastle family, was their unanimous choice. He proved to be stalwart in his commitment to the causes of which Pelham so strongly disapproved.[88]

There was a curious postscript to Richard's disappointment. In May 1825, Conington received the following letter:

'The Bishop of Lincoln having heard that sermons are about to be preached in your Chapel of Ease at Boston in aid of the Church Missionary Association, his Lordship has desired me to express his astonishment that you should lend your Pulpit at any time to a person, whom as you must well know, his Lordship would not licence to that very Chapel; and his Lordship therefore desires that you will without loss of time, inform Mr Sibthorp that he cannot be permitted to preach in your Chapel. The Bishop desires to add that he can foresee no benefit likely to result from a Church Missionary Association being established at Boston and that such an Association will never meet with his Lordship's concurrence in any part of his Diocese.'[89]

Dandeson Coates of the C.M.S. had some experience of these situations, and advised Conington:

'We much regret the tenor of the Bishop of Lincoln's letter, both as it respects Mr Sibthorp and the Society. We are quite unaware that there is anything in the principles or proceedings of the C.M.S., to give any just cause of offence to his Lordship or to call for the expression of his Lordship's unfriendly disposition toward the Society; neither are we acquainted with anything in the conduct of Mr Sibthorp which could have led us to expect that his Lordship would interdict him from preaching a sermon in your Chapel on behalf of the Society.

As however, it has uniformly been the practice of the Committee to conduct the Society's affairs with the utmost practical deference to the expressed wishes and feelings of the Bishops of our Church, I beg to suggest whether, as the case actually stands, that you yourself preach the proposed sermons, stating that circumstances had occurred which prevented Mr Sibthorp from fulfilling his engagement. We would not concede or invalidate the great principles on which the Society is founded but neither would we, where it can be avoided press those principles in a way that might be offensive or indecorous.'[90]

All this correspondence was conducted within a few days of the Sunday on which the sermons were to be delivered. The next day, 23 May, Richard wrote to Coates from Boston: ' I thought it my duty to appear on Sunday and show the cause why I did not occupy the pulpit was not my own backwardness.' He added that at that evening's public meeting he had vindicated the Society as 'valuable and in all points correct and orthodox,' and 'adverted only briefly to the reason why I did not preach – I stated it candidly. The Bishop has very little influence here and his opposition has no weight except with those who will not join it at any rate (*sic*).' [91]

The year 1822 opened with Richard still unsettled. Rebuffed from Boston, and surmising that he might soon be asked to resign Tattershall, he told Bickersteth of his plan to 'make a final attempt on the little less than Heathenism of this place.' Parting company with his curate he returned to the town, but did not mean to remain long. He said that if Fortescue failed to come he would look for another curate, 'to be ready to take my place here in God's good time.' This would set him 'more at liberty' to speak for the Society and pursue his Hebrew studies.[92] In February he arranged that the C.M.S. should provide a *locum* to free him, at the end of March, to tour the West Country, for it and the Bible Society. This arrangement however, depended on his health, for he was again suffering from his old complaint: 'exertion of my voice even in conversation for half an hour brings a hoarseness and uneasiness in my chest and . . . I am obliged to give up almost all private ministerial duties and my public ones, except one Sunday service.'[93] A few days later he was summoned to Canwick, where Coningsby's health was rapidly deteriorating, and on 7 March wrote from there to Tarn of the Bible Society, seeking to be excused from the planned tour. 'Your letter of the 4th followed me from Tattershall to this place whither I have been brought by the very alarming illness of my eldest brother. I lament to say that of his recovery there now remains no hope. He may have many days or he may be removed at any time.'[94] He died two days later. Charles de Laet succeeded him to the estates and in 1826, as member for Lincoln.

Towards the end of April, Richard joined Bickersteth and Joseph Hughes (of the Bible Society) for part of their West Country deputation, but subsequently remained in Lincolnshire, spending much time at Canwick.[95] Despite learning that John Fortescue, having been appointed to a Magdalene College living, would not be displacing him, he had begun to plan for the end of his ministry. In June, in declining a request for assistance from the Bible Society, he explained: 'My continuance at Tattershall is at present quite uncertain, but I rather expect I shall hold it at least for some months longer. Also I shall keep close residence and be as little as possible absent.'[96] In September, after another approach he agreed, reluctantly, to undertake an autumn tour of Yorkshire, although confessing himself unequal to advocating the cause in 'great meetings such as may be expected at Leeds.' He trusted he would be 'kept from saying anything really injudicious or unsuitable, yet it requires on such occasions a pleader of a different kind from myself . . . However, I shall not withdraw.'[97]

The Progress of the Gospel

To 'secure the gospel to Tattershall,'[98] by ensuring a suitable successor was now a priority and it appears that a curate designated to assume the incumbency arrived in 1823. Samuel Hillyard had been a schoolmaster at Almondbury, and in 1819 was ordained *literate*. He was a remarkable self-taught man, and a 'brilliant preacher.'[99] In 1821, his parish minister died, and he did not remain long under his successor.[100] It is possible that his neighbour H. J. Maddock – the first incumbent of Holy Trinity, Huddersfield, and a popular speaker for the Religious Societies – who would have known of his circumstances, recommended him to Sibthorp when they met in Yorkshire in October 1822.[101] With a curate in place, in August and September the following year, Richard undertook a major tour of the Midlands on behalf of the C.M.S. He was beginning to be seen as one of the foremost speakers on the Evangelical circuit. Archdeacon Spooner wrote from Birmingham that 'Mr Sibthorp's assistance in the cause in this neighbourhood has given very great satisfaction . . . For myself I cordially rejoice in having been so much with him and feel that my little endeavours are abundantly rewarded in having made an acquaintance, I trust I may say, formed a friendship with so ca. . .(pable?) a man and minister'.[102]

The gospel cause was making strides nationally, and in Lincolnshire too there were encouraging signs. In Louth, for example, where Robert Milne was appointed curate in 1822.[103] He was a man of decided and forceful views, whose preaching divided a town that had hitherto enjoyed a reputation as a rather somnolent home for a group of convivial clergy who served the nearby parishes. The *Mercury* wrote of his 'convulsive oratory' which, 'like an earthquake tears all up before it and leaves an impression never to be effaced.'[104] In December 1823, he contacted Sibthorp to tell him of an imminent meeting to establish a Church Missionary Association in the town, taking it for granted that he would attend and speak. Richard demurred and wrote to Bickersteth to explain why 'my attendance at Louth would rather hurt than forward the cause of the Missionary Society in that quarter.' He was surprised that the High Church establishment there had embraced Milne's scheme, putting it down to their ignorance. But should it be known that he was a supporter they would soon be disabused: 'to me, there attaches in this county the stigma of Methodism, Enthusiasm and all the other fearful isms, which are levelled at certain doctrines, and ways of proceeding, called evangelical. I feel afraid (humanly speaking) that I should raise alarm and suspicion by joining you on the Monday.' Moreover, the situation in Louth was very sensitive. 'Mr Milne, I apprehend on the balance between going and staying: that is, there is a strong party forming against him on account of his very warm zeal, to say the least: and a strong party for him on account of his general attention to the interests of his parish, his good character etc. Which will prevail time only can show.' He advised his friend to tread cautiously and 'address the people of Louth as you would address Dr. Gaskin only with this difference, that religion is beginning to work in this place to a promising degree and you may have far more hope of gaining them to help you than Dr. Gaskin.'[105]

The Meeting proceeded without him. A few days afterwards Milne wrote to Bickersteth: 'I had given particular directions to our friends not to allow any account of our proceedings to be published in the Newspapers lest it should excite hostility in certain quarters before we are able to stand a shock. But last night an article of considerable length appeared in the *Stamford Mercury*. This has caused me to feel no small degree of alarm for the consequences.'[106] Events thereafter took the course Richard feared and in September Milne preached his farewell sermon. According to the *Mercury*, there were emotional scenes, for he was leaving despite a declaration of support with 'upwards of 2600 names.'[107] The tenor of his final sermon may be gauged from the text: 'For I have not shunned to declare unto you the whole counsel of God.' Later published as *The Minister's Last Appeal*, it was a bitter attack on his clerical brethren, 'enemies of the gospel' who 'taught that men are not now to be made Christians . . . through the preaching of the Gospel . . . but by a simple ritual ceremony.'[108] In the weeks after his dismissal, Milne engaged in a flurry of activity on behalf of the C.M.S. In December, it was announced that William Wilberforce had presented him to the living of Swine in East Yorkshire. Yet he went, not to Yorkshire, but to London,[109] writing a series of letters to Bickersteth, with instructions about managing the Society's affairs in Lincolnshire and stipulating places that Sibthorp must visit. Towards the end of this correspondence, there is a hint that some glimmer of self-awareness had begun to dawn: 'I begin to suspect that my endeavours to promote the interests of the Society have been considered officious and I must keep a little at a distance for the future.'[110] His subsequent career was not distinguished. In 1833, proceedings were instituted against him for non-residence at Swine and five years later he was deprived of his benefice.

Nevertheless, the brief impression he made at Louth was remarkable. Evangelicalism was spreading in the county[111] and weakening Richard's sense of special responsibility towards it. Thus, he continued to unfasten his remaining links with his parish and at the beginning of 1824, told Bickersteth, 'I give you full leave to find me full employment' and as an earnest agreed to spend March and April on deputation. Thomas Sutton, the vicar of Sheffield, had recently asked him to succeed one of his curates, Thomas Cotterill, whose early death was widely mourned. It was a compliment, especially as Sutton had travelled to Tattershall to see him, but he had declined, 'For many reasons which appear to my mind duties . . . Mr Sutton may easily find one better suited to succeed him they have lost: nor does the continuance of the gospel in that church at all depend on my acceptance of it.[112] I must own to you that I consider the missionary cause as having the first claim upon me – the curacy of St Paul's would very materially confine me from giving that humble help to your cause that I am now able to give. I think of giving up my situation here and removing to London before the year has expired. There I shall be ready to give the Society any help it may require without becoming officially engaged to it at first. I shall be able to go on with . . . studies and wait to see whither the Lord would lead me. I feel no doubt so far as I can judge that I may leave my present post. I hope I desire not to have my own way, but to be and do what the Lord pleases.'[113]

But knowing God's will was problematical, particularly when

Bickersteth, now Secretary of the Society, presented him with a proposition. Administrative pressures at Missionary House were at boiling point, and when the Committee met on 23 April, it was agreed to create a post of Second Secretary and offer it to Sibthorp.[114] He replied a few days later from Newcastle in Staffordshire, where he was on deputation, explaining why he could not, at present, accept. He said he needed to devote time to 'securing the gospel' to Tattershall, which would require 'time and a little management.' It is not clear exactly what this meant, perhaps the patron was not happy with his choice of successor, or perhaps he felt that Hillyard needed further guidance. Feeling also a responsibility to remain near his increasingly feeble mother, he wrote of wanting 'that satisfactory proof to my own mind of the Divine will, which would enable me to join you with entire comfort.' Although anxious to help 'either travelling or in London,' he dared not become formally committed, 'without being satisfied in my own mind that I am fulfilling my duty as it respects all those who have a claim on me.'[115] His letter was read to the Missionary Committee on 30 April; the members recorded their regret, believing that the appointment would have 'materially promoted the Society's interests.'[116]

Leaving Lincolnshire

On 27 July 1824, Thomas Dykes preached at Tattershall School Anniversary, a celebration which effectively marked the end of Richard's incumbency. Within a fortnight he was back at Canwick and from there travelled to Nottingham at the start of another tour on behalf of the Religious Societies, after which he planned a brief stay at Tattershall and then removal to London. He told Bickersteth that he wished 'to help as I can, by way of correspondence etc. at Church Missionary House, and by Christmas I shall be able, I hope, to make a final decision to accept or decline the Secretaryship.'[117] By November his plans had changed and he wrote from Canwick formally declining the C.M.S. proposal. He was unwilling to set down his reasons, telling Bickersteth; 'Could I have some conversation with you and open my whole mind to you I am satisfied that even yourself, after all your solicitations, would approve entirely of my decision.' For the present, he must stay in Lincolnshire. 'My mother and her companion are both declining: and more than ever need my frequent visits: so that if there were no other weightier reasons for sojourning longer "amid the tents of Kedar," for so only my present station is, I should feel it a duty to do so. Thus I can most truly take up the language of the whole verse and say, "Woe is me that I am constrained."'[118] He said he would remain until the spring but then would be ready to assist the Society.

Richard had relinquished the incumbency; nevertheless, he renewed the lease of his Tattershall house for another year.[119] In the absence of any other pulpit in Lincolnshire, he regarded even a curate's role there as his appointed station, although he was ill at ease. He told his sister: 'But for wishing to be near them, (his mother and her companion), I should rejoice to leave a place which neither suits mind nor body; for here is no society whatever of any kind, and I think the air is too soft and relaxing to suit me.'[120] To Bickersteth he had written of 'weightier reasons' that detained him. These possibly had to do with concerns about his eldest brother, who on 9 August had duelled with Dr. Charlesworth following an exchange of insults at a turnpike meeting. Shots were exchanged, 'happily no injury was sustained.'[121] Charles had always been somewhat erratic, but in the opinion of the Lincoln diarist, Colonel Weston Cracroft, inheriting the estates did him no good: 'the change in circumstances changed the man and he became heartless and purse-proud, leading a life of intemperance, riot and wickedness.'[122] To his parliamentary colleagues he was to become a 'character', a Regency hang-over, and treated with amused tolerance.[123] But closer to home there was pain and embarrassment, caused especially by his notorious philandering, leading eventually to divorce.[124] On the evening of 3 November, unaccompanied by his wife, he had graced the Stuff Ball, the highlight of the Lincoln social calendar. The following day Richard wrote declining the C.M.S. post. Perhaps the events were linked?

These were difficult days. Early in November, Richard returned to Tattershall, but then, rather mysteriously, he got into some difficulty that made it expedient for him to leave and not return. On 27 December he wrote from Hull, where he had been staying for 'some weeks among my different friends' to assure Bickersteth that he was 'much better . . . in mind and body', adding 'I have had a narrow and very providential escape from evil of no common magnitude and trust to have cause for ever to praise and adore that grace which interposed to rescue me from some most unprincipled men.'[125] Having now 'entirely given up Tattershall . . . where I shall fix myself, I am at present quite undetermined . . . I propose, the Lord willing, to visit London in February and stay there for some little time. I will give you what help I can during this coming year, but you must not consider me pledged to anything because I know not what circumstances may occur to call me to other duties.'[126]

He probably delayed his departure to London, because by February his mother's health had so deteriorated that Mrs Hawkins was summoned to Canwick. However, the old lady defied confident expectations of her demise and by the early spring of 1825 was well enough for Richard to leave,[127] returning in May to deliver a farewell sermon at Tattershall. In common with many of his Evangelical colleagues, his thoughts were increasingly occupied with the apocalyptic and thus he pressed upon his old flock, the 'certainty and probable nearness of the Second Coming' as a clarion call to faith. Bidding farewell at Hull, he had hoped to meet his friends again, but in leaving Tattershall, he thought it probable that 'they may never meet again until that great day of final account.' Both sermons listed 'those great truths, on the right knowledge, belief and reception of which depend our present and eternal happiness . . . ' But there was a greater urgency now. 'Have you accepted the Saviour's invitation to come unto him? . . . Have you really sought the Lord? And have you so known and embraced the truth as it is in Jesus, that it has in a measure delivered you from the sin, the world and the devil?' He challenged his hearers to ask themselves whether they were truly 'in the faith.' This raised the thorny issue of assurance, much associated with the Methodists. The preacher was sure that it was in Scripture. 'Truly to desire the coming again of Christ, and for the purposes for which he will come, implies a solid well-founded hope of having a saving interest in him. It implies that assurance of hope which, however it may be abused, perverted and misunderstood, it is the duty of the Christian to seek and his privilege to enjoy.' Still some resisted the gospel. 'Drunkards, unchaste, Sabbath-breakers, profane, swearers, ungodly, worldly, sensual', all were warned: 'Tremble at the declaration of Christ, "I come quickly."' Yet he was quite sure that 'there are some here who desire and pray for the coming of the Saviour . . . ' He described the manner of life expected from them and concluded: 'May you be holy and unblameable! meek yet firm, gentle yet decided, zealous yet prudent, earnest yet cautious, pressing forward yet considerate, made all things to all, yet to all and before all, a Christian! condescending to the meanest yet before the highest, still recollecting you are a royal priest! active without hurry, serious without melancholy, retired without indolence, simple without affectation, singular without aiming to be so, ever seeking after and praying for the mind that was in Christ!'[128]

The sermon suggests some progression in Richard's Protestantism; the tone is distinctly individualistic, with no references to the place of the Church or her sacraments. Yet, the context must be borne in mind: his urgent desire for the conversion of those still untouched by his ministry. And his choice of the imminence of the Second Advent was more than an hortatory device: his conviction that the prophecies did indeed point to this gave particular force to these solemn parting words. He had been so much with Evangelicals; their language had become second nature. Yet, however deeply buried, Catholic thinking never really left him, and Tattershall had much that would have nourished a spirit always sensitive to the symbolic and mystical in religion. Twenty-five years later, no longer an Evangelical, he built thirteen bede houses. Was a seed sown during the time he lived among the old people who were the beneficiaries of Cromwell's charity? In the church were many reminders of a departed faith, including a magnificent rood screen and extensive chancel testifying to long traditions of Eucharistic worship. The former was used as a singing gallery, and the latter, equipped with a fine pulpit, had become the preaching place.[129] One reminder of departed glory still affronts every visitor: the despoliation of the splendid medieval stained glass. In 1754,

Lord Fortescue gave it to the Earl of Exeter, who paid for the reglazing of the nave in clear glass.[130] Not until the new century was the chancel re-glazed so that nearly all the richly carved wood in the choir had rotted away and much damage done to the stonework. Sibthorp himself expended a 'considerable sum' in collecting the remnants of ancient glass that remained and having them placed in the East Window.[131] Yet, despite these reminders, in 1825 Richard's Catholicism was but an ember, and he would surely have pointed to the clear glass as representing the light that shone upon the English Church, reformed in obedience to God's Word.

At Tattershall, Sibthorp proved his power as a preacher and lives were changed under his ministry. But he never felt at ease there, and to add to his regrets, his successor proved a disappointment. Nowhere in his farewell address does he commend to the people their new pastor, and as far as is known he never returned to preach. Hillyard's forceful rhetoric proved an unreliable indicator of his commitment to warm-hearted Evangelicalism. He did not support the Religious Societies, and was soon in conflict with his flock. In 1829, for example, the local newspaper reported a disappointing school feast and a dispute over the ringing of bells.[132] All this, at the time Milne was pursuing his erratic course, would have done nothing to assuage Richard's concerns, first voiced at Hull, about the potential unreality of high-sounding religious language.

Many lamented his departure. One was George Ranyell, who became a Methodist missionary. His official obituary (in the *Minutes of Conference* of 1884) includes the statement that in early life he was 'the subject of deep religious impressions.' This was in Tattershall during Sibthorp's incumbency. In February 1834, *en-route* to the West Indies and delayed at Portsmouth, he visited his old pastor at Ryde. Richard gave him a gift of books and asked why he and others had deserted his successor for the Wesleyans. Ranyell answered that when he left they had felt like sheep that had lost their shepherd.[133] Years later Sibthorp wrote feelingly about Anglicanism's inability to hold on to the poor, but in truth he found the realities of rural parish life frustrating and having 'planted the gospel' in this isolated part of Lincolnshire, felt he had come to the end of what he could usefully do. Where should he go? The missionary flame was burning lower, but the call to preach more insistent than ever. Excluded from Lincoln pulpits,[134] in London he knew he would be welcomed.

3

SEEKING DIRECTION
London and Oxford

On 7 May 1825, Richard Sibthorp preached at St. John's Bedford Row. It was probably not his first sermon there since moving to London some weeks earlier, but this time his words were taken down, and published in the *Pulpit* of 15 September. His theme was 'Providence' and the sermon was, according to the magazine, 'luminous and striking, according with the declarations of Divine truth, and borne out to the full judgement and experience of God's people.' His reference to the place of Providence in the history of the early Church is especially interesting:

> 'She has spread her conquests over the vast Roman empire. The imperial purple is seen bowing at her altar. She receives the homage of the nations of the earth. Then, in the midst of her territories, there rises up, *"the man of sin"*, calling himself, "the vice-regent of God" – assuming all the power of her lawful husband, and assuming it, not to bless, but to curse – not to preserve her as a chaste virgin, but to dress her out as a harlot – not to spread before her the letters of her Lord for her guidance, but to shut them up from her view – and to rule over her and oppress her thus the space of twelve hundred years!'[1]

It was being increasingly said that the 1200 years of oppression had ended. A few days later, in bidding farewell at Tattershall, Sibthorp explained why he too believed the End Times had come: 'the general spread of the gospel, the success of endeavours to convert distant nations to Christianity, the apparent approaching downfall of the Mahometan power; the present aspect of Popery rousing herself with extraordinary violence to a fierce and final contest against the Church of God.'[2]

Such was common ground among most students of prophecy, but there was disagreement as to what these signs portended.[3] The difference was largely one of generation. In the heady days that marked the end of the Napoleonic Wars, when the new Religious Societies were flourishing, it was easy to believe that a golden age was about to dawn. Maitland wrote in 1814 of 'the glories of the latter day . . . the Sun of Righteousness is now about to rise on a disordered and sin-distracted world.'[4] But with the harshness of the post-war years optimism became harder to sustain, especially among those not old enough to appreciate how far evangelical religion had permeated society.[5] It was hard, for example, to see the religious condition of London as an harbinger of a gospel millennium. In 1823, Haldane Stewart the minister of Percy Chapel had published *The State of the Metropolis*. Its tone was gloomy, even fearful: infidelity and vice were rampant, the Sabbath desecrated. This essay followed his extremely influential and widely-circulated pamphlet of two years before, *Thoughts on the Importance of Special Prayer for the General Outpouring of the Holy Spirit,*[6] which contrasted the hopes of 1815 with the 'extraordinary disquietude which now prevails.' Such was the political uncertainty, that 'men's hearts are failing them for fear, and for looking for those things that are coming on the earth.' Stewart pleaded that it would take more than money and efficient religious societies to usher in the millennium. He supposed that 'in no age of the world have so many benevolent attempts been made. . . . But what has been the effect produced by these societies? . . . It is a melancholy fact, that amidst the active operations of all our moral and religious societies . . . the Sabbath-day is openly violated . . . our prisons were never so full of culprits . . . infidel publications addressed to the lower orders, were never so numerous.'[7] The attempt to integrate this alarm into the interpretation of prophecy was leading to a rediscovery of the chiliasm of the primitive church, the belief that the millennium would not be the final flowering of the Church age, but a completely new dispensation. Christ, it was said, would soon return to earth to commence His reign of a thousand years, an event to be preceded by violence and judgements. Pre-millennialism, long out of favour because of the tumults of the Commonwealth, had never been completely abandoned; Bishop Newton for example did not discount it.[8] But it was perhaps when the charismatic Edward Irving began to proclaim his 'conviction of an approaching crisis in the fate of the world'[9] that the new theory moved from the arena of scholarly debate to become a matter of intense public interest.[10]

Richard's cousin, Sir Montague Cholmeley, was closely involved with the students of prophecy, and in March 1826 married the sister of Lewis Way, an early propagandist for the pre-millennial return. The latter's forceful advocacy of the cause had led to his resignation from the London Society for the Promotion of Christianity among the Jews, notwithstanding its dependence on his financial support; indeed it was largely his creation.[11] Although Richard never set out in detail his own beliefs regarding the millennium, he retained throughout his life a strong sense that the *Parousia* could come at any time. What did it mean for him to believe that it was more likely that his present life would be ended by the personal return of Christ than by death, and that this event would come suddenly and unexpectedly? At the very least, it would surely have fed his deep sense of accountability and the need to attend carefully to the promptings of the Spirit.'[12]

During the summer he supplied at St. John's Bedford Row, for Charles Jerram, who had recently taken over the lease from Daniel Wilson. It was the cynosure of metropolitan proprietary chapels, an impressive stage for the display of pulpit gifts. It stood or fell on the appeal of its preaching. *The Pulpit* was flattering: 'There can be no doubt that Mr Sibthorpe will prove a very acceptable supply to the hearers of St John's Chapel. . . . Mr S seems to have it in his power "to bring forth things new and old out of the treasury of God's Word", and so proves himself, "a wise and faithful householder." . . . There is something too, in Mr Sibthorpe's manner which renders his discourses very impressive. He uses notes but sparingly, if at all; and seems to have perfect self-possession, and an ability to avail himself of anything that is at all calculated to enforce or illustrate his various observations.'[13] But ministering there taxed his nervous energy to the limit. Both Wilson and his predecessor, Richard Cecil, were remarkable men, and they needed to be. The Church drew its congregation from the wealthy and influential, including the Clapham 'saints.' The Macaulays were noted 'Johnians,' and 'Mr Wilberforce was frequently present, with his son Samuel, "to take care of him."' Almost two thousand could be seated. 'Thirty or forty carriages might often be counted during the London season, standing in triple rows about the doors.'[14] Jerram found himself unequal to the challenge and there was some decline in numbers. He wrote that his time in charge was 'depressing . . . I became anxious to disengage myself from a service, to the discharge of which both my physical and mental strength were wholly unequal.'[15] Richard, who had once urged Bickersteth not to send him to 'great towns' to plead for the C.M.S.,'[16] would have sympathised.

On Jerram's return, Sibthorp moved to Percy Chapel, which seems to have been his 'home church' in London.[17] The link was through his cousin Jane Cholmeley, who in 1811 had married the solicitor William Forster. They were leading members of Haldane Stewart's congregation, and William's membership of the C.M.S. national committee, placed him at the heart of the 'religious world.' Richard lodged in Great Ormond Street not far from their home. In the autumn, he took over Stewart's pulpit to enable him to take his ailing wife to Scotland. On returning, the minister concluded that 'his congregation had been much edified in his absence.'[18] But this demanding ministry, after eighteen months of uncertainty and nervous excitement, exerted a price, and about the beginning of November, Richard became seriously ill. So intense were the symptoms of pneumonia that his life was feared for, and Mrs Hawkins was called to attend him. Memories of Coningsby's lingering death must have been in her mind when she wrote to her husband of arranging for her brother's return to Canwick for Christmas. She feared that 'mother will be dreadfully shocked when he does arrive, carried there, as he will be, just as if he was in his coffin.'[19]

Back in Lincoln he recovered slowly and in January wrote to reassure Lewis Hensley, his 'skilful and friendly'[20] London doctor. 'I walk about the room . . . and shall today get downstairs. The weakness is principally in my knees and my cough, which was the chief source of apprehension to my own mind, has quite left me.' He was concerned for his sister's spiritual welfare. 'She much deserves my prayers and she has them, that it may please God to admit her into his fold . . . She wants but one thing, but is not that the one thing needful?'[21] By the spring, he was well enough to return to London to attend Montague's wedding to Catherine Way.[22] But his mother's precarious condition soon took him back to Canwick, and he was there when she died in May. He recalled that it sent him, still enfeebled by fever, back to his bed.[23]

In July, the search for health took him to the Continent, but shortly before leaving he preached a commemorative sermon for the MP and publisher Joseph Butterworth, who although a Methodist, 'had a warm affection for the Church of England'[24] and often worshiped at St. John's. Richard spoke of his 'personal esteem and regard' for him. 'While he sought with zeal the interests of that body of Christians to whom he belonged, his spirit was truly catholic. He appeared to have attained to the right mean between indifference and intolerance: between that false liberality which sweeps away the essential distinctions of Christianity itself, and that bigotry which confines the privileges of the gospel to its own particular party.'[25] This tribute, given while he was still convalescing, underlined Sibthorp's esteem for the Methodists, and can be read as something of a lament for their separation from the Establishment. Two years before, Conference had decided, at Butterworth's request, that the centenary of Wesley's Anglican ordination in 1725 should be celebrated throughout the Connection, but opposition among the preachers was such that within months the idea was quietly dropped.

Butterworth's eirenicism did not extend to Roman Catholics. He was convinced that Emancipation would undermine religious freedom.[26] The issue had featured prominently in the recent general election, that saw Charles Sibthorp, supported by 'huge shoals of Revs and Right Revs,'[27] returned as the anti-Emancipation member for Lincoln. Richard, who supported his brother's stand, though concerned at the cost of the campaign,[28] now had the opportunity of examining Catholicism more closely, as he set off on a tour of France and Belgium.[29] Writing to his sister from Brussels, he described Paris and towns on the journey north. Cambrai he much admired: the 'residence of the excellent Fénelon: one of the most pious and enlightened members of the Church of Rome for the last three centuries.' There was less to approve at Hallé. He reported visiting a chapel of the Virgin, where 'waxen representations of all parts of the body were hung up in commemoration of the image's healing powers.' Sceptical, he nevertheless made a purchase. 'I bought a little wax leg as a recollection of the wretched folly of the scene . . . and a picture, which I was assured had touched the image: but I fear will communicate no benefit to me bodily or spiritual. Indeed since it has been in my possession I have had my face swelled up as if I had an apple within my cheek: perhaps Notre Dame de Hallé is angry with my incredulity.'[30]

Her anger continued. Returning to England, after brief visits to Brighton and to his sister at Bignor, continuing weakness took him back to Canwick, where convalescence was painfully slow. In November, he wrote to Charles Hensley, Lewis's brother, that he was 'soon wearied . . . my legs ache on the evening, as if I had walked many miles.' Yet his time had not been wasted, 'I have preached twice every Sunday, but the first, since I have been here – in small churches, however, such as required no particular exertion. After ten years exclusion I have obtained access to a Lincoln pulpit. I feel it a duty to embrace the opportunity, but I cannot but recollect that this is my own country and among my own kin, if I am a minister of the Gospel, as the term prophet may be understood.[31] But who can tell? It pleases God by the foolishness of preaching to save them that believe, and I sincerely pray that such may be the case with the inhabitants of a city which has long sat in darkness.' Notwithstanding his mother's death, there is now no further mention of missionary service, and it may be surmised that protracted illness had effectively closed this door. He told Hensley that he hoped soon to return to London, adding: 'All will, I hope be ordered aright respecting St John's.'[32] Jerram, who was anxious to quit, had offered Sibthorp the lease.[33] After he declined, Baptist Wriothesley Noel was persuaded to take on the chapel, and commenced his long ministry there in January 1827. Richard wrote to Hensley again on 27 December, saying he would be in London by the first Sunday in February in order to give Noel, 'any help he may desire.'[34] His real ambition, however, was to minister in his home city. 'It has pleased God to give me a measure of acceptance of Lincoln. Whether there will be a permanent opening for employment there I cannot at present see. I should hardly dare to refuse it, if offered.' Bishop Pelham, who certainly was an obstacle, did not have long to live.[35]

Returning to London, on 18 February Richard began at St. John's a series of Sunday evening sermons on the life of Abraham, finishing on 24 June.[36] Noel took the morning services. Both were able preachers, and the fall in numbers was reversed.[37] As regards pastoral work, Richard who lived near the church, was undoubtedly the more active.[38] He was now seen as one of the inner circle of Evangelical leadership. On 28 March, Daniel Wilson noted in his diary, 'We have had a most charming meeting of our Clerical Education Society; the best we ever had . . . The Bishop of Lichfield, Lord Teignmouth, Sir R. H. Inglis, Cunningham, the Noels, Sibthorpe and others.'[39] In May, invited to preach the Anniversary Sermon of the London Missionary Society, Sibthorp returned to a

favourite theme: the return of the 'glorified Saviour . . . infinity his domin-
ion – eternity the duration of his reign . . . when there shall be no longer
distinctions, divisions or differences in his church; but all shall be one
closely-united band . . . '[40]

The British and Foreign Bible Society

In view of the reputation that Richard Sibthorp later acquired for eccentricity, the moderating role he played in the Apocryphal Controversy
demands some attention. In the 1820s, the Bible Society was plagued with
dissension: another manifestation of the pessimism and loss of confidence
associated with pre-millennialism. The Society's opponents said that it
had 'lost sight of the end in the idolatry of the means'[41] and to this attributed its ineffectiveness. The long-feared split came in 1831, with the
formation of the Trinitarian Bible Society. A leading dissident, Henry
Melvill, in a famous speech ridiculed the notion that 'a Millennium is to
be manufactured by the outlay of a certain quantity of sheep-skins, and a
corresponding quantity of paper.' Rather, he said, the Society had actually done damage, had been 'the nurse of neology . . . The pounds of
English Nobles, and the pence of English peasants, have gone to the distribution of tenets, which, making Christ a man, and nothing more than a
man, leave the world in ruins!'[42] It was a frequently repeated allegation:
that in its overseas activities the B.F.B.S. had subsidised heresy. The
controversy had begun a decade before, when it became known that, as
a pragmatic response to representations that on the Continent only
Scriptures containing the Apocrypha would find acceptance, especially
among Roman Catholics, the Society had financed the distribution of
bibles containing the controversial books. The policy was brought to
public notice in August 1821, when Robert Haldane, a prominent Scottish
supporter, was invited to observe a sub-committee discussing the
Toulouse Bible.[43] He considered the Apocrypha as positively harmful, that
its presence contaminated Scripture truth, and in Scotland found many to
agree. His concerns also touched a chord among those who were coming
to believe that 'neologism' could be countered only by an uncompro-
mising insistence on the authority of the canon, its verbal inspiration, and
its literal meaning. Such was the furore that the Society was compelled to
decree that no more 'Apocryphal bibles' would be printed.

Unfortunately, the issue would not go away. Two years later a subsidy
was granted to Leander van Ess, the B.F.B.S. agent in Germany and a
Roman Catholic priest, to enable him to distribute bibles containing the
Apocrypha. When this became known, there were bitter recriminations
and the grant was rescinded. But in Scotland, confidence in the Society
was irretrievably damaged. A pamphlet war began, for in their instinctive
pragmatism the Society's leaders had powerful support, mainly from an

older generation: readers of the *Christian Observer*, and the Cambridge Evangelicals grouped around Simeon, who feared that a hard-line position would paralyse Scripture distribution in Europe. The Committee vacillated, but as Scottish Societies began to sever links, and with protests from all over the Kingdom, in 1826 the rules were amended to prohibit any support for the distribution of bibles with the Apocrypha. But it was too late, for by now the terms of the debate had widened. Demands were made that all links with the Continental Bible Societies should be terminated, on the grounds that these were dominated by 'neologians' and Socinians whose true agenda in supplying adulterated Scriptures was actually to discredit the authority of the canon. The Society's foes then opened another front, alleging misuse of funds. Robert Southey joined in the fun, and in *The Quarterly Review* undertook a detailed review of payments to van Ess, concluding that the latter's frequently expressed wishes, to forgo 'earthly emoluments,' had been 'cruelly outraged by the Directors.'[44]

According to Daniel Wilson, himself a pragmatist, nine out of ten of the Society's supporters were against the circulation of the Apocrypha,[45] but most of them believed that sufficient action had been taken and that it was time to move on. Edward Irving disagreed: he wanted public contrition, and at the Anniversary Meeting in May 1827, rose to rebuke the Committee, to demand resignations and the cessation of all links with the Continental Societies. His voice could hardly be heard above the protests. For Evangelicalism the *fracas* marked something of a watershed, and Gerard Noel spoke of 'his deep regret that for the first time the meeting . . . had manifested a want of Christian candour and courtesy.'[46] The Directors were shaken and felt a need to take urgent action. Supporters needed to be reassured. It had been alleged that covert support was still being given to the Apocrypha[47] and allegations against the Society's foreign agents required to be answered in detail: Dr Kieffer in Paris had been branded as unorthodox, and van Ess as a profiteer. On the other hand, although pledged to eliminate the Apocrypha, the Committee was anxious to counteract the adverse impact on bible distribution. Dr Pinkerton, one of the Society's most experienced workers, was therefore asked to visit the Continent: to confirm compliance with the new rules and investigate what could be done to encourage the taking up of approved Scriptures. Unfortunately, the critics regarded him as compromised. Not only was he complicit in the rejected policy, but was deemed to have been over-accommodating to doctrinal error. In 1821, following a visit to France to negotiate the removal of a controversial preface from the Strasbourg Bible, he reported that he had not read it 'in order to avoid discussion about its merits.' Robert Haldane's biographer deploring the dangers of 'being unequally yoked to unbelievers' commented, 'this narrative furnishes one of the most curious, and but for the melancholy occasion, amusing examples of the mimic State diplomacy then pursued.'[48]

It was in order to reassure the doubters that Richard Sibthorp, 'whose well known views on the subject of the Apocrypha, and whose standing at that time in the Society, it was thought, would give additional satisfaction to all its friends' was invited to go on the mission.[49] Amidst all the allegations of profligacy – Pinkerton's annual salary of £400 had been branded excessive – it was helpful that he agreed to defray his own expenses. On 5 July 1827, he wrote from his new lodgings in Woburn Place, accepting the commission, and pledging to keep 'the fundamental principles of the Society as now laid down and understood' invariably before him. His expressions of inadequacy were more than formal: 'I am very imperfectly acquainted with the details of the business . . . I know nothing of the German language, nor can I at present converse very fluently in French.' Yet, there was wisdom in his plea that in view of the likely difficulties, 'they should have definite instructions from the Committee to direct their measures.'[50] A few days later he was in Lincoln and, by the end of the month at Magdalen College, discharging his duties as that year's Dean of Divinity. On Thursday 26 July, he wrote to the Society's Secretary, Andrew Brandram, 'I hope to be in London this evening, as I shall leave Oxford as soon as the examination is over . . . this is the third day I have been seated in our College Hall examining candidates for scholarships etc., and I am really tired with work so strange to me. I hope to join my companions at Calais on Saturday.'[51] After some hectic travelling, arriving in London in the early hours of Friday morning, he reached Calais as planned, and by Monday he and Pinkerton were in Paris.[52]

During the following three months they visited over two dozen towns and cities in France, Belgium, Germany, and Switzerland. Primarily they went as auditors: to examine the affairs of the Society's agents, to ensure that no prohibited material was being subsidised, and that the Society's printers were producing bibles strictly as specified and on economic terms. But importantly, they also wanted to mend and to build bridges, and thus sought to negotiate with and cajole, not just local Committees, but anyone, Protestant or Catholic, who might further the distribution of the approved bibles. As regards the Continental Societies, their task was unenviable, for there was resentment at London's perceived arrogance. The Paris Committee, in their coldly formal response, set the tone for much of the tour. In the first of his regular letters to Brandram, Richard wrote that, 'They supply the Holy Scriptures without the Apocrypha to those who ask for them, but they could not undertake to recommend them. Beyond this they are not prepared to go in the circulation of Scripture without the Apocrypha. We asked them in what way the British and Foreign Bible Society could afford them aid – they seemed to think that at present no further aid was required.'[53] However, while most of the German Societies would not conform to London's policy, only a few such as those at Frankfurt and Stuttgart, effectively severed links. In many places, for example at Berlin, Leipzig, and Dresden, it was agreed that individual Committee members would receive and supply non-Apocrypha bibles. In Switzerland, and in the poorer parts of Bavaria, there was some success in persuading local Societies actively to distribute the approved Scriptures. However, despite the travellers' best efforts there was little enthusiasm for relinquishing long-standing practices and the years after 1827 saw a significant reduction in grants to the European Bible Societies.[54]

Part of the difficulty was theological; the travellers, who believed strongly in the integrity and inspiration of Scripture, had to negotiate with men whose views on the subject they found distasteful. After meeting the Paris Committee, Richard expressed regret that he had become involved at all.[55] From Halle, he wrote that despite its associations with Francke, the University was a 'nest of infidels,' and that of its 800 students, 'not more than 50 are entire believers in the Scriptures.'[56] He found the Bible Institute there, 'decidedly unfriendly.'[57] Meeting so many, pastors and theologians, who made him uncomfortable, he was quick to praise those who shared his views, for example, Tholuck, with whom he dined at Halle; the saintly Bishop Fabricius at Herrnhut; at Berlin, the Catholic priest, Gossner, recently converted to Evangelicalism; and at Wittenberg, Dr. Heubner, director of the Lutheran Seminary. All these men were active in distributing the Society's bibles.

In contrast to the difficult task of being tactful to those they judged virtually apostate, negotiating with printers was relatively straightforward. With Tauchnitz at Leipzig, and von Seidel at Sulzbach, quality was discussed and price reductions agreed, and it was impressed upon all the Society's suppliers how rigorous they should be in excluding any matter other than the canonical Books. At Basle compensation was agreed for the removal of the Apocrypha from Italian and French bibles and Pinkerton arranged for the condemned pages to be forwarded to England, in order, 'not to give needless offence.'[58]

A key objective was to confirm the good faith of the Society's agents. At Paris, Jean Kieffer was entirely approved. Although his translation of the Turkish New Testament had been criticised, the revised Turkish Bible that they saw being printed was considered quite acceptable. A larger cloud hung over van Ess's probity and meeting him at Darmstadt was a priority. But once there, they were met by bad news; 'we found this distinguished labourer in the Bible cause alarmingly ill, too much so to allow him to see us with safety or even have our arrival communicated to him.' This was a worrying development; 'we deemed it right to obtain the opinion of his physicians whose certificate of his state we enclose.' They were, however, able to audit his depot and found the bound bibles all in order, but were concerned that in a recent delivery of printed sheets six leaves of the Book of Judith had been included on the same sheet as two of the canonical writings.[59]

They decided to continue into Germany in the hope of speaking to van

Ess on their return, and after travelling eastwards as far as Berlin and then south to Basle, they arrived back on 20 October. Now they could see him, but learnt little, 'his mind is unquestionably greatly shattered: so much so as to incapacitate him at present from anything like business. His memory is much impaired, and there is altogether a degree of mental weakness (giving) rise to anxious fears as to the probability of his ultimate recovery.' The time was not, however, wasted. Conferring with van Ess's secretary, they examined his ledgers, with satisfactory results. As to the main concern – that he had made a fortune from royalties from the (subsidised) distribution of his own New Testament translation – they had already examined his printer's accounts and estimated that their agent's annual income from this source had averaged not more than £32. 'These then are briefly the facts of the case: nor, we confess, do we fear the result of the communication of them to the British Public.'[60]   van Ess was widely regarded as the acceptable face of Catholicism and there was some relief at these findings. Unfortunately, it was to be short-lived. In 1830 the Society's connection with him was quietly dissolved. Allegations were made as to his 'ambiguous domestic relationships' that could not be resolved because his 'oath as a Catholic priest precluded his making such explanations as might have cleared up the suspicions.'[61]

The two returned to England at the beginning of November and immediately briefed the Committee. They recommended that the Society should re-orient its approach away from reliance on local societies towards a system of direct distribution. Writing in the 1828 *Annual Report*, Richard pointed to the practical advantages that would result: both in avoiding errors and in achieving economies, adding that a central depot at Frankfurt would offer good communications and freedom from state interference. He ended by paying tribute to Dr Pinkerton, 'no other individual connected with our Society could have achieved so much in removing prejudice, softening angry feelings and in opening the continent in some degree to the reception of the Holy Scriptures as they are now circulated by us.' The proposed arrangements were implemented and in October 1830, Pinkerton assumed control of the Frankfurt agency. For their part, the Directors were most grateful and appointed Sibthorp a Life Governor; for his part, he pledged his continuing confidence in the Society as 'the First Institution of the Age.'[62]

The Catholic Controversy

For Richard the tour had tended to reinforce long-standing concerns. From Dresden, he wrote to Lewis Hensley: 'I think much . . . less favourably of the religious state of England than I did, contrasting it with the religion of Germany. There is much more infidelity than in England under various forms. . . . But there is a far stronger and more widely scattered body of pious persons than I expected to find here . . . and as far as I have seen the religion of these is of a more simple, holy, practical kind than the mass of profession in London. There is far less display, less knowledge of controversies and societies and preachers, and religious news – but there is prayer, love of the Saviour and his Word, Christian simplicity of life and manners and Christian godliness.' He had started to learn German, 'I feel a great anxiety to be well acquainted with it. I cannot say how useful it may hereafter prove to me, if spared.'[63] In after-years, it was said that meeting van Ess had fanned the flame of Sibthorp's latent sympathy for Catholicism. If this was so, it was not at a conscious level. Speaking at the 1828 B.F.B.S. Anniversary he recalled his pleasure at visiting Wittenberg, and lauded Luther's zeal for 'the universal circulation of the holy Scriptures.'[64] But at the same time, he could not have avoided noting how many Roman Catholics did value the Scriptures: at Cologne, for example, and at Constance, where the Vicar General responsible for half a million Catholics, actively promoted the distribution of the New Testament.

Those who condemned the Apocrypha were in the forefront of resistance to Catholic Emancipation. For the students of prophecy it was more than a political issue: Rome's growing confidence was seen as presaging some great crisis. The Reformation Society was founded in 1827 in the belief that the decisive battle with Catholicism was imminent.[65] Richard, agreeing that Emancipation would be blatant disobedience to the prophetical scriptures, undertook to contribute to a series of lectures arranged by the Society's St. Giles's Auxiliary. The intention was to bring the 'doctrines and principles . . . of Protestantism' to 40,000 Roman Catholics, 'sheep without a shepherd' . . . inhabitants of 'some of the poorest and most distressed *portions* of this *vast* city.'[66] On 20 November, he spoke on 'The Character and Tokens of the True Catholic Church',[67] and three months later lectured on the Papacy.

Although both were avowedly anti-Catholic, the two discourses illustrate Sibthorp's ambivalence towards the religion even at the apogee of his Evangelical career. The first sermon was moderate, not at all apocalyptic and covered familiar ground. He took from the Nicene Creed the marks of a true Church, and proceeded to demonstrate why the invisible company of 'real Christians' fulfilled these criteria, while Roman Catholicism did not. Much attention was given to demonstrating the late development of the Papacy and in explaining that the only head of the Church is the glorified Saviour. He urged that true unity lay in Trinitarian worship, not within 'the prison-house of her Superstition.' Nevertheless, he was prepared to acknowledge, 'the existence of real piety in a Church which . . . in her spirit and doctrines (is) hostile to it.' Moreover he denied that Roman Catholics could claim as their own, 'those holy individuals who adorned the first five or six centuries of the Christian era,' asserting that the Fathers of these times 'were in their faith and doctrines what the

Church of Rome now calls Protestant Heretics.' But this sanctity had decayed and he was certain of the higher morality of Protestant countries. Catholic immorality arose, he said, from antinomianism encouraged by the confessional and purgatory, whilst a Protestant's faith in Christ, 'is always, if genuine, productive of true piety.' In considering universality and apostolicity, he took the line mapped out in Milner's *History of the Church*: that a body of faithful Christians has always existed, and Protestantism was being successfully diffused all over the globe. The remainder of his lecture was aimed at demonstrating how far Rome had deviated from the Apostles' teaching. 'All therefore (it would appear from Scripture and the early Fathers,) who hold the Apostles' doctrines, may claim a succession from the Apostles, and a relation to that Catholic and Apostolic Church which they founded.'[68]

He appears to have consulted a number of Catholic sources, although Faber's recent *Difficulties of Romanism* was probably his main support.[69] Because he later became a Catholic there is a temptation to read underlying Catholic sympathies into the sermon, and such evidence is not hard to find, with references to Catholic saints and esteem for the Church of the first six centuries, a period he regarded as largely free from Roman 'corruptions.' This was slippery ground; G. S. Faber had questioned any doctrines arising later than the third century.[70] Moreover, Richard was prepared to accept extra-biblical material as normative, affirming that: 'in all the public confessions of Faith, drawn up in the first four centuries after Christ, all (true) Protestants agree.' This also was contentious, since some Evangelical colleagues would have questioned whether the creed of Irenaeus, which he quoted with approval, was fully compatible with justification by faith.[71] But at the time there was no reason to doubt his Protestant zeal and the *Christian Guardian* was enthusiastic about 'one of the most able argumentative discourses we ever read' to which 'many Roman Catholics listened with the utmost seriousness and propriety.'[72]

Of the Protestant credentials of his second lecture, *The Character of the Papacy as Predicted by St Paul in 2 Thess. II*, there could be no dispute.[73] As a young man, his eyes had been opened to see the Pope as the prophesied Antichrist, and fifteen years had done nothing to efface the impression. 'At some time,' he asserted, 'It matters not as to the precise era,' Papal Rome had become the 'chief seat of the power of the Beast.' For it was indisputable that the Papacy fulfilled all the relevant prophecies: '*On her forehead was a name written* (says St. John); *Mystery, Babylon the great, the mother of harlots, and of abominations of the earth.*' While willing to concede that an uncorrupted Church of Rome might in principle, exist separate from the Papacy, 'as it did for a considerable period after its first establishment' and that 'many have been and are saved, who live and die in its communion . . . It would be false charity to conceal the truth. The Papacy is the enemy of God, his cause and his people; and is to be destroyed with signal marks of his wrath. The warning voice of the Apocalypse proclaims, *Come out of her, my people, that ye be not partakers of her sins, and that ye receive not of her plagues.*' He stressed the urgency of the challenge: many of those present would live to see the return of Christ. 'Unquestionably great then, and imminent, is the danger of those who, in an age of scriptural light and religious knowledge, live and die in subjection to a power, and in the communion of a church, which God has declared he will judge, and visit with his wrath, even unto utter destruction; and whose judgments and visitations and destruction may now be *near, even at the doors.*'[74]

The Religious Tract Society

At Canwick for Christmas, Richard preached at Gainsborough on behalf of the Hibernian School Society on the 'injurious consequences of with-holding the Scriptures from the people' and repeated the sermon a few months later at Bristol, when the address was published. He was now almost an official defender of Protestantism having been appointed in August 1827, Anglican Secretary of the Religious Tract Society, following the death of Legh Richmond. Anti-Catholicism was written into the Society's constitution.[75] The appointment – which gave 'sincere satisfaction' to those 'familiar with his clear and faithful exhibitions of divine truth'[76] – was not an honorary one; because the Committee met weekly, it had been stipulated that the new Secretary should live in London.

As R.T.S. Secretary, Sibthorp's main emphasis was on making Christian literature available on the Continent. While travelling for the Bible Society, he had also contacted local Tract Societies and returned convinced that they could be stirred up to greater efforts. His overseas correspondence was to become a regular item on the Committee's agenda. As regards domestic concerns, his moderating influence, directed towards holding together conflicting denominational interests, was highly regarded. One contentious area was the New Testament Commentary, which Charles Bridges had been asked to write.[77] In December 1827, the issue of baptism came up and 'Mr Sibthorp was requested to correspond with Mr Bridges and report thereon.' At the same Committee, John Scott of Hull forwarded an objection to some phrases in a Tract dealing with regeneration, which was also passed to him.[78] The latter problem was easily resolved by a change of wording; the Commentary however, proved more intractable. In February, he and his fellow secretaries,[79] of whom one was a Baptist, were asked to co-ordinate the Society's position. Unfortunately, after correspondence with Bridges centring on the inter-pretation of Matthew 19 verses 13–15, agreement could not be reached and no Commentary from his pen appeared in the Society's Catalogue. But importantly there was no breach, and neither was there when the Committee directed that 'a manuscript Tract on the Sacrament of the

Lord's Supper . . . be submitted to the Rev Messrs Sibthorp and Hughes and brought up again.'[80]

During the first half of 1828 Richard combined itinerant preaching with attendance, each Tuesday at eight in the morning, at the R.T.S. Committee. His oratorical skills were in much demand, and during the May Meetings that year he appeared on the platform for the Tract and Bible Societies, as well as preaching for the Prayer Book and Homily Society, the Newfoundland School Society, and the Negro Education Society. It was not congenial work; he found the part of 'celebrity preacher' physically debilitating. In Germany, he had never felt better; in London, his health deteriorated, and he began to think of re-visiting the Continent on behalf of the Tract Society. In July he was at Canwick, and from there wrote to the Bible Society, explaining that 'to help my health and strength, which have been perceptibly to myself declining for some months' he would soon be leaving for Germany and the Netherlands and might also visit Austria, Switzerland, and Italy and offered to undertake commissions.[81] At his own Society's Anniversary Meeting he had raised the need for increased funding for overseas work.[82] Subsequently, the Committee supported his intention to visit the European Societies, and endorsed his planned departure date of 2 August.[83]

Yet, for reasons that remain unexplained, he did not go. It seems unlikely that there was any sudden deterioration in his health[84] because he continued to correspond on behalf of the Tract Society, and in September addressed a meeting of the Lincoln Naval and Military Bible Society at the Guildhall. Not only did he not visit the Continent; more significantly, he did not return to live in London. Although continuing as R.T.S. Secretary, thereafter he conducted its affairs at a distance, work that included an extensive overseas correspondence and the supervision of an abridgement of Keith's *Evidences of Prophecy*. He was closely consulted during a major crisis which arose in March 1829, when the anti-Catholic broadsheet, *Queen Mary's Days,* was castigated in the Commons as inflammatory. While the MP who raised the matter was mollified, the incident highlighted tensions within the Society, and some questioned whether its active hostility to Catholicism should be re-assessed. Richard wrote to the Committee on 18 April, 'stating his views on the course this Society should pursue in exposing the errors of Popery.'[85] Unfortunately, the letter has not survived.[86] Whilst undoubt-edly supporting the traditional policy – his brother was besieging Parliament with anti-Emancipation petitions – he would not have dissented from the Committee's determination 'to avoid any methods which are not fully consonant to the spirit of the Gospel of peace and love or which may incite or strengthen prejudices in the minds of those whom we are anxious to convince.'[87]

In 1829, Sibthorp was living in Oxford, from where, at the beginning of July he wrote to the R.T.S. committee announcing his intention to devote 'about two months to the promotion of its objects' on the Continent. A sum of £300 was placed at his disposal.[88] This time he did go, accompanied by Benjamin Wills Newton, a young fellow of Exeter College. During August they met with Societies and sympathetic individuals, at Brussels, Aix, and Elberfeld, before moving north to Bremen, Hamburg, and Schleswig. By the end of the month they were in Berlin, moving then to Leipzig before going to Dresden to visit the ageing Bishop Fabricius. From there they travelled south to Nuremberg, Stuttgart, and Basle, before commencing the long journey home via Strasbourg.

Their objective was clear: to promote the wide distribution of approved tracts, and to this end agreements were entered into with a number of Continental Societies. It was important that financial assistance should be linked to editorial control, and here the recent development of stereotype printing plates proved very helpful;[89] London would pay for and become owners of the plates, other costs being shared. The arrangement accepted by the Barmen and Wupperthal Society was typical. Sibthorp wrote that its committee would 'prepare and lay before the London Committee tracts to the amount of 72 pages . . . We will be at the expence of the stereotype plates for these, which are to become our property and entirely at our disposal, also of the printing of an edition of 3000 of each tract for them, to be done at Leipzic . . . they to be at the expence of the paper and carriage from Leipzic.'[90]

Some Continental Societies, such as those at Nuremberg and Stuttgart, would not co-operate. Some were simply inefficient. But there were other ways of getting tracts into circulation. For example, Richard had previously written to Professor Hahn in Leipzig seeking guidance about establishing a depot in the city for the circulation of literature throughout Europe.[91] Once there he negotiated with Tauchnitz arrangements for the making and holding of plates, and terms for printing. The travellers interviewed a number of individuals willing to distribute tracts. Among them was Fabricius, who also agreed to arrange for the translation of tracts into Polish and Bohemian.[92] Richard gave him a large personal donation.[93] He was impressed by Mr. Barth, a pastor from Calw, who published children's literature and in this case alone the Society made a cash grant of £20. Another key aim was to encourage the establishment of new Societies. In Basle, Blumhardt, the Director of the Missionary Institute was enthusiastic to begin a Society; in Leipzig supporters were encouraged to recommence the work on a sounder footing.[94]

Letters from Newton to his mother throw an interesting light on the journey. On 26 August, he wrote from Berlin complaining that 'We are hurried with such extreme rapidity from place to place, and when we are for a little stationary, have so much to do and see, that I find it extremely difficult to find anything like a quiet opportunity for writing a letter.' He described the dull countryside of Germany, and the unimpressive cities; Münster for example, 'The town itself is uninteresting and like most other

Prussian cities more like a garrison than a settlement of peaceable citizens.' Travelling was often tortuous; 'toiling through deserts of sand which covers the wheel above the axle-tree.' The picture he paints of Sibthorp is of an earnest, if somewhat naïve missionary, intent upon fulfilling a commission and suspicious of the pleasures of tourism. The youthful Newton regarded him, then aged thirty-six, as quite geriatric. He described how they and an English pastor had travelled from Hamburg to visit the Schleswig Tract Society. On the journey back,

> 'more rain had fallen, the roads were worse than before and we had not proceeded ten miles before we found our horses so spent with fatigue that they refused to draw us any further. We were ten miles from our nearest inn, yet in spite of our fatigue we were obliged to trudge it. The night came in very dark and we found it very difficult to discern the road, our postilion was old and asthmatic; our friend (the English Minister) and Mr Sibthorpe half blind, as my eyes were the best I took the lead – often cautioned by Mr S to beware of bogs on the right and ditches on the left. Indeed, it was exceedingly difficult to distinguish the ponds of water (which are large and deep) from the white sand which in the dark they so much resemble. To add to our discomfort we were pursued by a most portentous looking cloud which every now and then by a flash of lightning just gave us sufficient light to see its own blackness and our own unhappy plight. Poor Mr S had the misfortune to tumble into a pit full of water which – considering the caution with which he moved – was so exceedingly ludicrous that I could not help having a good hearty laugh, which considerably relieved me during the rest of the way.'[95]

Many years later Newton reminisced about his friend's earnestness:

> 'Sibthorpe never showed any tendency Romewards when he was with me. In fact, he and I were near being locked up in 1829 on the Continent. It was in this way. We left the hotel on Sunday morning for a walk. He turned back after some distance and I went on – prolonging my walk – on getting back, I found the street full of people, and also the hotel and even the staircase. I went in, wondering. On meeting Sibthorpe I asked him what it was all about and he said he had only given a tract to a man he met in the street, just as the people were coming out of the churches. I said, "Oh! How foolish, you may be put into prison. I won't go with you if you act so unthinkingly." Just then a message came from the Mayor, asking the hotel keeper who we were and what we had. The people flocked into our room with the hotel keeper and the officer. They examined our things and took away every tract and all our bibles. But we heard nothing more of it and went away quietly.'[96]

This was probably in Hanover.[97] Newton wrote that 'though the king is an Englishman, (it) is subjected to most tyrannical regulations with respect to the press and the circulation of every kind of writing. For every tract we distributed in this country we were in danger of being put into prison, so that as you may suppose we were somewhat cautious.'[98]

Returning to London at the end of September, they met the Committee, and Sibthorp gave a 'very lucid' statement, highlighting in particular the need for a German hymn book 'for use among Protestants and Catholics.' His fellow directors hoped the visit would open a new chapter in their European work: 'To Mr Sibthorp himself the Committee feel they cannot adequately express their sense of his valuable service.' For Newton, who was travelling on to Plymouth, there was a more tangible reward: his own set of the First Series of Tracts, and literature for distribution in Devonshire to the value of £1/1/-.[99] Following up on the tour, Richard set about arranging the production of Polish and Bohemian tracts, and collaborated with Pinkerton on the hymn book.[100] His greatest challenge was overseeing the satisfactory fulfilment of agreements. Problems were perhaps predictable because of the uncertain orthodoxy of some of the German committees. Nevertheless, in his account of the tour he was reserved: the publications of the Berlin Society were 'not as valuable as those of Hamburg,' and those published at Bremen seemed to 'want improvement.'[101] Newton wrote of visiting the Bremen Committee, 'eight or so clergymen regaling themselves with the never failing companions of every German – their tobacco-pipes . . . they have a great dread of Calvinism and on this account seemed to look with great suspicion on our offers of assistance from the London Society. I was not altogether pleased with the development of religious feeling among them. I have since heard that some of these are Universalists – I believe all were Arminians. Arminianism is a rank weed in Germany.'[102]

Most of the tracts submitted to London for approval were translations of those already published in England. The Society was meticulous in enforcing its policy that, 'the translation must be verbatim, most entirely correct and faithful translations of ours.'[103] This was not straightforward, and Richard spent many hours corresponding with the Berlin Society over the translation of *Sixteen Short Sermons*.[104] Even more problematical was the vetting of original material: of the six drafts submitted by the Berlin Society, only three were accepted, but not without revision. Among those rejected was *On Baptism and Confirmation,* to which there was an 'essential objection from the constitution of our Society.' Richard had tried to persuade Berlin to accept duplicates of plates being made for the Lower Saxony Society at Hamburg.[105] But there was a further complication when in May 1830 a letter was received from four members of the Hamburg Committee, stating that doctrinal views recently embraced by some other members had placed them in an embarrassing position. After consulting Sibthorp, the Assistant Secretary replied that the Committee 'never interfered in differences among its friends . . . we simply ensure the correctness of tracts.' Consequently, 'if faithful translations cannot be published our course is clear and the Committee will be under the painful necessity of declining assistance.' He urged, 'prayer, candour and forbearance.'[106] The problem with Hamburg was resolved, and the Society there continued to receive assistance from London. It was not so with Berlin. In August 1830 the President, Stobwasser, wrote objecting to stereotype plates and requesting that London would 'change their grant to a vote of money for them to print (in moveable type) the tracts already approved by this Society.' From Ryde, Richard wrote, 'expressing strong objections to making grants of money to Continental Tract Societies.' The Committee wholeheartedly agreed.[107]

In its *Jubilee Memorial,* the Society acknowledged its debt to Richard Sibthorp, who remained in office until 1836. 'The German Associations were watched with considerable anxiety . . . In 1830 (*sic*), the Rev R. W. Sibthorp visited several of them, and by his counsels and timely grants they were considerably revived.'[108] There were other enduring benefits of his stewardship, the distribution centre at Leipzig, for example. More generally, the impression that emerges from both his Continental tours is of a level-headed and shrewd agent, effective and business-like in discharging sometimes disagreeable tasks. It is noteworthy that the Tract Society, in many ways more vulnerable than the Bible Society to conflicting interests, was able to continue its work in Europe without experiencing the convulsions that tore the latter apart. During years of great anxiety, its Anglican Secretary was trusted on all sides.

Oxford Again

In retrospect, the fact that after his summer visit to Canwick in 1828, Richard did not return to London, was a turning point. Apart from some months in 1865, he never lived there again. The decision may have been linked to that sense of disillusionment with the 'religious world' evident in his letters to Hensley. Preaching in May 1828, he worried about the Religious Societies: 'They are apt to rest on their own force and wisdom: their supporters are wont to rest too much on human means . . . They are apt to attach too much weight to money, to popularity, to means of excitement, and not to depend sufficiently and simply upon God.' He was concerned also that a generation of children was imbibing a superficial fluency in religious knowledge, without any appreciation of the reality and power of Christianity; 'storing the head and memory with Scripture, may supersede close application of its truths to the conscience and heart.'[109] It is also much to the point that he found the life of a London pulpiteer both unsatisfying and exhausting.

The separate question of why Richard, so late in the day, changed his mind about touring Europe in 1828, cannot be answered. It may have been at the request of his sister-in-law, who had begun separation proceedings against her husband. More likely, it was linked to his wish to secure a permanent ministry in Lincoln, for an opportunity arose for him to minister at St. Peter's in Eastgate, and anticipating that the incumbent,

George Moore would appoint him curate, he bought a house close by in Minster Yard.[110] His preaching was very popular, 'the interior was filled by crowds, who stood and sat by turns, others hung like bees at the windows.'[111] In January, he began an acclaimed series of Sunday evening lectures.[112] But although a new and seemingly more sympathetic bishop was in office, he was refused a licence. Kaye's stated reason was a wish to enforce residence, but Elizabeth Massingberd, writing on April 9, hinted at other considerations:

> 'We had Mr Sibthorpe to do all the duty at St Peter's last Sunday, but I hear we shall have him no more, for he has got a permanent curacy near Oxford; and the reason the Bishop objected to Mr Moore having a curate was, as long as he held the curacy at Coleby he couldn't want one; that seems very obvious, but I believe Mr Moore is so unwell now that he cannot do any duty, so I know not who we shall have now.'[113]

The trouble was that Richard stirred up strong feelings in Lincoln. Many of the city clergy were uncomfortable with his zeal, especially perhaps, his neighbours in Minster Yard, the Cathedral Chancellor, George Pretyman and his brother Richard, the Precentor. As sons of the late Bishop Tomline, they had particular reasons not to welcome Sibthorp to a church standing in the shadow of the cathedral, and there are hints of organised opposition.[114] Kaye may have thought it politic to block this particular appointment, for by November his objections to Moore's wish had been overcome and a curate was licensed. Influential parishioners such as Charlesworth, who disliked enthusiasm, were to be disappointed; their new minister Mr. Pridham, a graduate of St Edmund Hall, was a zealous Evangelical.[115]

Yet, for Richard, after turning his back on London, the rebuff must have been unsettling. He cannot have been satisfied with what he had achieved after thirteen years in the ministry. There was a temporary feel to all he had attempted, a sense of plans made and abandoned. And now, approaching middle age, he still needed to discern the clear purpose of God in his life. What should he do? Where go?

His path became a little clearer after a visit to Oxford at the end of February 1829, where he had gone to vote against Peel and Catholic Emancipation.[116] Over the years, he had kept in touch with John Hill, the long-serving vice-president of St. Edmund Hall and at the centre of 'serious religion' in the University. A little over two years before when the curacy at St. Ebbe's, a ministry considered crucial to the Evangelical cause, became vacant, Hill had written to Sibthorp about it, perhaps asking him to consider the appointment.[117] It went, eventually, to Henry Bellenden Bulteel, whose forceful preaching made a dramatic impact.[118] Now, the vice-president was preoccupied by a serious setback to the gospel cause in the University. His friend Henry Bisse had been refused the College testimonials he needed to be licensed to the curacy of the newly opened

Kennington Church.[119] This was in retribution for an incident the previous November, when he and Joseph Philpot, both fellows of Worcester, had offended their colleagues by using a Common Room for bible exposition and extempore prayer.[120] It appears the matter was discussed on Richard's visit, because just a few weeks later he returned to take up residence as a fellow of Magdalen, and was soon preaching regularly at the little church.[121] Gladstone, in his first year at Christ Church, heard him there and in his diary noted one sermon as 'good' (10 May 1829) and that of the following Sunday, 'very good indeed on the gift of the Spirit.'[122] Fifty years later, he reminisced:

> 'The church was always full to the doors. Mr Sibthorp had no vestry; he put off his surplice and put on the black gown, which lay over the door of the reading desk, for the sermon, before the people . . . I have nothing more of the Oxford Sibthorp . . . than a soothing general recollection, a venerable visual image in the mind's eye, and a moral certainty that the preaching was, at the least, of singular grace and charm, which drew me again and again to walk some miles out of Oxford, where preaching was abundant, and *good* preaching was to be had. I may illustrate this, by saying that I never went out of Oxford to hear a preacher, except in this case and on one other occasion.'[123]

In old age, Richard remembered a spinster named Miss Dawson: 'She lived near the little chapel, and used to amuse Mrs. Hill and myself by her commendation of my predecessor there, as having a beautiful "deliverance."'[124] Besides parish work, he sought to influence the religious life of the University, moving cautiously at first, by inviting senior men to bible expositions in his rooms. On 18 May, Hill led the study.[125] Beyond his own College he found a like-minded supporter in Benjamin Newton, who in April, wrote to his mother about a letter he had sent to the *Record*, which had just been published anonymously. 'One of the fellows of Magdalen College – Mr Sibthorp, who has been rather a distinguished speaker and preacher in London, told me today he was exceedingly glad to see the subject taken up and asked me whether I had seen the letter: with which he said his feelings were quite in unison.'[126] This initial contact soon developed into quite a close friendship, which although brief was significant to the future of Evangelicalism at the University, and therefore deserves some attention.

Newton was closely associated with Bulteel. Both were from Plymouth and both had sat under Robert Hawker, one of the last survivors of the 'articulate, stubborn and tactless'[127] school of high-Calvinism. Gladstone said of the numerous undergraduates who frequented St. Ebbe's that their 'zeal appears to outstrip discretion. They have, it appears, adopted a very high strain of doctrine, and on this very high foundation, they seem to build all their notions of Christianity. They seem full of predestination and regeneration understood in a sense believed by others to be erroneous.'[128] According to Newton's somewhat contradictory reminiscences, he joined Bulteel's congregation in 1827, following a conversion experience.[129] But after a while his enthusiasm for the St. Ebbe's set began to wane.[130] The problem was a lack of intellectual stimulation, also of spiritual warmth and reality. He recalled, 'At first I gave my adhesion to the gospel receiving it very clearly and suffered a good deal for it, having left old friends whom I dearly loved and whose company I much enjoyed. But I found the evangelical circle I was in, to be ignorant, common-place, and narrow-minded and empty. No instruction in Scripture and nothing to occupy the mind or the soul's energies.'[131] Although strongly backing Bulteel when, in 1828, some College heads sought to discourage attendance at his church, he was troubled by the divisive implications of his friend's increasingly Calvinistic emphasis. He recalled that 'when it came to extreme High Calvinism I couldn't stand it. A Clergyman who preached High-Calvinism in his parish but did not preach it in the University was dining with our set and was asserting that Wesley was damned, I rose and left.'[132] There were other grounds for his unease. In April 1828, he received a letter in which his former tutor, Francis Newman, now teaching in Ireland and under the spell of J. N. Darby, asserted the coming millennium, and drew the conclusion that traditional religious concerns regarding, for example social morality, were beside the point. Newton found the antinomian and anti-intellectual implications of the new prophetical theory troubling.[133]

It was against this background that he befriended Sibthorp. 'It was at the time I parted from Bulteel: he was not what he had previously been and I took up with Sibthorp who was of Magdalen .'[134] Newton was a young man seeking to come to terms with the implications of his faith, still searching for an understanding of Scripture that would satisfy a restless intellect. However, journeying with Sibthorp for the R.T.S., he found the single-mindedness of his new friend somewhat daunting:

> 'I was travelling in 1829 with Sibthorpe one of the most popular preachers in London . . . He asked me if I would go with him in the summer to Germany. I went with him. And I used to go to cathedrals and objects of interest and converse with anybody I met. Sibthorpe remarked on this, "you're very worldly: you converse with everybody, and enter into everything, very worldly of you."
>
> I replied, "I don't agree with you one bit, I've done nothing wrong, nothing sinful; converse with mixed classes is not sinful."
>
> "Oh, but you're very worldly," he said.
>
> "Well" I replied, "I want to get near persons: in time, Christianity will affect the whole world, and the more I can do the better."' [135]

Newton added, 'I myself used to think God would in this dispensation improve the world, so I adhered to the world. Sibthorpe found great fault with me about it.'[136]

Returning from the Continent, Newton remained troubled in spirit, remembering it as a time of 'crisis.' He was unhappy with his friend's theology, recalling 'I did not like Sibthorpe so much by any means as I had liked Bulteel.'[137] He went to Plymouth, where his problems deepened: 'I saw this book which spoke of the ignorance of narrow Calvinism, but did it in a wrong way. Added to this I met a circle of worldly-minded professors, which furthered the bad influences of Taylor's book. So that I returned to Oxford much deteriorated.'[138] *The Natural History of Enthusiasm* had just been published.[139] He also recalled reading it in Oxford, and was left feeling that it confirmed a deficiency in his Christian experience, 'a void and that it ought not to be so . . . I remember walking up and down the High Street with Wigram and conversing with him on the painful subject and my sense of misery. Six weeks after that F. W. Newman introduced me to prophetic truth and it turned the whole current of my life.'[140]

After his return to Oxford, Sibthorp ceased to officiate at Kennington, and Peter Maurice of New College was eventually licensed to the curacy. From the Tattershall experience, it might have been predicted that he would not settle into a country pastorate.[141] He nevertheless remained busy with preaching engagements, waiting somewhat restlessly for a ministry appropriate to his gifts and uncertain longings. In November, Newton wrote to his mother, 'Bulteel is going on very comfortably. My time is so occupied that I only get a glimpse of him once or twice a week. Sibthorpe is wandering from Dan to Beersheba preaching. He set off yesterday to Leeds.'[142]

In addition to this itinerant work, there was another mission field closer to hand. Evangelicalism remained an alien plant at the University, although Gladstone who wrote of, 'four or five scattered individuals of the teaching or officiating body,' and 'a score or two of young men . . . nestled together in the small establishment of St. Edmund Hall' considerably overstated its rarity.[143] Charles Simeon had changed the religious climate of Cambridge, might something similar be attempted at Oxford? Sibthorp wrote to him seeking

'information and advice . . . I am designing to open my rooms once a week for what I may call, in one sense, an evening party . . . But the tea is only introductory to an exposition of Scripture which I propose to give myself. . . . Allow me to ask whether you open or close with prayer? With prayer, should the number exceed twenty, are we not in danger of being considered conventiclers? . . . I am sure that you will rejoice to hear that God is doing much in this University. There is a very goodly company of truly pious young men and an increasing one too.'[144]

Simeon, replying on 9 December, urged caution:

'Days are materially altered in two respects: much good is in existence and in progress now, so that the same irregular exertions that were formerly necessary do not appear to be called for in the present day; and our ecclesiastical authorities are more on the alert now, to repress anything which may be deemed irregular. I should be disposed therefore to carry my cup more even than I did in former days:[145] not that I would relax my zeal in the least degree, but I would cut off occasion from those who might be glad to find occasion against me. On this subject, I would not do anything which might subject me to the Conventicle Act. My own habit is this: I have an open day, when all who chose it come to take tea with me. Every one is at liberty to ask what questions he will. . . . We have neither exposition as such or prayer; but I have the opportunity of saying all that my heart can wish. . . . All this is unexceptionable; and if you fear your numbers will be too great, you may easily divide the Colleges into two or three parts, as you judge expedient, taking those on the one side of the High Street at one time, and those on the opposite at another.

I have one evening for the study of Composition making Claude my ground-work . . . I would do all the good I could; but in a place like Oxford, I would do it in the most prudent and unexceptionable way. At all events, I would recommend you *to feel your way*, not timidly, but wisely.'[146]

Whether, following this advice, Sibthorp opened his rooms is not recorded although he certainly attended religious gatherings in the rooms of undergraduates. On 10 March 1830, Gladstone noted in his diary, 'tea with Hanbury – introduced to Mr Sibthorp':[147] a meeting they reminisced about some years later.[148] The Prime Minister later remembered Richard with affection: 'an admirable representative' of 'ordinary Evangelical tenets' – in contrast to the St. Edmund 'School of ultra-Calvinism' – and an 'excellent preacher and devout, refined and attractive man.' Moreover, 'Mr. Simeon resembled Mr. Sibthorp. . . in his pure and venerable character'. Yet the former was endowed with, 'greater energy', helping explain the obvious fact that while Simeon attracted many adherents, Sibthorp's brief 'representation of the Evangelical party at Oxford was a purely personal representation.'[149]

Ministering to the spiritual needs of students did not prove to be Richard's vocation, and within three months of writing to Simeon, he had left Oxford for good. On 1 December, he had written to his sister: 'I am still within the walls of Alma Mater – lingering in it, rather than much liking it and stopping because I do not see any clear call of duty to go away. I cannot say its society has much attraction for me, but perhaps it may please God by me to do some good to those who are coming on in life; not a few to be ministers of religion. I am happy to find a considerable proportion of decidedly and consistently religious young men here and the number increasing, which promises well I trust, for England and for her national Church.'[150]

The Unconditional Freeness of the Gospel

Throughout the autumn term of 1829, Newton's faith continued unsettled. 'I was greatly tried in Spirit. All the freshness of Bulteel's ministry was gone and he was no longer preaching the Gospel, but two parties were formed, the one of High Calvinists led by Bulteel, and another more Arminian led by Sibthorpe. I was therefore greatly grieved at it.'[151] The great debate within evangelicalism on the issue of election, quiescent for some years, had recently been re-ignited with the publication of *The Unconditional Freeness of the Gospel* by the Scottish lay theologian, Thomas Erskine. Newton, who had a particular interest – his close friend G. V. Wigram of Queen's knew the author quite well[152] – was unconvinced by the book's strong anti-Calvinism. He lent it to Sibthorp, who read it during their stay in Hamburg: 'The book of Erskine's that Sibthorp had borrowed was *The Freeness of the Gospel*, I had met with it in Scotland the previous year and it had perplexed me much; but I had recovered. It was more to be dreaded than Arminianism.'[153] Newton recalled that at Leipzig Professor Hahn was translating it into German.[154] Sibthorp respected the professor as a pious man who had 'distinguished himself by his defence of Christianity against the infidel Neologians.'[155] His endorsement would have encouraged Richard, who found an echo of his own beliefs in Erskine's theme of universal forgiveness: 'I conceive all men to be in this state, that all are forgiven.' Not all, however, are saved. 'The limitation then is not in the pardon, but in the belief of the pardon.' Once the reality of unconditional love, of a pardon already granted, was firmly grasped, assurance of salvation, and sanctification would be sure to follow. Erskine's concern was to confront the 'religiosity' of empty words and conventional attitudes with the reality of Christian experience. He reflected 'it is perhaps, one of the chief snares and deceptions of our day to mistake the knowledge of religion for religion itself. . . . How different are those *forms* from the overwhelming reality with which the doctrines are animated in the bible. And oh, how different is the effect produced by them on the hearts of their partizans.'[156]

Not only would the new teaching have encouraged Richard in his instinctive, warm-hearted, Arminianism, but it provided a means whereby he could make better sense of his hitherto somewhat unsystematic theology. Unfortunately, the evidence for Erskine's influence upon him is largely inferential.[157] For example, most of the religious press condemned Erskine's book as heterodox.[158] It is therefore interesting that when Sibthorp moved to Ryde in 1830, it was whispered that his doctrine also was tainted. Fanny Oglander, although impressed by the crowds that flocked to hear him, observed, 'Mr S's preaching is extraordinary and is said to be not quite orthodox.'[159] Perhaps more persuasive is a letter of spiritual counsel written by Richard in 1832, that might have come from the pen of the Scottish theologian:

'I observe you frequently speak of losing an "interest in Christ." The term is a very common one; and has a correct meaning, but I fear it often implies an error in those who use it. I do not think that anyone can lose an interest in Christ, though they may not chose to profit by the interest they have in His work in common with every human being. You cannot . . . undo what Christ has done for you. You cannot stop His sacrifice on Calvary, nor the complete satisfaction He has made there for *sin*. Observe I say for *sin*, not for a certain or any number of sinners. The latter is a most lowering view to take of Christ's death, etc., as if God had put together the quantum of sin committed by a certain number, and then allowed Christ to pay the amount. No; it was for sin, as an evil against God . . . for which an atonement or satisfaction was required. And it has been made, and God is perfectly satisfied; and if all the world but ten persons (suppose such a case) were to refuse to take the benefit of this, it would not remove this, their interest in Christ. . . . Do not be anxious to *feel faith*, but endeavour to believe the satisfaction and work of your Saviour, just as you might believe any good news I might write you in this letter.'[160]

However, the strongest evidence of Erskine's influence is a sermon that Sibthorp delivered at St. Ebbe's on 6 December, in the aftermath of which he became briefly involved in the early history of Tractarianism. Newton recalled, 'Sibthorpe had a tendency to Arminianism, he would preach in the morning and Bulteel in the evening.'[161] Gladstone, who was in the congregation that Sunday morning, noted: 'Heard a beautiful sermon from Sibthorp . . . for the Ch. Miss. Society. Many Ch. Ch. men there. May he who ministereth seed to the sower sow it in us all & cause it to spring up & bring forth much fruit. Oh how unworthy am I to put up such a prayer. But there is a balm in Gilead.'[162] Writing in 1879, he recalled the scene of half a century before. 'For some purpose Mr Sibthorp preached on a Sunday morning to the crowded congregation who attended the parish church of St Ebbe's, under Mr Bulteel. I heard the sermon, an Evangelical sermon of a genial type. Mr Bulteel himself preached in the afternoon; and I well remember hearing at the time that he rebuked the error of saying that Christ died for all men, as in the morning his 'brother Sibthorp' had mistakenly taught them.'[163]

Only a few days before Gladstone had read and been captivated by *The Freeness of the Gospel*, describing it as 'an extraordinary book,' immediately taking up another by the same author.[164] For him, Sibthorp's sermon that morning either explicitly or implicitly touched upon issues raised by Erskine, and the next day he wrote to Edward Craig, a Presbyterian minister in Edinburgh, seeking theological guidance. The latter replied, 'Sibthorp is a very judicious man. Probably he and I would agree basically. But there are peculiarities in Erskine's book, which I cannot approve. I think the question may be settled by attentively studying – Our Lord's discourse to Nicodemus, Romans 5th and 10th. . . . ' He referred also to the 17th Article (on predestination.)[165]

Craig was not alone in questioning the preacher's orthodoxy. John Henry Newman felt compelled to write to John Hill – they were joint secretaries of the Oxford Church Missionary Association – about both sermons: 'considering that the doctrine reported to be contained in them, is not at all in necessary connexion with that professed by the Church Missionary Society, I am anxious to consult with you . . . about the propriety of adopting, if possible, some measure calculated to remove so erroneous an impression.'[166] Newman's aim was the restructuring of the C.M.S. on Church principles and the sermons presented a tactical opportunity.[167] Hill replied that as the offerings were unsolicited there was no cause for concern. He was however, prepared to comment on the theology of the preachers, and decided against Sibthorp:

> 'It is true that one of the preachers employed some expressions in his sermon which the other considered not to be altogether correct, who therefore felt it right to allude to the subject in the afternoon. But while it is open to the friends of each to converse with them on the subject according to their own judgment, surely the committee or secretaries of the Society are not authorised to interfere; as those opinions had no reference to the Society, nor were adduced as the sentiments of the Society. . . . Both the men are devoted servants of Christ, and actuated in an eminent degree by love of God and man – as their whole conduct and spirit testify. With regard to the point of difference between them, I conceive (so far as I can judge from the reports I have received of their sermons, and from my previous knowledge of their sentiments) that Mr. Bulteel is most correct, because more clearly adhering to the spirit and language of Scripture; yet I entertain at the same time a very high regard for the piety and usefulness of Mr Sibthorp; nor can I believe that the difference between them on the particular subject in question is so great as some casual expressions may have led some to suppose.'[168]

Newman persisted in seeking some formal disavowal, and even spoke to Sibthorp himself, shortly before the latter left Oxford to spend Christmas at Canwick. The matter was tabled for discussion at the February Committee. Hill reported to Bickersteth that he viewed his colleague's proposal, expressing '"thanks to those who had preached for the Society especially as they had done so without having received any application from the Committee". . . as a sting on our dear friends Bulteel and Sibthorp.' However, with the votes of local Evangelical clergy drafted in for the occasion, the resolution was 'happily thrown out.'[169]

Richard must surely have felt more isolated than ever. For a sensitive man it was painful to have been denounced from the pulpit, and probably to have known Hill's opinion of his theology. He could not have felt comfortable in an increasingly polarised and febrile religious climate, and may even have felt some sympathy with Newman, whose next move was to attempt to prune his Association's *Annual Report* of its 'conventional Evangelical phraseology.'[170] Bloxam recalled Newman as saying that of all his opponents at this time, 'Sibthorp was the only one who behaved like a gentleman.'[171] Certainly, Richard played no part in the *coup* that saw Newman expelled from the secretaryship.[172] At the heart of this plot was Benjamin Newton. Years later, he too found himself isolated, another victim of *odium theologicum*, which might explain why, in old age, he felt that he had let his travelling companion down. He recalled that, when Francis Newman was arranging meetings to discuss the new prophetical theory, and had asked about Sibthorp, he had advised against inviting him: 'I didn't believe it would do. . . .' Adding, 'I reflect sadly on that now. If it had been that he came it might have given him a light that would have prevented him going to Rome.'[173] It was however, not Frank Newman but J. N. Darby who converted Newton to radical Evangelicalism, when he visited Oxford in May 1830, some weeks after Sibthorp's departure. On meeting him, the issue that Newton raised first was the extent of atonement. Perhaps Sibthorp's views had unsettled him? If so he was reassured, noting with approval Darby's 'commitment to the tenets of Calvinism, but without the narrowness and exclusivity of Bulteel's high Calvinism.'[174] Only after being satisfied on this point did Newton turn to the question of prophecy.

Darby's zeal was central to the process that led to Newton's secession from the Church of England, along with that of Wigram and several others.[175] The religious climate in Oxford was becoming ever more heated, the pulpit at St. Ebbe's ever more strident. In June 1830, Bulteel's friend William Tiptaft wrote that he preached there, '*extempore*, without any premeditation. I was enabled to utter foolish things to confound the wise. I cut down false religion, and exalted Christ, to the great offence of the pious Pharisees.'[176] Hill felt increasingly isolated, having to apologise for reduced support for the C.M.S., 'our friends are gradually leaving Oxford . . . our own friends diminish and we find it difficult to raise new recruits.'[177] It was not a time for moderates and given his sensitivity to religious controversy, along with his unease in College society, Sibthorp's decision early in 1830 to accept the incumbency of St James's proprietary chapel at Ryde on the Isle of Wight is unsurprising. Did he regret turning his back on the Evangelical cause at Oxford? Forty years later, Charles Hole lamented that the departure from the colleges of 'scholarly men of earnest piety, who still clung to the doctrine of Scott and Milner' had prepared the ground for 'the new thoughts that issued from Oriel.' He believed the Church ultimately paid a high price because 'no centre of higher Christian intellect on the scriptural model was permanently and continuously visible in the Oxford pulpit; no schools of influential piety sanctifying men's studies had established themselves within the Oxford quadrangle.'[178] Yet, if Richard ever believed that this was his calling he was surely mistaken. The tide was set too strongly against it. Magdalen could never have nourished such a school, the *genius* of the place was against it.

4

A THEOLOGICAL REVOLUTION
The Ryde Ministry

St. James's Chapel at Ryde was built in 1827 in response to the resort's growing popularity, by William Hughes Hughes, a county magistrate and from 1830 MP for Oxford. In 1841, he explained how Richard Sibthorp became its minister: 'A younger brother of mine the Rev A. Hewitt (my name formerly) was the first minister I appointed to the chapel, and he only left it to take the curacy of the adjoining parish . . . being well acquainted with Mr Sibthorp as the then popular and highly gifted minister of St John's Bedford Row, I applied to him.' He must have declined, because Hewitt was followed by two curates, the second of whom left in February 1830, to become minister of Ram's Chapel, Homerton.[1] Richard was presumably approached again and this time accepted, provided he could purchase the freehold. Hughes Hughes said that in order 'to secure his valuable services' he reluctantly consented. 'Mr Sibthorp paid me under the valuation of three surveyors, £1000 less than the Church had cost me, owing, I believe very much to the pile-driving and other heavy expenditure attending the foundations.'[2]

The arrival, in April 1830, of such a celebrated preacher as Richard Sibthorp was undoubtedly a boost to the growing town,[3] which, said *Mudie*'s, could claim 'the most showy streets and buildings in the Island.'[4] Schemes were afoot to attract even more visitors. In June 1831 a new town hall and market-place were opened, and the following year work began to extend the pier 'so that steam packets may approach it at all times of the tide.'[5] Summer visitors, especially those designated 'families of rank and distinction,'[6] were crucial, and their arrival eagerly anticipated.[7] The eloquence of the new incumbent persuaded a number of well-to-do families to select Ryde for their summer residence, or even to reside there permanently, as in the case of John Fowler's informant: 'My first intercourse with Mr Sibthorp was in the autumn of 1830. I came to the island with a view to seek a residence on the southern coast for the benefit of my wife's health; but spending a Sunday at Ryde, I was so much struck with the preaching of Mr Sibthorp, that I determined to take a house there, which I did and have lived there ever since.'[8]

St. James's was built to accommodate 650, including 200 free sittings in the galleries.[9] Under the new minister, its popularity grew rapidly and there were defections from St. Thomas's, the Chapel of Ease[10] and from the Independent Church, including its organist.[11] Such was the demand for sittings that Richard was soon planning for enlargement and improvement.[12] On 28 October 1830, he wrote to his niece, Mary Anne Hawkins: 'for the last 8 weeks my chapel has been under thoro' repair, partly pulling down and enlarging, and I am anticipating 2 months before I have done with the builders. . . . The weather has been remarkably favourable for building and by Saturday evening I hope to have the roof slated in.'[13]

In the congregation the middle and upper classes predominated, with their servants taking up much of the free seating. 'Besides the townsfolk, there were many visitors in summer and county people from the neighbourhood who would drive in for the service; also the great families in Ryde itself . . . the Duke of Buckingham at Buckingham Lodge, Earl Spencer at Westfield House, the Simeons at St John's and many others.'[14] When the great Irish landowner Lord Farnham and his wife were killed in the Abergele rail disaster of 1868, Sibthorp remembered them as devout members of his congregation.[15] There was often a contingent of naval officers from Portsmouth in the congregation, and sometimes passengers from ships detained in the Solent. Although St. James's had no parish, its people were active on the pattern of the best Evangelical models. Fowler's informant wrote that 'Not much was done for the spiritual good of the town beyond Sunday services at St Thomas's Church. In consequence, Mr. Sibthorp established a society called the Provident Society to, in some measure, meet the needs of the place. The town was divided into districts, and two visitors from his congregation were appointed to each district.'[16] A savings scheme was operated, small deposits were collected, 'and the amount was returned twice in the year, with a bonus of 2d. or 3d. in the shilling, by an order on tradesmen for such things as the family may require.'[17] In 1836, a school was erected of which Sibthorp was a trustee, for the instruction of 'poor infant children.' The building also housed St. James's Sunday School, which by then must have outgrown the chapel.[18]

Without a curate, the minister was kept extremely busy. In addition to Sunday services and a Thursday evening lecture, weekly prayer meetings were soon commenced. Later a devotional meeting was begun on Tuesday evenings, and each Friday 'a little band of from ten to fifteen gentlemen,' met with him for discussion.[19] One priority was the compilation of a hymn book; published in 1831, it went through several editions; the chapel becoming noted for its congregational singing.[20] Henry Wilberforce, attending his dying sister on the island, wrote to John Newman (6 March 1832): 'Mr Sibthorp, who has a chapel at Ryde, had some kind of prayer meeting or such like almost every other day, but has nothing at all on Ash

Wednesday, because he is overworked. He is really a very nice man in many respects, but most lamentably low in all his notions.'[21] This was unfair: in 1828 he had preached before the Prayer Book and Homily Society on the value of the liturgy, and soon after arriving had sought advice about starting a monthly early Communion.[22] Under his zealous ministry, there was talk of a revival in the spiritual life of the town. Richard was hesitant: 'You may believe a tithe (or a twentieth) of what you hear about this place. There is some little good done . . . but it is an evil place and the general state of religious experience is low.'[23]

Many who sat under Sibthorp's early Ryde ministry remembered it as a golden time.[24] In 1833, his congregation presented him with a valuable collection of theological works, a 'tribute of affectionate regard.'[25] Over fifty years later, an elderly woman wrote to John Fowler saying that she still possessed four volumes of manuscript sermons, 'taken down by some of us (who were then young people) in short-hand and written out after.'[26] Week by week, their pastor preached systematically through books of the Bible, distributing printed summaries of the main points. In 1834, the collected notes on Jonah were published as *Pulpit Reflections*. In the following year, a commentary on Genesis – the distillation of many sermons – drew high praise from the *Methodist Magazine*: 'His explanatory remarks . . . bear a more striking resemblance to the terse and spirited Notes of Mr. Wesley on the New Testament than any other publication with which we are acquainted.'[27] Contentious matters, such as the issues raised by geological investigation, were avoided; the *Gentleman's Magazine* commented: 'We should consider Mr. Sibthorp to be a far better divine than philosopher.'[28] And indeed, he was happiest with the exposition of Scripture and urging his people on to practical holiness. On the island his spirits rose and he joked with his niece about the rebuilding work. It would, he said, make his chapel, 'both neat to the eye and convenient for use: being as the *Island Guide* would say "a substantial brick building of commanding size, and elegantly fitted up for the accommodation of numerous visitors who resort to this flourishing and improving town for the benefit of the sea air, and of that serenity of mind, which the exquisite scenery of the neighbourhood is so calculated to produce."'[29] His health steadily improved, although noting this in 1832, he was inclined to attribute it to his being 'more precise about exercise.'[30]

Slipping the Moorings

In May 1830, Sibthorp was in London, engaged to speak at the annual 'Western Meeting' of the R.T.S. Among the platform party was Dr. Milnor, an American, whose interest in *The Dairyman's Daughter*[31] took him in July to Ryde, where he spent 'one of his most comfortable and heavenly Sabbaths, under the ministry of the Rev. Mr. Sibthorpe.'[32] Also at the meeting was the missionary John Hartley, who in Oxford the previous March had impressed John Hill. He too was invited to Ryde, and spent much of August there.[33] Over the years there were many other visitors, drawn by their host's gracious company and compelling preaching, as well as the pleasures of the scenery. In 1832, Sibthorp moved from lodgings to a house in West Street and three years later purchased land two miles from Ryde where he built a mansion. There he was able to invite even more guests and its extensive grounds allowed him to indulge his taste for gardening. One visitor described *Holmewood* as 'delightfully situated on a hill commanding a view of the sea and surrounded by 30 acres of pleasure grounds etc.'[34]

Visitors kept him in touch with religious controversies. When the Bible Society divided, he wrote to Lewis Hensley, 'There always seems something novel in London, either in the way of doctrine or occurrences in the religious world'.[35] He was pleased to be away, writing in 1834, 'I am not surprised at your account of London. It has always been a nest of strange notions and novelties . . . I never thought the state of religion in its religious circles what it should be, and rejoice to keep out of them.'[36] At Ryde, his links with the Religious Societies gradually loosened, a process reinforced by the death of friends prominent in Evangelical circles. In August 1831, Jane and William Forster perished in the wreck of the *Rothsay Castle*.[37] It was a cruel blow,[38] as was the premature death of his friend John Sargent of Lavington two years later.[39] Yet the Solent could not protect him from all controversy, much as he might wish simply to preach the gospel and edify his people. His opinions had always been eagerly canvassed, although he could be disturbingly uncertain, even on key issues, baptism for instance:

'You could scarcely have asked me a question I find more difficulty in answering than the one you have put to me on the subject of infant baptism, if I may so express it. I have always found it very difficult to say what are the privileges of children of believers in this ordinance . . . I have always thought that a very peculiar obscurity rests on this subject, whether owing to the general prevalence of erroneous views, preconceived opinions, or attempts to reconcile different systems on a point where they seem to clash, or want of Scriptural clearness in our own Church services, I pretend not to say, but I have never yet been able to satisfy my own mind upon it.'[40]

It must have been a concern that there was an obvious contradiction between the idea of 'Scriptural clearness' and a fracturing Religious World, much of which considered Sibthorp's understanding of the atonement insufficiently biblical. For his part, believing holiness to be the touchstone of true Christianity, Richard found some aspects of contemporary Evangelicalism troubling, and worried that an overemphasis on 'instantaneous conversion' could lead to self-delusion, even hypocrisy. He warned Mary Anne Hawkins that 'eternal life is not given to a few faint wishes, breathed out in sickness or on a death-bed: but to holy diligence in doing the will of God.'[41] Fearful of antinomianism, he rejected Calvinism, but felt that the Wesleyan emphasis on feelings of assurance could be equally dangerous: 'Enthusiasts have mistaken and abused the doctrine of assurance. Some especially have saddened the hearts of sincere and humble believers, by affirming that without assurance none will be saved.'[42] The appeal of the *Unconditional Freeness* theology was its emphasis on practical holiness: the 'living personality of God must animate and fill out Christian doctrines, otherwise they only tend to add a fatal security to the sleep of the soul.' Erskine argued that faith's role was, 'to give the pardon a moral influence, by which it may heal the spiritual diseases of the heart.'[43] But this was all rather theoretical; it was hard to be confident that holiness was the inevitable consequence of embracing the Good News. Writing in 1830, Sibthorp stressed that salvation required the removal of two barriers. The one, external: the guilt of sin; the other, internal: 'my own evil heart.' The first 'the Divine Saviour removed when he died on Calvary;' the second, 'another Divine Being is ready to remove, and does from everyone who believing what Christ has done, applies to God as Father for the further benefit of the Holy Spirit's work.'[44] But there was a deeper problem with Erskine's theology, as the author acknowledged: 'The reader who is much accustomed to the ordinary technical language of theology will perhaps start at the idea of universal and unconditional pardon . . . as if it were removing the landmarks of the church and preaching a false peace to a world dead in trespasses and sins.'[45] Lurking behind the new approach was the spectre of Universalism, an implication that became clearer with the publication of the *Brazen Serpent* in 1831. Richard agonised about eternal punishment, but could never escape what he saw as the clear teaching of the bible.[46]

Whatever his final judgement on Erskine, Richard was open about his unhappiness with 'popular religion' and wrote of his concerns to his friend Mrs Hawkes, an elderly member of St. John's. She had grown up among the early Methodists, and had known the widow of John Fletcher of Madeley – Richard's *beau ideal* of a gospel minister. Mrs Hawkes agreed with him 'that Satan's mode of attack in the present day is by exciting an *outward,* rather than an *inward* work; especially by promoting an *apparent* zeal for God, in pursuing objects connected with the spread of the gospel.'[47] Sibthorp was no longer willing to tour for the Bible Society. It was taxing work,[48] but more importantly, he now rejected the kind of platform performance it demanded, telling Joseph Jowett in 1833, 'I will do anything for it rather than speak or make speeches . . . I cannot do this or essay to do it as once I did. The fault may be in me – certainly it is not owing to any less esteem or admiration of the First Institution in the world . . . But yet not altogether in me. I trust I shrink more from saying what may please an audience than once I did . . . So you may conclude you have little or no chance of aid from me.'[49] A later approach from the Assistant Secretary drew the stinging response that he 'was not enough of a Tertullus' to comply.[50] He did however, continue to chair the local Committee, and organised the supply of foreign language bibles to ships lying at anchor, as well as arranging Scriptures for those on the convict ships.[51]

Disillusion is not a good basis for a stable ministry, and it seems that it was not only as regards theology that Sibthorp was now slipping his moorings without having any clear destination. Rather startlingly, in October 1830 he recorded his approval of the 'July Days': 'To me it is no marvel that the mass of educated and enlightened should be dissatisfied with the state of things existing almost everywhere in Europe, but in our own famed country, and should desire charters and constitutional governments . . . In the events in France so far as they have gone, I cordially rejoice: because I trust that liberty, spiritual, intellectual, and political, will be promoted thereby.'[52] Was this evidence of the link that some detected between liberalism in theology and in politics? Orthodox Evangelicals had been swift to denounce the dangerous political implication of Erskine's theory. Hugh M'Neile, the rector of Albury, warned of the novel and false doctrine of 'universal pardon, independent of and irrespective of the person' which was being 'proclaimed by some in the church at this present time.' Only orthodoxy in doctrine, he argued, could guard against the corrosion of democracy, for 'the enemy has set with full power against the Established Church, in these realms.' One warning sign was evident, 'the loud praises of men who claim to be religious, which have been uttered in these last gone weeks, of a most irreligious, unjust, and ungodly act, as ever was performed by men calling themselves Christians.'[53] He meant the deposition of Charles X of France.

Actually, Sibthorp's views on French politics stemmed as much from the blow that he thought the Revolution would inflict upon Roman Catholicism, as from any wholesale adoption of radical politics, because he quickly added, 'We must pray for England. We have not George the 3rd on the throne . . . We have an irreligious ministry I fear and a turbulent Commons and a people more difficult to keep in order than 40 years ago.'[54] Thus he later rejected the Irish Church Bill; 'The diminution of Bishops I decidedly disapprove of and I feel by no means satisfied that it is the business of Parliament, a body of laymen, to do such an act. The next step of the Roman Catholics there will be to demand Government support, and then to be the Establishment. The Lord have mercy upon us!'[55] Yet, notwithstanding these fears, during much of his island ministry Sibthorp was identified with the Liberals. According to *The Times* he 'entered avowedly into politics at Ryde and represented the anomalous picture of a Radical clergyman.'[56]

It was a time of distancing from the Canwick heritage and from his brother Charles, who paid the price for his opposition to the Reform Bill by being rejected by the voters in 1832. He was returned the following year, and represented Lincoln continuously until his death in 1855, becoming one of the most frequently lampooned of parliamentary eccentrics: 'the embodiment of honest but unreasoning Tory prejudice.'[57]. Richard described him as 'a most strange being and unlike other people.'[58] Charles became notorious for his strong opposition to the railways: 'a degrading form of transport.'[59] An even greater dislike of foreigners prompted him to initiate (in January 1840) the successful motion to reduce Prince Albert's annuity from £50,000 to £30,000. His last and greatest campaign was against the Crystal Palace, which, he solemnly averred, Albert was organising in order to reduce the country to bankruptcy and to lure other foreigners into this once happy land.[60]

If Richard found his brother difficult, he was always susceptible to the influence of people he liked and respected, and on the island, those closest to him were Liberals by conviction. Hughes Hughes, for instance, was a Whig MP, a 'moderate reformer and in favour of shorter parliaments.'[61] A more significant friendship was with his nephew, John Heywood Hawkins, who in 1832 became the Radical member for Newport. Two years before he had extolled the followers of Captain Swing, who 'were exhibiting, in a practical way the fruit of 30 years of Tory government.'[62] Throughout his life, he remained on good terms with his uncle. Learning of his death, in 1877, Richard wrote: 'I very much esteemed and valued him.'[63] There was also a young clergyman, William Darwin Fox, Charles Darwin's cousin and scientific collaborator, who became Richard's *confidant*. From 1832 he regularly wintered at Ryde for the sake of his health, and seems to have undertaken some ministerial duties at St. James's. A committed Whig, in June 1832 he wrote to Darwin on the *Beagle*: 'By the time of your return we shall be better judges of the happy effects of our Reform Bill, at least if it is allowed to have its natural course in the correction of the abuses of Church and State.'[64]

Unfortunately, direct evidence of Richard's political involvement is elusive. What is known is that in 1835 he voted for a Liberal candidate, Sir Richard Simeon, nephew of Charles Simeon, a member of the St. James's congregation, and a strong supporter of the Bible Society.[65] Simeon had also struggled to secure the vote of Samuel Wilberforce, the rector of Brighstone on the south of the island, urging upon him 'with no small skill every conceivable ground upon which a clergyman . . . could give his support to a Liberal candidate.'[66] But Wilberforce was a High Churchman and an unbending Tory, who organised meetings of Church supporters at Newport to oppose Heywood Hawkins.[67] That Richard did not reject his friends' liberal opinions reflected his own deep concern for social cohesion. In later life, he severely criticised the Church of England for her inability to promote this. Her people, he said, were 'like a rope of sand, neither closely knit to each other, nor to the great body of the poor and humble classes, for whom especially the gospel was preached and the

Church instituted.'[68] From the same feelings flowed his willingness to regard all sincere Christians as brethren regardless of denomination. Although he was to reject Evangelicalism, he continued to work alongside the Independent Minister on the Committee of the Bible Society and as late as 1836, assured Jabez Bunting that he was happy to speak for the Wesleyan Missionary Society.[69] Thus, he supported the proposal to relax religious tests on Oxford entrants, although was not present for the vote in Convocation (May 1835) having paired with Samuel Wilberforce.[70]

The Rector of Brighstone

At Oxford, confronted with forceful and articulate Calvinism, Sibthorp was perhaps forced onto the defensive, but at Ryde things were different. His preaching was immensely popular, and he might have spent his remaining days quietly ministering the gospel to a devoted congregation, somewhat like his connection Charles Maitland, who had purchased a proprietary chapel in Brighton. That this was not to be was largely owing to the rector of Brighstone. Wilberforce was a man with a mission: he possessed 'an instinctive tendency to strike out from his own centre and gather others into a circle round him, with the practical object of enlisting and directing their force towards whatever aim he had in view.'[71] Personally ambitious, he had succeeded in making himself indispensable to the Bishop of Winchester, becoming his chaplain in 1832. Hurrell Froude wrote to congratulate him, saying he had heard that he was 'the μεγας διαλλακτης [great conciliator] of the Island.'[72] At Oxford, Wilberforce had become convinced that Church principles were the essential complement to Evangelical spirituality. It was a belief that he was determined to share, and he could be very persuasive. J. C. Ryle, a convinced Calvinist, described how 'one memorable night . . . he had a long discussion with me till a late hour about baptismal regeneration, in which he tried hard to turn me from Evangelical views on that subject.'[73] Ryle was unmoved, not so Walter Kerr Hamilton. In December 1838, Wilberforce informed W. F. Hook that he had just spent two or three hours with Hamilton 'and had much interesting conversation. . . . His Church views enlarge and clear themselves most hopefully.'[74]

On the island, the instrument Wilberforce fashioned to propagate his opinions was a monthly meeting of his clerical colleagues. The first was held on 1 January 1833, with Ordination as the subject for discussion. Richard did not attend, and at first resisted Samuel's invitations. Yet, in seeking to win his confidence, the latter possessed a number of advantages. The two men had much in common, their families were acquainted,[75] and the Evangelicals – despite growing evidence to the contrary – still considered Samuel as one of their own.[76] Both men had a strong sense of the apocalyptic. In January 1831, Wilberforce wrote that he could 'almost hear the coming chariot wheels of the Son of Man,' a view he was still expressing three years later.[77] Moreover, he genuinely valued Sibthorp's preaching, so that on the Sunday following the death of his sister at Ryde, he and other members of the family worshipped at St James's.[78]

However, Wilberforce's ultimate success derived less from his persuasive abilities than from Sibthorp's uncertain attachment to any coherent school of theology, and from the re-emergence, in the tranquillity of the island, of aspects of his religious personality more or less suppressed since childhood. When he became a Roman Catholic in 1841, a correspondent in the *Record* said that ten years before, Mrs. Hawkes had detected in him a tendency to misuse 'imagination' causing him to seek 'greater degrees of spirituality and elevation than the Scriptures authorize us to expect.'[79] In this connection, it is interesting that when William Phelps was at St. James's in August 1832, he noted that for his Thursday evening address Richard had chosen the unusual topic of 'baptism for the dead.'[80]

One belief at least, that Sibthorp had adopted in childhood, he had never abandoned: that devotional aids could nourish holiness. Writing in 1833 to thank Lewis Hensley for a gift, he made a remarkable admission:

> 'I was in Oxford when your letter came, and when the beautiful portrait of Fletcher[81] reached safely my dwelling here . . . (I have) given it a place in my study opposite a print (purchased by me in Basle) of that Divine Master whom he loved ardently and closely followed. It is well to have monitors of good men, and saints, and of the Lord of Saints. I am somewhat Catholic in my sentiments herein, and candidly confess I feel no horror whatsoever at a Crucifix but can contemplate one with much satisfaction. Such things were lamentably, yea awfully abused previous to the Reformation, and still are by many. They are very likely to be abused, man being glad to substitute anything for true spiritual service of God, but they may lawfully and properly be used. I cannot say I feel any disposition to worship them, or give them any undue honour, but I think I find the contemplation of them has a tendency to give seriousness to the mind and recall it to what is good, and I apprehend many will feel the same if they attend to their feelings.'[82]

He later acknowledged that the 'remembrance of devotional feelings' inspired by his youthful encounter with Catholicism, 'never entirely quitted me during subsequent years.'[83] Another example may be adduced. In 1837, he wrote to Newman that having just come across Tract 75 it had awakened a long-standing idea, 'that the Roman Breviary might be adapted to the use of Protestants, as an highly valuable Book of Daily Devotion. . . . *I have repeatedly, for many years, looked into it.*'[84]

Given all this, the fact that after only a brief exposure to Church views, aired forcefully at the clerical meetings, Sibthorp was converted to a High Church position may not be considered surprising. Encountering Wilberforce on several occasions during 1833, his reluctance to attend was gradually undermined. In March, both were visiting relatives in West Sussex, and met at the home of a mutual friend. Samuel wrote that their prayer and conversation was 'very pleasant.'[85] In August, they accompanied Bickersteth during his tour of the island on behalf of the C.M.S. By 1 December, Richard had succumbed and travelled with Wilberforce to the clergy meeting at Bembridge.[86] Thereafter, it was as though his submission to the High Church teaching was almost inevitable. Not only did it validate the soundness of his instinctive Sacramentalism, but also provided much-needed theological underpinning for his anti-Calvinism.

Peter Maurice bears testimony to Wilberforce's persuasive power. In *The Popery of Oxford* published in 1837, he recalled, 'in the latter part of 1833,' visiting an Isle of Wight friend whom, at that time, 'would not even *look*' at the Oxford Tracts, but was now 'carried away by their dissimulation.' This change was because, 'an individual, eminent himself, eminent too as the son of a father whose memory to English hearts will be ever dear, had adopted these erroneous and dangerous theories, and I augured what the result would be, and have lived to see it verified . . . if the *piety*, age, and the glowing and deep experience, of our clergy is not proof against these *Thyatira-like* innovations, what may we expect to be the necessary result in the case of our younger brethren.'[87] In a letter of 30 November 1836, Henry Wilberforce, a frequent visitor to the island, referred to the same circumstances, but drew a very different conclusion. He wrote to John Newman of:

> 'good news. Sibthorp is really become decidedly Apostolical. He was four years ago nearly the most hopeless X [Evangelical] in the world (except only that he was a thinking and reading man,) but hopeless as having been a Papist.[88] . . . I told you that three years ago he heard a very full exposition of the doctrine of Baptism from Sam at a clerical meeting, and seemed much inclined to adopt it. He told me some months after, that he liked it better the more he thought of it, *but had never heard it before.*'[89]

That an acceptance of baptismal regeneration was the trigger for Richard's theological revolution is convincing. But he had heard of it before. Preaching in 1818, he had dismissed it as 'the darkness of popery.'[90] Now he saw how it could resolve tensions in his theological understanding, and, most importantly, as Pusey sought to demonstrate in his three tracts of 1835, how it could be seen as a biblical teaching.

Unfortunately, not all aspects of High Church teaching could summon such direct biblical support. For Sibthorp – who never ceased to regard Scripture as uniquely authoritative – this was a problem, and may explain why he held back for some while before publicly avowing his new views. And when he did – at the Friday meeting of his close associates – he began, not with the sacramental, but the practical. One of those present told John Fowler, of Sibthorp 'advocating very earnestly the unity of the Church, and insisting upon its necessity. "For how," said he "could an epistle be sent to the Church in Manchester? to whom could it be addressed?"[91]

The potential stumbling block that the bible presented to the elevation of Sibthorp's churchmanship was dramatically removed with a discovery that he made, probably during 1836, whilst preparing a series of lectures on 'the Levitical law and institutions.' All agreed that the Levitical types pointed to Christ. But was this a complete explanation? Surely not: 'He, it is clear, was not the typified Israel . . . '[92] With great force, a new insight began to dominate his thinking: Richard became convinced that Israel, in its priestly orders, its worship and its ritual, was intended to foreshadow the Church of the New Testament. It was an interpretative method with exciting consequences. If the Church of which he was a priest was indeed called to be the antitype of the Jewish, then it was necessarily visible, ceremonial and sacramental. Thus were the religious tastes he had imbibed as a child confirmed as most sound, orthodox and biblical.

What first suggested typology to him as a Scriptural validation of Church principles is not recorded. He wrote that he found the topic seldom, 'more than hinted at in modern theological works.'[93] This was an exaggeration; it was a standard polemical weapon in defence of the National Church. For example, in a widely-read pamphlet of 1833, Michael Gathercole, a rather notorious dissenter who converted to Anglicanism had written, 'To the argument in favour of a National Religious Establishment, drawn from that of the Jews, no solid answer ever has been or ever can be given.' And in support of the three orders of ministry, he appealed to 'the Church of Christ as it existed throughout every period of the Jewish economy before his incarnation'.[94] In 1839, the anonymous author of the *Liber Redivivus,* proclaimed, 'The whole Jewish economy, its priesthood, sacrifices, altar and festivals were typical and shadowed forth better things to come . . . The Aaronic priesthood hath departed, and the Christian hath succeeded in its room.'[95]

Clear-sighted Evangelicals saw dangers in typology. They were unable to deny specific applications to the New Testament church, having to agree, for example, with T. H. Horne that the ark foreshadowed baptism, but most were unwilling to go further.[96] Patrick Fairbairn later summarised the reason for this caution, categorising Roman Catholicism as the offspring of the 'Judaizing Christians' who had striven 'to assimilate the New Testament economy in its formal appearance and administration to the Old.' While acknowledging that in her appeal to typology, 'Rome was able to avail herself of the authority of many of the more distinguished Fathers,' he argued that it was by 'means chiefly of mistaken parallels from Jewish to Christian times' that 'everything was gradually brought back from the apostolic ideal of a spiritual community, founded on the perfect atonement and priesthood of Christ, to the outwardness and ritualism of ancient time.'[97] Typology was thus a controversial tool, but where embraced enthusiastically meant that separation from the visible Church tracing its origin to the Apostles was a rejection of the authority of Scripture.

It was in the enthusiasm of his discovery that at a Clerical Meeting attended by Henry Wilberforce in November 1836, Sibthorp went into 'a considerable examination of Holy Scripture to show that the Succession of High Priests was a type of the Christian Episcopate.'[98] Typology was the motor that impelled the bible-loving incumbent of St. James's into the vanguard of the High Church movement. According to Henry, since accepting baptismal regeneration, Richard had

> 'gone regularly on, and is now *preaching* the Succession, the superiority of the Church prayers to preaching, – that "he will not say that those who are out of the Church *cannot* be saved, because he leaves that to God" etc. Last week at a clerical meeting he avowed his approval of Prayers for the dead! and renounced the X view of Justification by faith, saying that Wesley had done great harm by making people look for their personal comfort etc to their own feelings etc etc. instead of to their Baptism, and that the Evangelical clergy had fallen into the same!'

It was a triumph for his brother:

> 'All this is, under God, Sam's doing; I do not know what has rejoiced me so much. Is it not an omen of the power and force of Church Principles, when put out fairly? The Xs of Ryde are furious. They say they took their houses to be near Sibthorp . . . A great X refused to join the Meeting, saying that he had seen such bad effects produced on more powerful minds than his own by it, that he dare not trust himself. By the way, an X candidate for Orders came to consult Sibthorp about *Infant* Baptism, having scruples. S. replied, "Not only have I no doubt about the Baptism of Infants, but I am also convinced, which may perhaps surprise you, that that Baptism is the appointed instrument of obtaining regeneration"!!'[99]

Newman could not keep the news to himself. He wrote to James Bliss, 'Mr. Sibthorp of the Isle of Wight has publicly professed his adherence to Apostolical views to the full extent, to the great disgust of his people, who had taken their houses for the season on the ground of the opportunity of sitting under him. This is one way of teaching people not to trust to individual preachers – it will be curious if we teach them so by such a process.'[100]

The Rapid Transition of an Impulsive Mind

Sibthorp's publication in 1836 of *The Family Liturgy* can be seen, in its rejection of *extempore* prayer, to announce his departure from the Evangelical camp.[101] A process had begun with consequences few could have foreseen, but there was an early and startling portent. The Levitical Church had 'an impressive and magnificent ritual, every ceremony of which was symbolic and instructive, – adapted alike to the present infirmity of man . . . and to the glory and majesty of God?'[102] The worship of the New Testament Church, the worship at St. James's, must surely be based upon this glorious pattern. At the heart of the Temple worship was singing, and so, probably as early as 1836, Richard began to assemble a choir robed in surplices and cassocks.[103] He had long delighted in choral worship, but now felt that its introduction in his church was the path of obedience.[104]

Ollard dates the surpliced choir to 1839, affirming it was 'the first instance of such use in what was to all intents a parish church;' both statements are improbable, for there were other such choirs just over the Solent. In 1829, the *Gosport Herald* printed the following account of the consecration of the site of a new church at Forton. 'At 1 p.m. Divine Service was performed at the Parish Church, and the Collect for the 7th Sunday after Trinity well sung by the choristers.' The procession, which 'then moved to the intended site of the Church,' included 'children of the National and Sunday Schools of Alverstoke, two by two amounting to nearly six hundred' and 'the eight choristers of Alverstoke Church in their surplices with the organist.'[105] Henry Veck, the curate at Alverstoke, was Forton's incumbent-elect. In *A Selection of Psalms, Hymns and Anthems*, which he published the following year, he extolled the Psalms, so 'admirably adapted at the time of their composition to the rites and ceremonies of the Jewish worship.' It was his desire 'to promote the improvement of the Psalmody of our Church, which when properly and solemnly performed, is so noble, religious and delightful a part of divine worship.' In his new parish, he established a surpliced choir, and may have advised Sibthorp about forming his, for by the end of the decade their choristers were in friendly rivalry.[106] Other mainland clergy were also establishing choirs, John Craig for example, who had been an Evangelical, one of the very few influenced by the changes at St. James's. In 1836, he was appointed rector of Fetcham in Surrey and three years later moved to Leamington, where his choir benefited practically from Sibthorp's help.[107] In 1841, John Rouse Bloxam who was staying at Holmewood, wrote, 'We cross the water next week to assist in a solemn service at Forton Church near Gosport. Four choirs will meet on this occasion amounting to 60 choristers, with the addition of their organists, singing teachers etc. I heard them all practice the *Venite Exultemus* in the fourth tone of the Gregorian chant, and was delighted beyond measure with the effect produced by so many voices.'[108]

But in introducing choral worship at St. James's there was an obvious difficulty: the building was an auditorium rather than a sanctuary. In the redesign of the chapel and the evolution of ceremonial there, the part played by J. R. Bloxam, 'the real originator of the ceremonial revival in the Church of England,'[109] was critical. He first met Sibthorp at Oxford in 1835, both had been subject to Catholic influences,[110] and their initial acquaintance 'soon ripened into friendship.'[111] A Magdalen fellow, Bloxam became in 1837 Newman's curate at Littlemore, where with tastes 'antiquarian and ecclesiological rather than theological . . . he threw himself with enthusiasm into the task of adorning the little church and arranging its services.'[112] In November of that year Newman 'dined at Magdalen in order to meet Sibthorp,' probably at his new curate's invitation.[113] The following July, Richard was back in Oxford and must have discussed with Bloxam his detailed plans for the re-ordering of St. James's, because quite soon afterwards work to increase the capacity of the church, and to adapt it for choral worship, had begun. When it was completed, the organ had been enlarged, the flat ceiling over the body of the Church removed, and a chancel area designated by the addition of wooden gates and choir seats. Decoration was added, including painted shields on the gallery beams and texts on scrolls between the windows and over the chancel arch.[114]

The ornamentation of the chapel was a continuing process, and in the autumn of 1840, Bloxam wrote to the celebrated Catholic ecclesiologist Daniel Rock, seeking advice. He showed the letter to Pugin, who, being anxious to contact the Oxford divines, wrote directly to Bloxam offering to visit Sibthorp and 'give that gentleman any information of which I am posessed (*sic*) for the improvement of his building.'[115] On learning this, Richard wrote to him immediately[116] and seems to have asked the great Gothicist to design a triptych.[117] It was the start of a fruitful relationship. Pugin visited Ryde the following spring. His disappointment was predictable:

'I think his intentions *truly admirable*, but to speak the honest truth the sanctuary Looks amazingly (*sic*) Like one of those modern Catholic chapels – there is too much finery to produce a Solemn effect. for instance, the carpet is of a gay drawing room pattern & the flowerpots *on* the altar are quite *Parisian*. I feel truly anxious that we should avoid anything trifling, or too *gay* around the altar, it should be rich and devotional and in all revivals one must consult *antiquity* and not even glance at novelties. far be it from me to make these remarks in disparagement of Good Mr Sibthorps (*sic*) attempt. no one can appreciate his inttentions (*sic*) better than myself but I fear if not better Carried out they will only awaken protestant prejudice & fail to convey a true conception of Catholic solemnity, a modern altar always produces a mingled feeling of sorrow & disgust in my mind.'[118]

The *Ecclesiologist* was more charitable, after Sibthorp had left it conceded that he made the chapel 'in some respects more conformable than before to ancient usage.'[119]

'An Abyss of Error, Idolatry and Superstition'

Once St. James's had been refurbished, the new worship could be properly introduced and it was not long before Samuel Wilberforce, who in 1836 had been appointed rural dean of the north-east division of the island, became aware of complaints, and in March 1839, wrote to the bishop. Sumner was dubious that what was fitting for a cathedral was suitable to a parochial congregation, but felt the arrangements 'innocent,' and did not feel called to pronounce on them.[120] He soon changed his mind, having received an anonymous letter 'which may serve to shew Mr. Sibthorp that the whole of his congregation is not as contented as he would seem to believe. If they are I must say I cannot wish people to be content, or be so myself. The three crucifixes seem to me impossible – if there be anything which can be mistaken for this, it (*sic*) should be removed. To place actual crucifixes there at any time would, in my judgement be highly improper, but at the present time, when the question of popery within the Church is so prominent a topic, it would be so obviously injudicious that I cannot believe the allegation.' He was more prepared to credit complaints about the 'mode of reciting the Litany. If it be as stated, *at* (or near) the Communion Table, by the clergyman *standing,* with his back to the congregation, I think it wrong.' However, 'desirous of not giving Mr. Sibthorp pain unnecessarily' he asked Wilberforce to 'ascertain first whether there is any foundation' for the complaint, 'and only in that case transmit to Mr. S the letter and my views.'[121]

Responding to Wilberforce's reply Sumner confessed that he was:

> 'extremely concerned at the statement which Mr. Jackson gives of the actual interior of St. James's and have no longer any hesitation in requesting you to shew Mr. Sibthorp the anonymous letter and my remarks addressed to yourself. I think he cannot remove too quickly the three crosses, litany desk and fald stool. With respect to the latter, I certainly cannot agree that the litany is now said as required by the 15th Canon . . .
>
> If the arrangement of the Chapel be really according to your sketch I cannot conceive of any more injurious. The introduction of many ornaments is also most inadvised and even worse than that at the present time. But the most painful thing to me in the Church is that such a man as Sibthorp should be so blinded as to think himself, or suppose that others can think, that he places the cross on the altar rail for no other motive than to mark the centre! It is the straw, but indicates the hurricane.'[122]

Some action was taken. In March 1841, Pugin wrote to Bloxam, 'I had no idea of the shameful order against Mr. Sibthorpes cross – it is perfectly disgusting. I do not know what is to be done with these bishops, they seem terrible drags . . . '[123] Otherwise, the bishop's advice appears to have been ignored. In November 1839, Clara Cholmeley wrote of her sister's 'very strange accounts' of uncle: 'He has wax candles burning on the "High Altar" during the day on Sunday, he has three reading desks placed in different parts of the Church at which he reads different parts of the service and when reading the Litany he prostrates himself before the High Altar with his back to the people. All the service is chaunted. (I dont see anything wrong in that except that the congregation cannot join well), he has different texts of Scripture painted in all kinds of gay colours all over the walls of his Chapel which the person who gave the description to Selena said looked "tawdry" and several other odd things.'

She thought the account 'must be exaggerated though the gentleman was an eye witness and seemed to fear that Mr Sibthorpe was a little cracked he looked so wild and haggard.' Those who knew Richard well, never doubted his sincerity. Clara said her brother Stephen 'did not say he saw anything extraordinary.' She also reported what Thomas Woodroffe had said. He was rector of Calbourne on the island and previously a Secretary of the C.M.S., having taken up the office that Sibthorp declined in 1824. Her aunt, Sarah Cholmeley, had asked Woodroffe what he thought, saying 'she had heard some out of the way stories' regarding Sibthorp. '"I think" (he answered) "why I think nothing but love."'[124] His affection was shared by most of the St. James's congregation: unconvinced by the new theology, they remained intensely loyal, a fact attested by a local newspaper in January 1839:

> 'Such is the zeal manifested for the well-being of the inhabitants of our town, and much to the praise of the Revd. R. W. Sibthorp, Minister of St. James's Episcopal Chapel, that during the winter months, notwithstanding cold and rain, persons, and particularly those of the higher order, are seen two or three times a week, proceeding from all parts of the town to St. James's to worship, as early as 8 o'clock.'[125]

But for those at a greater distance, dogma was far too important to be sacrificed to sentiment. Criticism had begun even before the re-ordering of St. James's. On the island, Augustus Hewitt led the attack. Samuel Wilberforce, referring to an exchange at an S.P.C.K. meeting in July 1837, noted that he 'sneers at Sibthorpe and the tracts,' but added, 'I answered him with effect.'[126] A clerical meeting the following November became very heated, 'Davies vehement and confused . . . Holditch . . . timid . . . Sibthorpe good and clear.'[127] On the mainland, too, Evangelical sensors were quick to detect the new note being sounded at Ryde. In March 1838, Wilberforce was in London and wrote in his diary of having to 'defend Sibthorpe' against the 'Peculiars.'[128] The atmosphere became increasingly fraught. In November, at a Protestant Reformation Society meeting with Hewitt in the chair, there was a reference to 'local circumstances,' which 'almost all' present deplored 'as personal' and 'not borne out by fact.' The

Hampshire Telegraph added darkly that 'such allusion, if not refrained from must tend to put an end to all public religious meetings, in Ryde, at least.'[129]

However, it was the choral worship rather than the new theology that turned St. James's into a national scandal. The chapel attracted so many visitors with clear expectations that it was only a matter of time before the attention of the wider 'religious world' would be drawn to what was going on. On 24 August 1840, the *Record* – the voice of radical Evangelicalism – contained the following letter:

'While visiting the town of Ryde a few days ago my attention was directed to a bill announcing divine worship was to be performed and a sermon preached at St. James's Church on Wednesday, 12 August when a collection would be made for the benefit of some Society, for which *the Forton choir was to join that of Ryde*. Attracted by curiosity I went to the Church where I was struck by its appearance. I did not know at first to what denomination or sect it could belong. It was most profusely decorated with flowers from top to bottom in every direction,[130] and while looking on these I perceived as many little pictures of priests, beasts, fowls, crosses, crossed keys etc. etc. scattered all over the place, and in the centre was raised a formidable gilt eagle with its wings spread, highly ornamented with wreaths of flowers. I should have been tempted to think myself in some pagan temple, had I not, in advancing toward the top, discovered a small Roman Catholic chapel, such as those that are dedicated to some particular saints, which are to be seen in different parts of large Continental Romish churches. There was an altar with two raised candlesticks, a raised paten, and some books with golden crosses in front. Above it, as projecting from the wall, was seen a part of a cross, with women kneeling before it. And above that the picture of St. Jacobus surrounded with hieroglyphics. While wondering whether I was not in a Romish Church, I saw coming out from two different doors of the vestry, a clergyman at each door, followed by about twelve boys in surplices who solemnly walked down each aisle in procession, to the other end of the Church. When a signal was given, the music began to play, and the same procession came back with all the grimaces of a ballet-march, and then a musical service was performed. After the sermon six of the boys before mentioned went with plates collecting from pew to pew, and when that was done they brought the plates to the minister, who standing within the altar railing, took them, and having placed them on a crimson velvet cushion knelt down before them, lifting up his hands to his head and bowing down. Whether he worshipped the plates, or St. Jacobus, I cannot tell, but what I know is that anything but God was worshipped in that place. His holy name indeed was sung, but only as it would be in some opera, when it suits the purpose of the piece. After the performance was over some *Latin* anthem was chaunted. Upon my enquiring to what sect the Chapel belonged, I was told, "The Church of England." Is it so? I never beheld among Protestants such downright disregard of the first three Commandments.'[131]

The letter, signed by 'Protestant Foreigner,' was reproduced in several newspapers. After it appeared in the *Globe*, Richard feared, 'I shall be placarded as far as the East and West Indies.' Despite his not being 'aware of anything wrong on that day,' he was anxious. 'I own that the matter vexes and fidgets me a little . . . I have had some really violent letters, from individuals charging me with being a friend and abettor of heretics and schismatics, viz. the Oxford Divines. I am as much accused of preaching false doctrine as of superstitious practices. I wish they would direct a little of this pitiless pelting Oxford way, and not send it all to me, who has never printed a tract.'[132]

When the *Hampshire Independent* got hold of the letter, a preface had been added:

'The gewgaws of Popish ceremony have wondrous attractions, and possess undoubted efficacy in the estimation of Puseyism, and are therefore introduced, not only without the sanction, but against the positive injunction of the Book of Common Prayer. But what is the Bishop of the Diocese about? Has the Archdeacon, who is called the "Bishop's eye" seen nothing in these things to call for episcopal notice and reproof?'[133]

St. James's was a proprietary chapel and the bishop's authority was unclear. When a correspondent to the *Record* made this point, the editor suggested that the incumbent's licence could be revoked. Over the following weeks he printed several letters lamenting Sibthorp's fall from grace. One correspondent characterised the choral worship as 'little hirelings bawling and shouting to each other "how excellent," "how excellent" till you are wearied and disgusted.' But he also acknowledged the ambivalent attitude of the congregation, 'Considering however, their attachment, never perhaps in so large a congregation, were fewer people ever carried away by an erring minister.'[134] This was an accurate analysis, the great bulk of his people continued unconvinced but steadfast, and the *Record* received letters from several of them to the effect that Sibthorp was a sincere Christian and an eloquent preacher and should be indulged. None were published, but in November, the editor declared a truce: 'We do not intend at present to admit any additional letters on the subject of St. James's, Ryde. We believe the Pastor still introduces much of the gospel into his sermons; and it is only to be lamented that one who *in all things* adorned the gospel of God his Saviour should have been deluded to introduce sundry changes, many of which can be considered as small things, but all of which are indicative of a loss of perception of what constitutes the essential principles and properties of the gospel.'[135]

Despite this display of loyalty some in the congregation were unhappy, and would not have disagreed with the eighty-eight old Thomas Jones of Creaton, who visited Ryde in the summer of 1840, accompanied by George Bugg. He wrote of finding 'the very image of the beast' a church 'fitted up in so gaudy a manner, like a theatre. . . . The morning service lasts three hours: the organ takes up one hour of the three. It says "Amen" for the people every time it occurs in the service. . . . The Chapel is, on Sunday, very full, and has preaching in it nearly every day.' This puzzling popularity he solved by reflecting that 'many attended for entertainment.'[136] Some however, were not entertained and complained that the worship was too long and fatiguing. In November, Darwin Fox took up these concerns with Sibthorp, whose somewhat petulant reply hints at the pressure he was under:

'I hope I wish to act reasonably and to listen to reason: but I certainly require solid reasons and such as command themselves to whatever measure of plain sense I have. I have more than once thought over the subject you refer to, because the objection you speak of has on various grounds been made to me by more than one. I am obliged to say I can see not one good reason against such musical services as I have in my church – especially when the objection is placed to the account of *their length*.

1st What is there in my Church more than there is of the same kind at every Cathedral and College Chapel where there is a choir. *Nothing whatever.*

2. Why then is that so extremely and overpoweringly fatiguing at St. James's, Ryde which is not complained of as such elsewhere. *Give me a reason why.* But,

3. To come to particulars: because bodily fatigue is an effect of particulars . . . *Is it the anthem?* This you have at every Cathedral. . . . *Is it the Nunc Dimittis and Magnificat?* Have you any idea how long these take singing . . . Is it credible, rational to believe that a person cannot stand for 4 or 5 minutes at a time? But *is it the chanting of the Psalms?* I suspect it is. If so people should say so . . .

I want plain and solid reasons. I can find none.

If any one should say: "Oh, but your boys are not like the choir at Winchester, Oxford etc. If they were we should stand very well all the time as we do at these." I beg to reply 1st I don't believe if my boys were better than the Winchester or any other choir in England you would cease your objection. But 2nd . . . I do not hesitate to say, that my choir . . . is better than that of some cathedrals.

If I could see a solid reason for doing away with the musical services, I would not retain them. I do not think that the disposition of a certain, even a considerable number of persons in the congregation, is a reason of itself. It is a *reason* for a reason having weight – but no reason in itself for what is without other reason – on the contrary. I think the Church has suffered greatly from allowing the inclinations of a congregation to have influence.'[137]

Some yet believed that the erring brother could be won back to his former ways, Thomas Dykes, for instance, who visited him in 1840[138] and Francis Close of Cheltenham, who tried to persuade him to accept the incumbency of the new church of St Paul in the town.[139] Sibthorp must have accepted estrangement from former colleagues as inevitable, but even his new friends were uncertain. In October 1840, Newman wrote 'As to Mr Sibthorpe . . . I do not know him well. I doubt if Dr Pusey knows him at all. He has got his views for himself, and is no special friend of ours, much as I respect him. I do not know his Chapel at Ryde; if it is, and its worship what your friend describes, I am much concerned – but I suspect her account is exaggerated.'[140]

After many years of adulation and unused to being questioned, Richard found it difficult to cope with opposition; timid by nature, he undoubtedly felt isolated and anxious. Nevertheless, called to holiness, his pastoral zeal was unabated and his workload unrelenting, with services each day, most of which included a sermon. On Sundays, he left his home at 7 a.m. and did not return until 9 or 10 p.m. At 8 a.m., he had early Communion, then the normal Morning Service. In the afternoon there was a Children's Service, and at 6.30 full Evensong.[141] There was also the management of the Holmewood establishment, which included not only a large domestic staff, but also the resident choristers and often one or two visitors. Bloxam who was there in August 1841 described the daily routine:

> 'I am enjoying myself here exceedingly, our party consists of Mr. Sibthorp, his nephew, four choristers and their leader (a former chorister of Salisbury who plays and sings sacred music admirably). A bell is rung at an early hour and the boys assemble for prayers and religious instruction till 8 o'clock, when we all breakfast together. Then we walk down to Ryde about 2 miles off, where Mr. Sibthorp has purchased rooms, lately used for a Mechanics' Institute, now turned into a choral school, where Mr. Sibthorp catechises the remaining portion of his scholars, and tries over with them various services of the week till the hour of public daily worship, when we adjourn to St. James's Church where full cathedral service is performed. After which we return to Holmewood, and the remainder of the day is consumed in meals, school, recreation and prayers. Mr Sibthorp's quire consists of 16 to 20 choristers. We are today expecting 2 more to make up the number of 6 choristers (all sons of poor clergymen) whom he maintains and educates in his own house.'[142]

An Ideal Church

When Richard first told his congregation that membership of the visible and universal church was an essential aspect of biblical Christianity, someone remarked 'these views . . . must lead you to Rome.' His reply showed his sense of the apocalyptic to be undiminished: 'You are much mistaken. I believe from prophecy that Romanism is to make head again, and that this (the Puseyite) party is raised up to put it down.'[143] This exchange was probably in 1835, when he still describing Rome as 'Satan's Masterpiece.'[144] The study of typology however, made unequivocal condemnation much harder to justify. His reassessment of Catholicism must have been painful, but perhaps the more liberal views of island friends eased the process. Heywood Hawkins, who had visited France in 1830, had formed a largely favourable opinion of Catholic worship. Writing to Richard's brother, Humphrey, he described High Mass at Rouen Cathedral: 'general effect impressive, music monstrous but solemn, incense very agreeable; . . . the black and white costumes of the numerous ecclesiastics in the stalls very becoming. Congregations immense the whole morning, for there is a service every hour till 1 o'clock; women to men in the proportion 10 or 12 to 1, universal attention and much apparent devotion.'[145]

There are indications that as early as 1836 Sibthorp was modifying his views on Catholicism.[146] His resignation, in October of that year, of the secretaryship of the Religious Tract Society can be seen as a formal disavowal of crusading anti-Romanism.[147] Nevertheless, it seems unlikely that his new understanding of the bible would have led so rapidly to his conversion, without the contribution of the Catholic priest at West Cowes. Fired with zeal for the conversion of Protestants, Father Joseph Rathborne regularly regaled the citizenry of Hampshire and the Isle of Wight with polemical literature.[148]   He wrote to Sibthorp, disputing something he was reported to have said on the doctrine of purgatory. A correspondence ensued. When the priest denied Canterbury's claim to be a true part of the universal church and thus the validity of Anglican sacraments, Richard found himself at some stretch. So much so that in November 1840, he took the unusual step of appealing to Newman: 'What authority had Barlow or his co-consecrators for the consecration of Parker? I confessed I had never looked very closely into the matter and that I now feel myself at a loss to reply. – It was not done by the call or consent of the Catholic Church generally.' This was not an issue that particularly concerned Newman, but his reply must have been satisfactory for even as a Catholic, Sibthorp never denied the validity of Anglican orders.[149]

Rathborne's other, and ultimately more effective, strategy was to emphasise the evil consequences of the Church's shattered unity. Sibthorp confided in Newman his longing 'that an union might take place if possible between the Churches of Rome and England – or at least an attempt made to bring it about.' The priest had urged him, 'Depend upon it the Ch. of England will be a prey to dissent, unless it joins that Church which forms an impregnable barrier to the entrance of doctrinal division; that only looks to one object, *the presentation of ancient truth*.' He proposed that a team of scholars from both sides should examine the issues involved. '*Let all be done in charity. Let it be a contention for Truth only*: and let us see where *we can meet, not how much we differ*. Let our arguments be fairly and *kindly drawn* from Scripture, the Fathers, Ecclesiastical History; and Prescription.'[150] For Richard, distracted by controversy, unity was more than a typological imperative; it spoke of the Sabbath rest for which he longed. In March 1841, he wrote to Henry Wilberforce, 'Have you read Bowden's "Pontificate of Gregory 7?" It is one of the most deeply interesting books I have read for some time, and his views respecting the papal office, and its utility in past times, very striking. What a fearful rent did the Reformation make! and which exasperated feelings on both sides have kept open!'[151]

The following month Richard delivered before his University a sermon on *the Claims of the Catholic Church.* Asserting that the Church was the only 'divinely appointed sphere' in which to seek God's glory, he rejected any attempt to 'spiritualize Christ . . . to disembody Him, by making the union of His people . . . to subsist without the intervention of that Church, *which is His Body . . .* ' Separate from her the Christian life remained unfulfilled. 'As truly does the Catholic Church hold Christ within her, as the bark that bore Him on the sea of Galilee.' Yet, 'Never had the author of evil, a greater success against man since the Fall, than when he prevailed to break in pieces, as it is now broken, the Church's unity.' And so he mourned: 'Everywhere we see the effect . . . Our own charities show it, requiring a constant recurrence to every mode of popular excitement to supply their pecuniary resources. Our own poor feel it, indebted in age and destitution to legislative enactment for compulsory maintenance. The face of our country proclaims it, where boundless enthusiasm and untiring energy are shewn in everything more than (with some recent and admirable exceptions) the provision for the service of the Sanctuary of God.'

He pleaded with his hearers to 'seek after and ensue this unity.' But, 'Whether the time be yet come for a dispassionate consideration of the causes that have affected in past periods the Church's unity . . . is yet to be seen.' The obstacles to reunion were profound, but the prize was worth any hazard. 'There has not often been a period when men more needed, . . . a refuge from the tempest of the world's commotions, and from the devices of the world's master; a shelter from the assaults of infidelity on the one hand, and schismatical enthusiasm on the other.'[152]

Gladstone, who read it the following year, 'on the whole . . . thought it a beautiful and noble sermon.'[153] In June, on the Feast of St. John the Baptist, Oxford crowded into Magdalen Chapel to hear him preach again on *The Commemoration of Founders and Benefactors.* Looking back over the centuries, he spoke of illustrious names associated with the University; each was like the Baptist, *a voice in the wilderness,* 'how quick they pass away!' 'Theirs was the heaven-born love, which, first kindled in the waters of baptism (what cannot grace effect!) fed by the truth of the Holy Gospel, and by the body and blood of the Lord, and cherished by the element of the Church's Unity, burnt with steadiness and brilliancy . . . ' After eulogising three pre-Reformation benefactors, he turned to Sir Thomas White, the Roman Catholic founder of St John's College, who was 'loyal to his then much insulted, and to this day much calumniated, Sovereign, the first Mary . . . How did the voice of this upright, charitable, devout, consistent Christian life, *cry out in the wilderness!*' But what of the present? 'what would be the effect, if all the existing Collegiate establishments of

Christendom spoke one voice as to the doctrines, the discipline, and the government of the Church. . . What a testimony against the world, and infidelity, and heresy, and schism, and sin, and the Devil . . . One could weep to know the supposition so far from reality; and why? chiefly because want of unity in the Church renders so powerless this weapon of her warfare.'[154]

Reactions were predictable. When Ambrose Phillipps, a convert and leading Catholic layman, read the text he was entranced, 'it makes one burn with an indescribable desire to see the various Churches of Christ come once more at one together.'[155] Dr. Macray, who took over from Bloxam as Magdalen's chronicler, was in the congregation as a boy, and thought the sermon 'the finest I had ever heard.'[156] But the authentic voice of Protestant England sounded in a letter printed in the *Record*. 'Mr. Sibthorp emphatically introduced as the *calumniated* first Mary that Sovereign whose reign was deeply stained with the blood of the Reformers, and whom therefore all consistent Protestants have been accustomed to think and speak of as a bitter opposer and persecutor of the true Catholic and Apostolic Church of Christ . . . On leaving Magdalen Chapel many of us might well exclaim: "We have heard strange things today."'[157]

Both sermons caught a mood, a romantic yearning for an idealised past, an anxiety about change, so pervasive and so rapid. It was a climate of opinion that Nicholas Wiseman, recently appointed president of Oscott College and co-adjutor to Bishop Walsh of the Central District, sought to turn to Catholicism's advantage. In a pamphlet on *Catholic Unity*, published in September, he deplored the divisions rending modern society, which 'the modern phrenzies of Chartism and Socialism are doing their utmost to arouse into hatred and enmity.' He wrote of 'the miserable feeling of solitariness and separation' arising from 'the loss of ordinances, sacraments and liturgical rites; the extinction of monastic and ascetic feeling and observances; the decay of "awe, mystery, tenderness, reverence, devotedness and other feelings which may be especially called Catholic . . . "' The answer was clear, 'there is nothing . . . which can so securely penetrate to the principles of disunion, and heal them, and reunite the separated parts, as *religious unity*.' For the author this great goal, achievable only by a return to the ancient Faith, was no idle dream: was not 'the leaven' of Catholic feelings fermenting in many parishes?'[158] The pamphlet was an implicit challenge: unity with its attendant blessings was surely worth any sacrifice, and the first Anglicans prepared to pay the cost of 'going over' might become the essential catalyst. The preacher and the bishop shared one vision, and within just a few months the former, having responded to the latter's call, would be pleading with Anglicans to join him in repairing the ark against 'the desolating flood' of infidelity.'[159]

Wiseman also sought influence through Ambrose Phillipps, who dreamt of a reunited English Church and was in correspondence with the

Tractarians on how this might be achieved. In March 1841, he wrote to Bloxam, 'Our gaining Bishop Wiseman is an immense point. He is decidedly one of the first men in Europe. He "will do all in his power to promote the *reunion,* for which he will gladly give his life."'[160] Rathborne, like most of his co-religionists, dismissed any reunion short of re-submission. To hold out any other prospect was to encourage Anglicans in their schism. In April, he had published a pamphlet branding Wiseman and Phillipps as the dupes of 'Mr. Newman and Dr. Pusey and their associates.' These latter were 'wily and crafty, though unskilful guides' who were employing 'ingenious' means 'to prevent our numbers being increased by the accession of many great and good men.'[161] He then described how he was pressing Roman claims on 'a very enlightened and eminent clergyman of the Church of England, a high Churchman, but a man of higher honour.'[162] Frederick Lucas, editor of the recently established *Tablet*, shared Rathborne's hostility towards the Tractarians and their conciliators, and licensed the priest to air his views in its columns. Both had misjudged Wiseman who believed it his duty to win converts by any means.

Fishing with a Rod

Ambrose Phillipps, who regularly entertained Anglicans at his Leicestershire home, *Grace Dieu*, was especially anxious to meet Richard Sibthorp. On 15 September he wrote to tell Bloxam that he had 'a copy of the *Paradisus Animae,* which I will venture to present him on his arrival.' He was evidently still smarting from something that Rathborne had written in the *Tablet*: a 'contemptible attack upon Spencer, Bishop Wiseman and myself . . . it is gravely given out in certain quarters that *all three of us* are going to turn *Protestant*.'[163] Bloxam replied that his friend had had 'a long interview' with the author. 'He will give you an account of it when you see him – an opportunity of paying you a visit he is most anxious to avail himself of.'[164] The following month, Phillipps wrote again, 'Pray, when may we expect Mr. Sibthorp? I am longing to know. Bishop Wiseman told me that on the 28th of this month there would be the ordination of a priest at Oscott, would Mr. Sibthorp like to see it? If so, he could come here first – we would go together.'[165] Bloxam replied, 'You may expect Mr. Sibthorp soon, but he could not fix the time. He will probably call upon you suddenly.'[166]

Richard had his own reason for wishing to visit Oscott. He wanted to talk to Wiseman about Isabella Young, a member of the St. James's congregation, who was contemplating conversion.[167] E. B. Pusey, at her family's request, was attempting to settle her, although according to Lord Shrewsbury, with whom she corresponded, Sibthorp knew her 'almost as well.'[168] Pusey's efforts were apparently rewarded, for on 18 October

Newman wrote to him 'Thank you much for your cheering account. I hope there is no chance of her acting under excitement – else there will be a re-action.' He said that Sibthorp was in Oxford, 'and means to call on you and ask you some questions about her.'[169] That same evening Newman dined at Magdalen; an occasion he was to remember. 'I never was intimate with Mr. Sibthorp and never sympathized with him, though I always respected him, and admired him, in contrast to others, as a thorough gentleman . . . I did all I could without rudeness to show my dislike of his going to Oscott.' Richard was not to be persuaded, and when, at the end of the meal, he confirmed his intended destination, Newman said that 'there was a general laugh, as if it meant; "to Rome"; on which he exclaimed "O I have no such intention, you need not be afraid" or some such words.'[170] The following day or perhaps the day after, Richard set out on his mission.[171]

Few believed he was in any immediate danger. Certainly not Bloxam who on 21 October wrote to Phillipps speculating that just 'one or two individuals (Wackerbarth for instance)' were on the brink of conversion. Otherwise, he was optimistic: 'though I expect to see great blunders perpetrated shortly, yet the tide of Catholicism is flowing on in a manner that may possibly very soon efface the marks of precipitate error.'[172] His mood changed markedly when just over a week later Sibthorp returned to Oxford, 'looking worn and agitated, and no longer a member of the Church of England.'[173] Samuel Wilberforce, who wrote to his brother about 'poor Sibthorp's fall' said that it 'seems to have been hasty and, in all its circumstances, strange. He left his chapel unserved; for the fact of his having turned Papist had to be told to the assembling congregation by some boys who were standing round the closed doors. The consternation is complete.'[174] Newman, however, confided in Henry Wilberforce that he was not surprised: 'Before he went to Oscott he had no intention of conforming to Rome when there, I dined with him the day before.[175] But he was overcome. At the same time it was quite plain, it was but a matter of *time* with him.'[176] An anonymous observer of the Ryde scene drew his own conclusion: 'The event itself needs little comment. The cockatrice egg of Puseyism has been hatched, and out of it has come the fiery flying serpent of Popery.'[177]

Sibthorp has left no record of what happened at Oscott, perhaps because he did not fully understand it himself. Once there, it was as though he was caught up in a sense of inevitability: the unfinished business of his childhood could now be completed. He knew reunion was a pipe dream, and unable to deny that the Church of Rome was the true antitype, succumbed to the conviction that unity was a pearl worth all his riches. In seeking to explain the sudden, or as Newman later put it 'the "methodistical" character'[178]of the conversion, Richard's unhappiness at Ryde was probably critical. Official disapproval rankled, but more wounding was the desertion of old St. James's friends.[179] Three years before Wigram had lectured at Newport on behalf of the Plymouth Brethren and the cause continued to attract disgruntled Evangelicals.[180] The Brethren attack was intensified when, in 1841, an anonymous pamphleteer castigated those who remained at St. James's with 'fawning upon and flattering' their pastor. 'The doctrines professedly listened to with joy and gratitude in the year 1834 must have been either in themselves of little value, or have been imperfectly received, if they can be swerved from or denied in 1841!'[181] To Sibthorp, the new sect was a mockery of the unity that he now identified with the Age of Faith, an era that Pugin in his splendid Oscott chapel had deliberately sought to evoke. St. James's, despite all the changes remained what it was: a converted proprietary chapel, whose minister had 'sought in vain to satisfy the longings of my soul, by any combination of Catholic forms with Protestant doctrines – of Catholic devotions in private with the Anglican public worship.'[182] At Oscott, an alternative path seemed possible.

The conversion of Richard Sibthorp was a triumph for Wiseman, who wrote, 'it was not to educate a few boys that (Oscott) was erected, but to be the rallying point of the yet silent but vast movement towards the Catholic Church.'[183] And Richard was not the first; others had similarly visited the college and been overwhelmed. One Sunday, two years before, A. B. Granville, accompanied by 'an honest citizen of Birmingham,' attended Mass there, and wrote of what he saw:

'scores of priests, deacons, subdeacons and acolytes, the former in their splendid vestments of gold, the latter in scarlet tunics, surmounted by a short white surplice, were seated in pompous hierarchy, on dignified stools which rose gradually from the floor to the wall on each side of the inner or sacred space in front of the great altar – itself gorgeously decked and brilliantly lighted by massive candelabra, bearing lofty tapers around the tabernacle.'

He said of his companion, that when 'he beheld the high priest, followed by his two deacons and the acolytes, moving towards the altar; and there, after bowing before it, and going through many secret prayers and open ceremonies, he saw him incense the symbols of the Eucharist and the altar itself, to be himself, in his turn, incensed by one of the deacons – when the volumes of curling smoke from the censer rose and expanded through the church with a fragrance to reach where we were stood – when the full swell of the majestic organ, accompanying the human voice, was heard immediately above us, its cadences directing the melodious harmonies of the anthems, the ejaculations of the chaunting priests, and the responses of the congregation, – O then the protestant burgher of Birmingham stood enthralled, and marvelled at everything around him!' He determined to return, and wondered, 'that all the people of Birmingham do not flock to this place of worship.'[184]

Yet, according to Bloxam, his friend submitted on Saturday 23 October[185] 'after two days fishing with a rod, Sibthorpe was hooked at

Oscott, as unexpectedly by himself, as he told me, as a fish pulled out of the water.'[186] Attending High Mass must have been deeply moving, but only sealed a decision already made, thus giving the lie to Robert Wilberforce's acid comment. 'I suppose at Oscott Sibthorpe saw a show of Catholicity, just in the particulars which among us have been so sadly neglected, and was taken with a bauble, tho' the reality of Primitive truth and order were alike wanting.'[187] Did the discussion that made Sibthorp a Catholic focus on the Levitical types? If it did, then Wiseman was fore-armed. In his celebrated 1836 lectures, he had stressed the 'strong arguments of analogy which the old law gives us, for constructing the Church to be by Christ established.' Could any visitor to ancient Jerusalem mistake the Temple? 'the moment the stately . . . edifice, caught his eye, towering over every other pygmy building, exact in proportion, and unity of design, resting with untottering foundations upon the very spot where its inspired builder laid its first stone; above all, when he entered the vast court, and beheld the great High Priest still wearing on his forehead the golden plate which declared him "Holy to the Lord," in uninterrupted succession to the first Pontiff of his religion, and saw the Levites sacrificing on the same altar, and performing the same liturgy as were consecrated on the first solemn establishment of God's worship – surely upon seeing all this he would . . . pronounce himself assured that he had found the true house of God.'[188]

Schooled by Rathborne, Richard arrived at Oscott assured that the Council of Trent discountenanced superstitious devotional practices. This was important for someone so profoundly sensitive to what seemed alien to Scripture. The year before, when it was proposed that Magdalen should formally sponsor William Palmer in a mission to the Russian Church, he had protested strongly 'against this Society giving any encouragement to the idea of intercommunion with the *idolatrous* Greek Church.'[189] What therefore of the Papal Antichrist, the fear that had coloured so much of his life? In the excitement of those two days, was the matter even raised? If it was, his fears were allayed. Perhaps by arguments he would himself have used in other cases: many Scriptures are hard to explain, but in trusting where one cannot see, more light will be given. The issue, however, was not resolved. In the emotional crisis that led to the fateful step, it was put to one side.

As regards prophecy, Richard could accept that he might have misunderstood the bible, drawn wrong conclusions. As to the test of holiness, there could be no compromise. The sanctity consequent upon personal faith was ever at the heart of his religion and he had a nose for unreality. Thus, something that Peter Renouf noticed when, a few months later, he arrived at Oscott as a young convert, may help to explain why Richard was sure he had come to an end of his seeking. Renouf wrote to his parents: 'if you attended the daily evening service . . . you would fancy yourself not among Roman Catholics, or even among High Church

Protestants, but among Evangelicals.'[190] As Richard talked with Wiseman and with George Spencer, he sensed a piety that echoed his own soul, enough to still any lingering doubt.[191]

The decision made, he prepared for his reception. The *Records of St. Mary's College, Oscott* note for 27 October, 'The Revd. R. Sibthorpe a clergyman of the Church of England having made his Profession of Faith, received conditional baptism from the Rt. Revd. Dr. Wiseman in the College Chapel.' The following day a statement was issued: 'a reverend brother of Col. Sibthorp came here a few days ago to examine further into the tenets and practices of Catholics. After being satisfied by Dr. Wiseman, and the Hon. and Rev. Mr. Spencer, as to some of our difficult doctrines, he yesterday read his profession of faith in our Chapel, and had the happiness of receiving from the Bishop this morning the blessed Eucharist.'[192]

Responding to the news, Samuel Wilberforce was brutal. 'Poor Sibthorp! His head was, as you know, never a sound one. He had got entangled in a correspondence with a priest, a clever fellow, at Cowes, on some scheme of uniting Rome and England. He had exposed himself to temptation by long-formed habits of *grievous* self-will in religious matters, breaking out in his Low-Church excesses of old, and in mummeries of late, which he knew, grieved all his brethren.'[193] The Hull clergy detected strong temptation: 'you sank into the arms of the enchantress, with scarcely an effort at resistance, when none of your most intimate friends suspected it, and when, if report speaks truly, you had undertaken to enter on a contest against her claims.'[194]

5

HARLEQUINADE AND
PALINODIA

Having stayed at Oscott to be at Fr. Signini's ordination[1], on Saturday 30 October Sibthorp was in Oxford. He called on Newman, 'with a view' the latter recalled, 'to my conversion . . . like a fox that had just lost its tail and now wished all the other foxes to suffer a like loss.'[2] His presence was an embarrassment and he left for London the same day. Pugin, who on Sunday called at his hotel and accompanied him to High Mass at St. John's Wood, was delighted and surprised. He confided in Bloxam that, 'when I saw him at Ryde, he did not certainly appear to me to be as far advanced in Catholic principles as many others . . . it is altogether a great temporal trial for him but then so much greater gain, it is most consoling – and will do much in the way of stopping the senseless clamour raised by Rathbone (*sic*) and his party.'[3]

By Monday, Richard was back in Ryde[4] facing the painful task of winding-up his affairs and disposing of his property. Augustus Hewitt, who had just resigned his Newport curacy,[5] agreed to purchase the chapel in which he had once ministered. The *Times*'s amusement that the convert should sell it to a 'clergyman with views opposite to his own'[6] resulted in a letter from Hughes Hughes explaining that because of 'the affectionate and devoted attachment to the very last, of his numerous hearers' Mr. Sibthorp, 'instead of adding to their grief and loss through his secession, by the sale of the Church to the Papists (a body of whom, it is understood are greatly disappointed in not being able to purchase it) . . . and notwithstanding he had laid out probably upwards of £2000 on the enlargement and interior decoration of the Church, . . . offered it to my brother at the precise sum he had purchased it from me.'[7] The town's Catholics needed a church and must have been puzzled. They might also have noted that no one from St. James's followed their ex-minister. Indeed, under Hewitt, the chapel rapidly reverted to type and new trust deeds were drawn up to prevent any future departure from the doctrines of the Reformation. In January, the townspeople, 'urged on by their Protestant pastors . . . all but universally' signed a petition to the Archbishop of Canterbury, protesting against 'the dangerous errors proposed by certain members of the University of Oxford in the *Tracts for the Times*.' The petition set out a list of repugnant features, at its head: the 'arrogation of power by the clergy.' Action was demanded to counter the 'destructive doctrines (which had) already made such alarming progress among our clergy.' Archbishop Howley's reply was non-committal.[8]

Why Are You Become a Catholic?

Richard stayed at Ryde less than a week.[9] Back at Oscott, he wrote to Routh resigning his fellowship; a sacrifice, he said, 'of present ease, esteem and property and perhaps of future prospects' that he had willingly made for the Church: to 'promote her peace and unity, and recovery from her present distracted state.'[10] The ageing President, on reading it, 'burst into tears.'[11] Within a few days, the conversion was in all the newspapers, and faced with many letters of enquiry, Sibthorp decided to write a pamphlet. Completed during his final few days at Holmewood, over Christmas, *An Answer to the Enquiry; 'Why are you Become a Catholic?'* confirms that the deep spring of his conversion was a never-extinguished admiration for Catholic sanctity, and a feeling that only Rome could satisfy the devotional longings of his heart. As Luther had rejected the mechanical exchanges of mediaeval Catholicism, Sibthorp's soul found little nourishment in *sola gratia* and the simplicity of Protestant worship. He explained how, as a youth, he had observed among Roman Catholics 'an attention to religious duties associated with devotedness and earnest piety.' And now, in middle age, he craved to belong to the only Church that could satisfy his 'high, holy and heavenly desires and aims.'

He wrote of finding in his bible a united visible church so clearly foreshadowed that he was compelled to join himself to the 'true Israel of God': 'the Catholic Church in communion with the See of Rome . . . the close and perfect antitype of the Church under the Old Testament.' In ecclesiastical history could be seen the early outworking of the Jewish shadows. Proper study of it 'annihilates altogether the supposition that in the primitive church existed various differing denominations, some having sacraments, some none; some governed by bishops, some rejecting episcopacy; some having a form of worship, some abhorring it; some baptizing infants, some refusing to baptize them. There is not a shadow of ground for such an idea . . .' Moreover, typology validated Catholic ceremonial: in the sacrifices of the Temple could be discerned the Sacrifice of the Mass; the seven-branched candelabra foreshadowed the grace present in the seven sacraments. Doctrines hard to find on the surface of Holy Writ could be found, albeit veiled, in the Book of Leviticus. So, for example, to the eye of faith the succession of Jewish High Priests pointed to the papacy. But Sibthorp did not eschew more conventional arguments: did not a visible church require a strong central government? 'The development of this most wise and essential institution for the Church's well being, was in the nature of the case gradual. The strength, properties and usefulness of a plant, can only be developed as time permits its growth, and natural influences elicit its generic or specific characters.' He wrote that 'reluctantly and slowly' he had been forced to conclude that Rome had 'both Scripture and reason decisively on her side.' Tenets that he had once viewed as 'dangerous and opposite to the truth of the Gospel,' he now saw as 'parts of a beauteous and complete system of truth . . . the revelation and provision of infinite wisdom and love for the happiness and holiness of his creatures.' Yet withal, he could not deny the piety of many Protestants, Anglican, Wesleyan, and others, and their salvation was sure. 'Some . . . may belong to the soul of the Church, who are not of its body.'

Having dealt with Scriptural objections to Roman doctrines, he turned to the Anglo-Catholic assertion that 'the present Anglican Church is identically one and the same with that which St. Augustine planted in the sixth century.' This he could not accept; Archbishop Howley would certainly disagree with his predecessor on doctrines such as the Mass and purgatory, to say nothing of submission to the See of Rome. 'Can it be pretended that there is scriptural, visible unity, or any unity at all, in this?' As for Tract XC, its claim 'that the doctrines of the Catholic Church . . . are not really denied by the Anglican Establishment, but in principle, or tacitly, she admits them all' was 'one of the surprising discoveries of this age of discovery.' But it would not do. 'Suppose . . . that the Thirty-nine Articles are directed against certain abuses of the Catholic doctrines, not against the doctrines themselves; still it may well, I think, be asked of them: "Is this the way Catholic revealed truth . . . is to be held and set forth before the world, by his Church?"' Captivated now by the worship and pastoral discipline of Rome the Tractarian compromise was 'milk and water.'

Few who read the pamphlet could deny the author's eloquence or his sincerity. Sibthorp yearned to be holy. In the 'Catholic Church alone, in her glowing daily devotions, her hourly offices, her symbolic rites, her inestimable practice of confession, with its attendant sacramental privileges, her soul-engrossing intercourse with the spirits of the just made perfect' could the purpose of this earthly pilgrimage be fulfilled. In concluding – and here surely the influence of Wiseman may be detected – he appealed to Anglicans to join in repairing the ancient walls against the coming great battle with infidelity. 'Your return to me will be like health to the feeble and strength to the faint; like an infusion of young blood into an aged frame. You will be welcomed with gladness, and rejoiced over with singing . . . '[12]

Those he left behind were alarmed at the possible harm that might be done by such an eloquent appeal from 'a clergyman of exemplary piety and devotedness.'[13] Thirteen pamphlets were published in response to his:

from Evangelicals, pleading with him to return to his former paths, and from High Churchmen stung by the allegation that their beliefs had been taken to a logical conclusion. Others who had lately seceded from the Establishment were moved to vindicate their own radical views regarding religious unity. Although some wrote to gain recognition or further a career, overall the pamphlets throw an interesting light on the individuals and groups jostling for attention at the end of a decade of religious ferment. One or two contain little of interest. The Irish Methodist, Daniel M'Afee's address to the *Protestant Operatives of Belfast* on the *Apostasy of the Rev. R. W. Sibthorp* is a parade of routine anti-Catholic invective. R. P. Blakeney's production is perhaps more noteworthy,[14] not least because it marked the beginning of a long career of anti-Catholic controversy.[15] The author claimed that in Ireland Sibthorp's pamphlet was being distributed *gratis* as Catholic propaganda.[16] But extravagant abuse did not commend his cause. Sibthorp, he was sure, anticipated a lucrative bishopric, 'which, on account of the dulness (*sic*) and mediocrity of powers, he could never reasonably have expected in the Anglican church.' The types were 'ridiculous and foolish phantasms, fit only for the weak mind of Mr. Sibthorp, who could believe (professedly at least) in a *wafer god*.'[17]

The Old Testament basis of Sibthorp's argument drew the attention of a converted Jew who had become a minor celebrity in London religious circles. Ridley Haim Herschell was born in Poland, but as a young man living in Paris was drawn to Christianity, and on moving to London took a leading role in the Society for the Propagation of the Gospel among the Jews. It was because his 'Jewish instincts revolted against Catholic ritual' that he was led to write, *Reasons Why I, A Jew Have Become a Catholic and not a Roman Catholic*. G. E. Biber was out to impress and his *Catholicity v. Sibthorp*, issued as five long letters between January and March 1842, was soon followed by a second edition.[18] German by birth, he came to England in 1828, and having 'no settled convictions' decided to join the Church of England. Following ordination, he sought to build a reputation as an Anglican apologist.[19] In March 1842, Newman wrote to his brother-in-law, the editor of the *British Critic*: 'Don't flatter Dr Biber by speaking of him *graviter* – He is bent on writing himself into notice.'[20] The rather patronising and unoriginal *Remarks* of a *Clergyman of the Archdiocese of Canterbury* deserve little attention.[21] Indeed, Richard would not have been much troubled by any of the foregoing, but the bulky *Serious Remonstrance* from the Evangelical clergy of Hull, was a different matter. The signatories were Thomas Dykes, John King, William Knight, and John Scott. The last named was vicar of St Mary's Lowgate, having followed his father, under whom Richard had served as curate in 1817. Dykes was an even stronger link with the past. Although the arguments of these good men may not have disturbed him intellectually, he could not have read their heart-felt pleas without emotion.

Because Sibthorp had abandoned forever the Protestant understanding of justification and the Church, he would not have given great attention to the dissenting contribution to the debate, not even to the letter from Benjamin Wills Newton, now a leader among the Plymouth Brethren.[22] Seeking to restore 'primitive piety' and first-century unity, Newton pleaded with Christians to forsake the denominations – the wreckage of a failed dispensation – and assemble for worship in simple dependence upon the Spirit, waiting quietly for the imminent return of Christ. Another pamphlet from *Spectator* took much the same ground;[23] it was probably from the same anonymous pen as *Thoughts Suggested by the Present State of Religion in Ryde*, published a few months earlier. Both writers mourned over the divided state of Christendom. Newton wrote that he united with Sibthorp 'in believing that God intended His Church, i.e. "all who are sanctified by faith in Jesus Christ," to be VISIBLY one.' But the pretensions of Rome he rejected absolutely. She might not be *the* Antichrist, yet not only had her candlestick been removed, but 'her unchecked ambition has forced her into a position where she cannot pretend even to an outward likeness to the original order of the Church.' He believed the types would only become a reality during the millennial reign, and saw evil in Rome's adoption of antitypical garb. 'Satan well knows that these things are in Scripture, and therefore when raising up a candlestick of his own into the place of the candlestick of God, he wisely sets it in a position that *seems* to command the testimony of all the millennial Scriptures on its behalf.'[24]

Spectator avoided prophetical speculation, but in condemning all existing church structures was clear as to the mechanism of declension. 'It is unquestionable, that in the early era of the church, soon after the death of the apostles, "grievous wolves did come into the church not sparing the flock," and that it was their work of ravine chiefly to revive the wish for a Levitical religion, and to set up again an official priesthood equivalent to the old. This is in fact Judaism revived: from this heresy all darkness emanated, and in it all ecclesiastical darkness consists . . . '[25] Newton, agreed that 'the Churches of the second century . . . will have no more authority over our consciences than the practices of Israel in the days of Jeroboam!' But in turning to remedies, the Old Testament did provide guidance, 'We are not the first who have been placed amidst the ruins of a fallen dispensation: Nehemiah went out by night, to view the walls of Jerusalem . . . he laboured with the few around him, – he separated the Israelite from the stranger, – and sought to gather Israel together into the appointed place.' What was fallen was not restored, 'yet we know that his work was not unaccepted, . . . Can we see no analogy to the circumstances of the present hour?'[26]

Newton had seceded some ten years before, a few months after Bulteel, who had left Anglicanism in the belief that the re-appearance of spiritual gifts presaged the Second Advent. Edward Irving, the fountain-head of this teaching, had died in 1834. By this date leadership of the congregations that his preaching had inspired – soon to coalesce into the Catholic Apostolic Church – had already passed to others: men who taught that apostles had been restored to the Church, charged with proclaiming submission to authority and quiet preparation for the *Parousia*. One was the wealthy High Tory, Henry Drummond; an apostle himself, he wrote to chide Sibthorp that his extraordinary step was irrelevant sectarianism. 'To be really Catholic, it is necessary to recognise the unity of the Church: to remember that it is by baptism men become united to it, partakers of its privileges, and liable to its penalties.' Regarding Rome, he was ambivalent, although conceding that she 'contains every Christian verity of doctrine, if not practice,' he found much to condemn, especially the pretension of a foreigner who would interpose between a 'sovereign and her subjects'. Anglicanism was much to be preferred. All this, however, was beside the point; 'Catholicism is a higher region than sectarianism.' 'It is this whole Christendom which constitutes the Israel of God; it is this whole Christendom that has become one great Babylon; it is this whole Christendom that has fallen from its original standing . . . No one can essentially mend his condition by flying from one sect to another . . . What God is about to do now, none can tell; for few can see what He is actually working before their eyes; but there seems to be but one opinion, which is that the end has come to all things as they now subsist; and the fretful hurrying from sect to sect, will rather turn the mind from quiet consideration of and waiting for the events whatever they may be...'[27]

Who is a Catholic?

The seceders expected that a millennial Church would soon supersede a failed dispensation. Sibthorp, who also foresaw a crisis, was nevertheless confident: 'The ark of God is repairing, against the pouring forth of the desolating flood . . . She is calling upon all who are on the Lord's side, to secure themselves against the coming conflict, by taking refuge within her walls . . . '[28] But where were these walls? For two pamphleteers – the Irish High Churchman, William Palmer, and the London Tractarian, William Dodsworth – the position was clear. As members of the Church of England, they were already securely within the Catholic Church; any Anglican submitting to Rome was guilty of schism. In response to their arguments Sibthorp felt the need to publish a *Second Letter*, to which both replied, at which point the 'pamphlet war' concluded.

Palmer was a graduate of Trinity College, Dublin, and fellow of Worcester College, who in 1838 published a *Treatise on the Church of Christ*: the *locus classicus* of the 'branch theory' of Anglicanism. Perrone described him as '*theologorum Oxoniensium facile princeps.*'[29] Newman concurred, 'He was the only really learned man among us. He understood theology as a science. . .'[30] One of the originators of the Oxford Movement, he had been left behind by a determined commitment to the Reformation. In 1841, he wrote seven rather vituperative *Letters to N. Wiseman*, arguing that against the standard of Scripture, as interpreted by universal tradition, Rome had fallen into grievous error. Dodsworth, by contrast, was in the Movement's vanguard. Once a radical Evangelical, the study of prophecy had made him a High Churchman, and as incumbent of Christ Church, St. Pancras, he was one of the capital's leading Tractarians.[31] Preaching shortly after the news from Oscott, he had acknowledged that many would be alarmed by 'the recent conversion of a clergyman of well-known and popular talents and unquestioned piety . . .'[32] In congratulating him on his *Letter to Sibthorp* published soon after, Newman identified a significant *lacuna*. 'Your pamphlet pleased me very much, and promises to be useful, though you have not been led to dwell upon Sibthorp's main argument.'[33] This was probably because Dodsworth, like most Tractarians, agreed that ancient Israel did indeed typify the Church. Preaching about this time on *The Principle of Continuity between the Jewish and Christian Churches*, Newman was sure that, 'What took place under the Law is a pattern . . .'[34] The Hull clergy had explicitly rejected this 'Now your reasoning all turns on the false supposition that a *type* is the same thing as a *pattern* . . . In the law everything is minutely prescribed. Where is the Leviticus of the New Testament?'[35] Palmer, not wishing to concede any ground to Rome, leaned in the same direction. 'It is clear then that there must be *a difference of nature* between the types of the Law and their anti-types . . . the unity of the Jewish people, if it typified anything at all, must have typified something of a different nature from its own. It could not typify *the visible unity of the Church*: it *might* have typified its mystical union in the body of Christ.' Typology, he argued, was fraught with danger, 'The Law is indeed "a shadow of good things to come;" but it does not follow that *every* circumstance and ceremony is typical. Such a supposition leads necessarily to extravagance of interpretation, and probably to serious errors.'[36]

In his *Further Answer* Sibthorp dealt with Palmer's objections, citing a number of authorities to confirm his contention that both type and anti-type may be 'earthly, material and substantial; and in every respect similar, except the greater excellency and dignity of the latter.'[37] He also tackled the frequently expressed view that the promised glory of the Church pointed to its heavenly or perhaps millennial state. Biber had written, 'Your premises are correct, yet your conclusion is fallacious; because by the "Church under the New Testament, the mystical body of Christ," you understand . . . not the Church triumphant and perfect, which is in truth the antitype of the Levitical types; but the Church militant on earth, the imperfect, transient . . . external scaffolding . . .'[38] Richard accepted the Church triumphant as the archetype, but this did not preclude the Church militant as true antitype: 'the Jewish Church bore to the Evangelical the relation of a sketch to a finished portrait, as the latter bears to the Heavenly Church that of the portrait to the living original.'[39] Palmer's second pamphlet again insisted that his adversary's interpretation of the types was personal. 'Surely the mere existence of *some sort of similitude* between certain legal and certain Christian institutions, does not infer, with any sort of probability, the *typical* relation of the former to the latter . . . were we to follow Mr. Sibthorp's example, and without any guide but our own private judgments, proceed to determine great points of doctrine and morality on such grounds, it is impossible to say what amount of heresy, error, and schism might be the result. A real Catholic will found his belief and practice, not on uncertain applications of obscure passages; . . . but on the clear and certain declamations of the Word of God, received and upheld by the unanimous voice of the Universal Church.'[40]

In referring judgement to the 'Universal Church' Palmer did not think he was begging the question because he was clear that Rome had strayed from the purity of apostolic belief and practice. Thus the Church of England was a true branch although not 'identically one and the same with the ancient Church of England in all respects. She is now reformed . . . She is now pure, . . .'[41] Dodsworth although more appreciative of Rome, also pointed to her corruptions, unjustified on typical or any other grounds. 'We agree in desiring to see the Christian world united. We, with you, wish to have communion with the see of Rome, if Rome were other than she now is.'[42] He then threw down a challenge, 'Pray, either disprove the rule of Vincentius, or else shew us that those doctrines and practices which divide us from Rome were held in the first five or six centuries.'[43] In Sibthorp's reply to his two opponents and their subsequent pamphlets, there was much inconclusive debate as to whether contemporary Anglicanism or Roman Catholicism more resembled the Church of the sixth century and its beliefs. But the issue could not be decided in this way; Palmer and Dodsworth had found in Anglicanism what had eluded Richard. 'Could I find this typified Church on earth? The truth of God assured me of its existence. But certainly no Protestant sect presented the slightest correspondency with it. My own, the Anglican, which promised fairest, totally failed to prove her claim, if indeed she made it, to be in the world what the Jewish church was in the Holy Land.'[44]

Dodsworth, anxious to safeguard the *via media*, was grieved that his opponent – whose character 'forbids the thought' that he 'could *intentionally* write with disingenuousness' – had claimed that Tract XC asserted that the Anglican Establishment 'in principle, or tacitly' admits all the doctrines of the Catholic Church. Quoting the *Letter to Jelf*, he reiterated his leader's rejection of 'the doctrine of the Roman schools.' Dodsworth was clear why Sibthorp had fallen: in moving so rapidly from embracing Church principles to the investigation of Romanism,[45] he had not stopped to take in the Tractarian vision. His 'extreme unacquaintance with the writings of our best English divines' stemmed from that 'baneful influence of the school of ultra-Protestantism in which you have been trained.' Indeed, 'It is nothing new to say that one extreme leads to another, or that the way to Rome is through Geneva.' For 'Bible Protestants' like the Hull Clergy, the search for visible as well as spiritual unity carried little resonance. Churchmen like Biber and Palmer, secure in the purity of the 'English branch,' also seemed untroubled by division. Tractarians however, shared Richard's yearnings for unity; indeed Dodsworth was willing, in principle, even to accept the primacy of the Bishop of Rome. But there were limits. 'We are willing to confess, and do confess, that a large measure of the blame of disunion lies upon us; but we dare not add sin to sin by seeking union at the expense of TRUTH.'[46]

The principal debate – over the implications of typology – was ultimately inconclusive. It was not a 'knock-down' argument; some aspects of Roman Catholic belief were not even vaguely adumbrated. Henry Drummond pointed out, rather brutally, that such Scriptural arguments, although interesting, did not really explain his opponent's motivation. 'In the panegyric which you pass upon it (Roman Catholicism) . . . the ground of your approbation is personal, selfish, and uncatholic. It is what any close-communion Baptist or Wesleyan might say for his own sect. The end contemplated by you is purely your personal salvation, your personal holiness, your personal privileges, your personal feelings, your personal interests: self first, self middle, and self end.'[47] This was unfair. Seeking salvation and holiness is not selfishness, rather the Christian vocation. Yet, he was right in sensing that Richard's conversion owed more to a dream of Catholicism, than to a dispassionate investigation of its reality. Dodsworth said that his opponent's 'modified and spiritual' form of Romanism had blinded him to its true beliefs: about purgatory, the intercession of the saints and the like. He warned his readers of a system, 'comely and beautiful when stripped of its excresances, as it is by Mr. Sibthorp's eloquent pen – but having in it a "root of bitterness."'[48] He addressed his opponent directly: 'Why, my dear sir, your language is so different from that of your Church, as almost to lead to the hope that, after all, you are only half a Romanist.'[49]

The Religious World Responds

At the end of November, Pugin wrote to Bloxam, 'Mr. Sibthorpe gives the greatest edification at Oscott and has already done great good there,'[50] a somewhat ominous observation about a convert not yet confirmed. Wiseman administered this sacrament to him and to Wackerbarth – recently received by Father Gentili – at *Grace Dieu*, on 2 December. At Oscott a fortnight later he was ordained 'acolyth with the three preceding minor orders.' The congregation included Pugin.[51] Over Christmas, Richard was at Ryde arranging for the sale of Holmewood, and New Year took him to Southampton, to visit Kenelm Henry Digby, a celebrated convert. Just a few hours after his visit ended, on Monday night, 3 January, an intruder set fire to the premises, which were burnt to the ground. Digby's published deposition speculated as to motive:

> 'Notwithstanding the peaceful, amiable, disposition of the people of Southampton, several ministers of different persuasions, as the phrase is, have been accustomed, from their pulpits, to traduce the Catholic religion in the harshest terms, as if expressly, wishing to bring it into hatred; and on the Sunday preceding the fire, one of these gentleman is said to have animadverted on the recent apostasy, as he termed it, of the Rev. Mr. Sibthorp, and to have alluded to the fact of his having received the Holy Communion on that morning in the Popish chapel of Southampton . . . During his visit, while walking in the town, much attention was excited among persons who recognised him . . . While the fire was raging, many persons asked the servants of the family if Mr. Sibthorp had not been in the house, and many persons in the town, when they first heard of the fire, were impressed with the idea that the object was to destroy him.'[52]

None of the occupants was hurt, although a number of valuable manuscripts were lost. Digby's biographer remarked sourly, 'And the worst of it was that Mr. Sibthorpe was after all not worth the sacrifice, for he was a weak character, and presently reverted to Anglicanism.'[53]

Apart from this, there was little open hostility. Among friends who might have felt betrayed there was not 'the bitterness of anger but of grief.'[54] After reading his pamphlet, Robert Cholmeley wrote to his cousin, 'It reminded me of your sweet disposition, your gentle manners, your lively imagination and many of the charms of your pulpit ministry.' Of the convert's eternal security, he had no doubt: 'The Lord has a people in Babylon and you I doubt not are one of them.' Yet, his reasoning was surely 'the exercise of private judgement,' his Levitical theory 'nothing else than a resurrection of Judaism.'[55] Another friend, John Hunter, now Anglican chaplain at Nice, told W. W. Phelps that Richard had sent him 'a very affectionate answer ... His case is one of great peculiarity. Though he has joined the Roman Catholic Church, his views appear to be as evangelical as before he left Protestantism. I cannot enter into particulars, but I send you an extract of his letter of December 13, 1841: "I humbly trust that I have NO OTHER GROUND whatever of hope of eternal life but Jesus Christ and Him crucified: His atoning blood pleading before God is my sole confidence. I trust that I am conscious that without holiness I cannot see God and that by His grace I long after that holiness, and wish from day to day to follow after it."'[56]

Those Evangelicals who knew him only as a name were harsher. The *Record* recorded its vindication:

Dr Humphrey Sibthorp (1712–97), Richard's grandfather, Sherardian professor of botany at Oxford University, 1747–1784.

John Sibthorp (1758–1796) youngest son of Dr Humphrey. He succeeded his father as Sherardian professor and held the post until his death.

Richard's brother, Charles de Laet Waldo Sibthorp (1783–1855) in the uniform of a captain of the Fourth Dragoon Guards, a miniature painted in 1811. After inheriting the estates in 1822, he followed family tradition by becoming colonel of the South Lincolnshire Militia.

Richard Sibthorp in 1812, by the celebrated miniaturist, Andrew Robertson. Richard sat twice for this portrait after the original was stolen from the Royal Academy exhibition of 1811. Years later it was returned anonymously, with an accompanying note said to be in a female hand.

Martin Joseph Routh (1755–1854), president of Magdalen College, Oxford from 1791 until his death. Celebrated as the last man in Oxford to wear a wig.

1799 engraving of Tattershall castle and church (from a drawing by Thomas Girtin).

Sibthorp's close friend, John Rouse Bloxam (1807–1891). 'The real originator of the ceremonial revival in the Church of England.'

Richard Sibthorp in 1839, by Edward Turtle. 'We feel satisfied that the admirers of this eminent divine, especially the congregation of St. James's chapel, will be anxious to possess a faithful portrait of this highly gifted and talented minister.' (*Hampshire Telegraph*)

View of St. James's chapel, Ryde, in 1840.

St. James' Church, Isle of Wight.

Interior of St. James's chapel, Ryde, showing the 'gilt eagle' and other features to which 'Protestant Foreigner' took such strong exception (see page 94).

Samuel Wilberforce (1805–1873). As rector of Brighstone on the Isle of Wight, Wilberforce exercised a significant influence on Sibthorp's spiritual development. Sketch by George Richmond (1868).

A DANGEROUS CHARACTER.

Policeman Sibthorpe. "COME, IT'S HIGH TIME YOU WERE TAKEN TO THE HOUSE; YOU'VE DONE QUITE MISCHIEF ENOUGH."

'A dangerous character' – *Punch* (19 June, 1847) makes fun of Colonel Sibthorp's dislike of railways.

Engraving of St Anne's Bede Houses, Lincoln, shortly after their opening in 1848.

Contemporary view of St Anne's Bede Houses.

The Bede Houses chapel. After several false starts, Sibthorp engaged William Butterfield as architect.

Interior of the Bede Houses chapel, showing the brass plaques erected by Richard to members of his family.

Photograph of Sibthorp taken soon after his return to the Catholic priesthood (1868).

'The withdrawal of Mr. Sibthorp is not an unexpected event, certainly, but it is a solemn and remarkable occurrence and one big with instruction to many. Seldom have we been exposed to more severity of rebuke than we experienced from various members of Mr. Sibthorp's congregation when we ventured to remark on the lamentable change which had taken place in his ministrations and in the outward ornament and service of his church. Now, we presume, we shall be rebuked no more by that class of our readers in the Isle of Wight. The changes to which we objected and over which we mourned have now reached their just consummation.'[57]

The dissenting press took the opportunity to stir up unease about the Establishment. The *Evangelical Magazine*, detecting 'the insidious working of the Popish leaven' commended a rare honesty:

'The defection of so respectable an individual as Mr. Sibthorp, of Ryde, from the Protestant ranks, cannot fail to awaken pensive reflections in the bosom of every Christian patriot. Can it be that a minister whom we have heard denounce the Papal church as Antichrist, and from whose lips we have listened with delight to the most forcible statements of almost all those precious doctrines which Rome impugns, has himself merged in the great apostasy. . .? It is even so. The once honoured champion of evangelical truth is now a priest of Rome. . . . His honesty, somewhat tardily developed, makes us tremble for the destinies of our country, when we know that the same feeling of conscience would compel a formidable circle of clergymen to follow his example.'[58]

The *Methodist Magazine* took a similar line:

'The Rev. Waldo Sibthorp . . . well known to have been one of the most distinguished disciples of Dr. Pusey and Mr. Newman . . . had too much English and Christian honesty to play the hypocrite, by retaining the name and profession of a Protestant Clergyman, when he had abandoned the principles of the Reformation and become a Romanist at heart.'[59]

His colours were fairly hoisted; the real Jesuits remained behind, poisoning the young, infiltrating the parishes. At Oxford, C. P. Golightly, Newman's ex-curate, quickly enrolled him in his newspaper campaign against 'members of this University . . . taking advantage of their respective positions as Fellows of Colleges and Clergymen of the Established Church to propagate "Romanism."' For had not 'Mr. Sibthorp, when lately in Oxford observed to a friend that "there were about ten persons" holding his own opinions'?[60] Clearly, the conversion of a mature clergyman associated in the public mind with their teachings was an embarrassment for the Tractarians. Their opponents demanded that the bishops should act. Ryde was not alone in petitioning. In January, William Ward wrote to Ambrose Phillipps, 'What will be the issue of our present excitement it is impossible to guess; perhaps the most ominous thing we have yet seen is the Archbishop of Canterbury's answer to the address of the Cheltenham laymen. Considering his proverbial caution it looks as if something serious were really meditated against us.'[61] Pusey moved to counter the danger by addressing a *Letter to the Archbishop of Canterbury*; in Newman's opinion, 'the most magnificent thing he has written.'[62] It protested that the converts were not 'formed by any of us or by our writings. Those who have gone over, have been mostly persons, not at all instructed in the character of our Church, who sought in Rome what they might have found in our own Church . . . mostly out of Ultra-Protestantism, not at all from among us.' He argued that there was little difference between Sibthorp and the seceders to radical dissent, 'The argument on which Mr. Sibthorp justifies his secession to Romanism, is the same in principle, as that on which the Donatists and many modern sects justify their schisms. They urge the non-fulfilment of the note of Holiness, as Mr. S that of Unity.' However, wishing to make maximum use of Sibthorp, even at the peril of his main argument, Pusey hinted that any formal repudiation of Catholic principles might tempt 'young or susceptible minds' to follow his example.[63]

But there were no imitators: a fact that heartened Newman. He wrote to Keble: 'It has been taken here by persons one is anxious about, in a way which has put me in spirits . . . I fear I must say I am disgusted with Sibthorp, and I do not see any signs of sympathy for him.'[64] It was the 'methodistic character' of it that was wrong. As he told Henry Wilberforce, 'it seems to me that there is something most unnatural and revolting in going over *suddenly* – unless indeed a miracle is granted.'[65] Sensing a need to steady the ship, Newman delivered a series of Advent sermons urging loyalty to the Church of England.[66] The first set out her claim to the *Invisible Presence of Christ*. The following Sunday, 5 December, he spoke of the humiliation caused by secessions.

'The Church of God is under eclipse among us . . . And this being so . . . what a temptation is it to many such to be impatient under this visitation. . . . who can be so startled, not I, if a person here or there . . . leaves us for some other communion? Alas! and we, instead of being led to reflect on our own share in his act, instead of dwelling on our own sin, are eloquent about his; instead of confessing our own most unchristian divisions, can but cry out against his dividing from us; instead of repenting of our own profaneness which has shocked him, protest against his superstition; instead of calling to mind the lying and slandering, the false witness, the rejoicing in evil, the ungenerousness and unfairness which abound among us, our low standard of duty and scanty measures of holiness, our love of the world and our dislike of the Cross; instead of acknowledging that our brother has left us because we have left God, that we have lost him because we have lost our claim to keep him . . . can but enlarge on his impatience, or obstinacy, or wilfulness, or infatuation.'

Nevertheless there was moral culpability; for there were others, who 'have, in consequence of the miserable confusions of the time, been tempted to look out for the True Church elsewhere . . . but yet, when they proceeded on, and came towards, or upon, or over the border, they have one by one, though separate from each other, felt as if it were a nameless feeling within them, forbidding and stopping them.' Why then, had some fallen? 'This feeling has been something singular and distinctive, and of so cogent an influence, that, where individuals *have* left us, the step has commonly been taken in a moment of excitement, or of weakness, or in a time of sickness, or under misapprehension, or with manifest eccentricity of conduct, or in deliberate disobedience to the feeling in question, as if that feeling were a human charm, or spell of earth, which it was a duty to break at all risks, and which, if one man broke, others would break also.'[67]

Even as he wrote his sermons Newman was himself struggling with the 'strength of the feelings which draw one (to Rome),' and later acknowledged that his criticism of the converts' subjectivism was itself a 'sort of methodistic self-contemplation.'[68]

Of the traditional High Churchmen who knew little of these painful feelings, Gladstone was an able champion. In January 1842, he wrote to the *Times* expressing confidence that neither recent clerical conversion was attributable to the 'Oxford writings'. Wackerbarth, he dismissed. As regards Sibthorp, he mourned that 'a spirit so affectionate and devout could not be retained within the bosom of the Catholic Church in England.'[69] The letter was not published, but the following year, in a long article on *The Present Aspect of the Church*[70] Gladstone reaffirmed that his confidence in the benignity of the Movement was unaffected by the few secessions that had occurred. Among those who had left, only Sibthorp was a man of note, 'a popular and eloquent preacher. Much as we deplore the loss of a spirit so affectionate and devout, he was not one of those who had at any period acted in co-operation with Dr. Pusey and his friends; . . . it was on his passage from the avowal of Low Church doctrine to Romanism, that he, as it were, halted on their ground for a moment. He himself has ingenuously stated to the world, that his perusal of *The Tracts for the Times* actually delayed his removal into that communion of which he is now, we believe, for the second time, a member.' Yet, he detected danger signs. There was among some at Oxford an 'undeniable and substantial, estrangement from the heart of the actual Church of England. . . . ' For Gladstone the issue was clear, 'the Church of England either is the stewardess of the covenant of grace, or she is a counterfeit and a usurper.' No one may 'quit her communion without the most fearful guilt, unless she be the last.' Because he was certain of the former, there was no threat: 'as to bringing the millions of this Church and nation into harmony with actual Rome, in our view the perversion of Mr. Sibthorp and a few more, does not abridge even one inch of the all but immeasurable distance at which . . . such an event is set.' Not millions certainly, but the writer proved no prophet in arguing that the steady advance of

Catholic principles would lead to a 'gradual return' of the Romanising party 'to a more firm, cheerful, and harmonious tone of accordance with the institutions of the Church of England.'[71]

Roman Catholic Rejoicing

Bloxam was shaken by his friend's secession, and sufficiently angry to withdraw from the correspondence on reunion. He wrote to Phillipps on 31 October, 'My head is now throbbing with agitation caused by recent events and I must for a time remain calm and quiet. I speak candidly when I tell you that however desirous I may be of reunion I have never yet felt the slightest conviction that it is my own individual duty to leave the Church of England; and my repugnance to the notion is so great that I must decline any discussion of it.'[72] Unfortunately, Pugin, on first hearing the news, had written in triumph to him. He was soon in rapid retreat, assuring Bloxam that there was '*not one particle of exultation* in my feelings respecting the Rev Mr. Sibthorp . . . amongst *us* it will be productive of the greatest good and why not among you? at any rate it seems to Me to be positively (*sic*) wrong to give way to anything Like grief and pain at such an occurrence.'[73]

Anglican responsibility for co-ordinating the 'reunion correspondence' passed to William George Ward. He immediately remonstrated with Phillipps: any more such fishing could have the most harmful consequences.

'I spoke to Mr. S. on Saturday on what seems to Newman a particularly important subject, and which I will now go on to mention to you . . . To be anxious for individuals to join her [your Church] by short cuts (if I may use such an expression) is to take up a sectarian position, and seems rather to think of the temporal welfare of the Roman Church than of promoting God's glory, as He would have it. In proportion, on the one hand, as the Roman Church displays herself in her true colours as the visible image of sanctity and purity, and in proportion, on the other, as individuals advance in obedience and the spiritual life, in that proportion (if she be the Catholic Church) will they recognise her claims and join her, not from sudden impulse, but from the deliberate adhesion of their whole nature . . . Believing yourselves, then, to be the true Church, in consistency you must believe that the spirit working at present within the English Church is certain in God's good time to bring His elect to you . . . it is, therefore, much for God's final glory that you sympathise with and pray for those who through the English Church are preaching the true doctrine of the Cross . . . . than that you should show anxiety for the immediate union of some few individuals . . . In a word, in return for your charging me with Protestantism, I charge you with implicit and unconscious Lutheranism: no sympathy is felt for the inculcation of habits of self-denial and scrupulous obedience till they are developed into veneration of saints and love of ceremonial.'[74]

For Phillipps, this was to be expected; he was convinced that the ice had at last begun to move. On 11 November, he wrote to Lord Shrewsbury:

'I conclude you have heard some days ago of the conversion of the Rev. Mr. Sibthorp, one of the most prominent and eloquent defenders of the Oxford Party ... It has caused a great excitement in the University and generally in the country. What effect it will have I must wait a little longer before I can venture to conjecture ... The general feeling of our Oxford friends *is one of great embarrassment* but *they are not yet decided as to their course*, they may however come to a decision any moment. I presume, as things have *now been pushed so forward*, the *probable thing* is that a large body of Church of England Men *will join us*: should this be the case, it will be *very happy for them*, but as for the grand object of the reconciliation of their Church (that is of a national reconversion) I fear it must *then* (humanly speaking) be adjourned to the Greek calends.'[75]

A few weeks later, he was even more hopeful, although his reasons can only be surmised. 'The secession of such admirable Men as Sibthorp and Wackerbarth will make those who remain in the Anglican Church more and more anxious for Reunion; already practical men like Gladstone, Milnes, and others, Lord John Manners, for instance, Mr Bailly Cochrane, etc., are taking it up.'[76]

The *Orthodox Journal* announced the conversion on 13 November. 'One of the great consolations we experience in our capacity as a public journalist is the having occasion to record the return of an erring sheep to the one true fold, which is now happily becoming of frequent occurrence, and thus showing the undeniable spread of our holy religion.'[77] In the following weeks its readers were kept informed on the convert's progress with reports usually culled from other newspapers. For its part, *The Tablet* accorded Sibthorp minimal coverage, and on 27 November, published a letter on *The Prudence of Parading Converts*. The writer was disturbed at so much publicity: 'his going there, being seen here – of his selling his old church, and sitting down to study his new church – what his future prospects and projects are etc. etc., are faithfully recorded, and triumphantly heralded abroad. If I were wishing to enter the Catholic Church, I am sure the public exhibition would frighten me back ... True religion like its Divine Founder has "no respect of persons."'

Wiseman, of course, was delighted to be able to show that there was no policy of appeasing the Oxford leaders. But Sibthorp's conversion meant a good deal more to him than this. The convert laid the proceeds from the sale of his property before him. It proved most timely. More churches were needed, in December the bishop wrote to Lord Shrewsbury about the one that Pugin was building at Nottingham:

'It will be undoubtedly the *grandest* thing done yet, and the most reasonable ... There certainly was a moment when I was almost in despair about the work going on ... However, I had put my trust in divine Providence ... We have not been disappointed – within the last three days £3000 have been put at my disposal for the Nottingham church as a free donation. It will be paid in a few weeks and the work will go on in the spring.

It will, I am sure edify your Lordship whence the magnificent donation comes. It is the proceeds of the sale of Mr. Sibthorp's house and garden at Ryde, which he had resolved to donate to some church building. Now when at Grace Dieu (where I confirmed him and Mr. Wackerbarth, not *ordained them* as the papers have said) he saw his fellow townsman the Rev. W. Willson and formed at once a great friendship for him, and asked to have him for his godfather.[78] I thought of placing him when priest at Nottingham, where his preaching would be most efficacious. I mentioned this to him and we spoke about the new church and he, unsolicited, offered this sum.'[79]

Richard was most generous towards his new Church, and donated at least one set of fine vestments.[80] But the disposal of capital reduced his potential income, and he no longer received pew rents or fellowship proceeds. As a Catholic, he sometimes wrote of needing a stipend[81] and in the immediate aftermath of his conversion was anxious to receive his final fellowship dividend.[82] In the longer term, although proceeds from family sources were intermittent, he remained comfortably off and seems later to have been quite shrewd in capitalising on the railway boom.[83]

In May, Wiseman wrote again to Lord Shrewsbury:

'A few weeks ago we opened through Mr Sibthorp's liberality, a chapel at Erdington, a village two miles off, and Mr. Heneage, who has catechised and read prayers there on Sunday afternoon has a score or more under instruction . . . On Tuesday last I laid the cornerstone of Nottingham Church, quite privately, only a few clergy and Pugin being present . . . It will certainly be a splendid building, full of fine devotional effect and perfectly new in modern times. We are at present going on with Mr. Sibthorp's money and Myers has undertaken to carry on the building until your Lordship's payments can be made. It will thus be covered in before winter and gain in dryness and strength. Mr. S. has more than once signified his intention not to let it remain without a fine tower and spire.'[84]

Richard brought Catholicism another gift – perhaps even more precious – his pulpit eloquence; and no time was wasted in exploiting it. According to Wiseman, on the day of his confirmation, 'Sibthorp addressed the congregation at Grace Dieu and wrought the conversion of a Methodist preacher, a man of good sense. He also went to Shepshed and spoke to the people.'[85]

Undoubtedly, he was asked to give too much, too soon. Yet he received much in return; as the ancient faith, with its worship and deep certainties, ministered to his spiritual needs. He always looked back on the months at Oscott with affection, and was particularly enchanted by the staff. The devotion of George Spencer, with whom he undertook pastoral visitation, he especially valued.[86] He also befriended Henry Pelham Heneage, a member of a prominent Lincolnshire family,[87] once a diplomatist and now preparing for orders. Both friendships survived the later divergence of ecclesiastical paths. Of Wiseman, his memories were uniformly warm. Hearing of the Cardinal's death he said, 'Notwithstanding a pompousness of manner on public occasions, he was a very humble, kind, benevolent man, tender-hearted above most. I feel that I have lost a personal friend, one whom I could have applied to; and that always with very great confidence in his sound judgement and sympathy.'[88]

Finally disposing of all his interests in Ryde, Sibthorp returned to Oscott in January 1842. His chief occupation was the writing of his *Second Answer*, which, replete with patristic quotations, evidence of scholarly assistance, was published on Ash Wednesday.[89] Ten days later, on 19 February, he was ordained sub-deacon, following which he joined the staff of St Chad's, Pugin's splendid new church in Birmingham. On 1 March, he wrote to Darwin Fox:

> 'I am now resident at Birmingham, to be ordained deacon, D.V. next Sunday, being already sub-deacon.[90] There are four resident curates under the Bishop who is Rector of the Parish. Many thousand Catholics, principally poor, and Irish very numerous. There is dreadful penury such as you have little idea of in a poor country village . . . The work of the clergy is immense, at all hours every day – the poor, miserable, sick, dying, ignorant to visit, comfort, instruct and minister unto. But the labor (sic) is blessed. And not the least so because of natural repugnance to go amidst squalid poverty, filth and ignorance, not to say, vice.'[91]

'A Reed Shaken by the Wind'

Once in deacon's orders, Richard began preaching regularly, and as envisaged, non-Catholics flocked to hear him. He spoke twice at St. Chad's on St. Patrick's Day, looking forward to the ever fuller display of the glories of the Catholic Church, and the day 'when multitudes, now alienated from her, shall join her, and our dear native isle become once more a Catholic country . . . '[92] Thereafter he was kept relentlessly busy with his pulpit gifts much sought after for special occasions. On Wednesday of Easter week, 29 March, the day after the consecration of St. Mary's, Dudley, he preached there to a 'crowded congregation' and 'amongst other matters entered into his reasons for seceding.'[93] A few days later, writing to commiserate with Fox on the death of his wife, he told him: 'I am to receive full ordination at Pentecost, D.V. – I have constant work preaching twice sometimes thrice every week.'[94] In May, the newspapers reported sermons at Derby and at Nottingham when the foundation stone was laid for Pugin's new church there.[95] He was ordained priest on 21 May, and a few days later delivered two charity sermons in Manchester.[96] In June, he managed a fortnight's break in London, but on returning to

Birmingham wrote to Bloxam of 'much preaching and travelling.'[97]

Wiseman was delighted with his convert. But concern at the criticism directed towards him for requiring minimal preparation before ordination and for exposing Sibthorp to so much public attention, led him, in June 1842, to journey to Rome,[98] where he found the reassurance he sought. He later reflected on this time:

'How few sympathised . . . with the tone of soothing and inviting kindness which from the beginning Roman education had taught me to adopt – the voice of compassion and charity; and who needed these more? Newspaper assaults, remonstrances by letter (and from some of our most gifted Catholics) sharp rebuke by word of mouth, and resisting to the face, were indeed my portion, as though I compromised the truth and palliated error, as though I narrowed the distance between the two, by trying to throw a bridge over the hideous chasm, that men might pass from one to the other!

It had been usual to keep converts long under instruction and probation, even when prepared by previous study, fully convinced and painfully anxious to escape from the meshes of error. The practice of Rome was entirely opposed to this cold system, and I felt that I could not go wrong in adopting it at once. But with I think one only exception (good Mr. S.[pencer]) I do not remember anyone approving of it, but many blamed it. Many were the anxieties which I had to suffer on this account.

It was no small reason for me to go to Rome for the purpose of reassuring myself on this and other points connected with moral practical theology, in which I saw that my practice was at variance with that of others. I had almost become shaken in regard to them, by seeing myself so completely alone, and blamed accordingly. I consulted there those on whom I could rely and was encouraged by their answers.'[99]

Yet, the critics were surely correct, the convert had been too long a Protestant easily to absorb the *ethos* of obedience. His faith had been shaped by years of reading the bible through Evangelical spectacles. Dodsworth was right, but his insight was ignored. Just weeks after his conversion, Richard wrote to Fox that 'many of our Truths, such as Invocation of Saints and Purgatory, want, I believe, only explanation and consideration to show their reasonableness, and that they are not, at least, repugnant to Scripture.' And when the latter confronted him with the prophetic scriptures, he avoided the issue, referring to the Catechism of the Council of Trent: 'Say, as you read that book, whether we who hold it *submissively* are Antichrist.'[100] As a Roman Catholic, he preached as persuasively as ever, but some said that the content differed little from what had once so charmed the congregation at Ryde. Nevertheless, at Oscott all seemed well. From there, he wrote to Bloxam, 'I do not only not regret the step I took but would on no account have it otherwise. I can most truly say that I have found, and do find the Catholic Church the way of peace and holiness to my own soul: such as for years I have been a stranger to.' But then came a qualification: certainly the Church was 'an haven, whilst all Protestants seemed like vessels at sea,' yet 'it was the very nature of an haven to collect mud and require occasional cleaning out.'[101]

It was moving to Birmingham and experiencing fully fledged Irish Catholicism that made it much harder for Sibthorp to regard the things that so shocked Protestants with scholarly detachment. His memories were of the quiet restraint of English Catholics brought up under the Penal Laws. Circumstances had changed. Wiseman, who was actively promoting Roman practices, particularly devotion to the Virgin Mary, wrote in April 1842 to Shrewsbury about the miraculous conversion of Ratisbonne. It was 'intended to encourage feelings of confidence in the B. Mother of God at the very moment that Protestantism is making her the special object of its attacks.' But 'prudence may be very necessary to guard against the consequences of well-meaning enthusiasm in the mode of relating it.' And then, as if this thought was inspired by a particular concern, his next sentence was: 'Mr. Sibthorp proves indeed a most valuable acquisition, very able, eloquent, zealous and most devout.'[102]

The neophyte, instead of quietly learning the Faith, was required to teach. Thus, his itinerary for July included various speaking engagements in the North East,[103] at Leamington and at Little Haywood in Staffordshire, where he was to assist at the clothing of a nun.[104] Six years later, another convert F. W. Faber preached in Scarborough and from there wrote to J. H. Newman, 'I find that Sibthorpe preached here or in the neighbourhood as a Catholic priest, and gave great disedification by having nothing *distinctive* in his sermon, and so people *watched* me; however, I was lucky enough to give Mamma a good word or two, which Mr Walker tells gave unlimited satisfaction.'[105] Faber believed Marian devotion was the litmus test of sincere conversion. Thus he vowed 'to be her slave and to spread her devotion' and 'feared converts relapsing from want of that *gran segno di predestinazione.*' Not long after his conversion, he wrote to Bowden complaining his use of the term 'Mariolatry' had been misconstrued, grieving that 'it should be thought that I should be like one who *never* "warmed", as a Bishop expressed it to me, to Mary; and whose fall is considered to be owing to that.'[106]

Sibthorp could not accept the place of Mary in Roman Catholicism: she usurped the place of the Saviour. He might have winked at 'folk religion', but the devotion was everywhere and approved at the highest level. He considered George Spencer a model of sanctity, recalling an occasion on which, instead of joining him to sing High Mass at Leamington, he had sent a substitute, so that he could stay with a woman dying in the workhouse.'[107] But this just added to the mystery of his friend's devotedness to the Virgin. He afterwards told Bloxam: 'I cannot swallow all things down in the way that Mr. Spencer and some other later converts do. I have not so learned Christ and his truth.'[108] On 31 July, he preached at Alton Towers and was introduced to the American convert Pierce Connelly, who subsequently separated from his wife in order to enter the priesthood. In 1849 he repented this and began proceedings for restitution of conjugal rights. Seeing his name in the press, Sibthorp reminisced, 'I met him at Alton Towers and have a pretty lively recollection of him and of his Mariolatrous activities, which then amazed me.'[109]

On 23 August, Richard wrote to Bloxam who had just returned from the Continent:

> 'I feel a fear when a Protestant goes into Belgium or Italy of the effect that will be produced on him – and that the disunion should be widened instead of there being an increased desire for the healing of the Breaches of Zion. I think that it is only one who is a Catholic . . . that knows how to reconcile much which he finds among Roman Catholics with even the Council of Trent. The *disposition* to err in private judgement is not limited to dissidents from the Church. It has insinuated itself into the Church . . . if all Catholics thought, spoke, taught and wrote as the Church's own authoritative teaching is, scandal now existing too palpably would be removed: and though all Protestants would not join us . . . yet very many would. They would find that they might be true and sincere and devoted R. Catholics, and hold no unscriptural error.'[110]

Incomprehension at the honour given to Mary was Sibthorp's early and persistent stumbling-block. But there were other, more minor, problems. For example, after a lifetime running his own household, he found it hard to adjust to community life in the Birmingham Clergy House,[111] although this was not because of any distaste for his new colleagues. He invited Darwin Fox to visit, assuring him that he would find, 'neither dungeons, nor familiars, but well informed, gentlemanly and good men,'[112]and later wrote, 'I have a real regard for the clergy at Birmingham, Oscott and elsewhere – I met with nothing but kindness from them all.'[113] His fellow clergy were not 'rough Irishmen', as alleged by Christopher Sykes.[114] One of the Birmingham curates was the brother of Sir Charles Tempest, a wealthy Yorkshire landowner, whom Richard was invited to visit. The priest in charge, John Moore, was a strong supporter of the Gothic Revival, and largely responsible for introducing Pugin to Oscott.[115] More irksome was the fact that having long been used to running a parish,[116] he was now supernumerary and without clearly defined responsibilities. After visiting Ushaw in July, he wrote to the principal, 'I am at present as much abroad as at home and feeling very much like the apostle having no fixed dwelling place. In many respects this is well for me, to remember that a Christian is a stranger and pilgrim on earth. Yet I feel anxious to have my own congregation, to be commencing my own plan . . . for usefulness – forming my own little choir (the sacrifice of which was almost the greatest I made when quitting Ryde) and forming that acquaintance which there is between even the Protestant minister and his people, and how much more between a Catholic pastor and his flock.'[117]

The following day he wrote in the same vein to a Ryde friend:

'I am still here but still unsettled, I am not one of the clergy strictly speaking, of this station, having no proper pastoral duties. But I preach every Sunday and assist the curate of the church. I begin to feel anxious to get paid, and enter upon my own plan for usefulness, but this is perhaps the desire of ignorance, for I am persuaded we little know what is best for ourselves, and do well to let others whose office it is, guide and direct us; which as far as I have had the opportunity of judging, our Bishops and spiritual rulers do with kindness and consideration of circumstances and talents. A very beautiful new church is building at Nottingham, for which I am at present designed, but two years will elapse before it is consecrated, and how much may take place in that time. I often think of St. James, its services and congregation.'[118]

A prolonged state of religious excitement was, by the summer of 1842, beginning to tell on him. As a younger man, the life of a celebrity pulpiteer had affected his health, now in middle age, thrust into a community with all the pressures of daily social interaction, he was again called to the life of an itinerant preacher and a relentless preaching programme. After years of bitter anti-Catholicism, he needed time for adjustment, for study and reflection. But it was not to be. His duty was to proselytise. It thus comes as little surprise that weariness began to creep upon him and cause him to turn for consolation to long-treasured evangelical verities. In July, he wrote, 'I well nigh despair of becoming other than I am, a miserable defaulter in all holy and Christian duties, if it were not for the propitiation of Calvary, how could I lift my eyes to heaven! But thence I draw courage and hope.'[119]

A Parting of the Ways

On Thursday 4 August, Richard preached at the opening of St. Oswald's Catholic Church, Old Swan, near Liverpool. Awed by Pugin's glorious creation, he spoke of the eternal glory of the Church; such an 'excellent and eloquent address' was soon in print.[120] The following week he returned to Lincolnshire to spend some time with his clerical brother, Humphrey. The Catholic priest invited him to preach on both Sundays of his stay. The *Mercury*, in giving the substance of one address was moved to comment: 'The reverend gentleman appears to have greatly aged; arising probably, from the straits and anxieties of mind which he has had to pass through . . . nor does he use (if he possesses) that physical energy which made him so popular while a preacher in the "church by law established."'[121]

At the end of the month, he joined the family party at Bignor for the wedding of his niece, Mary Anne Hawkins.[122] Perhaps significantly, before going back to Birmingham, he visited Ryde.[123] Once returned, there was little time for him to settle into the house that he had taken at

Edgbaston,[124] as he prepared for another tour. On Sunday 11 September he preached at Preston, and the following Thursday at Skipton, staying at Broughton Hall, the home of Sir Charles Tempest.[125] He left on Monday, but only a few yards into the journey, there was an accident, alarming enough to be reported in the *Times*:

> 'The reverend gentleman was proceeding in a gig, accompanied and being driven by a servant of Sir Charles Tempest's, in order to meet the morning coach at Skipton, on his road homewards, when the animal, a very spirited one, took fright near Snaggill, and ran way at furious speed. The reverend gentleman and the servant were both thrown with great violence upon the ground. Mr. Sibthorp had a cloak wrapped round him at the time, and was unfortunately pitched upon his head with such force as to lay the front part above the right eye open and severely bruise the shoulder. He was immediately removed to the house of Mr. Marsden, surgeon, put to bed, and by prompt attention was enabled to be removed in the carriage to Broughton Hall where he now lies. The servant escaped with a few slight bruises.'[126]

In retrospect, the accident was a watershed. Before it, despite concerns, he seemed to be coping; afterwards his anxieties clouded everything. Wiseman never doubted that it led to his desertion, writing to Shrewsbury, 'Alas! Poor Mr. Sibthorp! I fear that I have no comfort to send further than my conviction that the fall, which he had at Skipton, by which his spine and the back of his head were injured, hurt his mental powers.'[127] Yet, at first, things did not seem too serious and within a fortnight, he was deemed well enough to return to Birmingham, and there at the request of Lord Shrewsbury, assisted in the *denouement* of Miss Young's spiritual struggles. Pusey had hoped she would enter an Anglican *mone* that he and Isaac Williams planned to establish at Bisley. But it was not to be, as Shrewsbury wrote to Ambrose Phillipps: 'Notwithstanding all his influence over her, she at last begged me to procure her admission into the convent at Birmingham *for a month*, that she might there pass a period of quiet reflection, and of course have the advice of a Clergyman. Pusey then wrote to me . . . which induced me to inform him that no violence should be done to her conscience, no controversy should be proposed to her, *her* questions only answered, *her* difficulties refuted. I gave him Mr. Sibthorp as the guarantee for this line of conduct being pursued towards her.'[128]

Well before the month had expired, on 28 October, Isabella made her profession of faith as a Catholic.[129] Pusey wrote to Williams in despair, 'There has been somehow a decided breach of promise on the part of the R.C.s and her mind is weakened and distracted and that has been acted upon by *extra ecclesiam nulla salus*, put in a strong personal tone. I arrived just too late.'[130] Shrewsbury denied any pledge was broken, 'I repeatedly told him that from the moment she entered the Convent I had done with her, that I left her in the hands of Mr. Sibthorp who . . . thro' me, assured

Pusey that she shd. not be hurried or forced into any thing.'[131] Undoubtedly flattered by the battle for her soul Isabella probably did not appreciate the emotional toll on both of her counsellors.[132] Pusey lamented, 'Having failed so miserably, I feel unfit to attempt anything new.'[133] Sibthorp told Bloxam he was puzzled, 'I regret with you Dr. Pusey's feelings and language towards us. I have had some little correspondence with him lately about Isabella Young and I own I know not what judgement to form of his mind. There seems a strange perplexity and I must say, sophistry in his view of the facts which rather surprises me. Such a sad disposition to put the worst construction on everything. He seems to me like a person who is *bewildered*.'[134]

On the day of Isabella's conversion, Richard wrote to the vicar of Canwick, 'I have been very poorly since I received yours, with inflammation in the head and eye, the consequence of a cold caught in church. But I am considerably better again, and my complaints are rapidly passing away. I am setting off (D.V.) on Monday next for Ryde, for some weeks of warm sea-bathing and sea air and quiet, which I have every reason to expect will, with God's most needful blessing, thoroughly recruit me. My surgeon says – what I judge from my own feelings quite correct – that this fall, though a fearful one, has prevented a much more serious illness which was hanging upon me; and brought it out at once in another form.'[135] He was over-sanguine. In December, Robert Cholmeley wrote to his son serving in India, 'Your cousin Richard Sibthorpe had an overturn in a gig in the autumn. It seemed at first of little consequence but from some symptoms which have appeared, it seems that his spine has got a shake which may prove very serious, the side and arm is much affected.'[136] Months later, Richard noted that he was still 'recovering from the lingering symptoms of my injury received last year . . . The hurt was too closely connected with a vital part – with both spine and brain, not (I myself apprehend) to leave its reminiscences while I retain my mortal coil.'[137] Wiseman may have been right in feeling that the trauma affected his convert's judgement. Recent investigation of the psychological effects of mild head injury shows that these can include 'a change in personality . . . loss of motivation . . . emotional lability.'[138] Certainly, Richard's letters of this time do show signs of some sapping of his resilience.[139]

He remained at Ryde until the week before Christmas. Robert Cholmeley hoped that staying 'among old friends' might be a turning point. 'I trust the Lord has stopped him for a season in his course that he may think on his ways and turn his feet again to his testimonies from Popery.'[140] His old congregation, sensing how much he missed his choir and his own flock, would have been eager to reinforce his unsettlement. Did he visit St. James's? If so, his feelings must have been sorely tried by the rapid return to Low Church fittings and worship. *The Ecclesiologist* for October 1842 noted:

'The church at Ryde . . . has lately been brought back to the original state, or a condition even worse. The pulpit etc. have been replaced before the altar and the east window made to open so as to communicate with the school room adjoining, and to render the church more useful in accommodating an audience to listen to religious speakers who occupy a platform in the said schoolroom. Other particulars also have been forwarded to us on the best authority which, if such things could be so, would be extremely diverting.'[141]

Richard attended the Catholic chapel at Newport, got on well enough with the priest there and in December preached for him.[142] But these weeks on the island were a time of introspection and brooding over concerns he felt unable to share. Perhaps Joseph Rathborne might have steadied him, but he had died in August, aged just thirty-five. Sibthorp longed for his own congregation and the freedom to minister according to his under-standing of the Catholic Faith. Whether Nottingham, for which he was still destined, would allow this was uncertain; in any case, it would be a long time before the new church was ready. His thoughts wandered to other possibilities, and he wrote to Bloxam seeking his 'opinion on my being placed at Oxford – would it be considered in a bad light as *impudent, unfeeling, intrusive, indelicate* etc. or with indifference?'[143] They probably discussed this when, on his journey back to Birmingham, he stayed at Magdalen. On 20 December, James Mozley wrote to his sister:

'There is a quondam member of the College visiting us just now, namely Sibthorpe; he is with Bloxam, and dines with the President to-day. I have not seen him, and probably shall not; though, I believe, he is prepared to receive callers. I cannot say, for my own part, that I have any great respect either for his character or his conduct, and, as I do not know much of him, shall not think it necessary to run any chance of an awkward interview. The President always was fond of him, though how far it arose from a partiality for old families that had tenanted the College, as Sibthorpe's, from time immemorial, it is impossible to say. It is supposed that if Sibthorpe had not resigned, it would have been a long time before the President could have brought himself to cross his name out. It is rather curious that S.'s fall from his carriage, seems likely, from what one hears, to have the effect of withdrawing him from a public and important posi-tion among the Roman Catholics. They say his head has been so much affected by it, that preaching will be a great exertion. Bloxam thinks that half from this, and half from not liking his new associates particularly, he will probably retire into private life. I hear Wiseman is much disappointed at the small chances of our all coming over. Mr Phillips (*sic*) had misled him by extravagant accounts.'[144]

A few days later, Newman wrote rather waspishly, 'Sibthorpe has been here, dressed very impressively and eating fish; else just the same. He dined in Magdalen College Hall with no embarrassment, I am told, on either side; he shutting his eyes and turning up the balls [N.B. This was habitual with him as a Protestant], and talking, and the scouts in waiting as grave and unconcerned as usual.'[145]

Soon after he left Oxford reports appeared in the press alleging that the convert was unsettled. Someone clearly wished to make mischief. On 5 January, the *Morning Herald* published a letter purportedly from Bernard Smith denying that he had converted.[146] Richard, who was at Smith's first communion on Christmas Eve, knew it was a forgery[147]and complained to Bloxam that he too had been misrepresented: 'tho' they cannot deny my being a Roman Catholic, they keep asserting, as if from certain and personal knowledge that I am about to leave the Catholic Church and am a very unhappy man.'[148] When the *Morning Herald* reproduced the speculation about Sibthorp, Wiseman decided to act. On 22 January, he wrote to the paper:

'My attention has been called to a paragraph in which it is stated that the Reverend Mr. Sibthorp is reported to have already serious differences with his brethren in the Romish priesthood; that he refused to pray to the Virgin, or to be a party to auricular confession; that an appeal is now pending to Rome for decision as to the absolute necessity of these practices; that the decision is looked for with great interest as a test of the probability of further concessions from Rome to converts from the Tractarians; and finally that should the decision be adverse, Mr. Sibthorp, it is said, will secede from the Romish Church.

. . . I feel it my duty to come forward, however reluctantly, and give a direct and complete denial in every part of the statement above quoted. It is not true that there has ever been the slightest difference between Mr. Sibthorp and his ecclesiastical brethren or superiors. It is not true that he has ever refused or hesitated to pray to the Blessed Virgin or to be a party to auricular confession (whether that mean to frequent or to administer the sacrament of penance); it is not true that any appeal has been made or is pending to Rome on any of these subjects, or any others connected with Mr. Sibthorp. . . . It is not true that any concession to converts has ever been thought of; and in fine, a shadow of fear of Mr. Sibthorp's secession from the Catholic Church has never been entertained by anyone connected with him.

Had there been the slightest ground for any one of the statements put forth in that paragraph, I must from my position have been acquainted with it, and Mr. Sibthorp, whom I have seen this very evening, is aware of my intention of writing this contradiction. Two topics have been particularly selected by the writer of the paragraph (as calculated to give currency to this fiction) for the subject of Mr. Sibthorp's doubts – prayers to the B.V.M. and auricular confession. As to the first, if the writer had been in St. Chad's Cathedral in Birmingham on Sunday last, he would have heard Mr. S preach upon that very subject in language which would have left him in no doubt as to the reverend gentleman's opinions and practices. And as to auricular confession I would only suggest to the same writer to enquire from Mr. Sibthorp himself what are his sentiments, as I am not aware he has publicly spoken on it. Nor do I think the trouble of such an application, sure as it is of being courteously met would save, what ought to be saved at any expense, the assertion of an untruth. But in fact, it would not have cost much trouble to ascertain that the Reverend Mr. Sibthorp occupies every Saturday, or even oftener, one of the confessionals in St. Chad's, where the enquiry, if necessary might have been made without danger of intrusion.'

The editor commented, 'The rumour which the Rev. Dr. Wiseman now contradicts has been in circulation so long without any denial, that it was generally believed to be well founded; we regret to find that it is not.[149] Sibthorp himself wrote to *The Tablet*, which had also picked up on the story:

> 'My attention having been directed to a paragraph in your paper of last week, extracted from the *Morning Herald*, I beg to assure you that so far as it relates to myself the statement it contains is as *false* as it is *foolish*. It is foolish to charge me with dissenting from the Catholic Church, because I will not worship the Virgin Mary. Assuredly, I do not WORSHIP her; but neither does the Catholic Church require me to WORSHIP her, or any but God. But I ask her intercession, and as you well know, must do so, many times a day, while saying my Breviary Office. And it is *foolish* to accuse me of disapproving of auricular or private confession as a practice of the Catholic Church, when the Protestant Church of England, at least commends it on some and frequent occasions. See her Communion Service, and office for the Visitation of the Sick.
>
> It is *false* that there are differences on these points between my clerical brethren and myself. And it is *false* that a reference or appeal has been made to the Pope etc. At least, if these statements are not false, I am at this moment not cognisant of any such facts.
>
> In short, the whole paragraph in the *Morning Herald*, as it relates to me, is a fabrication from the beginning to the end: the invention, probably of the same ingenious but not over scrupulous person, who lately forged the letter signed, "Bernard Smith," denying his conversion to the Catholic Faith.'[150]

The letters did little to dampen speculation,[151] for Richard was indeed unsettled. Yet, this was not the whole story. On Christmas Day, assisting Willson at High Mass, he said the music 'shook his frame.'[152] If he could only find a ministry where he need not be drawn into 'Marian excesses' all might yet be well. Unfortunately, considered in this light, Nottingham did not bode well. On Boxing Day he wrote to Bloxam, 'I want a post where I shall be to myself and having the sole direction of the congregation and the Church duties. And my health is not equal to much anxiety, – I need quiet and anticipate little at N.'[153] However, with Willson due to take up the bishopric of Tasmania, there was pressure on him to make a decision, and early in the new year Wiseman arranged to meet him in the town, where Bishop Walsh was now living, in order to finalise arrangements. Sibthorp was torn: his revulsion at 'Mariolatry' struggling with his desire again to be busy. Writing to Bloxam, he confessed himself strongly tempted: 'I can be happy anywhere, if only employed for God, and the salvation of souls. This is essential. I have too long been accustomed to daily duties around the Church to be without them.'[154] Having visited the town, his resolve was strengthened, 'I liked what I saw of Nottingham. It is a very fine town and magnificently situated. Our new church will be out and out Pugin's best work, except perhaps, Cheadle.'[155]

The Rankling of a Thorn

Little information survives from the early months of 1843, the crucial period in Richard Sibthorp's estrangement from Roman Catholicism. He took a house in Nottingham,[156] but was not happy and did not stay long. In January, Francis Cheadle, an Oscott Theology Professor, was appointed priest in charge, and there was a young curate from County Galway.[157] Dealing with them must have been difficult because his understanding of the Faith was so different from theirs. It seems there were differences of opinion, particularly as regards the design and appropriate decoration of the new church. Wiseman blamed the accident, 'He was never the same man after . . . All his ideas altered in a most extraordinary manner, as upon Church architecture etc.'[158]

Before the end of February Sibthorp seems to have decided that he could not join the staff at Nottingham.[159] Resuming his ministry at St. Chad's, he wrote to Bloxam of a retreat he had conducted. 'I found the quietness of the season and the employment useful and pleasant to myself'. He was now contemplating a further withdrawal: 'I often regret I so hastily parted with Holmewood – It would have let well and been a pleasant retreat for me, when I wished for one.'[160] At the end of April, in a melancholy letter to the Vicar of Canwick, he said he had 'entirely given up the idea of residence at Nottingham' and was 'like him of old, who went forth not knowing wither he went, in that one particular.'[161] The St. Barnabas invitation was not withdrawn; it was Sibthorp's decision not to go.[162]

On 17 May, he wrote to Bloxam, 'I returned last night having had a fortnight away in London, Brighton, Sussex, and Ryde. I went upon legal business in part, but in part to look for a residence in or near the Isle of Wight, having determined to retire into a more private position than I am likely to do here or at Nottingham. I have taken a house at St. Helen's about four miles from Ryde . . . a very retired but cheerful spot overlooking the sea, and in its full breeze, and in about a fortnight, D.V., I remove thither bag and baggage.' He would, 'if agreeable to the Bishop . . . have a small domestic chapel or oratory rather, where I shall say my Mass. There are very, very few Catholics in the neighbourhood, some three, or four perhaps. This is just what I at present wish . . . if I ever have a pastoral charge, I should like to form my own flock.'[163] In June, he moved to the island, and the first service at his chapel was on 2 July.[164]

Three months later Sibthorp renounced Catholicism. In 1866, he explained why: he had moved to St. Helen's 'not quite satisfied with one or two matters in the Catholic Church', but 'more dissatisfied' about some circumstances regarding his intended 'destination to Nottingham.' On the island he became 'morbid, and unhappy, and relaxed, and dispirited,' and in this frame of mind took the fateful decision.[165] This is unconvincing. Within a few days of returning to Anglicanism he wrote that he had decided before Easter 'to go into retirement' in order to 'leisurely reconsider the step I took (certainly hastily) in joining the Church of Rome.'[166] Far more was involved in a decision that cut him off from the ancient worship – above all, the Mass, now the heart of his devotional life – than he would later feel able to discuss. So why, given the profound implications for his soul's welfare, as well as for his reputation and future usefulness, did he conclude he had no alternative but to leave? And why did he not slip quietly away, but rather flee uttering prophetic denunciations?

In fact, prophetical fear was the only force powerful enough to transform nagging apprehensions into solemn recantation. In January 1842, he had described his new Church as 'the school of heavenly wisdom, and godly simplicity; of Christian dignity and childlike humility.'[167] By October 1843, she was 'the harlot and Babylon.' In the months after his accident, as Richard read and re-read the prophetic scriptures his unease about Marian devotion turned to dread. On the island, largely withdrawn from Catholic company, living 'almost literally, the life of a recluse,'[168] he became obsessed with the fear that he had united himself to the Antichrist. Years later, he told Francis Massingberd that he and Newman shared a painful legacy. 'He was in early years an Evangelical and certain views and feelings hence are partaken of, which in a system so opposite as is the Roman to that of the Evangelical school in the Church of England, will when they recur startle and trouble. He too early regarded the Roman Church as Antichrist, so did I; and as a thorn sharp and rankling, often leaves a point behind, which at times rankles afresh, so it may be in his case. It is in mine.'[169] The belief he said, was 'a recurring grief . . . the occasional rankling of a remnant of a thorn – which is felt when you make certain moves of the hand.'[170]

It was not a good time for this thorn again to rankle. Many bible scholars were convinced that the *Parousia* was imminent. In the United States, William Miller had persuaded thousands that the Lord would come in 1844, and his missionaries were at work in England.[171] Staid Evangelicals agreed with the thrust, if not the detail of their message. Among them was Edward Bickersteth, once a regular visitor at Ryde. On 5 November 1842, he delivered before the Protestant Association a celebrated sermon, entitled *The Divine Warning to the Church*. It quickly went through five editions. The tone was urgent; Bickersteth was sure that the present prophetic era – that of the sixth vial, a period of mercy – was approaching its end. God's forbearance had been abused and everywhere the Roman harlot was flourishing. 'We must not conceal from ourselves the fact that even zealous Protestant ministers have become priests of the Apostasy.' Soon the seventh and last vial would be opened: a period of suffering for the elect that would terminate 'suddenly and surprisingly,' with the execution of God's sentence against Antichrist. 'Oh! unhappy Babylon, Mother of Harlots and abominations of the earth. Equally sudden is the surprise of her destruction. . . . With what earnestness and tenderness ought we to urge upon our fellow-men, who have been deceived by her sorceries . . . the voice from heaven, "Come out of her, my people."' The preacher's conclusion was unequivocal. 'Here, as the Lord's watchman, in the centre of this vast Christian metropolis, I do give solemn warning to all who hear me of the speedy coming of the Lord from heaven.'[172] A few months before he had speculated about dates, and although speaking 'with hesitation and real diffidence' cited three prophecies that each pointed to 1843, as the time for the restoration of the Jews. This would then lead on 'at a comparatively brief interval, to those momentous events, which characterise the last days of the Gentiles, and the return of our Lord Jesus Christ to our world.'[173]For thirty years Bickersteth had been respected as a sensible and mature Evangelical leader, and was certainly no fanatic. Many equally respected bible students agreed with him; in 1845, Mourant Brock estimated that about 700 Anglican ministers were actively promoting the coming millennium.[174] Some of these men had assembled at St George's, Bloomsbury during Lent 1843, where they were addressed by the rector of East Retford, who, having carefully examined the 'signs of the Second Coming in the world at large' was sure that the Lord was 'nigh even at the door.' Haldane Stewart, who was also present, concurred, emphasising that the last times would come 'suddenly and unexpectedly.'[175]

Notwithstanding that St. James's had lapsed into 'semi-dissenterism'[176] Richard was on good terms with many of the congregation, and could not have avoided being reminded of how he too had once solemnly warned that Rome's 'destruction may now be *near, even at the doors.*'[177] Despite the elevation of his Churchmanship, his deep-rooted understanding of prophecy remained; unexamined and unrevised. The matter was therefore urgent. If Rome was the Antichrist, and if the Lord was at hand, his responsibility was clear. But how could he be sure? She possessed so much truth, so much to engage the heart. Yet, what was this, if not compelling evidence that once she had been the true spouse? And now? Marian devotion was unbiblical, idolatrous; was it so extensive, so highly sanctioned that the Bride had become an adulteress? Were these insistent thoughts, he asked himself, the voice of God urging him to flee from Babylon? Because very soon he might be called upon to render account. Grappling with this Sibthorp must have felt desperately alone. His circumstances were unique. No one, Catholic or Protestant, could plumb his conflicting emotions or see, as he saw, such imperfections in every denomination, or face the agonising imperative of obeying Scriptures that good men interpreted differently.

Bloxam, his closest friend, could be of little help. He visited St. Helen's in August, taking with him the books – the first Prayer Book of Edward VI and Nicholl's commentary on it – that his friend had requested.[178] It seems they discussed the evils of popular Catholicism, but not its apocalyptic significance,[179] perhaps because Richard thought his friend would not have understood. He must wait upon God alone.

The guidance he craved was not long delayed. It came in a letter that he received soon after Bloxam's departure: a well-intentioned and pressing invitation to return to the active priesthood. But the letter enclosed a print. Sibthorp wrote to Bloxam about it, using words in which his fear is palpable:

'We are going on just as when you were here – the same hours of prayer, of meals, of study, of exercise, save that I get a walk before breakfast every morning . . .

As it respects myself I can tell you nothing more than you know, as to any step I have taken. And your answer may safely and truly be, 'I don't know' to any enquiries, as to what I am about. I am asked to accept the chief chaplaincy of St. George's New Church, Westminster. There are plenty of poor people to visit, and this must be right and useful – ignorant to instruct, and this must be right and useful, plenty of opportunities I suppose, of speaking and advising and this cannot but be useful and right. And there could be much scope for self-denial, and this must be right. But then, look at the print, which accompanied the invitation, and you see the stumbling block. Is it the Church of Christ I should serve or of the Virgin Mary? Why protrude *her* figure at all? Why set forward *her* patronage? Why exhibit *her* mantle as protecting God's children? No: I believe that she and all the Saints of God do intercede for the Church Militant, but *protector, mediator, Refuge, there is but one* – the Lord Jesus Christ. But this is just the case – the Catechism of Trent on the shelf, *approved and neglected.* And *practically* the Blessed Virgin is made the Goddess of the Church and Christians are thus virtually led to repose trust in her which none but Christ may have. To this I cannot and shall not lend myself. It is idolatry and I dare not put out my little finger to uphold it . . . it is not evidently essential to the Church, but is something extraneous, the addition of individuals, and got so extensive I do not know how to keep clear of it.'[180]

Did the spirit of Antichrist now possess the Bride? The ticking of the prophetic clock meant that he must decide. Carefully observing providences, the accidental destruction of his oratory by fire must have seemed significant: 'the pictures, valuable prints, altar-linen, etc., were destroyed.'[181] In the end, the decision made itself. If his fears could not be quietened, the safer path was to leave. On Monday 2 October, he wrote to Bloxam:

'We have been so intimate and I believe feel so much regard for and interest about each other that I will not delay to communicate to you what will perhaps surprise you: tho' I scarcely feel it will *much* after the conversation we had together when you were last here. I have passed though a period of most painful anxiety. I think I could not much longer endure the mental conflict which every increased perception of the difficulties of the case caused me. Yesterday, I received as declaratory of my return to the Church of England the Holy Communion at St. Helen's from Dr. Young. During the last three weeks I have read and re-read, searched and re-searched, till I became satisfied I should not see more plainly than I did, as to material points, what must decide me and I must make up my mind on the knowledge I had, or never.

I have come fully to the conclusion that the R. C. Church is the πορνη μεγαλη of the Apocalypse. You will perhaps startle at this: and long was it before I could reconcile this with the manifest expression of Christian truths she makes. But I have not a doubt, considering both her doctrinal errors (mingled with the truth) and her *practical abominations.* Among the former I reckon, Transubstantiation: or that the substance of bread and wine are not remaining in the Holy Eucharist: her definition of the presence of Christ therein. Her doctrine of purgatory so far as relates to expiation made by suffering after death for sins that do not damn. The *Divine* authority of the Bishop of Rome: and her definition of the mediation of the Saints etc. etc. Among the latter I reckon; chiefly and fearfully, the worship of the B. Virgin, of which I send you a new and useful proof. This is idolatrous. And all her *beauties*, which are many, her endowments and attractions will not compensate for spiritual adultery. This is harlotry – a wife she is, but a wife that has become an adulteress.'[182]

'Thus Has Become Extinguished the Brightest Hope'

In July, Bishop Walsh had asked Willson, recently returned from Rome, to try and persuade Sibthorp back into active ministry.[183] The *Wesleyan Chronicle*'s island correspondent noted his failure. 'A few weeks ago a Romish bishop, lodging in the neighbourhood, in company with Miss J. Y paid a visit to the Rev. W. S. (as I understand it for special conference,) but the Rev. gentleman was not at home to the Right Reverend Father in God and his fair companion. This was perfectly understood by our young Popish converts. It was enough to blight their hopes in their tutelar priest. But the scene at St. Helen's on Sunday last gave the *coup de grâce* to all their expectations.'[184] When he learned of the tragedy Wiseman took to his bed. Walsh bid him remember his responsibilities, urging on him the example of Napoleon, who demanded to be woken immediately bad news was received:

'Why do you allow adversity to depress you to the injury of your health, and render your friends almost afraid to give you notice of what is going on wrong? The sooner such matters are made known to Superiors the better, that a remedy may the more speedily be applied to the evil.

If a misfortune, similar to the apostasy of Mr. Sibthorp assail us, let us

humble ourselves before God and beg his pardon for any share we may have
had in the scandal thus afflicting his Church, let us resolve to profit from the
experience thus purchased, and thus with holy confidence in the Father of
Mercies let us without loss of time courageously adopt measures to the best of
our power to counteract the evil.

My dear Lord, a Bishop, in this country more particularly, must be prepared
for many difficulties, and trials. But is not the sure way to Heaven the way of
the Cross: and are not those crosses which happen in the way of our Ministry,
the most valuable?

I believe that Mr. Sibthorpe has complained that the practice of Catholics is
sadly at variance with their profession. Let us learn even from this to be more
correct in our conduct.

For some time past his conduct has been mysterious to me. I hope either he
will repent of the step he has taken and return to his duty, or it will appear he
is not right in his mind. Let us pray for him and carefully abstain from all harsh
expressions in his regard. I said Mass for him this morning.'

The death of Bishop Baines, Vicar Apostolic of the Western District,
had created a vacancy and names were required for submission to
Propaganda in Rome. Walsh, however, said he 'would deprecate a
meeting of the Bishops at the present moment which might be construed
by the public into an alarm occasioned by the proceedings of Mr.
Sibthorpe, to which we ought not to appear to attach much importance.'
He then added a postscript: 'Would it not be well to obtain the prayers of
the *urchenessimi* for Mr. Sibthorpe and for someone from Oscott to write
kindly to him to enquire of him his motives for change, to tell him that
we shall all pray for him.'[185]

Willson met the two bishops on 12 October, and was asked to do what
he could.[186] Wiseman remained deeply depressed. Having invested so
much credibility in his convert, he felt betrayed. Later, he reflected on his
loneliness at this time, 'when one (and thank God! the only one) of our
good converts fell back, after receiving orders, and I was publicly taunted
with it, in newspapers and privately in every way, and when struck-down
and almost heart-broken by it, I was told by a friend he was glad of it:
because it would open my eyes to the false plan on which I had gone, about
converts, of hurrying them on. And yet I had been careful to consult the
Holy See, through Propaganda, before acting in this case.'[187]

Among Catholics generally, there was little animosity, rather regret and
sorrow. The *Tablet* noted, 'Every communication we receive upon this
painful subject breathes the gentlest and yet the deepest feelings towards
the unfortunate Mr. S.'[188] Now apparently vindicated, Lucas was
prepared to be generous, at least to the wanderer, if not to the bishop who
had acted so wrong-headedly:

'This is a melancholy termination to hopes that were once so bright. A small –
but yet all things taken into account, a considerable – number of converts have

joined us from Oxford, but of all of them, Mr. Sibthorp excited the most general and highest expectations. The pamphlets published by him . . . in a great measure confirmed the expectations that had been formed . . . nothing rash, extravagant or eccentric . . . a certain composed strength and unostentatious sobriety of mind . . . apparent richness and sweetness of thought seemed to afford the happiest omens of the future . . . it is certain that his accession to the Old Faith excited great expectations; and in none were they greater or more powerful than in poor Mr. S's ecclesiastical superiors. They at least can have entertained no doubt of his complete sanity. "Hands were imposed suddenly upon him" and quickly as he was ordained, he was, we believe employed in the preacher's chair, even before he was raised to the dignity of priesthood . . .

And thus is extinguished the brightest light that Puseyism has yet brought us . . . As far as it affects Mr. S, we of course, wish him nothing but good. But, as to us, we think it high time that a check was given to our boasting, a blow to our pride, a humiliation to our intolerable vauntings.'[189]

Ambrose Phillipps had also invested heavily. Writing to him on 10 October Ward sought to exploit his embarrassment. 'May I be allowed to observe that you Roman Catholics really don't know what you are doing when you endeavour to weaken the force of those feelings which restrain people from any change not distinctly placed before them by Providence; and that I for one should not be altogether surprised at other steps of a similar nature, if you were to succeed in your attempts to make converts in a similar manner.'[190]

By the time Wiseman was shown the letter he had recovered his equanimity, no doubt encouraged by Seager's recent conversion:

'I have not been disposed to take as discouraging a view as you have done of Ward's letter. . . . it is only expressing what we know to be their actual views, viz. that Providence has indicated a certain extraordinary or irregular, or perhaps rather abnormal, mode of acting, which they must follow in preference to the ordinary ways and rules. . . . Feeling that they advance in grace (as they hope) and that their efforts for unity are crowned, as far as they go, with success, they see in all this an intimation from Divine Providence not to move. . . . Now . . . were a Catholic who had the opportunity of bringing anyone into unity, to neglect it, on the ground that Providence seemed to work by exceptions, in the present state of things here, he would certainly sin . . . Mr. Ward's letter seems to me nothing more than a strong expression of the known views of his party, which were, indeed, likely to receive momentary confirmation from Mr. Sibthorpe's unfortunate fall.'[191]

Anglican reaction was much less sympathetic. *The Record*, for example, demanded that Sibthorp publicly affirm his adherence to the Reformed Faith. Until he made such atonement, he was not welcome: 'he may be honest in returning with a mass of false doctrines, which may make him the tool of Satan in luring men to the brink and preparing them to plunge into the stream of error.'[192] At the other extreme, the *English Churchman* was equally virulent. Its issue of 5 October summarily disposed of the apostate: 'We own that if we heard of this gentleman turning Mahometan it would have given us quite as much or as little surprise. . . . We presume that a very slight share of accountableness is possessed by Mr. S and there-fore we frankly own that no aberration however eccentric or devious can be considered out of his very remarkable orbit. . . . Having left us without our ballast and having acquired none in his eighteen months harlequinade it is not likely that Mr. S will bring much weight to any religious body he might espouse.' It then turned to its prime target, 'But with regard to the Romish divines, who with such blind alacrity and fatal haste seized upon and smothered the troubled conscience of this unfortunate person last Christmas twelvemonths, what can we say of a system which is so rapa-ciously eager of converts, at least of any name or standing, as to launch upon the full ministry of that Church and with unbounded *éclat* of special and unparalleled honours, one who was so loosely taught and imperfectly skilled in the new faith he was commissioned to propagate, as to be found worse than useless, before, if we are rightly informed, three months of his new profession had passed?'

This was but the beginning of Richard's troubles. On 30 October, the celebrated controversialist George Stanley Faber wrote to Golightly, 'I think a good deal may be made of Sibthorp's palinodia, touching Romish idolatry. I am sending a paper on the subject to the editor of the *Church and State Gazette*.'[193] His article was a polemical *tour de force*: 'Rome, for many years, has not received so fearful a blow as she recently has sustained from the secession of Mr. Sibthorp.' It confirmed her idolatry, and 'would act as a check to that strange and senseless monomania which leads so many in the present day, by a marvellous hallucination, to discover beauty in deformity.' Her apologists' 'eloquent plausibilities' were finally exploded, 'as soon as the veritable practice of the Latin Church was exhibited to him in its undisguised deformity, all Dr. Wiseman's painful explanations . . . vanished into thin air. Mr. Sibthorp after quitting England for Rome in the full honest belief that Rome *is not* idolatrous, finds it necessary to return from Rome to England on the equally honest, practical conviction that Rome *is* idolatrous.' He thus should be honoured for 'moral fortitude' in returning notwithstanding that 'In an evil hour . . . he rashly, because without sufficient enquiry, leagued himself with that "mystery of iniquity" the great demonolatrous apostasy.'[194]

The article was widely reproduced, significantly heightening the signif-icance of what had occurred. The *Morning Herald* agreed that Sibthorp's return was no ephemeral matter. 'It may be one of those mysterious arrangements of Divine Providence which become the hinge of the most momentous events – the source of phenomena which alarm the present generation and form indelible memorials to the future annals of the world.'[195] Curiously, six years later, in writing to Lord Shrewsbury,

Ambrose Phillipps also viewed the event as a turning point: 'Ever since poor Sibthorpe's unhappy relapse into Protestantism, I have felt damped in my hopes about the conversion of England. It seemed to be rapidly advancing up to that moment, the publick mind was more favourably disposed than it had been for centuries, but from that instant there has unquestionably been a retrograde movement; and this has been encreased by the very violent line which has been taken by some of the recent converts.'[196]

Of course, his hopes had been wildly unrealistic and Sibthorp was a convenient explanation when reality began to dawn. Nevertheless, the possibility that all the attendant publicity contributed to a cooling in attitudes towards Roman Catholicism cannot be wholly discounted. The conversion of such a zealous and bible-loving minister had caused some Protestants to reflect on their traditional prejudices and perhaps made the proposition that sincere Catholics could be 'real Christians' just a little more acceptable. For him to announce two years later that he had embraced 'the harlot' ensured a rapid return to, and strengthening of, the Protestant fortifications.

6

STRUGGLING TO SHORE

Although Faber's article greatly stimulated public interest in him, Sibthorp remained silent. Used to controversy, he probably found notoriety less of a cross than estrangement from old friends. Even good men saw him as the victim of mental infirmity. Thus, John Lingard thought him 'one of those weak men who consult others, and always feel disposed to agree with their last adviser. I suspect he will continue to oscillate between the two churches till the end.'[1] More painful still was the hostility and suspicion of those to whom he had returned. In Oxford, there was little sympathy. W. G. Ward spoke for many: 'How unspeakably dreadful: it makes one sick to think of it.' He assured Ambrose Phillipps, 'His reception among us will be, I fully expect, of the most repulsive character; I for one will decline any intercourse with him whatever.'[2] Among the few who did welcome the prodigal's return was his own elder brother, the member for Lincoln.[3] But this did little to raise Richard's spirits and on 21 October, he replied dejectedly to Bloxam, who had told him that some were calling his behaviour 'criminal'.

> 'With you I wish I had the power to recall matters to the position they were just two years ago . . . when I was a Fellow of Magdalen College and had my chapel. . . . But regret is useless, and I can now only move from day to day as the way seems before me. I find very few can sympathise with me. The R. Catholics of course do not – condemning (though most gently and charitably, as yet, at least) my apostasy. The Evangelicals do not – condemning what they call my Puseyism. . . . the Old High Church Party do not, because I will not join in a wholesale condemnation of the Roman Church. The *English Churchman* does not . . . in a most bitter and uncharitable article it put forth about me. I judge that yourself and a few more do. So that you may well suppose I feel my position a somewhat solitary one and I occupy a corner in one of the great forlorn pews in St. Helen's Church where all is dull and cold and deadening beyond my power to express and I feel as isolated in sentiment as I am in bodily position.'[4]

He was writing from London, having gone there to escape being 'pestered by a set of the Plymouth Brethren,' one of whose 'ringleaders' lived near him on the island. But here too, he was 'worried greatly by the Evangelicals' and tried to keep out of their way. Oakeley's Chapel was however, a 'great comfort.'[5] The newspaper attacks were unremitting. Faber, in his article, had challenged him to 'set me right' if idolatry was not the reason for his withdrawal. But speaking publicly was impossible, because Richard was soon plagued by the thought that he may, in his excitement and haste, have mistaken the will of God, and could not shake off the conviction that he remained a Roman Catholic priest. He had given up so much that was manna to his soul. Responding to puzzled Catholics, to some he opened his heart. George Spencer received such a letter and on 6 November, wrote about it to his cousin: 'what is most remarkable in an *apostate* is that he declares that all his affections are yet with us, that he feels desolate where he is, that when he took the step, and after it, that it was done after much deliberation and prayer, he doubted and still doubts whether it was right.'[6] Beset by doubts as to the path of obedience, Richard found it impossible to explain himself in a way that would satisfy either side.

In the event, he did not need to respond to Faber, because Edward Bickersteth answered for him. In September, hearing that his old friend 'wavered in his apostasy' he had written to him, and had sent a copy of Sibthorp's reply to his bishop, asking him to suggest a suitable clergyman, who might correspond with, and possibly help to 'recover this wandering sheep.'[7] On the same day, 2 October, he wrote to Richard again, in rather harsh terms. Certainly, God's dear children were to be found in Rome, for did not Revelation 18 v. 4 charge them to come out? As for the visible unity that his old friend valued so highly, this must await the Second Coming. The Tridentine doctrine of inherent righteousness, as he understood it, Bickersteth strongly condemned. The reply was not long in coming and contained the most heartening information. On 5 October, Sibthorp wrote that he had found the evidence that Rome was 'the Babylon of the Apocalypse . . . too strong to allow the many valuable truths and practices I see in her to retain me longer in her Communion.' Mariolatry, he said, was 'the grand decisive feature which makes her spiritually a strumpet, from whom separation is a clear and bounden duty.' The remainder of the letter – a lengthy and elaborate defence of the doctrines he had assailed – Bickersteth would have found less pleasing. Lutheranism was rejected and the Tridentine *Capita* on justification eulogised as 'admirably thorough and scriptural,' indeed substantially what the Puritan, John Flavel had taught: 'It is Christ in you that is the hope of glory. Till thy heart be opened, Christ with all the hopes of glory stands without thee.'[8] Regarding unity, whilst its external manifestation might have to wait 'until Christ shall come,' it was 'the sin and shame of Christians that such should be the case, and not a matter to glory in.'

Bickersteth's invitation to Watton was politely declined; Richard sought only 'quietness, stillness and retirement.' He ended, 'I may perhaps please no party from Dr. Pusey at the top to Baptist Noel at the bottom. But I think to please God.'[9]

At a meeting of the Church Pastoral Aid Society in Bath, on 14 November, Bickersteth 'read part of a letter he had received from the Rev. Waldo Sibthorp.' Just the first few sentences were sufficient for his purposes. It was a signal victory; confirmation, he said, of 'the value of prophetic testimony and how important was it to have this divine armour given them in the Word of God to meet the apostasy of Rome.'[10] Lucas was considering his response to Faber's article when he learnt of Bickersteth's disclosure. Thus, in the *Tablet* of 18 November, he conceded that this information did indeed seem 'to be decisive as to Mr. S's opinions on 5 October; and possibly Faber may be entitled to glory in the bastard-orthodoxy of that eventful day.' But he had a trump card, another letter; one sent by Sibthorp to 'an intimate friend – a Catholic clergyman.' And from it Lucas quoted the writer's sorrowful admission: that although he had 'passed from the torrid to the frigid zone . . . his love for Rome is not changed into hatred, but rather he thinks, remains love still.' The editor expressed bewilderment, 'Love for a harlot, Mr. Sibthorp, how is this?' and then drew a sorrowful conclusion: 'Mr Faber insists strongly upon it, that Mr. Sibthorp is honest in these changes. We believe the general opinion among Catholics is more or less to the same effect. We wish certainly to hold to this opinion if practicable, but after the present *exposé* Mr. Faber will, we are sure, see there is no way of saving his *protégé's* honesty except by giving up his sanity.'[11] The following week's paper reproduced another letter in which the apostate eulogised the Catholic Church for her, 'daily devotions, her hourly offices, her symbolic rites', ending, 'Yes, my mind upon all these things is *unaltered*. But as yet, I dare not retrace the step I have taken.'

Lucas succeeded in turning Protestantism's champion into a laughing stock. Even Faber was forced to concede: if his reported sentiments 'be genuine it will lamentably evince Mr. Sibthorp to be as unstable as water.' Nevertheless, if he was so well disposed to Rome why did he not retrace his steps unless he was indeed, 'prevented by a wholesome dread of personally ascertained idolatry?'[12] Again, Faber challenged the convert to explain himself. To Bloxam, Richard complained forlornly of a 'great violation of the confidence of private correspondence'. Faber had indeed 'misunderstood and misrepresented' him, but he shrank from the ultimatum 'of either *writing publicly*, or being considered to have had *such and such motives.*' The press demanded simple explanations, but paralysed by uncertainty he had not the words to satisfy either camp. 'I am like a man who, passing over some narrow causeway, has put out one foot and neither dares bring it back again, nor bring up the other after it.'[13]

Other newspapers joined in the sport. At the end of November the *English Churchman* solemnly averred that: 'the Reverend Mr. Sibthorp has never abandoned the Roman Communion, that he is still in its pale, and that he is undergoing a course of penitential discipline under the superintendence of Dr. Wiseman, preparatory to his readmission to full privileges.' It then quoted at length from an editorial in the *Morning Herald*:

> 'Mr. Sibthorp's somnambulism, or *mesmeric fit*, or if there be any more apposite phrase for the reverend *bachelor's* perversion, began however, to give way after 18 months confessing of *male* and *female*, *married* and *single*, according to the most approved usages . . . and suspicions of his hankering after the *flesh pots* of Egypt shot through Dr. Wiseman's far-searching perceptions, and all plans and prescriptions were proposed for the mortification of this mortal sin.'[14]

The *Churchman* advised the *Herald* to leave theology and concentrate on sporting matters![15] Yet, returning to the subject on 16 December, the latter displayed a rather deeper insight than the religious press. It said the unfortunate Sibthorp was 'too much of a Protestant to remain in the Church of Rome and too truly a Papist to return to the Church of England, and withal too honest to do, or seem to do, anything inconsistent with what he believes the prescription of duty.' The newspaper, however, knew its own duty, which was to abuse the Church of Rome. Through the confessional Dr. Wiseman was 'thoroughly acquainted with all that is weak or susceptible' in the deserter's character. 'Mr. Sibthorp has yet to feel the power of that terrible engine under the operation of which he has come, and we venture to predict that the reverend gentleman will either return to the Roman Communion more entirely its slave than he was before, or will end his days in a lunatic asylum.'

Because of the continuing furore Richard abandoned a planned Christmas visit to Oxford, telling Bloxam it would 'add to the false and absurd reports appearing in the papers for the last two months.' He complained 'Of all the papers, the *English Churchman* has been the most unkind and malignant. It was that paper which first declared that I was mad, as suggested to the *Tablet* (ever ready to take up anything personally abusive)'.[16] Only with the new year did respite come; the newspapers found fresh quarry and Richard's name slipped from their pages. Although occasional references appeared, he never again achieved such notoriety. He was largely forgotten.

Antichrist or Bride?

Richard might have hoped for sympathy from President Routh. He wrote to him the day after his return 'desiring to be the first to communicate what I hope will have your approbation.' But, even Routh's goodwill must have been taxed by the prodigal's painful honesty:

'I will not trouble you with my reasons for this step; but neither will I conceal from you that it has cost me an intensely severe struggle to satisfy myself as to the duty of returning to a Church which, though as it seems to me free from the adulteration of truth, is not in some points (by no means unimportant) in such accordance with the primitive Church of Christ as I could wish her to be. I have been obliged to rest a good deal on this conclusion, that *perfection* is not to be looked for, and that, in the present broken and divided state of Christendom, freedom from positive error is what one must be satisfied with. If I must choose one to be united with, there can be no question where the choice must be, between an adulteress, which I verily regard the Church of Rome, and one who, though wanting in not a few embellishments and agreeable endowments (to say the least), is yet chaste and true and faithful.'[17]

Oxford was puzzled. On 6 October, Mark Pattison noted in his diary 'Bloxam walked up to church yesterday afternoon, and brought confirmed account of Sibthorpe's apostasy. He has received the communion in our church at St. Helen's I.O.W. but to what communion he will attach himself is not so clear. Says Rome is Babylon, etc., and the strange thing is all that he alleges as the ground of his change are the trite objections about idolatry, etc., which he must have heard and got over often enough before his conversion.'[18] Writing to his sister a month later, J. B. Mozley made the same point, 'Sibthorpe is expected here at Christmas. He has suffered, Bloxam says, amazingly throughout. But there are some persons who privately enjoy these spiritual uneasinesses and doubts, and I half suspect he is one. Mariolatry is the point on which he has started. I have no doubt there are things to astonish any one in that way, but he might have anticipated them.'[19]

Such surprise was understandable. Richard was probably present when, in 1827, William Vance, the curate of St. John's Bedford Row, lecturing *On the Invocation of Angels and Saints,* had criticised the ambiguity of Rome's position: 'some Roman Catholic writers have candidly acknowledged that the difference between the latria due to God, and the hyperdulia and dulia paid to the virgin Mary and other created beings, was not understood by the illiterate multitude, it follows that the worship rendered to angels and saints, and especially to the Virgin, is really rendered to them as Divine.'[20] In 1841, William Palmer made the same point in his *Letters to Wiseman.* The answer given to him, was the answer accepted by Sibthorp: 'Mr. Palmer has no . . . right to force upon us, as part of our religious and dogmatical system, doctrines, however popular (if they exist), which differ from *the Creed* of Pius IV, our standard on these matters.'[21] Convinced that Rome was the prophesied new Israel, Richard had trusted Wiseman, and thinking back to his youth could not recall being troubled by Marian devotion. But thirty years had wrought a change in Roman Catholicism. Also in him: believing the bible had come to mean viewing the world through the prism of prophecy. He never doubted that Rome was married to Christ, still beautiful with her bridal adornments. This was just the problem. He told Darwin Fox that he had a mind, 'so constituted probably, as not only to see acutely, but to dwell strongly on deficiencies and evils, which others, looking at the more general and large result allow . . . to go by. But . . . the very fact of that predicted adulteress being a Christian Church seems to require that her idolatry . . . should have some plausible covering, which requires a closer examination of the case to be satisfied of the guilt attaching to her than the majority of persons are aware of.'[22]

Among the Anglicans anxious to learn more about his motivation was Joseph Oldknow, the vicar of Bordesley. Sibthorp told him that although he could have avoided 'Mariolatry,' 'as a Pastor in her Communion, I was influential to bring others within its influence and from this I shrank. Besides I certainly felt, and do feel, an apprehension to say the least, that the Roman Church in this respect, perhaps in others was brought under those very fearful prophetic denouncements . . . I did not dare stay with the evil I saw and the anxieties or suspicions it produced.'

He had other concerns. In particular, his inability to ' take in Rome's view of the real *corporal* presence in the Holy Eucharist.' He believed that 'the *Body present* is the Body that was broken, not the risen . . . Body of the Lord, as that cannot be (being a natural body like ours) present in many places at once: it is really and truly present in a mystical sacramental kind; so as to render the Bread, after the consecration no longer common bread, but sacred and not only sacred, but figurative of a most sacred thing and more than that – not only figurative, but truly in a mystical, sacramental and to human understanding, inexplicable kind, the Body of the Lord – for a special season there, and kept there . . . that this may be a commemoration of the merits of Calvary – a representation of it – in some sense a continuation and renewal of it – a festival of it – therefore in itself a sacrifice.' There were other failings. Rome's use of Latin 'not merely in the actual Sacrament, but at other times (a practice gaining ground I apprehend in England)' was a 'serious error.' There was also a 'danger of *formality* in the most weighty sense of the word – of both pastor and people in the vain *performance* of sacred duties – The confessional may really become death instead of a life-giving ordinance.'

Yet none of these other considerations would have moved him. Indeed, much of the letter was taken up with the 'indescribably rich things' of Rome: 'the piety that has been and still is, in her – her mass of truth – the devotional tone of her services and liturgy – the real honour paid to Christ . . . – her strict holding of the three great Creeds. . . . If a pastor in her communion kept himself and others to the Catechism of Trent as his guide in doctrine, and piously laboured to bring the whole system of *Catechising, Sacraments,* and *Ceremonial,* especially the *Confessional* to bear on the spiritual health of his people, I can conceive nothing more admirable, more perfect.' The tragedy was that, in thrall to a particular understanding of prophecy and haunted by the spectre of Antichrist, he dared not return. 'Violent embittered men on either side will blame me – I only hope for the pardoning and forbearing mercy of God. I cannot condemn the Church of Rome where I do not see her wrong – if the Spirit that dictated the Apocalypse was at my call to whisper its true key, I would no doubt see my course very clearly one way of the other. As it is I can only judge by what I know or seem to know.'[23]

'A Rope of Sand'

Sibthorp longed for a settled assurance that he had heard and obeyed the voice of God, but prayer and study brought no light and the passing days no rest. In December, he wrote to Bloxam that he had 'not enjoyed one peaceful hour' since leaving the Church of Rome, but added, 'I cannot get over the apocalyptic prophecies – *this is my stumbling block*. And really I sometimes doubt whether I shall get over the continual conflict caused by my perception of the deficiencies of the English Church for practical usefulness and for comfort and my *apprehension of the harlot character of Rome*. You, who have not been in the latter cannot know what the deprivation of the Eucharist is, as the grand centre, the vital matter of public worship. Without it, all to me is cold and statue-like.'[24] However, in the absence of further light, the safest path must be to remain a penitent member of the Anglican Church: 'a most cold, repulsive, unamiable, but chaste old maid, or rather wife.'[25] To Oldknow, he listed the symptoms of her 'desolate state': 'Sacraments undervalued and abridged – catechising neglected – ceremonial scarce – confessional obsolete – ministerial dignities and privileges unrecognised and laughed at – the people in this case like a rope of sand – in the other like a strong well woven cable.'[26]

Stirred to respond, Oldknow sent him a sermon he had delivered the previous November 5: *The Duty of Maintaining Christian Unity*. Whilst urging a positive attitude to the Roman Catholics – he was himself on good terms with the Oscott clergy – he had no doubt about the superiority of:

'our own most favoured portion – which gives to her members greater opportunities of becoming acquainted with God's Word than any other upon earth – which expounds that Word, in her formularies, according to the sense (derived, no doubt, from the Apostles) of the earliest and purest times, and shuns not faithfully to declare His counsel, without curtailment or addition – which instructs her children to worship their God in forms, most of them derived from remote antiquity, to which, for beauty of expression, solemnity of tone, and fervour of devotion, our language can produce none equal; and disdains not to provide for the reverent celebration of His service, by minute directions of posture, place, and manner, tending alike to the edification of priest and people.'[27]

Richard's reply, disagreeing profoundly, illustrates some of the concerns that had shaped his life:

'I have thought a good deal for very many years (at times more than others) on the Church of England . . . from my earliest ministry in her I sensibly felt some great deficiency in her to make her (what is one grand requisite of the Church; one main purpose of her institution) a centre of unity, and Communion unto holiness for mortals. Her people are like a rope of sand, neither closely knit to each other, nor as to the great body of the poor and humble classes, for whom especially the gospel was preached and the Church instituted. Therefore as a means of keeping together Christ's sheep she is . . . a *failure*, and signally so, beyond any other existing Church or denomination . . . The mass of people have but with the greatest difficulty . . . been retained in her. In spite of the piety of many of her clergy and others . . . She has had and has very little hold on the affections of the great bulk of the people who yet belong to her: and every minister knows the difficulty, when any of the middle or lower classes are made earnest about their salvation, to keep them from leaving her. There seems a want, an utter want (in) retaining and uniting and cementing people in her.'

She had failed because she had turned her back on her Lord's institution:

'Her view of the Blessed Eucharist seems to me sadly defective and at variance with the primitive view. In all the ancient liturgies the Eucharist was a sacrifice: not of praise and thanksgiving only, or of prayers or alms: but a commemorative repetition in figure of that of Calvary: and presented *to God* not before men only. It was Calvary in mystery and without blood shedding, repeated, renewed in the eyes of God for our benefit. It was also not an occasional adjunct to prayers and sermons, but the grand central point of the worship of the Church . . . the Communion Service is different from this view, and hence from the defectiveness of this Divinely instituted bond of unity, comes a want of feeling of unity, and unity itself. An early morning Communion may do a little to remedy the evil, but I consider the deficiency a radical one and not to be remedied without a return to a close conformity with the Primitive Eucharistic office.'

This was at the heart, but other factors were linked:

'The almost total absence of ceremonies is a great cause of the want of attachment to, and interest in, the Church of England . . . the mass who are not truly spiritual, the uneducated, the poor, the children, all want something external to keep alive their interest in religion and pleasure in going to the House of God. The Roman Church possibly exceeds as respects ceremonies – but the total defect is far the worst extreme. I know experimentally the powerful hold these have on all the above classes in the Church of Rome, while their symbolic character makes them exceedingly precious and beneficial to the more spiritual, I do think the charge just, of a dull monotony in the English service.'

The spiritual authority of the priesthood should bind people together, but the 'English clergy have almost wholly lost caste so to speak and the people have lost all sense of their sacerdotal dignity. We are preachers, parsons, instructors, perhaps valued according to our capabilities as such, if indeed at all. We are no longer priests, having power (which even kings have not) to confer grace, to administer holy mysteries – to absolve and to retain sins. The total falling into disuse of the power of the keys and of the exercise of confession is another powerful cause of the low state of the Church of England. . . . True the power exists as to the letter in the Church. But who dare exercise it? Who dare invite the people to come to confession and who would come if he did?'

In essence, the problem was that the 'Catholic Church is since the 11th Century a wreck, a vessel broken up, like St Paul's ship at Melita: and the crew, God's people, are seeking the shore, some on one plank, some on another. . . . ' Thus how could he be blamed for investigating whether some other raft 'may not be better adapted for the preservation of souls?' However, having made the experiment, 'it is quite a distinct point whether any other . . . Church or Denomination really is better qualified. . . .' He had returned to the Church of his baptism, because 'There is no falsehood in her doctrines. Her fault is in my opinion defectiveness. If I cannot be her devoted admirer, I can be her sincere well-wisher and if such be the Divine will, her humble minister. If she is but a raft . . . I can see no longer the perfect vessel anywhere – and in so sad a wreck may be thankful for such a help to get to shore and aid others to get there.'[28]

Sadly, he was now unable to aid others. Preaching was his life's work, but every pulpit was closed to him. His old Isle of Wight friend, Sir Henry Thompson, now vicar of Fareham, had early approached the Bishop of Winchester on his behalf. The latter's reply, dated 19 October, was not encouraging:

'I am much obliged for your report of Mr. Sibthorp's present feelings. . . . As regards his officiating again I do not think it would be at all desirable at present, even if it were possible. But happily I have no discretion in the matter, for the regular rule is, that ministers of our Church after quitting it for another Communion shall bring testimonials for the three last years before he (sic) can be re-admitted to officiate and I think such probation most necessary in order to give proof of stability before one who has been notoriously known to have left us, shall be permitted to act again as a Teacher of others in our own Church.'[29]

A Broken Vessel

Seeking solace, in January 1844 Richard returned to London and in February received Communion from Routh in Magdalen Chapel. But back at St. Helen's he wrote gloomily to Bloxam, 'I find myself *now*, somewhat, to use a scriptural expression, "like a broken vessel" without occupation, pursuit, and I had almost said, prospect. For you know, and can understand my feelings about a parochial charge. I am sometimes most painfully depressed, when my mind dwells on these matters and here I have no one who can sympathise with me . . . Wednesday brought me anonymously, 2 tracts on the outpouring of the Holy Spirit, marked for my edification and admonition. Yesterday a letter of objurgation that I erred in the journey that led me to Popery, accompanied by a Tract of scriptural passages also marked for my special notice. Is not this too bad? enough to disgust anyone with *Evangelical Protestantism*. And to me, harassed and desolate at present it is most annoying.' He added that the weather was so bad that the previous day he had had difficulty getting to Church, 'It was like going to Church in one of the islands in the vicinity of Spitzbergen.'[30]

On Easter Eve, he wrote again: 'What a Holy Week, what a contrast to last years! . . . Pugin never made a more true . . . remark than when he said, "a cope and two candlesticks do not make a Catholic." All the external attraction in the Church of England has to me a most unmeaning, empty appearance. The one thing, the "Holy Sacrifice," which for 1800 years has given weight and solemnity to the House of God (the Word of God, of course gives much) is not there distinctly recognised . . . We are like shipwrecked mariners on a raft escaping to the shore. All is gloomy, sad, depressing, but where can we go, and what can we do that is better.'[31]

After Easter, he visited Hull, and wrote from there that 'every succeeding week only seems to increase my dissatisfaction with the Church of England, I fear I shall never be satisfied again. In vain do I see this and that church, stone altars, stencilled roofs etc. It is like the adorning of a corpse to my afflicted soul. The vitality of the Body and Blood of Christ in the Eucharistic Sacrifice is wanting – a communion is not a sacrifice. I declare to you, it seems to me, that the "one thing needful" the grand mysterious rite, which Christ Himself appointed to perpetually remind God and man of His one Great Atoning Sacrifice, and to cause the blessing of the whole Trinity to rest upon the whole family of God . . . is omitted, wilfully omitted; or reduced to a mere shadow of that substance that it ought to be. How then can I be at ease or satisfied, having been so differently placed.' He bemoaned the Low Church atmosphere of Hull, although a new church built by Mr Lockwood, an 'evident Puseyite,' was 'really gorgeous' within.[32]

In June, the St. Helen's lease expired and in the absence of any clear leading, Sibthorp took another house, at Spring Vale, near Ryde. Months spent pondering over what the Word of God required of him had led to stalemate. 'Oh that Rome were better or worse! That I could sweep her Mariolatry and other evils out of her as with a besom, or else could view her the coarse and depraved harlot of the Apocalypse . . . May God pardon me the thought that I sometimes wish the Book of Revelation either had not been written or had spoken out plainly and not made so obscure and difficult to perceive what is yet so deeply important to understand.' He had acted because he could not convince himself that Rome was not Antichrist. But, if Bickersteth and the others were correct in their understanding of the prophetic chronology, then he could take some comfort in the thought that, 'Time and the events of time will doubtless develop who and what is the Man of Sin.' He told Bloxam he had invited Heneage to stay, 'my soul is with such men, and I am sometimes sick at heart I am not with them in body too.'[33]

The visit had, however, to be cancelled when 'mental disquietude' began to affect his health. Taking his physician's advice by the end of July he was at Harrogate. Yet what could the waters do? His illness was spiritual, having to do with an almost physical distaste for Anglican worship: 'I can only reconcile myself to it by the feeling that in the present state of things *we are called to mortification and penance even in public worship.*'[34] The Harrogate churches were 'unbearable' and he left after three weeks, telling Bloxam, 'Mr Digby the clergyman of one, is a cousin, or as he said, has the misfortune to be, a cousin of Kenelm Digby. He is an Irish Evangelical and I need say no more.' At the resort, he was an object of 'public gaze.' Believing himself still a priest, he dressed as one, with 'no small scandal taken at my dress i.e. *my Roman Collar.*' He fled to Ilkley, 'famous for its hydropathic establishment,' putting himself 'into the hands of the German physician who presides over it.'[35] Remaining there, he shared his griefs with Bishop Longley, an old school-fellow, and visited Sir Charles Tempest to meet Bishop Brown of the Welsh District, 'who did not succeed in removing my leading difficulties.'[36]

Sibthorp left Ilkley at the end of November, and spent the next month slowly travelling south. Visiting Hull, he noted a hardening in Evangelical attitudes, 'suspicions, uncharitable surmises and reports – unsparing abuse and speaking evil of dignitaries, spiritual and temporal.'[37] Staying with Mrs. Allenby at Kenwick Hall, 'a very holy and devout woman' brought some comfort. Meeting her reminded him of 'Oakeley's argument in favour of the Church of England drawn from the holiness of its members, and as a proof that God's grace is at work in a peculiar manner in these latter days.'[38] His last Lincolnshire call was at Wragby, whose High Church vicar, George Yard, had married his niece Agnes Hawkins. Arriving in London on Christmas Eve, he attended Communion at Margaret Chapel, meeting Oakeley and Ward.

Richard spent much time studying theology, both ancient and modern, Catholic and Protestant. In October 1843, for example, he was reading Chemnitz's strictures on the Council of Trent, and Möhler's recently translated *Symbolik*, and thought both able works. John Wesley continued to fascinate him. Taking up the *Journal*, he was again struck by the extent to which the early Wesleyans looked to the Primitive Church; 'the Tractarians are not the only people who have evinced a regard to *Festivals* and *daily Communions* – the very Methodists preceded them in these Popish observances: as they did in an avowed regard to fasting on the appointed Fast Days and Vigils – But prejudice is blind, and passion is deaf as a stone.'[39] Books that helped strengthen his resolve to remain an Anglican merit special mention. In July 1844, he purchased Ward's *Ideal of a Christian Church*, and was reading it in the lounge of the Berners Hotel[40] when the author walked in. Prophecy was discussed but, as he told Bloxam, Ward had 'given no consideration to the grand point which startles me in the Apocalyptic predictions and the reasons for their application to Rome Papal.' Thus he found the book disappointing, concluding that although 'he well points out the deficiencies of the English Church . . . he does not *know the Roman* . . . from the view he seems to take of the B.V.M. I quite dissent.'[41] This was perhaps negative comfort. Not so, E. B. Elliott's monumental *Horae Apocalypticae*[42] published the same year, which provided a mass of evidence reinforcing the prophetic case against Rome. Richard found it, if not totally compelling, yet very disturbing and advised Bloxam to read it, 'slowly and patiently.' If Rome was not Antichrist, 'what else is or can be, that has yet been seen on earth, I cannot discern. . . . Elliott seems to me, notwithstanding a good deal of partisanship and manifest prejudice the most able work on this important subject yet written . . . It does not convince me . . . But it distresses me and would, as one reason among many have deterred me from leaving England for Rome, had I read it and duly weighed it four years ago.'[43]

From now on, his anxiety about the prophecies began to wane, as though after absorbing Elliott's three volumes, little more could be said. He would however, have noted that the author was among those whose re-calculated chronologies now allowed a further twenty years or so before the final collapse of Papal power.[44] In January 1845, he summarised where he stood. 'I admire much in Rome, and tho' I think I could minister in her with a good conscience, and tho' I sometimes doubt whether I have acted right and agreeable to God's will, in leaving her altars, yet I do believe her awfully (*sic*) corrupt, and I fear incorrigibly so.'[45] A few weeks later he found a surprising ally: 'I am struck with Dr. Arnold's views respecting Rome, they do so express many of mine; especially his insight into the difference in her case between practical error such as idolatry and dogmatical rules. . . How just is Dr. A's remark on the "absurd confusion between what is really Popery and what is but wisdom and beauty adapted by the Roman Catholics and neglected by us."'[46]

Excluded from the pulpit Sibthorp took up the pen. Seeking to infuse into Anglicanism something of the primitive beauty he believed she lacked, in 1844 he published a service book recasting the Anglican Eucharist as an act of sacrificial worship.[47] He later said it was the 'effort of a mind uneasy and scarcely knowing where or how to find what it needed.'[48] The following year he re-worked his 1836 *Family Liturgy* into

An Office of Family Devotion or a Catholic Domestic Liturgy and also produced a short *Summary of Christian Doctrine adapted for both Old and Young Christians.* These books were expensive to produce, and only a few copies were printed. Authorship was an unsatisfactory occupation. He told Bloxam: 'I cannot write much, it produces a feverish excitement and coldness of the feet, the result I surmise of a flow of blood to the head, which forbids me sitting long at my pen.'[49] Yet these 'silent years' did produce one 'best seller,' an anonymous exhortation entitled: *The Dream that had a Great Deal of Truth In It, Or a Few Hints for Church-Goers.* First published in 1846, it went through several editions, which might not have been the case had its authorship been known.[50]

Apprentice to a Cobbler

Finding Spring Vale far too close to the 'the circle of Ryde Evangelicalism,' in January 1845 Sibthorp moved to Winchester. He thought the climate would be healthier and was attracted by the city's appearance 'of ecclesiastical antiquity and past ecclesiastical splendour.' He was soon disabused. 'I have begun attendance at the Cathedral – but alas! my pleasure in English church music is all but gone – I miss the fine Gregorian chants – the Birmingham Mass and Vespers, the order and decorum and solemn impressive ceremonial of the Church of Rome.'[51] Here was no consolation at all: the Cathedral services were 'discomfort and vexatious desolation, even desecration.' He said the bishop had set himself against 'all that is helpful and beautiful' making it scarcely possible that 'I can ever officiate as an English clergyman in this diocese . . . I regret now more than ever my first abandonment of Ryde: to get such another posting anywhere else seems impossible.'[52] Telling Bloxam, 'I almost nauseate the Cathedral services'[53] he spent much of the spring in London, returning occasionally to receive visitors such as Fr. Spencer. In July, he was in Ilkley, from where he wrote to Bloxam, who was to join him, 'It is positively needful for my health that I cast off as much as I can, anxiety such as I have had for the past two years.' He added that travelling there he had been impressed by the worship at Leeds Parish Church: 'full choral service, it pleased me on the whole. There is some life and vigour in the way it is gone through: – also order and reverence and the organ is played well and wisely.'[54] It helped to persuade him that Anglican worship could approach the minimum level he felt essential for spiritual stability.

As his doctor recommended sea bathing, after Bloxam returned to Oxford, Richard removed to Redcar, passing through Leeds on Sunday, 7 September. It was a significant day. He wrote of attending morning worship at St. James's Episcopal Chapel, 'a miserable octagon building and poorly attended – but the service the best conducted I have ever seen in the Church of England . . . 9 clerks and 10 choristers all in surplices.

. . . They walked from the Vestry up the middle aisle in procession and with a seriousness and decorum all but Roman – when they came up to the bottom of the sanctuary, all knelt down – and filed off very nicely to their places.' He drew a little plan of the Chancel, and continued. 'Service began with the Litany at the fald stool, as of old at St. James's Ryde. All the service chanted, and very nicely: better than at the Parish church and without the organ, tho' there is a large one in the gallery. Why it was not used I know not: *but the effect was very good indeed.* . . . The sermon (one third of it excepted, which was a kind of pure rant,) impressive and Catholic in tone and matter and delivery. In short I never expected to see what I saw that morning. A Mr. Aitkin (*sic*) is the minister, who, I believe has been a Wesleyan – but I have nothing of his history. I suspect he is not in good order with Dr. Hook and his friends. The whole service here came more up to what my idea is of what should be, than I have seen anywhere, *not excepting* St. Margaret's London, for there was more life and impressiveness and solemnity.'[55] Aitken had indeed been a Methodist, a revivalist, but like Sibthorp, a convert to High Church principles, and was now Hook's curate.[56]

Afternoon worship was at the recently consecrated St George's and here again he was not disappointed. 'Psalms and amens, responses etc. well chanted, and organ very tastefully played – made me more out of sorts with Winchester tasteless service than before – and instead of a sermon, catechising children from the altar – nicely done, really wanting surplice instead of black gown to have made it very Catholic.' In the evening, he attended St. Anne's Roman Catholic Church, 'and heard Latin Vespers – followed by English night prayers, of which latter, tho' very near the top of the Church, I scarcely heard ten words. Catechising of children followed by a short discourse. I was not well satisfied here. The music and singing I did not think equal to that at either of the two other churches; tho' the style of it was more Catholic.' More seriously, his doubts about popular Catholicism were re-awakened. 'The instruction I thought positively erroneous on the subject of the sufferings of Purgatory – a subject always in my opinion better avoided – and on which the Priest in this case, as very commonly, went into minuteness very painful.'

It was a salutary day. 'I confess that I came home with the conviction that both the morning (*sic*) services were more rational, edifying, and suited to promote the good of the people, and the glory of God, than the evening service: at which I greatly apprehend full one half of those present were rendering a mere bodily service or exercise. They could not join in the Latin or hear the English. This is bad and my quarrel with the Church of Rome is that she lets this sort of thing go on – and so long as the Chapel is full rests satisfied with the formal attendance of the people – not regarding their real spiritual profiting.' But about Anglicanism it was hard for him to remain cheerful long: 'then comes the painful thought: How long will this last. Already the flame of mob interference has broken out at York, and who can say if it will not reach Leeds, and the forced inter-ference of the Bishop alter things, and restore them to their former dull and wearisome monotony.'

Rumours of Newman's imminent secession were rife. Richard, although clear that 'with all her deficiencies, the Church of England has paramount, unalienable claims on all who belong to her,'[57] did not consider it a matter of great significance. With the fear of Antichrist receding, he could see no vast chasm between Canterbury and Rome; just two flawed institutions, of which either could be an ark of salvation. Wearying of Redcar and its 'extreme dullness', he moved at the beginning of October to Whitby. Autumnal despondency hindered his writing to Bloxam. 'My mind has been so sore troubled during the last ten days . . . I sometimes think my heart will break under the burden of conflicting desires and anxieties. Nor do I gain, except very occasionally any comfort in prayer: or seem to gain the least guidance, or light on my path. I long to preach the gospel of Christ and yet seem to shrink from either of the two churches, which, alone of all present denominations could, I feel, be my church. And whether I turn to the Roman and seek sympathy from its priests, or to the Anglican and seek it from her clergy, such as formerly were my chief acquaintances, I am alike disappointed: such exclusive views, such narrowness, such prejudices, meet me that I am ready to cry with David, "I am as it were a sparrow that sitteth solitary" . . . there is no employment or pursuit of any kind, to give the comforting reflection that one is not living in vain or to no purpose. I would rather go appren-tice to a cobbler than be thus unoccupied.'[58]

Such was his despair that he thought again of the Roman ministry.[59] But impulsiveness had been replaced by its opposite. At Redcar, he could not even bring himself to enter the Catholic Chapel. 'I went to the door half a dozen times and had not courage and resolution to go in: Strange, you will say, after what I have done. But so it is: and my very acquain-tance with the Church of Rome has made me thus timid and irresolute.' Continuing in the Church of England was, he said, 'the *self-denying path* for me to take.'[60] Reluctant to return to Winchester, he decided to visit Scarborough. Passing through York, he found Dr. Gentili giving a retreat, and joked, 'I made my retreat, in another sense.' Perhaps because it lent some retrospective credibility to his own action, when news of Newman's conversion arrived, his gloom began to lift. He felt able to attend Catholic worship and meet with the resort's priest, John Walker. He told Bloxam, 'The Mass service is always edifying to me' but was sure that the converts had 'left the *less* for the *more* corrupt.'[61]

Deciding he could delay his journey south no longer, on Sunday 16 November he was again in Leeds, and worshipped at St. James's. This time his admiration was more muted, 'I have seen nothing like it. Still there are sad deficiencies. The Holy Eucharist is administered every Sunday: I did not stop but long enough to see all the choir going out previously: so that of course the Communion Service would be dull and puritanical as elsewhere.' The following day he visited Aitken, 'a very singular person – one of no common mind – and very acute in his views on Church matters – on Rome etc. I also visited and dined with the Clergy of St. Saviours, who are living in a sort of monastic way: edifying, self-denying, and simple. It reminded me of the monks of St. Bernard's. The Church itself *is very beautiful*, the paragon of new English churches – and one only regrets that so much beauty is lavished to set forth such a dull, monotonous stale service. It is like providing a Court dress for a kitchen wench. The Bishop of Ripon appears to have behaved very kindly and moderately – ours of Winchester would, I suppose, have fled from the Church as from Rome herself. I had some talk with Dr. Hook specifically on Confession.'[62]

In London, he met Oakeley, now 'enjoying the most solid satisfaction, to use his own term . . . He, I think has been *driven* into Rome, but I do not feel that others, Ward or Newman, for instance can say the same. Dr. Pusey will be *driven* out, *if at all* and I cannot quite accord with you that there is such persecution as to compel any one to withdraw from the Church of England and no persecution should do this if the Church of England is decidedly in the right.' Perhaps the secessions could mark a turning point? 'I confess I am not without a hope, and an idea, a sort of expectation, that things have come to the worst, as to the opposition in the Church of England and that now gradually matters will mend. If so, what will be the issue? Surely, a split between the Evangelical and the Catholic parties.'[63]

For their part, the converts thought much about Sibthorp. From talking with him, Oakeley believed that his heart was with Rome. George Spencer urged a season of prayer. Newman wrote to F. W. Faber on 7 December: 'They are beginning tomorrow at Oscott a Novena for Sibthorp, whose state is more deplorable than ever, according to Oakeley, who has seen him, sorry that he joined the Church, sorry he left it, and averse to add another change to his past movements.' The little group at Littlemore also united in the intention, and their leader noted in his diary for Monday 8 December, 'mass at St. Clements – received as all of us, for Novena for Mr. S.'[64]

An Imaginary Via Media

The *Essay on Development*, which Sibthorp read soon after its publication, did not tempt him back to Rome; rather the opposite. Newman proposed his book as 'a solution of such a number of the reputed corruptions of Rome, as might form a fair ground for trusting her.'[65] Richard was not convinced; he thought it special pleading, which, although it would please some, was over-subtle. From Winchester, he wrote to Bloxam about it:

'Before I left town I got Newman's work, and have since been reading it, anxiously and deliberately. It has not much affected my mind, because it does not dwell, except accidentally, on my own objections to Rome; one excepted, the *cultus,* as N calls it, of the B. V. Mary: respecting which I confess his reasoning is not to me satisfactory. I think his argument . . . is sophistry.[66] Nor am I convinced that his main argument, on development, is not erroneous. I mean that a *corrupt* development is just as probable, if not more, considering the corruption of the world, of human nature, of the Church herself from the first, in many aspects, and the power of Satan, to say nothing of the argument from analogy from the Old Testament Church, as a *pure and sound* development. Considering the soil in which the Vine was planted I should have looked for it to develope itself in a degenerate form rather than in a pure one. Of course, the question is, which of the two is the fact. Or there may be a mixed case: a development in part pure, in part corrupt – which would be rather what I consider the case. N seems disposed to go the whole hog (to use an American phraze, (sic) with the Roman Church: with her practice. And it was this which first caused the move at the period of the Reformation, and if that event had been content with rectifying the practical abuse, it had been an unmixed good. Still the work seems to be a very remarkable one and an able and learned one – deep beyond my capacity to understand in several parts. And I think it will prove a *clencher* as they say; *retaining* in Rome all who have joined her of late – and gradually bringing others in. But time will show. '[67]

If Sibthorp could have accepted the infallibility of the Church, how much easier his course would have been. But the Spirit, the inner voice, had convinced him that the Church was shipwrecked. The evidence of imperfection seemed so clear that he could not give Rome the obedience she required. Forced thus to compromise, by early 1846 he had arrived at a sort of unstable equilibrium, which he explained in a long letter to the Rev. J. M. Gresley.[68] He had joined Rome from preference, thinking her better adapted 'for furthering the present and eternal happiness of men . . . (not) under the conviction which most converts to her, have, that she alone is the true Church – I don't mean to say I never entertained this notion, but the contrary was *my deliberate conviction*; regarding always the Anglican orders as valid, consequently the administration of the Sacraments, such.'
The unfortunate implication of this was that the question of

'whether I was justified in the sight of God in leaving the Church of my Birth, Baptism, Confirmation, Ordination etc. for another Church on the ground of preference only' remained open. And when misgivings arose I had no doubt (but I say this tremblingly under a deep – would it were deeper – sense of my own immense evil and unworthiness) that I had known GOD, served Him, and been helped by Him in the Church of England, as well as that I had been called of the Holy Ghost into her ministry. I could by no means then answer the question, "have I done right in leaving her?" *affirmatively.* I became *satisfied, beyond a doubt* that I had *done wrong,* simply on the above ground: that I should have abided in my calling, seeing it a lawful one; and believed by me to be such.

I left the Church of Rome, *in part* because further acquaintance with her did not justify my feeling of *preference* for her. . . . I will specify . . . three grievous deficiencies of the Roman Church: A sound scriptural form of "common prayer" for the congregation, such prayer, *and the administration of the Sacrament*, in the tongue understood by the people. Sound evangelical preaching, and exposition of Holy Scripture: by which the truth of God may be enforced in the heads and consciences of men . . . wherever the Gospel of Christ is kept back from, or partially applied to, the people, the result must be most pernicious. I may add a fourth defect: The great neglect both among Clergy and Laity, of the reading of the Holy Scriptures in private . . . It is not true that "it was the finding so much wickedness tolerated and disposed of by the Clergy" which made me leave her . . . but . . . I am strongly of opinion, *that there is less real and scriptural holiness in her, than in the Church of England*, or indeed in the Protestant Bodies generally. . . . I could not then affirmatively answer another question; "am I helping to promote the cause of God and of scriptural truth and piety on the earth, by joining with the Church of Rome, rather than with the Church of England?" but negatively.

I left the Church of Rome, *in part*, because the extent to which Mr. Newman calls the *Cultus* of the B.V. Mary, is carried, was intolerable – It was idolatry in which I could not participate. . . . Her name is put on a level with His, and practically, she is more looked to – oftener invoked, than He. The result is that a life of communion and dependence by faith on Jesus Christ, as made to the Christian, all in all, is obscured . . . the principle is asserted, that God designs to put special honour *now* on the B.V. Mary as a recompense for the dishonour put upon her since the Reformation, *Mariolatry is in progressive development*. Mr. Newman has done wisely to introduce or develop, his doctrine of Development, for this *Cultus* can be justified on no other ground. And I cannot but think he sees as much: and that if S.S. or the Early Church are to decide the question, the Roman abuse is indefensible . . . I am aware that it is not absolutely necessary for a Roman Catholic to participate in the practice, but, to *say nothing of the tacit sanction given to it*, by every one who does not protest against it, it would be most difficult, I conceive, for a Priest to keep himself clear of it.

In not a few other points the practice of the Roman Church exceeds her dogmatic teaching. Popular Romanism and Tridentine Roman Catholicism are not the same thing.'

Gresley had specifically asked Sibthorp whether he believed Papal Rome to be the Antichrist. His answer shows that this demon, whilst not exorcised, no longer had the power to terrify. Anxious study had convinced him that the whole shipwrecked Church, like Israel of old, was upon her trial. There was idolatry in Rome, but Richard no longer believed in her incurable apostasy, God had not abandoned her, indeed pleaded with her still. Moreover, no denomination was immune to Satan's beguiling voice, some had fallen, but each could be purified and reformed:

'On another topic, to which you have referred, I almost fear to say anything – namely the application to Rome of certain fearful appellations found in Sacred Scripture – and of certain aweful (*sic*) prophetic denunciations. . . . It seems aweful (*sic*) to charge a portion of Christ's Church, and so large a portion; and so venerable for antiquity and for so much that is good and beautiful with incurring the guilt these . . . infer. Yet some of the Fathers so applied it, and not to Rome Pagan. . . . I must say that recent endeavours to disprove this application seem to me total failures, while much (not all) that has been written by such writers as Bishop Newton, Mede, Elliott, Faber etc. etc. seems to have considerable force. If the terms set forth in 2 Thessalonians chapter 2, and in Revelation XVII do apply to Rome, it is to her conduct, not her doctrines as dogmatically set forth. This distinction seems to me exceedingly important. For it is an accident, so to speak, which may be separable from her without any or much change of her doctrines or discipline, and might become applicable to any other Church whose conduct should resemble hers in three respects – Idolatry, Intolerance unto persecution, and gross Secularity with corruption of manners. But in all these three respects, Rome does seem to me guilty, pre-eminently guilty . . . (yet) . . . It is an accident, from the evil attachment of which a Church may be purified. I think it has been so, and will be perhaps, yet more so, with the Church of England. It may be so with the Oriental Churches – It might be so with the Church of Rome – Perhaps she is now upon her trial. If she will clear herself from these evils, and reform, she will yet be the acknowledged, honoured spouse of Christ. If she will not, but will persist in aggravating her sins in these three respects, from having been once a faithful wife, she will become and be treated as an harlot. Her case will be similar to that of the Old Testament Jerusalem as set forth by Jeremiah and Hosea. Now I acknowledge that such was my apprehension: and is . . . I felt it safer to be out of her: at least not to help her. But on such an awful, mysterious, difficult subject, I beg to be understood as holding only an anxious opinion – open to change, if ground for change arises. Much would it rejoice my heart, if I could see such ground.'

He was certain that those in the Church of England should stay where they were and 'hold fast the pearl of great price, which is in her.' But his own circumstances were special, and from what he then said Gresley would not have been much surprised that Sibthorp died a Catholic. 'I had no doubt that anyone erred greatly who left the Church of England, committed a great mistake, to use as mild a term as I can find. But when a person has left her it becomes another question, whether he ought to leave again the Church of his (however mistaken) adoption: seeing that she is also a portion of Christ's true Church – in which is salvation: and, at worst a Church upon trial. For it is a solemn thing to take vows in any Church, especially in one, which with all corruptions, has so many excellencies and whose corruptions are all practical, rather than dogmatical. Therefore, it became to me, a decision between difficulties whether to go back; or stay and endeavour to serve God where I had put myself. I had to balance many things and I think I judged rightly in deciding to return.'[69]

In the same month, February 1846, he wrote in similar terms to the Rev. Edward Jackson, soon to succeed Aitken at St. James's, Leeds.[70] He left Rome after coming 'to the conclusion . . . that it would be the safer line of conduct, more pleasing to God, one that would give me more content in the hour of death, as well as in this life . . . I formed the best judgement I could and stepped back, God knows if I was right, but I feel very much more satisfaction and conviction that I was than once I did. If not an unbroken conviction, it is, unless I am mistaken, a growing one, and becoming settled on grounds so solid and having so much to do with the life of the soul and peace of heart, that I am not ashamed of it.' Moreover, 'the more the Church of Rome had full influence in any country the less effective was she in the sanctification of man,' and again he spoke of his repugnance at 'Mariolatry.' However, he paid warm tribute to the Catholic clergy, 'patterns of devotion in their work,' and ended by reflecting wistfully on the many great and holy men found in Rome, notwithstanding her evils.[71]

Understandably, these rather formal letters underplayed a continuing unease. He was more open with Bloxam. 'My own mind remains as it was: in a state of miserable dissatisfaction with the Anglican and of repugnance to the practices of the Roman Church, so that I live in a kind of imaginary *via media;* which must necessarily be very unsatisfactory, in as much as it is imaginary; and the soul wants solids, not imaginatives, to rest in.'[72] This effectively was the terminus of his spiritual pilgrimage: while at times his unhappiness would be assuaged, he never secured the satisfaction he sought.

Reinstatement

During 1846, Sibthorp spent more time in Winchester, although with frequent visits to London. As the end of three years' 'penitential regret'[73] approached, his health improved markedly, and applying to the bishop for reinstatement, he assumed it would be a formality. It was not, and he was bitterly disappointed. Sumner was concerned about 'Romanizing' influences. So too was Samuel Wilberforce, lately his Archdeacon, but now elevated to the see of Oxford. Three years before, Wilberforce, alarmed to discover that his own nominee for the curacy of a new church at St. Helen's proposed to introduce a stone altar, fald stool, and eagle, had requested him to withdraw from the appointment. 'Let me remind you that the introduction of these was a prominent step in poor Sibthorpe's unhappy career. . . . I feel certain that you would never regain the confidence of the people, shocked as it has been by Sibthorpe's defection, & that the attempt would be a cause of stirring up strife & increasing Division.'[74]

In May 1847, in a long letter to Routh, Sibthorp summarised the position regarding his return to the Anglican ministry. Sumner had demanded, 'some more satisfactory proof than he possessed of my entire conformity with the doctrines of the Church of England, especially on the points of difference between her and the Church of Rome.'[75] Richard said that it was painful to be 'called upon for subscriptions or declarations or documents not required of others similarly circumstanced: namely, clergymen who had left the Church of England and returned to it.'[76] In reply, he had described the bishop's request as 'vague,' although expressing a willingness to answer specific questions. Sumner's response, when at length it came, caused consternation. He had been informed 'on the authority of a Romish priest,' of circumstances of which he had hitherto been 'altogether ignorant': 'that I had since the beginning of that year, been present at the Romish worship, and that he required from me to know whether it was so or not.' The information was correct; Sibthorp did attend Catholic worship, but, in his innocence could not fathom why these 'occasional acts of indiscretion . . . which might after all be attributed to many other motives than any wrong attachment to the Church of Rome' should be regarded as significant. He thereupon withdrew his application: the bishop had been prejudiced by 'reports designed to injure me, and prevent the success of my application.' Richard felt deeply the price he had paid in returning, in 'reputation, ease and friendship', and was 'not prepared to be dealt with otherwise than tenderly and gently, as respected the position I had just quitted, as a Minister, an ordained Presbyter, of another branch, however corrupt, of Christ's Catholic Church.'[77] Years later, reading of these events in Sumner's biography, he reflected ruefully that a visit to Warwick Street Chapel in 1846 'did not favourably move me towards the Roman Church. I came away rather annoyed and disgusted than otherwise at the service as then conducted.' However, 'good and pious Bishop Sumner was disposed to catch, I fear, at anything to stay the hand of reconciliation in my case. He in fact never gave me the slightest encouragement to return, quite in contrast to the R.C. Bishops.'[78]

In the pain of rejection, Richard may have again explored the possibility of his return to the Catholic priesthood. In November 1846, he withdrew a longstanding application for his name to be restored to the books of Magdalen College.[79] But, if he did waver, it was only for a moment. He dared not act hastily again, and by the following February could re-assure Routh, 'I feel more than I have ever yet been, confirmed in my decision to abide in the English Communion, if she will permit me . . . while I acknowledge a sympathy with some of the doctrines of the Roman Church, with many of her ceremonies and much of her discipline, I do most conscientiously believe the Church of England to be doctrinally far purer, more Scriptural, and more in accordance with true Catholic practice as witnessed by the Primitive Church.'[80] Nevertheless, there were reports that he had been reconciled. On Ascension Day 1847, Newman wrote from Rome, to David Lewis, 'As to Sibthorpe, I see the *Tablet* announces his return to the Church absolutely.'[81] A few days before, Richard had complained to Bloxam, 'I have my suspicions . . . of the party whence these reports emanate. I certainly can trace a strong attempt making to get me back into the Church of Rome or out of the Church of England.'[82]

Early in 1847, Sibthorp moved from Winchester to Carlton, a pleasant suburb of Nottingham and since 1837 in the diocese of Lincoln. Perhaps Bishop Kaye would 'regard my case more favourably, and, I think I must add, less rigorously, than the Bishop of Winton.'[83] Determined to use whatever influence he could, he enlisted Routh's help, 'At my request, my eldest brother is applying to the Primate for my re-admission to officiate in the Church of England. I apprehend he will consult with Sir Robert Inglis (a Parliamentary friend) . . . I ventured to tell my brother that I thought you would give me a favourable testimony and in this I hope I have not erred.'[84] At first, Howley wanted Richard to publish his reasons for returning; which he was reluctant to do. At length, a compromise was agreed, which Sibthorp explained in a letter to Bloxam: 'after one or two further communications with the Bishop, through a friend and connection in this neighbourhood, I resolved to write a letter. . . . This I offered to publish, provided it had the previous approval of the Archbishop and the Bishop; printing a limited number at Lincoln, some for the Bishop, some for any friend who might desire one. The result was a communication from the Archbishop that he was quite satisfied with the letter, and would merely require its entry on the register of the Diocese. Thus all publication and going to press was, I am happy to say, needless. And on Tuesday last [21 December 1847] on taking my testimonials to the Bishop, he informed me that I might now officiate as formerly.'[85]

The testimonial, asserting that 'for three years past the applicant had lived piously, soberly and honestly' was signed by Humphrey Sibthorp, George Yard and George Quilter, and dated 15 December. Sibthorp's Letter of Retraction reads:

'My Lord,

In the autumn of 1841, I quitted the communion of the Church of England for that of Rome. The step was a hasty and erroneous one, taken without due and prayerful consideration. The reasons which I soon after published, under the title 'An Answer to the Inquiry, "Why are you become a (Roman) Catholic?"' I consider to have been altogether insufficient to justify the step and I deeply regret their publication. Nor have I seen any reasons put forth by those who, either lately or at any former period, have quitted the Church of England for that of Rome or any other communion which appear to me to justify them in so doing. I consider the Church of England to be, as regards her doctrines, government and formularies, a sound and healthful portion of Christ's Holy Catholic Church; worthy of all respect for the Truth's sake that is in her, and of the faithful adherence of all her members: and with whose existence and welfare are bound up, not only the best interests of our own land, but of the world at large – in fact, the glory of God, in the happiness and salvation of man, by the extension and influence of the Religion and Kingdom of Jesus Christ.'[86]

The Lincoln Ministry

During his quarantine, reflecting on an appropriate ministry for a peni-tent, Richard's thoughts had turned to the establishment of a charity, modelled on the almshouses at Tattershall. Perhaps a visit he made whilst at Redcar in 1845 played a part in reawakening memories of Pugin's enthusiasm for the recreation of such institutions. He had toured 'Kirk Leatham Hospital – an endowment of about 200 gns. for 10 old men, 10 old women, 10 boys and 10 girls – and very well kept up in a retired village in a retired corner of Yorkshire.' Although there was much to lament: 'if any such institution can be marred and curtailed in the Church of England, it is: and the pious intentions of the founder as much as may be, diverted. It is however, a munificent charity – and better kept up than most. There is Chaplain, Organist, Surgeon . . . Mistress, Porter, all on the establishment.'[87] In October 1846, using money from a Waldo legacy[88], he purchased land near the edge of the Lincoln escarpment, looking across the valley of the Witham to his birthplace.[89] The following March, he informed Routh that soon he would move to the city, 'to super-intend a little charitable foundation I am purposing (D.V.) to raise there, I trust *ad majorem Dei gloriam,* but especially in memory of my mother, who, a widow herself, took a particular pleasure in relieving the distress of other widows, who were in less affluent circumstances. I hope to have it finished before the next year, and to be able to send you a sketch of the building, which is not to be raised without the aid of Mr. Pugin's taste, though I only employ his builder.'[90] Work commenced in April, and well before the official opening in July the following year, thirteen elderly women and one male porter had taken up residence.

President Routh was in his ninety-second year, but well able to give scholarly advice. Soon after the building was started, Sibthorp wrote to him, 'Thank you for giving me an inscription for the Bede Houses. It will by the end of the year occupy its designed place in a central gable of the building . . . there is one expression . . . with which I feel some difficulty – the designation of St. Anne as *parentis* – mother of the B.V.M. – as distinctly recognised in the Office of the Church of Rome. The mention of her in Holy Scripture would not as it seems to me warrant the conclu-sion of such a relationship between the Virgin and the Saint: rather the contrary. But you know how far the testimony of ecclesiastical history decides the point and if you can satisfy me upon it I shall feel an addi-tional obligation: and I fear in this place, with so many eyes upon me to do or say what may give occasion of cavil and not be prepared with my defence.'[91]

When the building work began Richard moved to Lincoln, to a house close by. Having no clerical duties he personally superintended the construction and was an exacting employer, still finding fault long after completion. Pugin wrote rather irritably to Bloxam in January 1850, 'I am truly sorry to find that Mr. Sibthorp has so many matters for complaint as regards his Bede Houses, but as I never acted as architect in the building but only supplied the drawings for a contract arranged through Mr. Myers I cannot consider myself responsible for the defects that may have occurred in the execution of the building . . . I must say that I thought Mr. Myers price too low, making it difficult to enable him to build in a solid manner in which this kind of structure should be raised.'[92] Sibthorp appointed trustees to join him, and in August 1847, the property along with £1000 invested in consols, was assigned to them. In December, at their first meeting, £7000 of a £12000 mortgage was transferred, the balance following three years later.[93] Such heavy expenditure meant that the chapel, an essential feature, had to be delayed, and it was not until February 1850 that Pugin – whom Richard said he liked 'much, with all his peculiarities'[94] – met him at Lincoln and supplied drawings for this and a warden's house. Unfortunately, the price was deemed too high and the architect would not compromise.[95] The following year, the trustees borrowed £1500, and various other architects were consulted, before the commission was awarded to Butterfield.[96] Commencement was delayed until 1853, with the chapel being consecrated by Bishop Jackson in September the following year. Richard appointed himself Chaplain-Warden.

The Bede Houses still fulfil their original purpose although the residents are now drawn from a wider area, and are no longer required to wear the blue uniform that their founder designed. They remain as a testimony to a life given over to charity. For Bishop Bagshawe, preaching at Sibthorp's Requiem, in St. Barnabas's, Nottingham, on 15 April 1879, this was the keynote of their founder's life: 'He was always kind and gentle to others, and in charity – the great and beautiful virtue of almsgiving – who so distinguished as he? They all knew what they owed to him in the completion of that church by its spire, which was his gift, and they knew further his many works and boundless charity among the poor, – how he gave to the Sisters, that they might feed the poor children; how he gave to the poor box, that the priests might be helped to give; how he assisted the hospital, dispensary, and other charities, besides his own large personal distribution of charity to the poor of Jesus Christ.'[97] In death, Richard's only substantial bequest was a porcelain collection, accumulated over many years, so that it might be sold for charity and the proceeds divided between the Bede Houses and the Asylum for the Insane at Earlswood.[98]

Once re-instated to the ministry Sibthorp served the city churches. On 4 July 1848, he wrote to Bloxam apologising for being unable to attend the College anniversary. 'In the first place, it falls on a Saturday, a day peculiarly inconvenient to those who have Sunday duties, as is now my case, and will, I expect, at that time be fully so. I am daily expecting to be licensed to the cure of St. Peter's-below-Hill. I am to take the morning service and sermon, and have an assistant to read and take the afternoon duty.[99] Besides that I shall have the evening service at another church, so that my time will be full. . . . This city is in a low, dead, uncomfortable state, full of party politics, worldly businesses; and the greater part of what is better being of that vague Evangelical sort, that, though savingly useful to individuals, produces no lasting strength to Christ's mystical body, the Church.'[100]

The power had gone from his voice, and the years of mental turmoil were written in his face, yet when he spoke of the reality of the spiritual world the effect remained solemn and impressive. In December 1848, *The Lincolnshire Chronicle* reported his occasional ministry at St. Peter's: 'This Church is now well filled each Sunday morning, people coming from every part of Lincoln to hear the Rev. R. W. Sibthorp. This extraordinarily gifted pulpit orator has, for an extempore preacher, the greatest power and readiness of language, we have ever heard. His digressions always tend to elucidate the passage of Scripture brought prominently forward. The earnestness of the preacher fixes the attention of the entire congregation, and feeble as is the voice of the messenger, every word seems to be, as it were, caught by the congregation, whilst an almost death-like silence prevails.' His theme was the nearness of the Second Advent. 'The sermon is, even now, the subject of general conversation, and is allowed by all who heard it to have been the most profound and brilliant pulpit effort we ever heard in Lincoln.'[101]

Something prevented him being licensed to the curacy of St. Peter's. It was an avenue he did not pursue; coming to believe that he could not 'with any comfort or quiet of conscience undertake a parochial charge.' In 1849, he refused the incumbency of St. Martin's when Bishop Kaye offered it to him,[102] and once his chapel opened was not often heard in the city. In the 1851 census he was content to describe himself as 'a clergyman without cure of souls'. He was not a solitary, often entertained guests, and kept up an extensive correspondence with friends of all persuasions. Yet, some visitors noted an indefinable air of melancholy. Samuel Cooper Scott, son of the vicar of St. Mary's Lowgate, at Hull, said that all his family 'had a great veneration for him, and regarded his character as one of the most delightful they had ever known, and they talked frequently of his beautiful, unselfish, and devoted life.' As a child in the early 1850s, he remembered being taken to see 'Mr Sipthorpe.' 'I had often heard of him, and my father, who on this occasion was with me in Lincoln, took me to call . . . A large picture hung in his room with a curtain in front of it. When he came in, he brought an air of mystery and stillness with him; he had the face of an ascetic and dark hair. He asked very kindly after the members of our family and everyone he knew in Hull, but I think there was a certain air of restraint about things, and I think I was not the only one of the party to whom the close of the visit brought relief.'[103]

The Path to Sainthood

Sibthorp spent seventeen uneventful years in Lincoln: penitential years, lived in an imaginary *via media*, with the spiritual and material needs of his alms-folk, and the regular Chapel services, filling the long hours. He drew closer to his family, occasionally travelling to London to care for his brother Charles, who, despite age and infirmity, had not ceased be an embarrassment.[104] The latter's death, in 1855, marked a further loosening of Richard's links with outside society. While 'the world' and its preoccupations had never much concerned him, with advancing years, eternity filled his mind. He wanted to be a saint. Confessing that 'I scarce do touch with my toes the threshold of this sanctuary', he resolved, 'God helping me, to go further in.'[105] Throughout the Lincoln years he had before him the strangely parallel life of Thomas Harris, who also as a young man had been deeply attracted to Catholicism. He, too, had been diverted into a different channel and in 1827 became a Congregational minister at Alford. At last accepting that he had mistaken his path, Harris began to correspond with the Tractarians and at the end of 1841 resigned his ministry.[106] Later, through Mrs. Allenby, he contacted Sibthorp, who was at first suspicious. 'I may be much in error, but giving Mr. H. full credit for very real piety, and for a degree of Christian devotion, I have not; still there is a peculiarity, not to say eccentricity about his mind, which I confess rather repels me.'[107] But when Harris decided to become a Roman Catholic, Richard repented, saying he had 'got into a good Port: whence I trust he will be both happy and useful. I should have little doubt that he shares some of my difficulties. God give me more of his piety.'[108]

After a very brief priesthood, Harris died in March 1849, and a year later, in an article in the *Dublin Review* he was eulogised as a pattern of sanctity. The writer included extracts from Harris's letters and sermons, designed to show how each aspect of the Catholic system had assisted his quest for salvation and concluded: 'Thus quietly, and unseen by men, expired in the midst of mighty London, one whose virtues and holiness of life might elsewhere have shed a mild lustre on the Church of God, in this her darkened hour.'[109] Sibthorp must have been moved, and perhaps disturbed to read of the dying convert's joy. He described him as a '*sacerdos sanctificatus . . .* a very remarkable person.'[110] Now quite certain that only Rome could make saints, he could never be satisfied as an Anglican. He wrote to Fowler, 'the great desideratum for every one is union with the Lord, participation of His nature, oneness with Him; and this is given through the sacraments especially. They are the channels through which and by which Jesus comes to us.'[111] The Anglican sacraments, though valid, could not meet his need. 'It is impossible almost not to feel that strict adherence to her office all but negatives weekly, and still more frequent, communion, while the Mass invites it.'[112] The *Dublin*

Review had said of Harris that his sense 'of the Divine Presence in the adorable Eucharist was most vivid, and his devotion, in consequence, towards It was most profound and tender.'[113]

It may be surmised that Roman Catholic friends with whom he kept in touch during the Lincoln years, did not seek to mitigate these yearnings. These included Robert Willson, who visited him when on furlough from Tasmania in March 1854, and George Spencer whom he met the following year.[114] In 1860 he told Bloxam, 'I had a visit the other day from Mr. E – who is now in my old quarters at St. Chad's, Birmingham. I never think of Birmingham without a kind of affectionate remembrance, mingled with sadness.'[115] Through these contacts, and correspondents such as Heneage, he was sure that: 'The Church of Rome is making tremendous advances. I speak from knowledge.'[116] Men of real learning and piety continued to join her; outstandingly H. E. Manning who agreed to consult Sibthorp before taking the final step.[117] But the conversions of those close to him made a greater impression. In 1855, his Magdalen friend, William Wheeler[118]'went over' and in 1863, George Yard, who had been contemplating the move ever since his wife's death in 1857. According to Orlando Forester, Yard 'never left a stone unturned until he had drawn Sibthorp again into the Roman net.'[119]

As he grew older, Sibthorp thought more and more of the Church that increasingly engaged his affections. In 1864, he read *The Life of the Curé d'Ars* and was deeply affected by 'a Christianity so high, so genuine, so divine, so beyond all I see around, that in reading it, I seem lifted into a higher atmosphere – I can only look up, and wonder and then pray – my soul be with such, wherever they are in heaven or on earth. The common clerical life I see around me, is as much below this of the Curé d'Ars as the Fens of Holland are below Mt. Blanc, in elevation above the earthly level.'[120] Reading the *Apologia* as it appeared in monthly parts seemed to underline the sanctifying power of Rome. Ever since their unhappy meeting in October 1841, he had been suspicious of Newman and thus it was 'pleasant to observe the coming on of gentleness and tenderness of feeling, and lowliness over the sharp, cold atmosphere of the Fellow of Oriel. If he becomes a Roman Catholic, he becomes a Christian. . . .'[121]

Sibthorp, who well understood Newman's 'false conscience' that Rome was Antichrist, was now convinced – intellectually at least – that the Protestant theory was partial. According to the revised prophetical chronologies of Elliott and others, the Papacy should be tottering, heralding the Second Coming.[122] It clearly was not. But there were ominous signs of the depredations of Antichrist much closer to home. In 1851 Richard had warned, 'If they meddle with the Athanasian Creed, I think my way will be clear . . .'[123] Having sacrificed so much for doctrinal purity, the publication in 1860 of *Essays and Reviews* was unsettling.[124] But two years later came something far worse: an Anglican bishop, Colenso of Natal, who impugned the trustworthiness of Exodus.[125]

Sibthorp delivered and then published a sermon asserting that it was of 'the first importance that we have neither wavering or hesitation of doubt respecting the Divine authority of any portion of that Holy Book of Books.'[126] As he wrote to Fowler: 'If Christ treats Moses' writings generally as the Word of God, it is infidelity to deny they are so; as this Bishop does.'[127] Episcopal unorthodoxy was far worse than popular superstition and unimaginable in Rome.

At the end of August 1864, Richard handed over his chaplaincy to his deputy John Fowler,[128] and moved to London.[129] It was not a prelude to re-conversion, simply a flight from deep unhappiness. He could no longer cope: either with ministering in the Bede Houses and the constant remembrance of failure and regret, or with the stifling atmosphere of Lincoln society, where no one knew quite how to treat him. Desperate to escape an increasingly oppressive situation, he closed his ears to every plea: 'no doubt, the old women miss me, at the Bede Houses. They would miss any one who was kind to them . . . But when you speak of *the grief of my late congregation* allow me to say that to use a common proverb, "there is more cry than wool" in this; in other words, tested by the reality of the case, it amounts, this grief, to very little. For what was my late congregation? Exclusive of the 14 or 15 Bedespeople, it consisted of about 12 or 14 females and some half a dozen of the other sex.'[130]

There was little surprise that in London, Sibthorp 'began to resume intercourse . . . with Roman Catholic ecclesiastics, and to frequent Roman Catholic services.'[131] He had never denied what lay at the root of his unhappiness. In October, he wrote to Bloxam 'God knows how I have felt the change from Rome to Anglicanism! I have scarcely known a day of mental or heart peace since I made it.'[132] But what duty required was another matter, and of this, he was still unsure. Writing in December, to Francis Massingberd, he mentioned one matter 'on which I wish to speak very plain . . . If in the Church of England I would never resume my ministry at Lincoln or in its neighbourhood. I am sorry I ever came to live at Lincoln and if I saw it my duty to minister in the Church of England *my very first step would be the entire removal of my residence from it.*'[133] He spent the dying weeks of 1864 agonising over what to do. Those who 'doubted whether he had ever really laid hold of the principles on which the English Church makes good her claim to be considered a national branch of the Catholic Church'[134] did not understand the real dilemma. Dean Jeremie's lament that it was futile 'to meet *feelings by arguments*' was nearer the mark.[135] What held him back? Not ridicule, for the vocation of saints was to be 'fools for Christ's sake,' nor any feeling that he would not be happier as a Catholic. As he told Massingberd, 'Thoughtless people will scoff at the notion that a Roman Catholic priest may not feel very well satisfied as a Protestant minister in the Church of England. But oh! I could tell them how far otherwise it is! that there is not an act of that ministry that will not cause a pang. . . . The Communion Table at St.

Anne's has witnessed, if it could speak, some of my feelings of a very painful kind.' Time had worked no healing: 'no one who, seeking to walk with God in holy communion and to serve Jesus Christ in the salvation and sanctification of his own soul, and of the souls of others, has been in the Church of Rome (I mean in her ministry,) will ever feel at peace elsewhere.' Even if the deserter had concluded that 'Rome is unscriptural and altogether in the wrong,' 'he would find it a hard struggle to be happy again.' 'But' he added, *what if he holds Rome to be right on those points?*'[136]

Past mistakes and two decades spent in penitential reflection made it hard to act. Yet, there was really only one possible outcome. As he wrote to Fowler, 'I am actually an ordained priest (and this my last ordination) of the Roman Church, with all her obligations on me: excommunicate, not actually but virtually, every time that I officiate at the Holy Table in the Church of England.'[137] A few days before his re-submission he wrote to him again, 'Are my ordination vows of the Church of Rome binding on me? And is the Church of Rome right or wrong on the points of difference between her and Protestants?'[138] Fr. Dessain noted that 'Sibthorpe became a Catholic again at the end of 1864, his censure being removed by Manning on January 8, 1865.'[139] The former statement must be qualified; when he wrote to Bloxam on Thursday, 5 January, Richard's mind was still in turmoil, 'I am passing through a great conflict. You can understand the nature of it, without my entering on it. The announcement, which you might have come across in the papers, was premature, and drew on me both condemnatory and congratulatory letters, all of which, or nearly so, I could only pass over *sub silentio*. The fact is, I fear to do wrong. Conflicting claims pull me first one way and then another.'[140]

'Let us Gather up the Fragments of Time on Earth that Remain'

Once taken, the inevitable decision brought him peace. It cheered also the last days of the dying Wiseman, who 'insisted that the first Mass said by the Rev. R. W. Sibthorp, after his long absence of 20 years from the altar, should be celebrated in his private chapel. When that Mass was said, on the Feast of the Conversion of Saint Paul, the Cardinal was too ill to see Mr. S, but his gratification at the good news was heartfelt.'[141] Restoration to the priesthood brought an Indian summer to the old man's ministry. A burden of worry and anxiety was lifted, and participation in the Eucharist brought longed-for spiritual refreshment. He wrote of finding, 'what I did not find elsewhere; and an attested presence of Jesus with me and in me, which sometimes amazes me.'[142] His preaching was re-invigorated, and at an age when others would have looked to rest, he was anxious to redeem wasted years. But first, he needed to heal broken relationships and in

February set out on a 'grand tour.' He visited Bernard Smith at Great Marlow, and at Birmingham he met Bishop Ullathorne. Staying at the Oratory he was reconciled with Newman. At Oscott: 'I occupied my old room . . . in which I slept at that memorable time in October, 1841, when, notwithstanding Dr. Newman's warning, I *did* stop at Oscott. He quite remembered it all.'[143] Then he had to go to Lincoln for a difficult visit, but his family was 'very kind.'[144] At Nottingham, he was pressed to join the Cathedral staff. But there were problems, not least painful memories: 'Nottingham has several recommendations, but also some (to me) serious drawbacks, though Bishop and priests invite me thither.'[145] His inclination was for London, but whilst frequently officiating at St. Charles's, Ogle Street, and other places,[146] no regular post opened up, and in the autumn he decided to accept Roskell's offer.[147] It may have been an act of atonement, because an ailing Willson, had returned to his old parish to end his days. In September, Sibthorp rented a house near to his, 'in order to care for him'[148] and in December, began work as a Cathedral priest.[149] Willson, who regarded his old friend as 'one of the most able preachers in England,' was 'all affection.'[150] He died in July the following year. Sibthorp administered the last rites, and stood on the pulpit steps during Ullathorne's moving tribute. Hearing him speak of Willson's indebtedness to Bishop Milner, his 'holy father in Christ,' perhaps he reflected on the beginnings of his own search for holiness, and the strange ways of Providence.[151]

As old age crept upon him, Sibthorp sought 'to gather up the fragments of time on earth that remain to us.'[152] He thought much about the values he had early acquired – a sense of community centred on the parish church, devoted biblical piety, and quiet unobtrusive Catholicism – and felt a duty to urge these on a rapidly changing society. In Nottingham, he became well known as an old-fashioned Tory gentleman and a stout defender of the Establishment. He campaigned for Anglican candidates at School Board elections, and urged his fellow citizens, 'stick to your Church . . . although it is not mine, I love her. Can I forget the Church that nourished my younger years, the Church that watched over me in my youth . . . No! I admire her learning; I admire her increased piety. I would say do not for a moment help to bring down those beauteous village churches.'[153] His last appearance on a public platform was to assail the 'spoliationists' at a meeting of the Liberation Society in March 1876. According to a friendly account, 'a feeble tottering figure,' rose to speak, and when the 'well known, strongly marked, powerfully intellectual, yet eminently benevolent face' was recognised, the hall seemed to 'vibrate with welcoming applause.' And he did not disappoint, '"I should say it," said he, "though I stood at the Pope's right hand, the Church of England contains a magnificent mass of truth."'[154]

He was outraged when Trinity College awarded a Fellowship to Newman. 'I love the Church of England with all her faults and defects.

And I consider our Universities as bound up with the Established Church; and, therefore, to place the greatest injurer of that Church, in one of her Colleges, and as a Fellow, is an insult to the Church of England, and a very serious injury.'[155] He believed the continuing vitality of the English Church helped to restrain the excesses of his own, and never doubted that the Reformation had been needed: 'The Church had become dreadfully corrupt; a Jehu was wanted.'[156] Seeking a strong Establishment that it might continue its 'disinfectant' role he regarded Ritualism as pernicious,[157] and dismissed talk of reunion, as an 'idle dream, – no other.'[158]

In politics, he was active in the Conservative cause, frequently embarrassing his fellow clergy, as when he argued strongly against disestablishing the Church of Ireland. He feared Liberalism and viewed Gladstone with suspicion. At an election meeting in 1873, he exaggerated slightly in remembering that 'in early life he attended my rooms at Oxford and received some religious education from me.' But, despite these links, in disestablishing 'the Church of a neighbouring land he struck a vital blow at this fair country.'[159] He was wary, too, of Manning whose visit to Nottingham in August 1876 he anticipated with some anxiety. But things passed well enough and he was asked to second the vote of thanks. It was 'one of those stirring speeches in which the spirit now seems to soar above its now feeble tenement.   He was severe on the false diamond of Liberationism and the counterfeit peal of Secularism, and demolished Mr. Chamberlain in a single sentence: 'I beg to say we don't want Brummagem ware here.'[160] He viewed all change with apprehension – 'Nottingham is no worse than any other place . . . but the amount of vice and profligacy is tremendous'[161] – and saw in it a prophetic significance. 'The symptoms of the last days, both the good and the bad signs, are developing.'[162]

Ministry at the altar was a great comfort, and he delighted in the solemn worship. Some devotions still made him uncomfortable, but they no longer aroused visceral fear. Rather it was ultramontanism that troubled his last years. He deplored it in all its aspects, lamenting for example, the trend toward Roman vestments. By 1875, the threat was at his doorstep: 'As yet we keep to the Pugin Old-English vestments here; but some, I doubt, will not rest till they have got rid of them, and brought in the Warren-blacking style of dress at Mass, – stiff, ungainly, untasteful, un-English.'[163] He saw deeper dangers, and in a rare conjunction with Gladstone, feared Papal Infallibility as a threat to national security, linking it with his long-standing distrust of France. The *débâcle* of 1871 made no difference: 'She was far more a degenerated nation at the commencement of the revolutionary wars of 1790 . . . yet what did she not do, under the influence of strong determination, and of democratic impulse? . . . She is gathering her strength now for a great struggle. . . . It will be a religious war.'[164] What then? 'Will the Infallibility of the Pope make German Catholics, Irish Catholics, American Catholics, antibellicose (to coin a word)? . . . This test of Catholic loyalty has not yet come;

and therefore, all the replies to Gladstone, which dwell on present Catholic loyalty, of which but few will doubt . . . are evasions.'[165]

In 1870, Sibthorp described his life as a Cathedral priest. 'I say Mass daily, and preach frequently, hear confessions, and visit a few sick.'[166] It was an influential ministry, appreciated by both Catholics and Protestants, and prolonged until November 1874, when the appointment of Bishop Bagshawe was the signal for him to retire from the 'active list,' although he continued to serve in the Cathedral. The following year he moved from Wellington Circus to the house in East Circus Street in which he was to die. Slowly he was becoming a man apart. He blamed deafness, but his isolation was spiritual, in striving for heaven the externals of ecclesiastical life seemed increasingly irrelevant. All that remained was to salvage 'what remains after the wreck. Be it much or little, it is well to secure it; not to lose the little time and broken strength, and failing powers yet remaining after so much waste and irreparable loss.'[167] Still displaying the 'Fletcher-like spirit' noted fifty years before, he longed to impart the religion of the heart to his own people: to deepen devotion to the Saviour portrayed in Scripture. 'I want to reach our Catholics, and to bring them to discern things that differ, and not to rest in the shell, but to get to the kernel, which is Christ.'[168] His task was 'to put forward Christ our Lord before our own people here, and win, by God's grace, their hearts for Him.'[169] Although there was among some Catholics, 'a true spirit of deep piety,' he lamented that: 'Too many of them are better satisfied with repeating and hurrying over the beads and the Rosary, than prayerful reading of the Scriptures.'[170] Thus, soon after retiring, he began work on a book of devotional studies, based upon his weekday addresses in the Cathedral. The result called *Daily Bread* was published in February 1876.

Sibthorp was not satisfied with it, and began work on a book of readings for every day of the year; he reached No. 358 before his final illness caused him to lay down his pen, and the book also called *Daily Bread* was published posthumously. It is a fitting legacy, as the *Tablet* – in describing it as 'written in what is almost a foreign language'[171] – unconsciously acknowledged. As a young Anglican minister he had protested against unreality in religion and so he pleaded still: 'remember not to rest in any privileges of Church-membership . . . nor in external rites and ceremonies . . . God requires and looks for . . . His grace in operation in our hearts.'[172] In *Daily Bread,* the Sacraments are rarely mentioned and there is nothing of the intercession of Saints. Of the Virgin Mary, he wrote that union with her was possible only through Christ: 'Happy are we . . . to have that relationship to Christ and through Him to His Blessed Mother.'[173] There are no references to purgatory; indeed Sibthorp regularly reassured grieving Protestants that their loved ones were with the Saviour.[174] His politics are not concealed, the establishment of religion being lauded as a bulwark against 'learning and science which shall put Christianity and Christ on one side . . . the spirit of infidelity . . . marking the close of the dispensation.'[175] He wrote as a penitent, 'I have to redeem dreadful waste, such as only Christ can atone for.'[176] *Daily Bread* was the work of an old man who longed 'to get to Jesus.'[177]

Despite warning against reliance on feelings in religious matters, Sibthorp was sure that 'It is not unbecoming in a Christian to endeavour and pray for the assurance of his own salvation.'[178] Sadly, while struggling to complete the book, a dark cloud hovered over him, for the comforting and guiding voice, which throughout his life, he had strained to hear, deserted him. He wrote in *Daily Bread* of the 'danger of despair of salvation possessing our minds.'[179] It became his own soul's cry. Eight months before his death, he wrote to Bloxam: 'I find my want of the Holy Spirit, witnessing with my spirit: a very sad and humbling and alarming care for me daily to attend to. There are very solemn, awful statements on this great matter. It brings me on my knees. Pray for me.'[180] He regarded the witness of the Spirit as above any system or institution. In its absence, he became, almost, what he had never been, a Calvinist. 'I have not a rag of righteousness, but only His, to cover my nakedness, my wounds, my leprosy. If I live at all before God, it is not I, but Christ liveth in me.'[181] Why he asked, had some, close to him, subject to the same influences, been so completely taken up with the world, yet it had not been so with him? He wrote to Mrs. Bodley, 'My great want is the continual Presence of His Holy Spirit . . . There are and have been from the first, from Abel and Cain, the sons of God and the sons of men, as declared in Genesis early, – two great divisions of the human race. There lies at the back of this a deep, fathomless (at present) mystery. But it is so. Can we say, "We are on the way to God?" There was this our way and its result in His Eternal Mind, when He created the world by Jesus Christ. But what are we, to have such a call? Alas! I may say for myself, how little have I responded to it!'[182]

In December 1878, becoming very ill, he told the rector of Gedling: 'I don't believe in Churches, but in my Lord Jesus, who of God is made to me Wisdom, Righteousness, Sanctification, and Redemption; for that is all my hope.'[183] The pain eased, but in March, it returned with increasing intensity. 'My sufferings are very great, – continual painful irritation: but if God seals my pardon, and my redemption from my iniquities, all will be well. I am full of fears and doubts. "Jesu, mercy!"'[184] In the last few days, as memories of family and childhood reclaimed him, he turned to the Anglican Prayer Book for comfort.[185] Now taken up with an idealised past, he grieved what he saw as an act of betrayal: 'I have not a doubt that Dr. Newman is quite wrong in taking the Cardinal's hat.'[186] It was his last comment on matters ecclesiastical. Toward the end of the month, the pain was 'almost past expression.'[187] It then receded. He received the Last Rites, and died on Maundy Thursday, 10 April 1879. In the hours before his death the clouds mercifully divided, and he said, 'I am going to heaven.'[188] At the Requiem the following Tuesday, Bishop Bagshawe delivered a warm, if somewhat guarded tribute; afterwards the coffin was taken by train to Lincoln and rested in Canwick Hall overnight. Shortly before nine o'clock the following morning, Richard Sibthorp was buried in Lincoln Old Cemetery, in the valley between Canwick and the city. In accordance with his careful instructions, John Fowler read the burial service of the Church of England.

Fowler then began to record the life of his friend, using the biographical material that Bloxam had assembled for the *Magdalen College Register* and a great number of recent letters. He wrote to Gladstone seeking information about the Oxford days, and telling him of the Anglican burial. The great man was much comforted. 'The circumstance you have mentioned respecting his interment is most soothing, most touching. Doubtless, his peace is now deep, and his light abundant. I can never think of him but as a simple, rare, truly elect soul.'[189] In April 1880, notwithstanding the rigours of an election campaign, he found time to read the biography, noting in his diary how it was, 'singularly adapted . . . to my very peculiar condition.'[190] In thanking the author, he confessed himself pained how a 'most saintly devotion of character' could nevertheless lack 'any proportionate accuracy of perception in . . . some elementary questions of justice and injustice.' Yet the uncongenial politics were 'a scarcely perceptible' drawback, 'so pure, beautiful and holy is the character, and with such grace and natural truthfulness.'[191] Other Anglicans were similarly comforted. Dean Church compared Sibthorp with T. W. Allies: both were 'men of honour and high purpose,' but while Allies grew bitter in controversy, Sibthorp's course, despite 'strange vacillations' was marked by 'patience, sweetness, equity . . .'[192]

Catholics were puzzled,[193] and Anglicans comforted, by Fowler's opinion that at the end the wanderer had returned to the Church of his baptism.[194] This may be doubted. In truth, he had found no 'continuing city,' whether in Canterbury or Rome, Ryde or Nottingham; nor in Lincoln, although in death he wished his body might rest there. As for his spirit, he longed to be with Jesus, not in some awful agony of purgation, and the Book of Common Prayer promised him that 'the souls of the faithful, after they are delivered from the burden of the flesh, are in joy and felicity.'

Bloxam presented a copy of the biography to Newman, who a year later wrote to thank Fowler for including a denial of the assertion in the *Life of Bishop Wilberforce* that in 1841 he had accompanied the convert to Oscott. As regards Sibthorp himself, the Cardinal was less generous than the Prime Minister. 'He had a hundred good and high qualities, was devout, single-minded, and kind hearted, but what spoils him to my mind (may I say it without offence?) is the perpetual, "I, I, I" all through his letters. If he would but forget himself, and cease to remind his readers of his own central position, his letters would be charming. Thus I account for his changes.'[195] Fowler said he could not 'take the least offence . . .

There is no doubt that my venerated friend never got rid of this extreme subjectivity of religious belief with which in early life he had become imbued.'[196] There is a mystery here. Fowler, who visited the old priest during his last illness was moved to write of how suffering brought out 'the pure quality of his gifts and graces: the depth of his humility, his forgetfulness of self, his anxiety for others, his wish to "preach Christ" even to his latest breath.'[197] And this truly is the impression left by the letters. Writing to a relative in December 1877, Sibthorp referred briefly his poor health and 'many little trials,' before immediately adding, 'Enough of this, and of what concerns self. Oh that we may sit more closely at the feet of Jesus, and have His precious Word more deeply engraven within our hearts! I think I want to say, "To me to live is Christ." But it is a conflict.'[198] Naturally introspective, what Evangelicalism gave him was a burning sense of accountability, the eternal significance of each passing hour. Struggling with *Daily Bread,* he wrote, 'I wish to consider nothing that I have as my own. Time, talents – such as they are – intercourse with others by word or letter; – all belong to Him who grants me the use of them, as a steward of His property.'[199]

In July 1877, Sibthorp wrote of a friend, probably his nephew John Heywood Hawkins who had recently died, that 'he had hard cards to play in life.'[200] So did he. Called to holiness he was unable to compromise, unable to hand over responsibility for his soul to another. Struggling to the shore, clinging to the wreckage of a shattered vessel demanded all his courage, all his strength. If his life was a scandal, so to the Jews was the preaching of the Cross. Perhaps Samuel Cooper Scott, who at the end of the century, reflected on the affection in which Richard Sibthorp was held by his parent's generation, can speak for the very many, whose lives he touched. 'In which Communion he died I do not know, and to those who knew the man it mattered very little, for he was good and true, and only wanted perfection too soon. He was disappointed then, but not, surely, now. There was nothing worldly or ambitious about him; he only wanted to know what he ought to do, and, having no definite vision, he went on his way with the refrain always on his lips, "Lead, kindly Light, amid the encircling gloom, Lead thou me on."'[201]

The Sibthorp Family

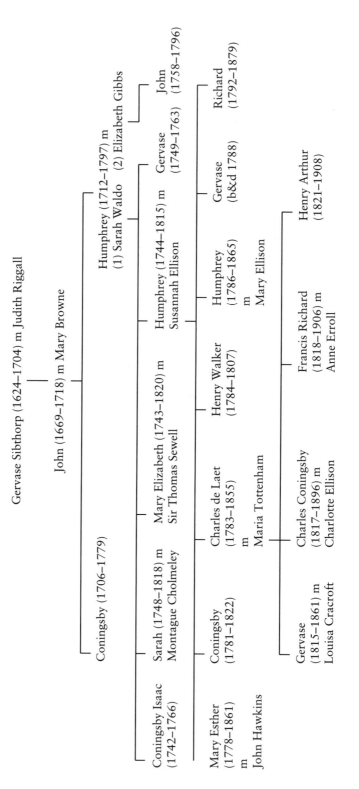

Gervase Sibthorp (1624–1704) m Judith Riggall

John (1669–1718) m Mary Browne

Coningsby (1706–1779)

Humphrey (1712–1797) m
(1) Sarah Waldo   (2) Elizabeth Gibbs

Coningsby Isaac
(1742–1766)

Sarah (1748–1818) m
Montague Cholmeley

Mary Elizabeth (1743–1820) m
Sir Thomas Sewell

Gervase
(1749–1763)

John
(1758–1796)

Mary Esther
(1778–1861)
m
John Hawkins

Coningsby
(1781–1822)

Charles de Laet
(1783–1855)
m
Maria Tottenham

Henry Walker
(1784–1807)

Humphrey (1744–1815) m
Susannah Ellison

Humphrey
(1786–1865)
m
Mary Ellison

Gervase
(b&d 1788)

Richard
(1792–1879)

Gervase
(1815–1861) m
Louisa Cracroft

Charles Coningsby
(1817–1896) m
Charlotte Ellison

Francis Richard
(1818–1906) m
Anne Erroll

Henry Arthur
(1821–1908)

NOTES

Chapter One   *The Sibthorps of Canwick*

1   Noted in Sibthorp family bible, [Sibthorp Papers] 4 Sib 3.

2   'We need not wonder Mr. Editor at the increase in dissenting chapels when the clergy of the Establishment pay so little attention to their duties; and which seem to become heavier as they have become possessed of the loaves and fishes of which this gentleman has caught his net full.' [*Lincoln, Rutland and Stamford Mercury*] *L.R.S.M.*, 22 August 1817.

3   By 33 votes to 8; Mercers' Company, *Acts of Court*, 1818–19.

4   [C.] Sykes, [*The Damascus Road*, in *Two Studies in Virtue*, Collins, London, 1953,] p. 20.

5   A Sibthorp pedigree is included at Appendix 1.

6   J. Bateman, *Great Landowners of Great Britain and Ireland*, University Press, Leicester, 1971 (reprint of 1883 edition), p. 407.

7   [A. R.] Maddison, [*An Account of the Sibthorp Family*, James Williamson, Lincoln, 1896,] p. 27.

8   *Ibid.*, pp. 40, 41.

9   His father wrote to him on March 4, 1768: 'Have I submitted to every Denyal for the Raisment of my Family. . . and suffer you to eclipse the Credit of your Family, and see an Estate delivered down by our Ancestry increased even in Age of Dissipation by the greatest Virtue, decent Frugality the Mother of Generosity, shuffled away in the Hands of Gamblers?' *Ibid.*, pp. 57–58.

10   [Sir F. Hill,] *Georgian Lincoln*, [Cambridge University Press, Cambridge, 1966,] pp. 129, 137.

11   J. A. S. L. Leighton-Boyce, *Smiths the Bankers, 1658–1958*, National Provincial Bank, London, 1958, p. 139, see *Georgian Lincoln*, p. 137. For Abel Smith see [D.] Newsome, [*The Parting of Friends*, John Murray, London, 1966,] pp. 22, 120, 121. Smith's granddaughter married John Sargent, rector of Lavington, which was close to Bignor Park where lived Mrs. Hawkins, Richard Sibthorp's sister.

12   The son of Elizabeth Gibbs.

13   2 Sib 4/3.

14   Maddison (pp. 68–69) sympathises with Dr Sibthorp. 'Miss Ellison did not

bring at once a large fortune with her, neither was there any prospect of one, for she had at least three brothers living, which would render it improbable that she would ever become the heiress of her family.' The Ellison family had not then attained to the great wealth it ultimately acquired.

15   *Ibid.*, p. 28.

16   Quoted by C. Webster in L. S. Sutherland & L. G. Mitchell, *The History of the University of Oxford*, 1986, Vol. V, *The Eighteenth Century*, Clarendon Press, Oxford, p. 720. Smith, who edited John Sibthorp's *Flora Graeca*, may have been a little harsh on Humphrey who corresponded with the Swiss polymath, Albrecht von Haller, and in 1754, was appointed a member of the Russian Academy of Sciences. Sir Joseph Banks, a gentleman commoner at Christ Church finding in December 1760, 'that no lectures were given in botany, he sought and obtained from the professor, permission to procure a teacher to be paid for by the students'. [Sir L. Stephen, *Dictionary of National Biography*, Oxford University Press, Oxford, 1963–64 (reprint of first edition 1897–1898),] *D.N.B.*, Vol. II, pp. 1049–53, article by B. D. Jackson.

17   A. Chalmers, *The General Biographical Dictionary*, J. Nicholson, London, 1816, p. 495.

18   [J.] Fowler, [*Richard Waldo Sibthorp, A Biography, Told Chiefly in his Own Correspondence*, W. Skeffington & Son, London, 1880,] p. 7. For Canwick Hall library catalogues for 1800, 1806, and 1807, see Sib. 1/1, 1/2, 1/11.

19   'On 27 April 1804, Turner brought to a view of the Royal Academy "Coll. Sibsthorpe."' S. Whittingham, 'Turner's Lincolnshire Connections: Prospects, Progeny and Politics,' *Lincolnshire History and Archaeology*, 29 (1994), pp. 39–44.

20   Following Charles Sibthorp's death, Christie and Mason auctioned his 'Choice Collection of Works of Art and Vertu' (9–14 April, 1856.) D. & J. Mills, M. J. Trott, ['New Light on Charles de Laet Waldo Sibthorp,' *Lincolnshire Journal of History and Archaeology*, 36 (2001),] pp. 31, 32.

21   Davies Gilbert, P.R.S., quoted in *Gentleman's Magazine*, N.S. 16 (1841), p. 322.

22   John Hawkins was the uncle of Edward John Trelawny. Born a month after Richard Sibthorp, Trelawny was the intimate companion of Shelley and Byron, and living until 1881 was venerated as the last survivor of the great age of Romanticism. See D. Crane, *Lord Byron's Jackal*, HarperCollins, London, 1999. A Hawkins pedigree is included in F. Steer, *I Am My Dear Sir*, West Sussex County Council, Chichester, 1958.

23   Maddison, pp. 21–22. If John Sibthorp had Catholic sympathies, they were well disguised. In July 1710, he joined a group of Lincolnshire gentlemen who expressed their determination to, 'Deliver our Constitution entire to the most serene House of Hanover.' (*Ibid.*, p. 23.)

24   [H. D.] Beste, [*A Sermon on Priestly Absolution, Third Edition with Notes and Other Autobiographical Writings, by J. Richard Digby Beste*, Longmans, London, 1874,] pp. 173, 174.

25   Sib. 2/4/1.

26   W. M. Honnybun, *Register of Poor Clare Nuns at Gosfield*, Catholic Record Society, *Miscellanea* IX, 1914, pp. 25–27.

27   Willson E. J., *The history of Lincoln: containing an account of the antiqui-*

ties, edifices, trade and customs of that ancient city; an introductory sketch of the county; and a description of the Cathedral to which is added an appendix comprising the Charter, and a list of mayors and sheriffs, Drury and Sons, Lincoln, 1816, p. 153.

28 [R. E. Leary,] *The Date Book for Lincoln [and Neighbourhood from the Earliest Times to the Present*, R. E. Leary, Lincoln, 1865], p. 231.

29 Maddison, p. 72.

30 In Wexford, the rising had 'an essentially religious character . . . the rebels . . . regarded Protestants in general as their enemies, to be attacked, plundered and even slaughtered, simply for being Protestants.' J. C. Beckett, *The Making of Modern Ireland*, Faber and Faber, London, 1966, p. 263.

31 3 December 1798, 2 Sib. 5/6.

32 See Canning's letter to him, 26 April 1803, 2 Sib 4/134 and R. G. Thorne, *The House of Commons 1790–1820,* (vol. V, Q-Y), Secker & Warburg, London, 1986, p. 173.

33 Letter undated (September 1804), 3 Sib 1/15.

34 Opposing Ewart's Public Libraries Bill in 1851. T. Kelly, *A History of Public Libraries in Great Britain*, Library Association, London, 1977, p. 14.

35 27 April 1812, [Cholmeley Papers] C.P.

36 *Archivists' Report, No. 22, 1 April 1970 – 23 March 1971*, Lincolnshire Archives Committee, 1971, p. 46.

37 In 1802, Wilberforce wrote questioning the propriety of his again addressing Lord St Vincent. (2 Sib. 4/101.) Three years later Henry queried the result of his father's interview with the Prime Minister (17 July 1805, Sib. 2/ 4/36) and after a few weeks wrote again, suggesting alternative action 'should Billy Pitt forget his promise which these great men have a habit of doing.' (1 September 1805, Sib. 2/4/38.)

38 *The Date Book for Lincoln*, p. 307; Maddison, p. 83. Humphrey died on 4 November 1865.

39 Fowler, p. 8

40 Undated (probably summer, 1801), [Hawkins Papers] H.P. J3/7/1376

41 8 February 1821, [Church Missionary Society, Special Collection, General Secretary's Correspondence] C.M.S. (S.C.)G./A.C.3.

42 Fowler, p. 246. The game was called 'Stags free round the benches.'

43 9 April 1800, scene described in *The Date Book for Lincoln*, p. 231. See also *The Sun*, 21 April 1800, and *Georgian Lincoln*, p. 220.

44 Maddison, p. 75.

45 In the chapel of the Lincoln Bede Houses built in 1854.

46 His daughter Sarah Cholmeley wrote to him a few weeks before his death: 'we are much obliged by your offer of providing for one of our sons in a mercantile line, but we have none to bring up in that profession. Therefore if what you thought of bestowing on them in Trade, with your approbation, you can please to bestow on them in any other branch will be equally acceptable.' (12 July 1797, 2 Sib. 4/41.) No descendant fulfilled the conditions, and after lengthy proceedings in Chancery, the money went to Magdalen College.

47 The letter is headed, 'Lincoln, July' and was written either in 1800 or 1801, H.P. J3/3/252. Hawkins married Mary Sibthorp in August 1801.

48 His opponents sang: 'The wearied Member's gone to bed/Empty purse and

empty head/Deficient strength and failing voice . . .' *Georgian Lincoln*, pp. 220,221.

49   [M. C.] Jones, [*Notes Respecting the Family of Waldo*, printed for private circulation, n.d.,] p. 16.

50   His father and two elder brothers, 'presided over estates bound up in a web of debt and interrelated mortgages.' D. & J. Mills, M. J. Trott, p. 36.

51   Charges in his favour were; marriage settlement of Col. Humphrey (1777) £1500, will of Col. Humphrey (1815) £8000, will of Coningsby (1822) £8000. *Ibid.*, p. 35.

52   Twenty years after his mother's death Richard was still receiving payments from the estate. See letter dated 11 March 1845 [Burton Scorer papers] B.S. 12/3/1/3/230.

53   22 June 1804, Sib. 2/3; see Jones, p. 19.

54   Negotiations over the will demonstrated Humphrey Sibthorp's hard-headedness. On 9 December 1842, the Rev. Robert Cholmeley (the only surviving son of Sarah Sibthorp) wrote to his son Montague: 'Your sisters have told you of old Mrs. Waldo's death by which I become heir to a share of her husband's money. It is in Chancery. . . whether six or seven are entitled to the money . . . Humphrey Sibthorpe who under the Will of Mr Waldo is entitled to the Landed property thinks he has a claim also to a share of the Money. We think he has no right to both and so we shall get some Chancery Judge to settle the dispute.' [G. H.] Cholmeley, [*Letters and Papers of the Cholmeleys from Wainfleet*, Lincoln Record Society, Hereford, 1964,] p. 78.

55   Letter to John Hawkins, 7 October 1820, H.P. J3/5/593.

56   Letter, 18 December 1820, C.P.

57   *The Times*, 14 November 1821.

58   D. & J. Mills, *Interim Report on the Sibthorp Estates*, privately circulated, 1998, p. 3.

59   'Letter to a relative' 1871, Fowler, p. 20.

60   [R. W. Sibthorp,] *Daily Bread*, [1879,] p. 676.

61   The *Lincolnshire Chronicle* (15 April 1879) printed this anecdote from an unnamed source. 'I can give you the reason for the Reverend Gentleman's attachment to the Roman Church. His father, although always a staunch Protestant, was very kind to French Roman Catholic priests who were so mercilessly driven into exile in the Great Revolution of 1793 and although he had placed the Reverend Canon at a tender age with one of them it was with a strict understanding that his religious tenets were not to be interfered with. But the Colonel calling one morning found his son at prayer in the Oratory, in which was a silver crucifix, and in consequence of this breach of trust took his son away with him. Meeting, when he came out his friend William Wilberforce, ex-MP for Hull he told him of the circumstances and Wilberforce made this prophetic reply. "Depend upon it Sibthorp, that boy will one day become a Roman Catholic."'

62   Beste, pp. 174–6, 216–18.

63   *Ibid.*, p. 4.

64   Bishop Milner's journal, entry for 20 October.

65   Fowler, p. 10

66   [W. T.] Southerwood, [*The Convict's Friend*, Stella Maris Books, Tasmania, 1989,] p. 4.

67 J. Gillow, *A Literary and Biographical History, or Bibliographical Dictionary of the English Catholics, from the breach with Rome, in 1534, to the Present Time*, Burnt Franklin, New York, n.d. (first edition, 1881–1903), Vol. IV, pp. 496–500. In 1824, William Eusebius Andrews noted that the Protestant sick in Bloxwich and Walsall 'never think of sending for their parson when death makes his appearance, but for the Catholic pastor (Martyn) who prepares them in the best manner as time and circumstances will permit to appear before their God.' G. Every, 'The Catholic Community in Walsall 1720–1824,' *Recusant History* 19, 1988, p. 325. Martyn left Louth in July 1807 and was replaced by an émigré priest.

68 [R. W. Sibthorp,] *Some Answer to the Enquiry 'Why are you Become a Catholic?' [In a letter to a Friend*, 1842], pp. 4, 5.

69 He 'played the fool' (Fowler, p. 12) perhaps a compensation for shyness?

70 Canwick, 27 February 1810, [Magdalen College Archive] M.C.A. Ms. 465, [*The Sibthorp Correspondence.*] Wainfleet was the birthplace of the College's founder.

71 Bath, 1 September 1810, *ibid.*

72 Fowler, p. 20.

73 In Oxford, Sibthorp was remembered as having been a Catholic. Peter le Page Renouf wrote to his father in 1841, 'When he came here first to reside as undergraduate he was a Roman Catholic. I don't know whether he had any scruples. . ..' [K. J.] Cathcart, [*The Letters of Peter le Page Renouf, 1822–1897, Vol. I, Pembroke College Oxford, 1842–1846, St. Mary's College, Oscott, 1842–1846*, University College Dublin Press, Dublin, 2002,] Vol. 1, p. 76.

74 Kiddington, where Rock had been since 1788, was just a few miles from Oxford and Holton.

75 Fowler, pp. 13,14.

76 Letters to Bloxam, 19 April and 19 June 1875; Fowler, pp. 282–84. Bloxam explained how Biddulph gave the game away. 'Mr. Sibthorp's father entreated him to go to him, merely to ascertain, as he said, that all was well. Biddulph did so, but was secretly followed by a detective and his brother Coningsby, who brought him back to his father.' [J. R.] Bloxam, [*A Register of the Presidents, Fellows and Demies of St. Mary Magdalen College, Oxford*, 1881, James Parker, Oxford Vol. VI.,] p. 212.

77 This sentence is omitted in Bloxam's transcription of the letter (*ibid.*, p. 213).

78 Sudbrooke Holme, 7 November 1811, M.C.A. Ms. 465 (Canwick Hall was being rebuilt and Sibthorp was staying with the Ellisons.) 'During the consternation caused in the household by his flight, a search was made among his miscellaneous properties'; perhaps this was when Rock's letter was found. Fowler, p. 14.

79 *Ibid.*

80 [*Observations on Richard Waldo Sibthorp's 'Answer to the Enquiry "Why are you become a Catholic?"' by A*] Spectator, [Groombridge, London 1842,] p. 23.

81 Beste, p. 220.

82 7 November 1811, M.C.A. Ms. 465.

83 Beste, p. 217; see also H. D. Beste, *Four Years in France or a Narrative of an English Family's Residence there During that Period. Preceded by Some*

Account of the Conversion of the Author to the Catholic Faith, Henry Colburn, London, 1826, p. 60.

84 Paris, Archives des Affaires Etrangeres, Vol. 616 fo. 230 (I am grateful to Dom Aidan Bellenger for this reference).

85 Letter to Routh, Sudbrooke Holme, 15 January, M.C.A. Ms. 465.

86 Vicarage House Eltham, 30 January 1812, *ibid.*

87 *Ibid.*

88 Sudbrooke Holme, 1 April 1812, M.C.A. Ms. 465.

89 In 1813 Collins was Public Examiner and awarded firsts to Hampden and Arnold. In 1815, he was presented to the rectory of Barningham in the North Riding. (Obituary in *Yorkshire Post and Leeds Intelligencer*, 9 May 1870) His son Henry was received as a Roman Catholic at Grace Dieu in 1857 and became a Cistercian at Mount St Bernard in 1861, and was the spiritual director of Mrs. Phillipps de Lisle. (Pawley M., *Faith & Family – the Life and Circle of Ambrose Phillipps de Lisle*, Canterbury Press, Norwich, 1993, pp. 287, 417.)

90 Letter to her sister, Mrs. Cholmeley, C.P.

91 9 April 1816, Bloxam p. 216.

92 Emeris Papers, Em. 41/6.

93 *Some Answer to the Enquiry 'Why are you Become a Catholic?'* p. 5

94 Farnham was an Irish landowner, a zealous Protestant, who sought to convert his Catholic tenants.

95 [T.] Pinney [(ed.), *The Letters of Thomas Babington Macaulay*, Cambridge University Press, Cambridge, 1974], Vol. 1, pp. 218, 219.

96 *Langhton Priory – A Novel in Four Volumes by Gabrielli*, Minerva Press, London, 1809, Vol. IV, pp. 333, 334, 339.

97 *Second Homily for Whitsunday.*

98 [E. S.] Purcell [& E. de Lisle, *Life and Letters of Ambrose Phillipps de Lisle*, Macmillan, London, 1900], Vol. I, p. 23.

99 [T.] Newton, [Dissertations on the Prophecies which have Remarkably been Fulfilled and at this Time are Fulfilling in the World, (Revised by Rev W. S. Dobson,) Scott & Webster, London, n.d. (1754),] p. 416. 'The Thessalonians, from some expression in the former epistle, were alarmed as if the end of the world was at hand, and Christ was coming to judgement. The apostle, to correct their mistakes and dissipate their fears, assures them that the coming of Christ will not be yet awhile: there will be first a great apostasy or defection of Christians from the true faith and worship. This apostasy all the concurrent marks and characters will justify us in charging upon the Church of Rome.' (p. 402.)

100 From Rev. 11: 2,3 and 12: 6,14; see also Dan. 7: 25.

101 Newton, pp. 576, 617.

102 Cholmeley, p. 6. In 1813, Robert Chomeley married Maria Miller, Maitland's wife's sister.

103 February 1814, N.S. 1, pp. 127–140.

104 The respected Anglican commentator, G. S. Faber concurred, see: *A Dissertation on the Prophecies that have been Fulfilled or will Hereafter be Fulfilled*, F. C. & J. Rivington, London, 1810.

105 [Capt. Maitland, RA,] *A Brief and Connected View of Prophecy [being an Exposition of the 2ⁿᵈ, 7ᵗʰ and 8ᵗʰ Chapters of the Prophecy of Daniel together*

with the 16th Chapter of the Revelation to which are added some Observations Respecting the Period and Manner of the Restoration of the Jews, J. Hatchard, London, 1814], pp. 5, 21.

106 'Richard Sibthorp' in *D.N.B.*, Vol. XVIII, pp. 190, 191 (article by T. Cooper).

107 *Some Answer to the Enquiry 'Why are you Become a Catholic?'* p. 5.

108 Letter to Sarah Cholmeley, undated but probably June 1813 (C.P.) John Natt, incumbent at St Giles from 1809 to 1828, made it a centre for Evangelical teaching. Yeadon was also an Evangelical.

109 T. Barclay, *Light – A Sermon Preached in the Parish Church of Backwell Somerset on Sunday afternoon December 4 1842 on the Occasion of the death of the Rev. Zachariah Henry Biddulph, BD*, Hamilton Adams, London, 1843, pp. 9–12.

110 [C.] Hole, [*The Life of the Reverend and Venerable William Whitmarsh Phelps MA*, Hatchards, London, 1871,] Vol. 1, pp. 122, 123.

111 'Another strand consisted of Evangelicals in the Church of England and their associates. Few were Methodist converts or even touched by Calvinistic Methodism.' D. W. Bebbington, *Evangelicalism in Modern Britain: A History from the 1730s to the 1980s*, Hyman, London, 1989, p. 30.

112 Later re-named Stoke Rochford.

113 'The honoured spiritual father of Dr. Ford was John Wesley.' [V.] Wing, [*Reminiscences of Rev. Thomas Ford, LLD Formerly Vicar of Melton Mowbray*, William Darley, Melton Mowbray, 1864,] p. 23.

114 [N.] Curnock, [*The Journal of the Rev. John Wesley, A. M.*, Standard Edition, Charles Kelly, London, n.d.,] Vol. VI. p. 69. When away from his parish Ford would preach for the Methodists. He remained at Melton until 1820. (Wing pp. 22, 24.)

115 On 14 August 1782, adding: 'You would have been very welcome at our Conference. Mr. Pugh and Mr. Dodwell were present at it; and I believe are more determined than ever to spend their whole strength in saving their own souls, and them that hear them.' *The Works of the Rev. John Wesley A.M.*, Vol. XII, Wesleyan Conference Office, London, 1872, p. 508

116 Curnock, Vol. VI., pp. 327, 328.

117 B. Biggs, 'Two Lincolnshire "Methodist" Parsons', *Lincolnshire Journal of Methodist History*, 5, 4 (1995), p. 52. Pugh's ministry ended in 1799.

118 [T.] Cocking, [*The History of Wesleyan Methodism in Grantham and its Vicinity*, Simpkin, Marshall & Co., London 1836,] pp. 143, 144, 293.

119 Vol. XXX, pp. 295–347.

120 Vol. XXXVI (1813), pp. 822–30.

121 November 13, 1809, [Methodist Archives,] P.L.P. 34/35/1.

122 *Memoirs of the Life of the Rev. Peard Dickinson*, quoted in Cocking, pp. 203, 204.

123 Another notable curate was Daniel Corrie. At Stoke Rochford from 1802 to 1806; he went to India as a chaplain and became the first Bishop of Madras. Visiting England in 1815, he recorded a visit to Easton Hall. A. Macnaghten, *Daniel Corrie, His Family and Friends*, Johnson, London 1969, p. 68.

124 [A.] Stevens, [*The History of the Religious Movement of the Eighteenth Century called Methodism*, William Nicholls, London, n.d.,] p. 323.

125 [W. T.] Gidney, [*The History of the London Society for Promoting*

Christianity amongst the Jews, from 1803 to 1908, L.S.P.C.J., London, 1908,] p. 52. Cholmeley was made a baronet in 1806; his son, was a firm Anglican but in 1835 gifted land at Colsterworth to the Methodists for the construction of a chapel. J. Clarke & C. Anderson, *Methodism in the Countryside*, privately published, 1981, p. 165.

126 To Mrs. Miller, October 4, 1813; Cholmeley, p. 6.

127 *Ibid.*, p. 15.

128 In 1827 Lincolnshire ranked third (after Cornwall and Yorkshire) in the proportion of its population who were Wesleyan Methodists (5%). J. Stephens, *Chronicles of Wesleyan Methodism*, John Stephens, London, 1827, Vol. II, p. 249.

129 At Marston, a few miles north of Easton, the rector George Thorold was a committed Evangelical. He was the grandson of Sir John Thorold, an early friend of John Wesley.

130 Cocking, p. 184.

131 To Bloxam, 29 January 1845, [Ollard Papers] O.P. XIX.

132 15 October 1864; Fowler, p. 152.

133 He wrote in his journal on 3 July 1788: 'Thence we went to Raithby; an earthly paradise!' Curnock, Vol. VII, p. 412.

134 'Mr. Brackenbury had a considerable library, the sight of which set my soul on fire.' T. Jackson, *Recollection of My Own Life and Times (Edited by Rev. B. Frankland,)* Wesleyan Conference Office, London, 1873, p. 77.

135 Stevens, p. 505.

136 14 May 1845, O.P. XIX. Mrs Brackenbury was a generous supporter of Methodist causes, and in 1838 helped to fund the mission to Fiji. A. Birtwhistle, *In His Armour*, Cargate Press, London, 1954, p. 57. Family members remain unimpressed; C. E. Brackenbury described her as 'ungenerous, though deeply religious'. *The Brackenbury Memorial Lecture, 2 July 1983: The Brackenburys of Lincolnshire – A Sketch for a Portrait of a Lincolnshire Family*, The Society for Lincolnshire History & Archaeology, Lincoln, 1983, p. 9.

137 Letter from John to Sarah Cholmeley, June 1813, C.P.

138 Canwick, 8 July 1818, M.C.A. Ms. 465.

139 Sibthorp told his sister that he had caught a cold in the chapel of Buckden Palace, and that he was not impressed by Tomline who 'had not the civility to ask us to dinner . . . indeed a more uncouth being I never saw. I like him neither as a Bishop or a gentleman'. Letter dated 21 December 1815, [Hunt Collection] H.C.

140 Fowler, pp. 22–23.

141 15 April 1879.

142 [A] Watmough, [*A History of Methodism in the Neighbourhood and City of Lincoln*, Mason, London, 1829,] pp. 60–61.

143 *Ibid.*, p. 61.

144 G. Barratt, *Recollections of Methodism and Methodists in the City of Lincoln*, Charles Akrill, Lincoln, 1866, p. 20.

145 Fowler, pp. 25, 26.

146 G. Tomline, *A Charge Delivered to the Clergy of the Diocese of Lincoln at the Triennial Visitation of that Diocese, in May, June, July 1812*, F. C. & J. Rivington, London, 1813, p. 8.

147 26 June 1790. 'And is it a Christian, yea a Protestant Bishop, that so persecutes his own flock? I say, *persecutes*, for it is persecution to all intents and purposes.' H. Moore, *The Life of the Rev. John Wesley, AM*, John Kershaw, London, 1825, Vol. II, p. 385.

148 According to Wilberforce, Pitt's prejudice against Evangelicals 'arose out of the confidence he reposed in the Bishop of Lincoln' (who had been his tutor). R. I. & S. Wilberforce, *The Life of William Wilberforce*, Murray, London, 1838, Vol. II, p. 364.

149 R. F. Scott, *Admissions to St. John's College, Cambridge*, Cambridge University Press, Cambridge, 1931, Part IV, p. 163.

150 *L.R.S.M.*, 14 July 1815.

151 *Remarks upon that part of the Bishop of Lincoln's late charge to the Clergy of his Diocese relative to the Bible Society and to intercourse of Churchmen with Dissenters*, Longmans, Hurst, Rees, Orme & Browne, London, 1815, p. 8.

152 According to Coningsby's obituary in the *Gentleman's Magazine* 92 (1822), p. 281: 'He was a true friend also to the doctrines and disciplines of the Church of England and those inroads which its pretended friends, but in reality its worst enemies are perpetually making upon it, were always discountenanced by him.' It is unclear why Ford K. Brown includes him among the 'Saints' in the Parliament of 1818. [F. K.] Brown, [*Fathers of the Victorians*, Cambridge University Press, Cambridge, 1961,] p. 271n.

153 *L.R.S.M.*, 29 November 1816. One city clergyman was present: 'The Rev. Mr. Hett . . . censured in strong terms the expression, and said that till these words were spoken he had been much gratified by what he had heard, and that he (and his brethren) were not hostile to the Society.'

154 Letter to a newspaper regarding Sibthorp's obituary included among the biographical material assembled by J. R. Bloxam, M.C.A. Ms. 492, (*Rev. R. W. Sibthorp*.) The Toleration Act (1812) made it illegal for more than twenty persons other than immediate family to meet for religious worship in any building but a consecrated church or licensed dissenting chapel.

155 Canwick, 7 August 1817, M.C.A. Ms. 465.

156 W. Dixon, *History of Freemasonry in Lincolnshire: being a record of all extinct and existing lodges, chapters, &c.; a century of the working of Provincial Grand Lodge and the Witham Lodge; together with biographical notices of Provincial Grand Masters and other eminent masons of the county. With an introduction by W.J.Hughan*, James Williamson, Lincoln, 1894, p. 185.

157 Faculty Book 4, 127a, 135a, L.A.O. See J. Towers, *An Excursion into Waddington's History – Methodism*, printed for the author, Waddington, 1998, p. 8.

158 'Every incumbent must be presented . . . The presentee may be refused by the bishop. . ..' J. M. Dale, *Clergyman's Legal Handbook & Church Warden's Guide*, Seeley, Jackson & Halliday, London, 1881, pp. 22, 23.

159 Attesting to his orthodoxy, it was signed by twelve clergymen, endorsed by the Archbishop of York, and dated 'June 19th 1818'. M.C.A. Ms. 465.

Chapter Two   *The Tents of Kedar*

1   I. Milner, Practical Sermons by the late Rev. Joseph Milner M. A., Master of the Grammar School and Vicar of Holy Trinity Church in Kingston upon Hull. To which is prefixed an account of the Life and Character of the Author, E. Matthews, London, 1804, pp. i–lxviii.

2   [J.] King, [*Memoir of the Reverend Thomas Dykes, Incumbent of St John's Church, Hull*, Seeley, London, 1849,] p. 96.

3   On 20 April, he was at St. Mary's, Beverley. *L.R.S.M.*, 25 April 1817.

4   Hole, p. 154.

5   *L.R.S.M.*, 17 October & 19 December 1817, 9 January 1818.

6   W. Knight, *The Christian Pastor's Removal from Earth to Heaven. A Sermon Preached at St John's Church Hull on Sunday evening August 29, 1847 on the Occasion of the death of the Rev. Thomas Dykes, Incumbent Minister of that Church*, John Hutchinson, Hull, 1847, p. 21.

7   *Commonplace Book of John Scott.*

8   T. Scott, *Remarks on the 'Refutation of Calvinism' by G. Tomline, Bishop of Lincoln*, L. B. Seeley, London, 1811.

9   *Commonplace Book of John Scott.*

10   [R. W. Sibthorp,] *A Sermon, Preached at St. John's Church, Hull [on Tuesday evening, May 19, 1818. At the Close of a Temporary Residence in that Town*, Topping and Dawson, Hull, 1818], pp. 5, 7, 8, 9.

11   Letter to James Hervey, 15 October 1756; (J. Telford, *The Letters of John Wesley AM, Sometime Fellow of Lincoln College, Oxford*, Epworth Press, London, 1931, Vol. III, p. 372.)

12   J. Scott, *An Inquiry into the effects of Baptism, according to the Sense of Holy Scripture, and the Church of England in Answer to the Rev. Dr. Mant's Tracts on Regeneration and Conversion*, L. B. Seeley, London, 1815. See W. J. C. Ervine, *Doctrine and Diplomacy*, unpublished PhD thesis, Cambridge University, 1979, p. 65.

13   In 1817, Scott had published *The Principles of 'An Enquiry into the effect of Baptism' defended against the animadversions of the Rev. Richard Laurence LL.D.* (L. B. Seeley, London.)

14   Along with Bishop Randolph, Tomline had revised the notes submitted by D'Oyley and Mant for the *Family Bible* published by S.P.C.K. in 1814.

15   A. C. Oustler, *The Works of John Wesley*, Vol. II, Abingdon Press, Nashville 1985, pp. 410–11(Sermon 57, *On the Fall of Man.*) See C. W. Williams, *John Wesley's Theology Today*, Epworth, London, 1960, p. 55.

16   Romans 8: 14.

17   *A Sermon preached at St. John's Church, Hull*, pp. 10, 11, 12, 17, 20, 21; (italics in the original).

18   J. Scott, *Extracts from Letters Written to Various Friends during the Progress of his Last Illness*, printed for private circulation, Hull, 1834, pp. 4, 5.

19   Samuel King Scott, the architect's brother, see Sir George Gilbert Scott, *Personal and Professional Recollections*, Paul Watkins, Stamford, 1995 (first edition 1879), pp. 241, 243.

20   Fowler, p. 28. Dr. and Mrs. Bodley retired to Brighton. Of their children, William Hamilton entered the Anglican ministry and converted to Rome in 1851; George Frederick was the celebrated church architect.

21 In 1829, King, p. 131.
22 'a great event in Hull' [S. Cooper Scott,] *Things That Were*, [Christophers, London, 1923,] p. 96. [T. R.] Birks, [*Memoir of Rev. Edward Bickersteth, late Rector of Watton, Herts*, 1852,] Vol. 1, p. 323.
23 Although it was an Anglican Society, Tomline would not countenance it, and in 1814 gave a very frosty response to a request that he would ordain its missionary candidates. C. Hole, *The Early History of the Church Missionary Society Society for Asia and the East to the end of A.D. 1814*, Church Missionary Society, London, 1896, pp. 373, 464.
24 Story Street, Hull, 27 February 1818, C.M.S. (S.C.)G./A.C.3.
25 *Report of Lincoln Association of the Church Missionary Society*, July 1823. On 22 February 1822, Sibthorp wrote to Bickersteth that he was anxious 'to learn something of my namesake at Regent's Town and to do something privately for his welfare.' C.M.S. (S.C.)G./A.C.3.
26 *Doncaster Chronicle*, 22 May 1818.
27 3 October 1818, C.P.
28 22 May 1818, C.M.S. (S.C.)G./A.C.3.
29 To Sarah Cholmeley, 3 October 1818, C.P.
30 Birks, Vol. 1, p. 329.
31 *Ibid.*, p. 330.
32 Brown, p. 495.
33 H. Fortescue, *Diary, March 1811 – June 1818*. In 1817, the incumbent T. T. Roe, a local magistrate had accepted the near-by living of Bennington. Tattershall itself was worth £70 p.a. not enough to support a curate with a family. (See Sibthorp's letter to his sister, 10 November 1824, H.C.)
34 [M. A.] Pickworth, [*A History of Tattershall, Lincolnshire, with its Collegiate Church & Castle*, Akrill, Ruddock & Keyworth, Lincoln, 1891,] p. 101.
35 J. Harvey, *Gothic England*, Batsford, London, 1947, p. 102.
36 Cromwell died before the work was completed, and William Waynflete, the founder of Magdalen College assumed responsibility.
37 A fragment of a fifteenth-century brick building survives in the village, and is known as Tattershall Old College. The Tudor composer, John Taverner, was a chorister here and Master of the Choristers in 1524.
38 In 1792, troops were called out to suppress a riot by navvies working on the Bain navigation to Horncastle. Pickworth, p. 100.
39 Pickworth, p. 99.
40 *L.R.S.M.*, 12 June 1818.
41 Letter to Bickersteth, 18 November 1818, C.M.S. (S.C.)G./A.C.3.
42 *Ibid.*, 26 January, 1819.
43 Letter to Sarah Cholmeley, 3 October 1818, C.P.
44 [R. W. Sibthorp,] *An Address to the Inhabitants of Tattershall* [*in Lincolnshire, on entering upon the Living of the Parish*, 1818.] The *Advertisement*, is dated Hull, 21 May 1818.
45 *Ibid.*, pp. 9, 11, 12.
46 J. Obelkevich, *Religion and Rural Society: South Lindsey 1825–1875*, Clarendon Press, Oxford, 1976, p. 127. Obelkevich refers to an attack on private baptism by Archdeacon Bayley in 1826, but says that it was still common thirty years later (p. 128).

47   *An Address to the Inhabitants of Tattershall*, pp. 17, 18.

48   R. W. Sibthorp, *A Sermon Preached in St John's Church, Hull, on Tuesday Evening, June 26, 1821 for the Benefit of the Church of England Sunday School Association*, 1821, p. 26.

49   [F. M.] Yglesias, ['Richard Waldo Sibthorp at Tattershall, 1818–1825,' *Lincoln Diocesan Magazine*, Vol. XIV, No. VIII, August 1948.] Yglesias later became the incumbent and worked closely with Lord Curzon (who purchased the estate from Fortescue) in the restoration of Tattershall Castle.

50   *L.R.S.M.*, 16 August 1822.

51   *An Address to the inhabitants of Tattershall*, pp. 19, 20, 21.

52   26 January 1819, C.M.S. (S.C.) G/A.C.3.

53   Fowler, p. 29.

54   *An Address to the inhabitants of Tattershall*, p. 4.

55   In the 1788 preface he wrote, 'I thank God, I have not yet seen cause to alter my sentiments on any point . . .' J. Wesley, *Sermons on Several Occasions, With a Life of the Author by the Rev. John Beecham*, John Mason, London 1838, Vol. III, Sermon CI, pp. 140–41.

56   Yglesias.

57   A correspondent to *Notes and Queries* (Seventh Series, Vol. 1, p. 31) placed Neale in Hull in 1824, and his novel, *Living and Dead*, contains references to the Rev. John Scott, implying personal acquaintance.

58   The day after she died, he wrote: 'I can safely say that not a day has passed for years in which she has not been in my thoughts. With her every place was pleasant and without her all seemed to be unsatisfactory and void.' Letter to J Hawkins, 13 May 1826.

59   Letter to Bloxam, 12 March 1844, OLL XIX.

60   *Morning Herald*, 21 November 1843.

61   After a visit to Canwick in 1857, Anderson wrote: 'it is quite delightful to see how the young Sibthorps revere their Uncle Richard, and the pleasant terms they are on. He is quite charming.' (Wilberforce Mss., 8 November, 1857. Quoted in [Sir Francis Hill,] *Victorian Lincoln* [Cambridge University Press, Cambridge, 1974], p. 175.)

62   [E.] Neale, [*The Bishop's Daughter*, W. H. Dalton, London, 1842,] pp. 285, 196, 191.

63   R. W. Sibthorp, *A Second Address to the Inhabitants of Tattershall in Lincolnshire, Upon the Commencement of a New Year*, 1819, p. 8.

64   *Ibid.*, pp. 13, 18–19

65   Neale, pp. 195, 285.

66   *Ibid.*, p. 286.

67   Perowne was unable to reach Tattershall in time and the church was closed on Sunday, 18 July. He sailed to Bengal the following year, becoming Principal of the C.M.S. schools in Burdwan, returned in 1827, and from 1835 to 1863, was incumbent of St John's, Maddermarket, Norwich. He had three distinguished sons: J. J. S. Perowne, Bishop of Worcester, E. H. Perowne, Master of Corpus Christi, Cambridge and T. T. Perowne, Archdeacon of Norwich.

68   British and Foreign Bible Society, (B.F.B.S.) Home Correspondence – Inwards (H.C.-I.,) 7 April 1820.

69   Cotterill is remembered as a hymnodist. 'Some members of St Paul's

resenting Cotterill's evangelicalism, argued that hymn singing was illegal in the Church of England and arraigned him before the Diocesan Court of York. The case more or less legalised hymn singing. . .' (Article by J. S. Andrews in [D. M.] Lewis, [Blackwell *Dictionary of Evangelical Biography*, Blackwell, Oxford, 1995,] Vol. 1, p. 257.)

70 November 16 1820, C.M.S. (S.C.) G/A.C.3.

71 Letter to Bickersteth, 8 February 1821, *ibid.*

72 Goe was appointed in 1817, A. M. Cook, *Boston – Botolphstown*, The Church House, Boston, 1934, p. 111.

73 [H.] Porter, [*Boston, Some of the Happenings in its History, 1800–1835 or Thereabouts*, n. d., unpublished typescript in Lincoln Central Library,] p. 71.

74 The Act provided that all the original subscribers and pew holders should become freemen of the borough, or at least entitled to a freehold vote. After the Reform Act of 1832, the pews were traded for at least £10.

75 Porter, p. 72.

76 8 February 1821, C.M.S. (S.C.)G./A.C.3.

77 M. J. Trott, 'Political Assassination in Lincoln?', *Lincolnshire History & Archaeology*, 34 (1999) pp. 38–40.

78 Although, his sister, Mrs Hawkins spent much time at Canwick from 1821 to 1826, even to the neglect of her own family.

79 6 March 1821, C.M.S. (S.C.)G./A.C.3.

80 One of the greatest linguists of the nineteenth century, Samuel Lee was born in 1783. Raised as a carpenter, he showed remarkable aptitude for language and studied at Cambridge under the aegis of the C.M.S. and Isaac Milner. Graduating in 1818, he was Professor of Hebrew from 1819 to 1848.

81 Lee to Bickersteth, 19 & 21 March 1821, (S.C.)G./A.C.3.

82 Letter to Bickersteth, 22 March 1821, *ibid.*

83 *Cambridge Chronicle and Journal*, 11 May 1821.

84 Letter to Bickersteth, 30 June 1821, C.M.S. (S.C.)G./A.C.3.

85 Letter to Jowett, 31 October 1821, *ibid.*

86 See Thorold's obituary in *Wesleyan Methodist Magazine*, Vol. LXII, April 1839.

87 Gladstone was confirmed by Pelham at Eton (1 February 1827.) He urged the boys to, 'maintain the practice of piety, without luke-warmness, and above all, without enthusiasm'. A. C. Benson, *Fasti Etonienses*, p. 500, quoted in [P. J.] Jagger, [*Gladstone, the Making of a Christian Politician*, Pickwick Publications, Allison Park, Pa., 1991,] p. 83.

88 The subscribers voted on 18 October (Porter p. 73) Conington was appointed on 5 January (L.A.O. P.D. 178/9). The latter was the father of celebrated sons. John (1825–1869) fellow of University College, became Corpus Professor of Latin in 1854. His evangelical conversion, in the same year, according to Mark Pattison made 'shipwreck' of 'the most distinguished scholar whom the University had turned out.' His brother Francis (1828–63) was a fellow of Christ Church and a chemist. Both died at their father's home in Boston.

89 From the Bishop's Secretary, Richard Smith, Buckden House, 17 May 1825, C.M.S. (S.C.)G./A.C.3.

90 May 1825 (office copy) *ibid.*

91 23 May 1825, *ibid.*

92 18 January 1822, *ibid.* It is unclear what happened to Mr Llewellyn but as he is reported addressing Bible Society meetings in the county well into 1823, he may have obtained another curacy.

93 22 February 1822, *ibid.*

94 B.F.B.S. H.C.-I.

95 Sibthorp met Bickersteth at the Lincoln C.M.S. Anniversary in May, but did not write to him again until 4 February 1823.

96 6 June 1822, B.F.B.S. H.C.-I.

97 17 September 1822, *ibid.* A further letter of 30 September illuminates his transport arrangements, 'I think it uncertain whether I can reach Sheffield on Tuesday morning . . . It depends upon the Newark coaches. But you should remember I live at the heart of this county – no public conveyance within many miles but the steam packet which would not carry me to Lincoln till between 4 and 5 in the evening of Monday.'

98 Letter to Bickersteth, 28 April 1824, C.M.S. (S.C.)G./A.C.3.

99 F. Boase, *Modern British Biography*, Frank Cass & Co., London, 1965 (first edition 1892–1921) Vol. 1, col. 1478.

100 C. A. Hulbert, *Annals of the Parish of Almondbury*, Part I, 1882, p. 73, *Supplementary Annals of Almondbury*, Longmans, London, 1882–1885, p. 16. The new curate, Lewis Jones became vicar in 1824, and divided his huge parish into 14 livings, appointing a Welsh Evangelical clergyman to each one. (Article by R. L. Brown, in Lewis, Vol. 1, p. 623.)

101 A. S. Weatherhead, *Holy Trinity, Huddersfield*, 1819–1904, J. Broadbent, Huddersfield, 1913, p. 33.

102 Letter to Bickersteth, 18 September 1823, C.M.S. (S.C.)G./A.C.3. Wilberforce had a high opinion of his brother-in-law, writing of Spooner as 'so truly good a man that it must be useful to be his associate'. Newsome, p. 26.

103 Little is known of his background. In 1817 Robert Milne, 'formerly a private soldier' published in Dublin and dedicated to Robert Peel: *An Attempt to Defend the Church of England against an Attack made on her Fundamental Principles by Thomas Kelly* (printed for the author, Dublin). The British Library catalogue identifies the author with the curate of Louth.

104 *L.R.S.M.*, 5 September 1823.

105 17 December 1823, C.M.S. (S.C.)G./A.C.3. George Gaskin was Secretary of the S.P.C.K. and not well disposed to the C.M.S.

106 10 January 1824, *ibid.*

107 *L.R.S.M.*, 17 September 1824; R. Gilbert's *The Clerical Guide or Ecclesiastical Directory*, Rivington, London , 1829 gives the total population of the parish of Louth as 6012.

108 R. Milne, *The Minister's Last Appeal to His People*, J & J Jackson, Louth, 1824, p. 21. On the title page is John 8: 46, 'Which of you convinceth me of sin? And if I say the truth, why do you not believe me?'

109 To a curacy at St. James's Church, Clerkenwell, where a sermon he delivered on 21 August 1825, was favourably reviewed in *The Pulpit*, 5, 126 (22 September 1825), pp. 145–48.

110 Letter Milne to Bickersteth, 15 April 1825, C.M.S. (S.C.)G./A.C.3.

111 In 1822, Lincoln College appointed William Yeadon, the Evangelical incumbent of All Saints, Oxford to Waddington.

112 A correct forecast. In 1830, an American visitor (Rev. J. Milnor) noted that Sutton's curates were, 'giving a more powerful impulse, moral and religious, to this populous town, than is, perhaps, found in any other manufacturing centre in the kingdom.' ([J.] Stone, [*A Memoir of the Life of James Milnor D.D.*, American Tract Society, New York, 1849,] p. 390.

113 29 January 1824, C.M.S. (S.C.)G./A.C.3.

114 23 April 1824., C.M.S. Minutes of the Committee of Correspondence (G./C.1/1/2).

115 28 April 1824, C.M.S. (S.C.)G./A.C.3.

116 30 April 1824, C.M.S., G./C.1/1/2.

117 2 August 1824, C.M.S. (S.C.)G./A.C.3.

118 4 November 1824, C.M.S. G./A.C.3. The allusion is to Psalm 120: 5,6: 'Woe is me that I sojourn in Mesech that I dwell in the tents of Kedar! My soul hath long dwelt with him that hateth peace.'

119 He wrote to his sister that he was now the curate, and Hillyard the incumbent, 'as I have obtained the church for him.' (10 November 1824, H.C.)

120 *Ibid.*

121 *L.R.S.M.*, 13 August 1824; Sir Francis Hill comments, 'There is no surviving account by Sibthorp, who did not write much though he talked incessantly.' *Georgian Lincoln*, p. 278.

122 *Victorian Lincoln*, p. 17.

123 Charles Greville wrote: 'M'Intosh, in the course of the recent debate, went one day to the H. of C. at eleven in the morning to take a place. They were all taken on the bench below the gangway, and on asking the doorkeeper how they happened to be all taken so early, he said, "Oh, sir, there is no chance of getting a place, for Colonel Sibthorpe sleeps at the bawdy house close by, and comes here every morning by eight o'clock and takes places for all the saints."' *Greville Memoirs*, ed. Lytton Strachey and Roger Fulford, Macmillan, London, 1938, vol. 1, p. 287.

124 T. B. Macaulay's dismissal of him was brutal, '. . .that hairy, filthy, blackguard, Sibthorpe'. Pinney, Vol. 2, p. 174.

125 Both his politics and his willingness to condemn non-Christian behaviour could have made him enemies in Tattershall. In 1816, shortly before he left, the previous incumbent's wheat stacks were set on fire, and his horses poisoned. *L.R.S.M.*, 13 September 1816.

126 C.M.S. (S.C.)G./A.C.3.

127 C. Sibthorp to J. Hawkins, 15 February 1825; J. Hawkins to M.E. Hawkins, 11 March 1825; H.P. J3/7/748; J3/12/1357.

128 [R. W. Sibthorp,] *Farewell Sermon Preached in the Parish Church of Tattershall* [*Lincolnshire on Sunday May 15, 1825*], pp. 10, 15, 20, 44, 46, 53, 56, 57.

129 *Gentleman's Magazine*, 91 (ii), October 1821, p. 308.

130 Some of it may be seen in Burghley House and some in St. Martin's Church, Stamford.

131 Letter from Sibthorp to his sister, 10 November 1824 (H.C.) See also a brief autobiographical note (A.N.), written for J. R. Bloxam. M.C.A. Ms. 492 (*Reverend Richard Waldo Sibthorp*).

132 *L.R.S.M.*, 7 & 14 August.

133 Yglesias (who gives Sibthorp's reply, 'Some on boards, some on broken

pieces of ship, but still they escaped all safe to the land.') See also Pickworth, p. 100 (the author was Ranyell's niece.)

134 'I doubt whether as matters stand between me and a certain Rt. Rev. personage, I should easily get another station in the county or neighbourhood of Lincoln.' Letter to sister, 1 August 1822; H.C.

Chapter Three   *Seeking Direction*

1   *The Pulpit*, 5, 126, (15 September 1825), p. 130.

2   *Farewell Sermon Preached in the Parish Church of Tattershall*, p. 21.

3   In 1821, Cambridge University Press published a New Testament with a bound-in *Synopsis of the Visions of St. John*. It was unequivocal: 'The pouring out of the VIth vial commenced in the present year, 1821, upon the Empire of the Othmans.' Then will follow 'the Seventh vial . . . the last convulsions of the Political World. To this terrible tempest succeeds, the Kingdom of Christ upon Earth, or the Tranquil Millennium; a period of years during which the power of Satan will be suppressed.'

4   *A Brief and Connected View of Prophecy*, p. 5.

5   Two sermons, both delivered on 30 January 1831, may be contrasted. In Bath, William Jay exclaimed, 'Had I died the day after my ordination (he was celebrating 40 years in the ministry) and lately been raised from the dead. . . .. I should have been perfectly astonished at the change; and have exclaimed, "What hath God wrought!"' While at St Luke's Chelsea, H. Blunt bewailed, 'a downward course of impiety and profanity.' *The Pulpit*, XVI (1831), pp. 170,318.

6   The pamphlet was taken up by the Religious Tract Society and by 1855 almost 90,000 copies had been sold. [D. D. Stewart,] *Memoir of the Life of the Rev James Haldane Stewart M.A.*, [Hatchard, London, 1856], p. 98.

7   [J. H. Stewart,] *Thoughts on the Importance of Special Prayer [for the General Outpouring of the Holy Spirit*, Hatchard, London, 1821], pp. 7, 8, 9.

8   'In short the doctrine of the millennium was generally believed in the three first and purest ages . . . it sprung up again at the Reformation, and will flourish together with the study of the Revelation. . . . We should neither with some interpret it into an allegory, nor depart from the literal sense of Scripture without absolute necessity for so doing.' Newton, pp. 591, 592.

9   Address to the Continental Society, 1825, [Mrs. Oliphant,] *The Life of Edward Irving [Minister of the National Scotch Church, London. Illustrated by his Journals and Correspondence*, Hurst & Blackett, London, n.d. (first edition 1862)], pp. 105, 106.

10 An Anglican proponent, Henry Gauntlett, Vicar of Olney, published in 1821 an *Exposition of the Book of Revelation* (Seeley, London.) It had about a thousand subscribers, 'nearly half of whom were clergymen of prominence, and the rest writers on prophecy, educators and men of affairs in national life.' [L. E.] Froom, [*The Prophetic Faith of Our Fathers, Vol. III – The Historical Development of Prophetic Interpretation*, Review & Herald, Washington, 1946,] p. 430.

11 In 1824, A. M. W. Stirling, *The Ways of Yesterday, Being the Chronicles of the Way Family from 1307 to 1885*, Thornton, Butterworth, London, 1930, pp. 271, 272. The articles Way wrote about prophecy, in *The Jewish*

Expositor (1820–22), were published in 1826 as *Thoughts on the Scriptural Expectations of the Christian Church*, *(*A. Panton, London). (Froom, pp. 418–19.)

12   On Sunday evening, 15 May 1831, Sibthorp was preaching on 'the feelings which the thought of Christ's second Coming to judgement excited, as being a good test by which to try the reality of faith: when a most vivid flash of lightning lit up all faces, and the tremendous crash of thunder which followed made everyone start.' Fowler, p. 382.

13   *The Pulpit*, 4, 126, pp. 133–34.

14   [J.] Bateman, [*The Life of the Right Reverend Daniel Wilson, D.D.*, John Murray, London, 1861, (first edition in two volumes, 1860,] p. 101.

15   [J.] Jerram, [*The Memoirs and a Selection from the Letters of the late Charles Jerram, M.A.*, Wertheim & MacIntosh, London, 1855,] p. 305.

16   'let them be for great men.' Letter to Bickersteth, 20 June 1819, C.M.S. (S.C.)G. /A.C.3.

17   In the *Proceedings of the Church Missionary Society* for 1821/22, Richard Sibthorp is noted in the list of contributors from the chapel.

18   *Memoir of the Life of the Rev James Haldane Stewart M.A.*, p. 142.

19   6 December 1825; H. P., J3/7/770.

20   Sibthorp's letter to his sister, 12 January 1826; H.C.

21   18 January 1826, M.C.A. Ms. 492.

22   At St. Marylebone on 18 March 1826.

23   He wrote to his sister on 23 May, the day after the funeral: 'How providential that I was at Canwick that week: that I was in the house at the time of her dissolution; I really seemed guided homeward at the very moment, for I had only just got up stairs, when I was summoned to witness her removal from suffering and infirmity to heavenly bliss. Had I prolonged my absence 10 minutes, I had been too late – I heard her dying declaration of simple confidence in Christ.' H.C. See Fowler, p. 40.

24   [R.] Watson, [*A Sermon on the Death of Joseph Butterworth, Late M.P. for Dover, Preached at Great Queen Street Chapel, July 9, 1826*, Kershaw, London, 1826,] p. 14. Watson was from Lincolnshire and a convert of William Dodwell in 1795. See: Wesleyan Methodist Church, *Official Handbook of the 182nd Conference held at Wesley Chapel, Lincoln, 15 to 28 July, 1925*, Ruddock, Lincoln, 1925, p. 112.

25   R. W. Sibthorp, *The Substance of a Sermon Preached at St John's Chapel Bedford-Row, London, on the Sunday Following the Interment of Joseph Butterworth Esq., Late M.P. for Dover*, 1826, p. 18.

26   Watson, p. 26.

27   *Georgian Lincoln*, p. 231.

28   Letter to his sister, 23 May 1826, H.C.

29   The Forsters probably travelled with him.

30   To M. E. Hawkins, 28 August 1826, 3 Sib. 1/15.

31   Matthew Ch. 13 v. 57.

32   2 November 1826, M.C.A. Ms. 492. In 1827, Hensley became a curate in Gainsborough; the following year, Thomas Cooper, the Chartist, wrote that his preaching, 'gentle as it was, touched cords within me. . . .' *The Life of Thomas Cooper – Written by Himself*, Hodder & Stoughton, London, 1897, p. 77.

33 A.N., *ibid*. Noel acquired a sub-lease; the principal lease (from the Rugby Estate) remained with Wilson.

34 27 December 1826, *ibid*.

35 Pelham died on 7 February 1827.

36 Except on Sunday 17 June, when he visited Manchester and Wilmslow for the C.M.S. (M.C.A. 492).

37 D. W. Bebbington, 'The Life of Baptist Noel', *Baptist Quarterly*, 24, 8, (October 1972), p. 391.

38 'He has gone through St. Giles at all hours', (Fowler, p. 39.) In 1830, an American visited Noel's 'charming residence' at Walthamstow. It was some distance from the Church, and to this, the visitor attributed his 'remissness in visiting . . . a frequent complaint among the laity.' (Stone, p. 306.)

39 Bateman, p. 130.

40 R. W. Sibthorp, *Sermon Preached at the Parish Church of St. Clement Danes, Strand, on Friday May 11 1827, at the Thirty-Third General Meeting of the London Missionary Society*, 1827, p. 28.

41 [A.] Haldane, [*The Lives of Robert and James Haldane*, Banner of Truth Trust, Edinburgh, 1990 (reprint of first edition 1852),] p. 525.

42 On 7 December 1831, quoted in J. King, *The Comparative Claims of the British and Foreign Bible Society and the Trinitarian Bible Society Calmly Discussed*, 1832, Isaac Wilson, Hull, pp. 26–28.

43 He had called on the Society's offices in Earl Street to reclaim his umbrella!

44 *The Quarterly Review*, 36, 71 (June 1827), p. 5.

45 Speech at 24th Anniversary of B.F.B.S., *Christian Observer*, May 1828 (Supplement No. 130).

46 *Official Report of the Speeches Delivered at the Twenty-third Anniversary of the British and Foreign Bible Society, on Wednesday, May 2d, 1827*. Reprinted in *The Wesleyan Methodist Magazine* N.S. VI (1827), pp. 551–52.

47 A. Brown, *The Word of God Among all Nations – A Brief History of the Trinitarian Bible Society, 1831–1981*, T.B.S., London, 1981, p. 11.

48 Haldane, p. 538.

49 [G.] Brown, [*The History of the Bible Society from its Inception in 1804 to the Close of its Jubilee in 1854, Compiled at the Request of the Jubilee Committee by the Rev. George Brown, during 21 Years one of the Secretaries of the Society*, B.F.B.S., London, 1859,] p. 364.

50 To A. Brandram, B.F.B.S. H.C.-I.

51 *Ibid*.

52 Where he met a number of friends, 'Mr Dealtry of Clapham; Mr. Thornton, the Treasurer of the Bible Society; Mr Bickersteth and his wife, Mr. Coates; – Mr Lewis Way is residing here.' Letter to Mrs Rowlett, 6 August 1827, M.C.A. Ms. 492.

53 8 August 1827, B.F.B.S., Foreign Correspondence – Inwards (F.C.-I).

54 Grants to Central Europe in the period 1818–1826 were £51,918, during 1827–1834 they amounted to £12,026. [W.] Canton, [*A History of the British and Foreign Bible Society*, John Murray, London, 1904, Vol. 1,] p. 443.

55 To Mrs. Rowlett, Paris, 6 August 1827, M.C.A. Ms. 492.

56 To Mrs. Hawkins, Berlin 5 September 1826 (*sic*), *ibid*.

57 *Ibid*., (the Canstein Bible Institute).

58   Letter to A. Brandram, 16 October 1827, B.F.B.S. F.C.-I.

59   20 August 1827, *ibid.*

60   22 October 1827, *ibid.*

61   Canton, p. 441.

62   Letter to A. Brandram, 'Woburn Place, 17 December, 1827', B.F.B.S. H.C.-I.

63   Lewis Hensley was Charles Hensley's brother. Letter, 14 September 1827, M.C.A. Ms. 492.

64   *Christian Observer*, May 1828 (Supplement No. 130,) pp. 131, 132.

65   Founded by Edward Irving, Lewis Way, and C. S. Hawtrey, Froom, p. 726.

66   [R. W. Sibthorp,] *The Character of the Papacy* [. . .to which is appended a Report of the Proceedings of the said Auxiliary Society* 1828,] pp. 27–29. The *Report* said that the lectures were, '*on the whole*, well attended.'

67   Preached at Tavistock Chapel, Drury Lane, on 20 November 1827.

68   [R. W. Sibthorp,] *The Character and Tokens of the True Catholic Church*, [1829,] pp. 33, 34, 35, 41, 56.

69   For example 'I have carefully reviewed the original language of Cyprian (regarding the episcopate) and am satisfied that Mr Faber's remark to this purport is correct.' *Ibid.*, p. 21.

70   G. S. Faber, *The Difficulties of Romanism*, John Murray, London, 1826, p. viii.

71   *The Character and Tokens of the True Catholic Church*, p. 24.

72   January 1828, p. 37.

73   Delivered at St. John's Bedford Row, 11 February 1828.

74   *The Character of the Papacy*, pp. 3, 4, 8, 10, 22, 23.

75   In 1825, the R.T.S. had adopted Edward Bickersteth's resolution: 'That this meeting considers it most important fully to recognise the principles upon which this Society has hitherto proceeded; namely "the evangelical principles of the Reformation in which Luther, Calvin and Cranmer were agreed . . ."'

76   [W. M. Jones,] *The Jubilee Memorial of the Religious Tract Society*, [R.T.S., London, 1850,] pp. 83, 84.

77   Charles Bridges (1794–1869) wrote various commentaries and a standard work: *The Christian Ministry with an Enquiry into the Causes of its Inefficiency*.

78   19 December 1827, R.T.S., Executive Committee Minutes (M.E.C.)

79   Joseph Hughes (Baptist pastor) and Dyer, Secretary of the Baptist Missionary Society.

80   19 February and 17 June 1828, R.T.S. M.E.C.

81   To A. Brandram, 14 July 1828, B.F.B.S. H.C.-I.

82   His resolution that, 'the numerous applications from many foreign countries for increased assistance require the friends of the Institution to use more active endeavours in aid of its funds' had been endorsed unanimously. *Report of the Twenty-ninth Anniversary Meeting*, 16 May 1828, R.T.S. M.E.C.

83   22 July 1828, R.T.S. M.E.C.

84   Although according to Fowler, 'He was in such a state of nervous excitement that his friends became really alarmed'. (Fowler, p. 41.) Unfortunately, this is not dated but loosely associated with the St. John's ministry. There is no

indication of any serious breakdown during the London period, other than that of 1825.

85   21 April 1829, R.T.S. M.E.C.
86   Many of the Society's records were destroyed by enemy action during the night 10–11 May, 1941.
87   10 April 1829, R.T.S. M.E.C.
88   7 July 1829, *ibid*. This was for tracts, Sibthorp paid his own expenses; (31*st* *Annual Report of the Religious Tract Society*, R.T.S., London, 1830).
89   'The aid granted by him (Sibthorp) being in stereotype plates of Tracts approved by your Committee will prevent the diffusion of error by the funds of the Society, and will also be a great saving in expense.' (*Ibid.*)
90   1 September 1829, R.T.S. M.E.C.
91   17 April 1828, R.T.S Foreign Correspondence.
92   15 September 1829, R.T.S. M.E.C., letter from Leipsic (*sic*), 1 September 1829.
93   Letter to Fabricius, Ryde, 30 June 1830; R.T.S. Correspondence.
94   29 September 1829, R.T.S. M.E.C, *Statement Received from R. Waldo Sibthorp Respecting His Recent Tour on the Continent of Europe*. In October 1830, Sibthorp wrote to Basle, complaining that no Society had been established. [T. C. F. Stunt,] *From Awakening to Secession*, [T & T Clark, Edinburgh, 2000,] p. 215.
95   Letter copied into the *Fry Collection* of B. W. Newton papers, in the Christian Brethren Archive, (C.B.A.) 7049, pp. 180,181. Newton's reminiscences in old age include the following humorous account. 'It was dreadfully bad travelling in Prussia as there were no roads until 6 miles around Berlin. We walked a good part of the way from Hamburgh to Berlin, sending our luggage by vehicle which bumped over the roots of trees. It was then that Sibthorpe fell in the dark into a hole and having his hands in his pockets he naturally pulled them out quickly as he fell and out came most of his money and he was groping about to find it. I quite lost sight of him and called to him as to what he was about. That night I remember we had such unwholesome black rye bread only fit for horses that made both of us ill. We could not digest it. (C.B.A. 7049, p. 183.)
96   C.B.A. 7049, p. 182.
97   1 September 1829, R.T.S. M.E.C.
98   C.B.A. 7049, p. 177. In December 1829, a decree was issued by order of Baron von der Decken, the provincial counsellor of the King of Great Britain and Hanover. 'It has come to our knowledge that for some time past, there have appeared in our jurisdiction foreign missionaries, who not only form conventicles, but have also distributed little tracts, which are partly filled with quibbles upon the articles of Christianity, or at least of such a nature that they cannot be understood by the common people or young persons . . . The distribution of tracts by foreign missionaries is in future entirely prohibited, and can only take place by the dignitaries, superintendents and ministers of religion; and all other persons found transgressing the above decree, by distributing tracts, will be punished as the law directs . . .' *The Jubilee Memorial of the Religious Tract Society*, p. 351.
99   29 September 1829, R.T.S. M.E.C.

100 27 April 1830, 21 February 1832, *ibid.*
101 *Statement Received from R. Waldo Sibthorp Respecting His Recent Tour on the Continent of Europe, ibid.*
102 Letter to his mother, 29 August 1829, C.B.A. 7049, p. 178–9. In Newton's understanding, Arminianism was, 'nothing more than varnished Pelagianism.' (Letter to his mother, 13 January 1828, C.B.A. 7049, p. 143.)
103 Letter to Rev. H. C. Burke (Thailfingen); Ryde, 3 June 1830; R.T.S. Correspondence.
104 Sibthorp asked for the phrase '*Dir mitgiltheilten*' to be removed. 'I trust that you and our other dear friends in Berlin will recognise in this suggestion the same spirit of a wish to prevent misconceptions without at the same time sacrificing any part of Divine Truth. . . .' He seems to have made little progress with his German, confessing, himself 'ill acquainted' with the language. To Rev. Stobwasser, Ryde, 26 April 1830, *ibid.*
105 To Rev. Stobwasser, Canwick, 8 January 1830, *ibid.*
106 28 May 1830, *ibid.*
107 12 October 1830, R.T.S., M.E.C.
108 *The Jubilee Memorial of the Religious Tract Society*, p. 334.
109 R. W. Sibthorp, *A Sermon Preached at St. Paul's Church, Covent Garden, on Tuesday Evening, May 13th 1828, before the Newfoundland School Society*, 1828, pp. 22, 32.
110 Fowler, p. 47. 'I have seen Mr Cropper here for an hour – he is I am sure a genuine devoted Christian. He lives above Hill in Mr Sibthorp's house.' Abel Smith to Alexander Leslie Melville, March 2, 1830, [National Westminster Bank Archives] (N.W.B.A.), D.6404.
111 Fowler, p. 47.
112 *L.R.S.M.*, 9 January 1829.
113 Mass. 1/32.
114 On 13 February the *L.R.S.M.* contained this announcement. 'We beg to correct a misstatement which has been made in this city respecting the evening lectures at St. Peter's in Eastgate: we have authority for saying that the lectures will be continued, that the church is permanently fitted up for the purpose, and that there has been no interference tending to suppress such a valuable system of instruction for the Sabbath evening.'
115 '(Mr Cropper) gives a poor account of spiritual things even Mr Moore the best Minister does not either preach or go to Bible meetings, but he believes he has got a pious curate in Mr Pridham. Mr C. knows Mr Sibthorpe very well and likes him very much.' N.W.B.A., D.6404. Under Pridham a plan was brought forward to enlarge the Church, which his opponents acted to thwart, 'we took the alarm only just in time to save ourselves from the play of a (masked) battery on our parish purse. The dissimulation of the saints is odious and frightful.' Dr. Charlesworth to Sir Edward French Bromhead, 19 May 1831, *Georgian Lincoln*, p. 299.
116 W. R. Ward, *Victorian Oxford*, Frank Cass, London, 1965, p. 75.
117 26 September 1826, [Hill's Diary, St. Edmund's Hall] (S.E.H.) Ms. 67/6.
118 Bulteel became curate in December 1826.
119 S. Gillam, *Kennington History – St. Swithun's Church*, Kennington History Project, Oxford, 1994, p. 3. In 1828, the Rector of Sunningwell built the new church on the site of a ruined chapel.

120 7 November 1828, S.E.H. Ms. 67/7. [J. S. Reynolds,] *The Evangelicals at Oxford,* [*1735–1871, A Record of an Unchronicled Movement,* Marcham Manor Press, Abingdon, 1975,] pp. 103–104 (additional contents.) See also, [T. C. F. Stunt,] 'John Henry Newman and the Evangelicals,' [*Journal of Ecclesiastical History,* XXI, 1(January 1970),] pp. 65–84; p. 70.

121 Hill records meeting Sibthorp on 10 &12 March 1829, S.E.H. Ms. 67/7.

122 [M. R. D.] Foot, [*The Gladstone Diaries, Volume 1, 1825–1832,* Clarendon Press, Oxford, 1968,] pp. 241, 242.

123 27 July 1879, Fowler p. 46.

124 Letter to P. Maurice, 14 April 1877, Fowler p. 334. The predecessor was presumably Bisse.

125 S.E.H. Ms. 67/7, Grantham and Bell were there, Hill expounded from 1 Corinthians.

126 28 April 1829, C.B.A. 7179 (6) & C.B.A. 7049, p. 169. Newton had criticised some statements on the Fall and eternal punishment in Blanco White's *London Review. From Awakening to Secession,* p. 216.

127 Brown p. 171.

128 Note of March, 1829; [D. C.] Lathbury, [*Correspondence on Church and Religion of William Ewart Gladstone,* John Murray, London, 1910,] Vol. 1 pp. 3, 4.

129 Burnham argues it was a conversion to 'some form of Calvinism' – Newton had already imbibed the moderate Evangelical Anglicanism of his school teacher, T. Byrth. [J.] Burnham, [*The Controversial Relationship Between Benjamin Wills Newton and John Nelson Darby,* unpublished D. Phil thesis, Oxford University, 1999,] p. 55.

130 C.B.A. 7049, p. 138, & 7060, p. 86. Any chronology – based upon the reminiscences of an old man – must be conjectural. See, *From Awakening to Secession,* pp. 197–198.

131 C.B.A. 7049, p. 79. See H. H. Rowdon, *The Origins of the Brethren, 1825–1850,* Pickering & Inglis, London, 1967, p. 62; *From Awakening to Secession,* p. 198.

132 C.B.A. 7049, p. 139; the incident cannot be dated. See Burnham, p. 61

133 C.B.A. 7049, pp. 62–65. *From Awakening to Secession,* pp. 210,211. 'To devote good talents to write history or investigate nature, was simple waste: for at the Lord's coming, history and science would no longer be learned by these feeble appliances of ours.' F. W. Newman, *Phases of Faith,* Leicester University Press, Leicester, 1970 (first edition 1850), p. 23.

134 C.B.A. 7049, p. 140.

135 C.B.A. 7064, p. 35.

136 C.B.A. 7049, p. 183.

137 *Ibid.,* p. 140.

138 *Ibid.*

139 In 1829.

140 C.B.A. 7049, p. 79.

141 Perhaps Sibthorp's frequent absences from the pulpit were seen as an obstacle to his being licensed. Writing to the B.F.B.S. on 7 July 1829, he seems to have had no thought of leaving; saying that he would leave for the Continent, 'provided I can suitably provide for the care of my church during my absence'. (B.F.B.S. H. C. – I.).

142 12 November 1829, C.B.A. 7049, p. 190; Richard was preaching for the R.T.S. substituting for Haldane Stewart.

143 Reynolds describes the period 1807–1831, as one of expanding evangelical influence; *The Evangelicals at Oxford* pp. 77–101, *passim*.

144 Letter undated, probably November 1829, H. C. G. Moule, *Charles Simeon*, Methuen & Co., London, 1892, p. 205.

145 Nehemiah 1: 11.

146 W. Carus, *Memoir of the Life of the Rev Charles Simeon*, Hatchard, London, 1847, pp. 641, 642.

147 Foot, p. 288. Gladstone also was unsure about the proprieties and wrote to Edward Craig enquiring whether it was permissible for students to meet for prayer in one another's rooms. 15 December 1829, Add. Ms. 44352 fol. 141.

148 'I had indeed forgotten the introduction to Mr Hanbury's rooms to which you refer.' Letter to Gladstone, 23 September 1844; [Gladstone Papers] Add. Ms. 44361 fol. 237.

149 [W. E. Gladstone,] *Gleanings [of Past Years*, John Murray, London, 1879, Vol. VII], p. 212.

150 H.C.

151 C.B.A. 7049, p. 236.

152 'Wigram's was a broader mind and more intellectual. He also had a wide circle of Christian friends in different parts of England – some too who were very objectionable; for instance Erskine, one of the letters in Erskine's *Freeness of the Gospel* is addressed to Wigram "My dear Friend."' CBA. 7049, p. 262. [T. Erskine, *The] Unconditional Freeness [of the Gospel in Three Essays*, Waugh & Innes, Edinburgh, 1828], p. 262.

153 C.B.A. 7064, pp. 35, 36.

154 C.B.A. 7049, p. 181.

155 R.T.S. M.E.C., 29 September 1829.

156 *Unconditional Freeness*, pp. 54, 62, 68, 69, 81.

157 Writing in 1878, Mrs Bodley asked Sibthorp whether he had read the recently published life of Erskine. Fowler, p. 337.

158 See the summary of reviews in N. R. Needham, *Thomas Erskine of Linlathen, His Life & Theology, 1788–1837*, Rutherford House, Edinburgh, 1990, pp. 160–209. The *British Critic's* reviewer feared that Erskine was 'on his way to universalism.' (*Ibid.*, p. 175.)

159 To Col. Henry Oglander, Meerut, India, 14 January 1831; Oglander Papers, O.G./C.C./ 310.

160 Letter to a relative, October 1832, Fowler, pp. 58–59; this may have been Mary Anne Hawkins who was prone to depression.

161 C.B.A. 7049, p. 139.

162 Foot, p. 272.

163 Fowler, p. 46.

164 Foot pp. 270–271, he read *Remarks on the Internal Evidence for the Truth of Revealed Religion*.

165 15 December 1829; Add. Ms. 44352 fol. 142.

166 (11) December 1829, [A.] Mozley [(ed) *Letters and Correspondence of John Henry Newman During his Life in the English Church*, Longmans, Green & Co., London, 1891,] Vol. 1, pp. 215–16.

167 'a society . . . availing itself of the name of our Church, yet actually conducted

on principles so widely different from those which her doctrines and disciplines imply . . . is doing secret injury to her highest domestic objects . . . '. J. H. Newman, *Suggestions Respectfully Offered to Individual Resident Clergymen of the University in Behalf of the Church Missionary Society*, 1830. In *The Via Media of the Anglican Church*, Longmans, Green & Co., London, 1885 (first edition 1877), Vol. II, p 11.

168   12 December 1829, Mozley, pp. 216, 217.
169   Letter to Bickersteth, 20 February 1830, C.M.S. (S.C.)G./A.C.3
170   'John Henry Newman and the Evangelicals', p. 68.
171   M.C.A. Ms. 89 (*Cardinal Newman*) quoted in R. D. Middleton, *Newman at Oxford: His Religious Development*, Oxford University Press, Oxford, 1950, p. 34.
172   At the C.M.S. Annual Meeting, 8 March 1830.
173   C.B.A. 7064, p. 35.
174   Burnham, pp. 63, 64.
175   See W. G. Turner *John Nelson Darby*, C. A. Hammond, London, 1951, p. 70, *From Awakening to Secession* p. 219.
176   To W. T. Keal, 9 June 1830; J. H. Philpot, *The Seceders*, C. J. Farncombe, London, 1930, p. 146.
177   10 December 1830, C.M.S. (S.C.)G./A.C.3 .
178   Hole, p. 363.

Chapter Four   *A Theological Revolution*

1   Byers was the first curate, the second, Thomas Griffith. Among the latter's London congregation was George Gilbert Scott, the architect nephew of John Scott of Hull.
2   Letter to *The Times* of 16 November 1841.
3   'The Rev. R. Waldo Sibthorpe Esq. has lately been licensed to the Chapel of St James by the Bishop of Winchester. The Rev. Gentleman has already commenced his labours and intends to establish a lecture on Thursday evenings.' *Hampshire Chronicle*, 17 May 1830.
4   R. Mudie, *Hampshire*, D. E. Gilmour, Winchester, n.d., pp. 208–209.
5   *Hampshire Chronicle*, 29 September 1832.
6   *Ibid.*, 17 August 1833; visitors already arrived included, 'the Countess of Craven, Lady Louisa Craven, the Earl of Rathdown', etc.
7   'This delightful watering place has received a considerable accession of visitants during the past week, but there are still very many houses unoccupied and arrivals are daily anxiously looked for.' *Hampshire Telegraph*, 10 July 1830.
8   Fowler, p. 49.
9   *Hampshire Telegraph*, 9 July 1827.
10   The parish church was at Newchurch, some miles away.
11   Fanny to Henry Oglander, 14 January 1831, O.G./C.C./310. J. W. King, *The Independent Church of Christ Assembling in George Street Chapel Ryde*, printed for the author, Ryde, 1945, pp. 22, 23.
12   *Portsmouth, Portsea and Gosport Herald*, 27 June 1830.
13   H. P. J3/14/1.
14   [*St. James's Church Ryde, 1827–1927*] *Centenary Souvenir* [– *Being a Short History of the Church and District*, Mellish, Ryde, 1927], p. 9.

15   'Let us hope all thus called away were as ready as Lord and Lady Farnham, whom I remember thirty years since at Ryde, with her good mother old Lady Despencer.' Fowler, p. 198.
16   Fowler, p. 49.
17   *Centenary Souvenir*, p. 11.
18   *Ibid.*, pp. 11,12.
19   Fowler, p. 49. It seems unlikely that all these activities were held every week for any prolonged period.
20   *The Record*, 24 September, 2 November, 1840.
21   [I. Ker & T. Gornall,] *The Letters and Diaries of John Henry Newman Vol. III*, [Clarendon Press, Oxford 1979,] p. 30.
22   Letter to Mr. Hensley, 6 June 1831; M.C.A. Ms. 492 (seeking information on the practice at St. John's.)
23   4 April 1834, *ibid.*
24   F. Lyell wrote to Bloxam (7 January 1885) of a mutual friend: 'Sibthorp himself was the means of awakening religious life in (his) mind in those good Ryde days, before the clouds came'. *Ibid.*
25   B. Taylor, note in *Lincoln Diocesan Magazine*, XXIV, VII (July 1958). See Fowler, p. 50.
26   Mrs Henrietta Hawksley (daughter of Lady Jackson,) 21 April 1886, M.C.A. Ms 492.
27   *The Wesleyan-Mathodist Magazine for the Year 1835*, N.S. XIV, p. 289.
28   N.S. III, (May 1835), pp. 516, 517.
29   Letter to Mary Anne Hawkins, 28 October 1830, H. P. J3/14/1.
30   Letter to Mr. Hensley, 21 November 1832; M.C.A. Ms. 492; Fowler, p. 52.
31   Published in 1810, it recounts Legh Richmond's experiences when curate of Brading and Yaverland on the island.
32   Stone, p. 343.
33   Hartley informed the C.M.S. Committee that he was delaying his return to the Levant, because he wished to find a wife. (August 14 1830, C.M.S. (S.C.)G./A.C.3.) He eventually left for Corfu with Mrs. Hartley on 6 June 1832.
34   J. R. Bloxam, 7 August 1841, M.C.A. Ms. 335 (*Reunion*). King p. 177.
35   6 June 1831, M.C.A. Ms. 492.
36   4 April 1834, *ibid.*
37   They were returning from a visit to Haldane Stewart in Liverpool: he wrote movingly of their death in *Letters to a Friend of the Late W. M. Forster Esq.*, Seeley, Hatchard & Nisbet, London, 1831.
38   Sibthorp wrote, 'the intimacy had been long, close, confidential. Their home had been my home, whenever I chose to make it so and there were not many days in which they had not some of my thoughts.' Letter to Mrs. Hawkins, 21 September 1831, H.C.
39   M. Hawkins wrote to her mother, 'How grieved Uncle Richard will be – and so are all of us in whatever situation who knew him – his loss will be felt more and more.' H. P. J/2/9/2057 (undated, Sargent died on 3 May 1833.)
40   To L. Hensley, 2 November 1826, M.C.A. Ms. 492.
41   28 October 1830, H. P. J3/13/1.
42   *Farewell Sermon Preached in the Parish Church of Tattershall*, p. 47.
43   Erskine, pp. 79, 24.

44 To Mary Anne Hawkins, 28 October 1830, H. P. J3/14/1.

45 Erskine, pp. 129, 130.

46 'While on the one hand, with his loving heart, he would that all men might be saved; yet, on the other he desired to bow his head to the doctrines of the Church, so far as they are declared in her interpretation of Scripture.' Fowler, p. 340.

47 June 1831, C. Cecil, *Memoir of Mrs. Hawkes, late of Islington*, Robert Carter & Bros., New York, 1851 (first edition 1837), p. 348.

48 On 12 August 1833, he wrote to Tarn of the Bible Society, pleading that his nerves were unequal to the effort of speaking. (B.F.B.S. H. C.- I.).

49 27 February 1833, *ibid.*

50 12 August 1833, *ibid.* See Acts 24 2. Tertullus's 'speech is made up of flattery and falsehood; it calls evil good and good evil'. (*Matthew Henry's Bible Commentary*, Marshall Morgan Scott, London, 1960, p. 531.)

51 25 February and 25 March, 1831, B.F.B.S. H. C.- I.

52 28 October 1830, H.P. J3/14/1

53 Sermon, 17 October 1830, *The Pulpit*, 15, 409, (28 October 1830), pp. 297–305. Newman wrote to his mother (20 August 1830,) 'This Revolution seems to me the triumph of irreligion.' I. Ker & T. Gornall, *The Letters and Diaries of John Henry Newman, Vol. II*, Clarendon Press, Oxford, 1979, p. 283.

54 Letter to Mary Anne Hawkins, 28 October 1830, J3/14/1.

55 To Jowett, 27 February 1833, B.F.B.S. H. C.- I.

56 *The Times*, 10 November 1841.

57 *Ibid.*, 17 December 1855. Charles de Laet Waldo Sibthorp was unseated in the election of 1832, but returned in 1835, he continued to represent Lincoln, until his death in 1855.

58 Letter to Mr. Hensley, 21 November 1832, M.C.A. Ms. 492.

59 C. Sykes, 'Colonel Sibthorp: A Festival Centenary' in *History Today*, May 1951, p. 17.

60 *Ibid.* p. 18.

61 M. Stenton, *Who's Who of British Members of Parliament: A Biographical Dictionary of the House of Commons, Volume 1, 1832–1885*, Harvester Press, Hassocks, 1976, p. 204.

62 Letter to Humphrey Sibthorp, 30 November 1830, 3 Sib. 1/20.

63 27 June 1877, Fowler, p. 324.

64 F. Burkhardt & S. Smith, (eds.) *The Correspondence of Charles Darwin, Vol. 1, 1821–1836*, Cambridge University Press, Cambridge, 1985, p. 245.

65 Poll Book 75 (Isle of Wight Records Office.) Fowler p. 180.

66 [A. R.] Ashwell, [*Life of the Right Reverend Samuel Wilberforce*, Vol. 1, John Murray, London, 1880,] p. 78.

67 *Ibid.*, p. 72.

68 To J. Oldknow, 18 January 1844, Add. Ms. 44360 fol. 325.

69 To Jabez Bunting, 25 April 1836, Methodist Archive, P.L.P., 97–10–7.

70 Wilberforce to Sir C. Anderson, 21 May 1835, Ms. Wilberforce, d. 25.

71 Ashwell, p. 53

72 1 October 1832, *ibid.*, p. 63.

73 This was in 1842 or 1843; M. L. Loane, *John Charles Ryle, 1816–1900*, Hodder & Stoughton, London, 1983, p. 41.

74   7 December 1838, Ashwell, p. 131; Hamilton was Bishop of Salisbury, 1854–1869, 'a saintly adherent of the Oxford Movement', S. L Ollard & G. Crosse, *A Dictionary of English Church History*, Mowbray, London, 1912, p. 543.

75   In 1828, Sibthorp had provided letters of introduction for Robert Wilberforce to use in Germany. (Letter, 27 May Ms. Wilberforce c. 2.)

76   In October 1832, Wilberforce was among the select group who gathered in Cambridge to celebrate Simeon's fifty years of ministry; Birks, Vol. II, p. 37.

77   Letters to Anderson, 4 January 1831 and 12 September 1833; Ms. Wilberforce d. 25.

78   Wilberforce diary, 11 March 1832, Ms. Wilberforce e. 5.

79   *The Record*, 18 November 1841.

80   Hole, vol. II, p. 103.

81   John Fletcher of Madeley, Welsey's designated successor.

82   24 June 1833, M.C.A. Ms. 492.

83   *Some Answer to the Enquiry 'Why are you Become a Catholic?'*, p. 4

84   Diary entry, 22 September 1837; [G. Tracey,] *The Letters and Diaries of John Henry Newman, Vol. VI*, [Clarendon Press, Oxford, 1984,] p. 138, n. 1 (italics added).

85   Samuel accompanied by Mr. Sargent, dined with Sibthorp at the home of James Tripp, rector of Upwaltham (14 March 1833, Ms. Wilberforce e. 5.)

86   *Ibid.*

87   P. Maurice, *The Popery of Oxford, Confronted, Discovered & Repudiated*, Seeleys, London 1837, p. 72. The preface is dated 29 May.

88   Henry Wilberforce's misapprehension was quite widespread, see note 73, p. 193, *Vide supra*

89   [T Gornall,] *The Letters and Diaries of John Henry Newman, Vol. V*, [Clarendon Press, Oxford, 1981,] p. 386.

90   *A Sermon preached at St. John's Church*, p. 12.

91   Fowler, p. 50.

92   *Some Answer to the Enquiry 'Why are you Become a Catholic?'*, pages. 5, 6.

93   *Ibid.*, p. 12.

94   M. A. Gathercole, *Letters to a Dissenting Minister*, R. Groombridge, London, 5th edition (first edition, 1833), pp. 165, 330.

95   *Liber Redivivus, or the Booke of the Universall Kirke Reopened, by a Presbyter*, John Symington & Co., Glasgow, 1839, p. 40.

96   T. H. Horne, *An Introduction to the Critical Study and Knowledge of the Holy Scriptures*, T. Cadell, London, 1828, Vol. II, p. 456. In 1836, the Evangelical chaplain to Bishop Sumner, Alexander Dallas, preached eighteen sermons on 'The Israelites a type of the Church.' *Incidents in the Life and Ministry of Rev Alex. R. C. Dallas, by his Widow*, 1873, p. 313. See also Marsh, p. 79.

97   P. Fairbairn, *The Typology of Scripture. . .Viewed in Connection with the Whole Series of Divine Dispensations*, Evangelical Press, London, 1975 (first edition 1847), p. 161.

98   *The Letters and Diaries of John Henry Newman, Vol. V*, p. 386.

99   *Ibid.*

100 3 December 1836; *ibid.*, p. 389.

101 R. W. Sibthorp, *The Family Liturgy, being a Course of Morning and Evening Prayers for a Family arranged and compiled on the Plan of a Liturgy*, 1836.

102 *Some Answer to the Enquiry 'Why are you Become a Catholic?'*, p. 9.

103 'After he had been 5 or 6 years at St James' Mr. Sibthorpe established a surpliced choir of 24 boys with one man as a leader. . .' *Centenary Souvenir*, p. 12. S. L. Ollard, *A Short History of the Oxford Movement*, Mowbray, London, 1915, p. 169; N. Yates, *Buildings, Faith and Worship*, Clarendon Press, Oxford, 1991, p. 137.

104 'The musical parts of the divine service were at all times his delight.' Fowler, p. 54. The choral services at Magdalen were 'thought much of.' B. Rainbow, *The Choral Revival in the Anglican Church (1839–1872)*, Barrie & Jenkins, London, 1970, p. 203. At Lincoln, Beste recalled, 'pomp and solemnity . . . *disjectae membra ecclesiae*'. At Magdalen he found, 'in a smaller space the same ceremonial'. Beste, pp. 7, 8.

105 12 August 1829; *Portsmouth, Portsea and Gosport Herald*, 16 August 1829.

106 There is reason to believe that such choirs existed in other unlikely parishes. 'When the future William IV visited Brixham in August 1828, H. F. Lyte accompanied by a surpliced choir met him on the landing stage.' B. G. Skinner, *Henry Francis Lyte*, University of Exeter Press, Exeter, 1974, p. 77. See W. F. Hook, on the *Principles of the Reformation* (1838) in *The Church and her Ordinances*, Richard Bentley & Son, London, 1876, Vol. 1, pp. 89–93.

107 When Sibthorp's choir disbanded in 1841, his choirmaster went to work for Craig, taking the surplices with him. Letter, Sibthorp to Bloxam, 23 August 1842, OLL XIX.

108 To Ambrose Phillipps, 7 August, M.C.A. Ms. 335. In old age, Veck was a bitter opponent of Rome. See *Eight sermons published at the request of the parishioners having been preached in the Church of St John Forton 1866*, by Anglo Catholicus (Veck.) J. Parker, Oxford, 1866.

109 A. Symondson, *Theology, Worship and the Late Victorian Church* in C. Brooks and A. Saint *The Victorian Church – Architecture and Society*, Manchester University Press, Manchester, 1995, p. 195.

110 'I fell in with the Tracts and read them, when second master at Broomsgrove School in Worcestershire, before I came up to reside at Oxford as Fellow of Magdalen College in 1836. I liked them, though I knew nothing of the authors. But a Roman Catholic priest, who lived at Grafton near Bromsgrove, had previously put some good Catholic notions into my mind, without, as he said, any intention to convert me to Romanism.' [R. D. Middleton,] *Newman and Bloxam* [*An Oxford Friendship*, Oxford University Press, Oxford, 1947], p. 29.

111 Bloxam heard him preach in a little church' (Kennington?), Bloxam, p. 224. In July 1835, Sibthorp twice visited John Hill (S.E.H. Ms. 67/10).

112 *Newman and Bloxam*, p. 39.

113 23 November 1837, *The Letters and Diaries of John Henry Newman, Vol. VI*, p. 172.

114 *Centenary Souvenir*, pp. 12,13. Some of the texts remain *in situ*. On 14 September 1840, Richard wrote to Bloxam, 'Will you be so kind as (to) send me a small piece of that violet wool which forms the ground of part of your

altar cloth . . . My cloth is in progress . . . I have put up two new texts (part
of the 1st chapter of St. John's gospel) on each side of the vestry doors. They
are painted in Red, Black and Blue letters on a parchment ground – and I
think the best executed work in the Church.' And again, on 5 December 'The
painter has finished your four scrowls and sent them off yesterday.' OLL
XIX.

115 7 September 1840; [M.] Belcher, [*The Collected Letters of A. W. N. Pugin,
Vol. 1, 1830–1842*, Oxford, Oxford University Press, 2001], p. 140.

116 14 September 1840, OLL XIX.

117 As Pugin told Bloxam, 'a tryptick *with nothing in it*!!!' 28 February 1841,
Belcher p. 212.

118 8 May 1841, *ibid.*, pp. 235–36.

119 *Ecclesiologist*, October 1842, *Depredations of Churches*.

120 20 March 1839, Ms. Wilberforce d. 46. On 27 March Charles Jerram wrote,
'I am told that – has thus paid homage to the beast, nor am I much surprised.
I am sorry he is not singular in this rapid change from ultra Protestantism
to ultra Romanism.' Jerram, p. 450.

121 23 March 1839, Ms. Wilberforce d.46.

122 26 March 1839, *ibid.* Wilberforce visited Sibthorp the following day, Ms.
Wilberforce e. 7.

123 2 March 1841, Belcher, p. 214

124 Letter to Katharine Cholmeley; 25 November 1839, G. Cholmeley, pp.
71,72.

125 *Hampshire Telegraph*, 5 January 1839.

126 Diary, 10 July 1837, Ms. Wilberforce e. 7.

127 *Ibid.*, 8 November 1837. On 8 March 1838, he wrote, 'A poor account of
the clerical meeting – great danger of its becoming too *disputatious*. Holditch
pugnacious and Hewitt overbearing. . . .' *Ibid.*

128 24 March 1838, *ibid.*

129 *Hampshire Telegraph*, 2 November 1838.

130 The flowers could have come from Holmewood, where several gardeners
were employed; Sibthorp and Augustus Hewitt vied for honours at the
annual exhibition of the Isle of Wight Horticultural Society. (*Hampshire
Advertiser*, 26 September 1840.)

131 *The Record*, 24 August 1840.

132 14 September 1840, OLL XIX.

133 *Hampshire Independent*, 12 September 1840.

134 *The Record*, 24 September 1840.

135 *Ibid.*, 2 November 1840.

136 J. Owen, *Memoir of the Rev. Thomas Jones, Late of Creaton,
Northamptonshire*, Seeley, London, 1851, p. 176. The author added, 'He
tells us after he returned home he had some correspondence with the
minister: "he thought him a good man in a fit of insanity."' Sibthorp
described Jones as, 'bitter against the Oxford men', and sent him a pamphlet
by Sewell. (Letter to Bloxam, 5 December 1840, OLL XIX.)

137 6 November 1840, OLL II. Fox had become rector of Delamere in Cheshire.

138 King, pp. 176–179.

139 *Berrow's Worcester Journal*, 18 November 1841.

140 To Miss Holmes, 19 October 1840; [G. Tracey,] *The Letters and Diaries of*

John Henry Newman, Vol. VII, [Clarendon Press, Oxford, 1995,] p. 409.

141 *Centenary Souvenir*, p. 10

142 Letter to Ambrose Phillipps, 7 August 1841, M.C.A. Ms. 335. One chorister with whom Sibthorp kept in touch was Edward Hill, who entered Magdalen Choir School in 1843, and in 1865, was presented to the parish of Ashurst, becoming a neighbour of J. R. Bloxam (by then vicar of Upper Beeding).

143 Fowler, p. 50 – the exchange at a Friday evening meeting is undated.

144 *Ibid.*

145 Letter, 30 November 1830, 3 Sib 1/20.

146 William Marsh writing to Charlotte Leycester, in February 1836, was probably referring to him: 'I admire Mr. S.'s charity. I can exercise it with him to the same extent towards some of the members of the Church of Rome, and approve as he does, of some sayings from their writers. . . . (but) . . . There can be no union for the Church of England with the Church of Rome till the points referred to are given up. . . .' [C.] Marsh, [*The Life of William Marsh, D.D.*, James Nisbet, London, 1881,] pp. 126, 127.

147 Letter, 11 October 1836 (R.T.S. M.E.C., 1 November.) Sibthorp said he could no longer give the office the attention it required. The previous February, he had tried to link the Society more firmly to the Church of England; at his suggestion, its Annual Report was sent to every bishop. At the Committee Meeting of 24 January 1837 a 'French manuscript' sent by Mr. Sibthorp was not considered 'adapted for publication by the Society.'

148 Rathborne was born in London on 11 May 1807, and ordained in February 1830. R. E. Scantlebury, *Isle of Wight Historical Registers*, Catholic Record Society, London, 1968, p. 319.

149 Newman's reply is not extant, he noted in his diary (16 November 1840) 'wrote to . . . Sibthorp', *The Letters and Diaries of John Henry Newman, Vol. VII*, p. 444.

150 Letter from Sibthorp to Newman, 11 November 1840, Birmingham Oratory.

151 Newman's letter to Bowden, 11 March 1841; [G. Tracey,] *The Letters and Diaries of John Henry Newman, Vol. VIII* [Clarendon Press, Oxford, 1999,] p. 65.

152 [R. W. Sibthorp,] *The Claims of the Catholic Church* [*A Sermon Preached in the Chapel of St Mary Magdalen College before the University of Oxford on the Feast of St Mark the Evangelist*, 1841], pp. 10, 11, 19, 25, 26, 28, 29.

153 25 November 1841, M. R. D. Foot & H. C. G. Matthew, *The Gladstone Diaries, Vol. 3, 1840–1847*, Clarendon Press, Oxford, 1974, p. 159.

154 [R. W. Sibthorp,] *The Commemoration of Founders and Benefactors* [*A Sermon Preached before the University of Oxford in the Chapel of St. Mary Magdalen College on the Feast of the Nativity of St. John the Baptist*, 1841], pp. 13,16,19, 25.

155 19 July 1841, M.C.A. Ms. 459 (*Phillipps*).

156 [W. D.] Macray, [*A Register of the Members of St Mary Magdalen College, Oxford*, Vol. V, Frowde, London, 1906,] p. 165.

157 5 August 1841, this letter from *A Priest of the Church of England* was originally printed in the *Oxford Herald*.

158 N. P. Wiseman, *A Letter on Catholic Unity addressed to the Rt. Hon. the*

Earl of Shrewsbury by Nicholas Bishop of Melipotamus, Dolman, London, 1841, pp. 7, 9, 17, 21.

159 *Some Answer to the Enquiry 'Why are you Become a Catholic?'*, p. 35.

160 29 March 1841, *Newman and Bloxam*, p. 134.

161 J. Rathborne, *Are the Puseyites Sincere? A Letter Most Respectfully Addressed to a Right Reverend Catholic Lord Bishop, on the Oxford Movement*, T. Jones, London, 1841, p. 4.

162 *Ibid.*, p. 24.

163 M.C.A. Ms. 459.

164 18 September 1841, M.C.A. Ms. 335.

165 10 October 1841, M.C.A. Ms. 459.

166 12 October 1841, M.C.A. Ms. 335.

167 For information on Miss Young see *The Tablet*, 4,142 (28 January 1843); E. B. Pusey's letter to Isaac Williams, September 13 (1842), Lambeth Palace, Williams deposit, (W.D.) 3/114; [O. W. Jones,] *Isaac Williams and his Circle*, [S.P.C.K., London, 1971,] p. 85, 86.

168 [E. S. Purcell,] *Life and Letters of Ambrose Phillipps de Lisle*, [Macmillan, London, 1900,] Vol. 1, pp. 273–74.

169 *The Letters and Diaries of John Henry Newman, Vol. VIII*, p. 302.

170 Letter to J. Fowler, 12 April 1881, [C. S. Dessain & T. Gornall,] *The Letters and Diaries of John Henry Newman, Vol. XXIX*, Clarendon Press, Oxford, 1976,] p. 363. Another version is given in Fowler (p. 63) 'before he started on his Oscott errand, he met J. H. Newman in the cloister at Magdalen College; who on being told where he was going said, "Mind you don't stop there"'.

171 There is some confusion about dates. On 19 October, Wiseman wrote to Bloxam, saying that he would be 'most happy to receive Mr. Sibthorp on the date you mention (28 October).' (Bloxam p. 224) See [W. Ward,] *The Life and Times of Cardinal Wiseman*, [Longmans Green & Co., London, 1897,] Vol. 1, p. 396.) According to Newman, Sibthorp left Oxford on 19 October (letter to H. Wilberforce, 8 November 1841, *The Letters and Diaries of John Henry Newman, Vol. VIII*, p. 321.) Bloxam wrote to Phillipps on 21 October, saying that Sibthorp had left him the day before (M.C.A. Ms. 335.) Whichever is correct, it seems unlikely that there was enough time for Wiseman to have been consulted about Sibthorp coming earlier than he expected.

172 M.C.A. Ms. 335.

173 Bloxam, p. 224.

174 Letter undated, Ashwell, p. 202; Wilberforce heard the news on Friday 5 November; *ibid*, p. 204.

175 Newman later added "(in company)".

176 8 November 1841, *The Letters and Diaries of John Henry Newman, Vol. VIII*, p. 321.

177 *The Church and the Chapel*, [or *Thoughts suggested by the Present State of Religion in Ryde*, London, R. Groombridge, 1841,] p. 28.

178 Letter to Fowler, 12 April 1881, *The Letters and Diaries of John Henry Newman, Vol. XXIX*, p. 363.

179 *The Church and the Chapel*, pp. 3,4.

180 *Hampshire Telegraph*, 18 August 1838. According to Benjamin Newton, the

Countess of Clare, one of the St. James's congregation, 'was very near to becoming an Exclusive. A long while she oscillated between Rome and Darby.' (C.B.A. 7049 p. 249.) She became a Roman Catholic in 1842.

181 *The Church and the Chapel*, p. 13.

182 *Some Answer to the Enquiry*, p. 32.

183 *Spiritual Memorandum* (1847) quoted in *The Life and Times of Cardinal Wiseman*, Vol. I, p. 348.

184 This was on 27 October 1839; A. B. Granville, *The Spas of England and Principal Sea Bathing Place*, Henry Colburn, London, 1841, pp. 191–92. W. G. Ward visited in July 1841 and his delight at its 'truly Catholic ethos' did much to move him Rome-wards; *Newman & Bloxam*, p. 156.

185 On a letter from Ambrose Phillipps (22 October), Bloxam wrote, 'Mr. Sibthorp went down to Oscott direct from Oxford and was admitted into the Church of Rome on 23 October 1841.' M.C.A. Ms. 335.

186 Letter Bloxam to Dr. Lee, quoted in H. R. T. Brandreth, *The Oecumenical Ideals of the Oxford Movement*, S.P.C.K., London, 1947, p. 26.

187 Newsome p. 287.

188 N. P. Wiseman, *Lectures on the Principal Doctrines and Practices of the Catholic Church, Delivered at St. Mary's Moorfields, during the Lent of 1836*, Joseph Booker, London, 1836, Vol. 1, pp. 89, 331.

189 R. D. Middleton, *Dr. Routh*, Oxford University Press, Oxford, 1938, p. 80.

190 'Thursday in Holy Week' (24 March) 1842, Cathcart, p. 96.

191 John Lingard remarked of Spencer, ' I never met with so methodistic a looking man.' [M. Haile & E. Bonney,] *Life & Letters of John Lingard*, [*1771–1851*, Herbert and Daniel, London, 1911,] p. 310.

192 [*The London and Dublin Weekly Orthodox Journal*] (*L.D.O.J.*) XIII, 333 (13 November 1841), pp. 317–18.

193 Letter to Charles Anderson, 30 November 1841, Ashwell, p. 203.

194 [Hull Clergy, (Dikes T., King J., Knight W., & Scott J.),] *A Serious Remonstrance [Addressed to the Rev. R. W. Sibthorp B.D., formerly curate of St Mary's Church Hull, Occasioned by His Recent Publication Entitled "Some Answer to the Inquiry – Why Are you Become a Catholic?" By those of the Hull Clergy who were Personally Known to Him*, Seeley, London, 1842], p. 73.

Chapter Five   *Harlequinade and Palinodia*

1 *The Life and Times of Cardinal Wiseman*, Vol. 1, p. 396.

2 Fowler, p. 63. Newman wrote to Henry Wilberforce, 'I saw him afterwards as he passed through Oxford from Oscott to Ryde, and did not like his manner.' *The Letters and Diaries of John Henry Newman, Vol. VIII*, p. 321.

3 31 October 1841, Belcher pp. 279, 280.

4 *Ibid.*

5 'To oblige' the vicar, Dr. Henry Worsley, *Hampshire Advertiser*, 16 October 1841.

6 13 November 1841.

7 Letter written from Ryde on 15 November published on 16th.

8 *Hampshire Telegraph*, 22 January, 5 February, 1842.

9 Letter, Spencer to Wilkinson, 5 November 1841, Passionist Archives, File 15, 'W'.

10   10 November 1841, M.C.A. Ms. 465.

11   Bloxam, p. 225.

12   *Some Answer to the Enquiry 'Why are you Become a Catholic?'* pp. 5, 11, 14–15, 19, 20, 23, 25, 26, 27, 28, 30, 32, 35.

13   [W. Dodsworth,] *Remarks on the Second Letter [of the Rev. Richard Waldo Sibthorp, B.D., Entitled 'A Further Answer to the Inquiry etc,'* James Burns, London, 1842], p. 3.

14   [R. P.] Blakeney, [*A Voice from Ireland in Reply to the Rev. R. W. Sibthorp's Pamphlet styled, 'Some Answer to the Inquiry etc.,* Wiliam Curry, Jun. & Co., Dublin, n.d. (1842.)]

15   Blakeney had recently graduated from Trinity College Dublin. J. Wolffe ascribes his animus to 'some imperfectly documented personal tragedy, relating to his wife, for which he held the Roman Catholic Church responsible'; see *The Protestant Crusade in Great Britain 1829–60*, Clarendon Press, Oxford, 1991, p. 109. See article by S. Gilley in Lewis, Vol. 1, pp. 107, 108.

16   Both Sibthorp's *Answer* and his *Further Answer* went through several editions; in the United States they were bound-up together as, *The Path for the True Churchman Wandering in the Mazes of Protestantism.*

17   Blakeney, pp. 4, 25.

18   Retitled: *The Catholicity of the Anglican Church Vindicated and the Alleged Catholicity of the Roman Church Disproved.*

19   He had previously published, *The Standard of Catholicity, or an Attempt to Point Out in a Plain Manner Certain Safe and Leading Principles amidst the Conflicting Opinions by which the Church is at Present Agitated*, 1840.

20   19 March 1842, *Letters and Diaries of J. H. Newman, Vol. VIII*, pp. 488, 489.

21   *A Few Remarks on some points contained in Mr. Sibthorp's Letter to a Friend by a Clergyman of the Archdiocese of Canterbury*, John Ollivier, London, 1842.

22   [W. B. *(sic)*] Newton, [*A Letter to R W Sibthorp B.D., Late Fellow of Magdalen College, Oxford on the Subject of his Recent Pamphlet*, D. Walther, London, 1842.]

23   *Observations [on Richard Waldo Sibthorp's 'Answer to the Enquiry, "Why are you become a Catholic?"' by a Spectator*, Groombridge, London, 1842.]

24   Newton, pp. 3, 9, 14.

25   *Observations*, p. 8.

26   Newton, pp. 23–24.

27   [H.] Drummond, [*Reasons Wherefore a Clergyman of the Church of England Should Not Become a Roman Catholic in Reply to the Rev. R. W. Sibthorp*, J. Hatchard, London, 1842,] pp. 35, 49, 50, 56, 57–58.

28   *Some Answer to the Enquiry 'Why are you Become a Catholic?'*, p. 34.

29   F. L. Cross, *The Oxford Dictionary of the Christian Church*, 1957, Oxford University Press, London, p. 1009.

30   [J. H. Newman,] *Apologia Pro Vita Sua*, [Longmans, Green & Co., London, 1890 (first edition 1864),] p. 40.

31   In 1829, he was at the Albury Park Conference, from where Edward Irving wrote to his wife, 'Mr. Drummond says that if I and Dodsworth had been joined together we would have made a Pope Gregory the Great – he to

furnish the popish quality, not me.' *The Life of Edward Irving*, p. 273.

32 W. Dodsworth, *Allegiance to the Church*, James Burns, London, 1841, p. 3.

33 1 February 1842, *The Letters and Diaries of John Henry Newman, Vol. VIII*, p. 448.

34 [J. H. Newman,] *Sermons Bearing on Subjects of the Day*, [Rivington, London, 1843,] p. 230.

35 *A Serious Remonstrance*, pp. 6, 7.

36 W. Palmer, *An Examination of the Rev R. W. Sibthorp's Reasons for his Secession from the Church*, Parker, Oxford, 1842, pp. 10, 11, 12.

37 [R. W. Sibthorp,] *A Further Answer to the Enquiry* [:'*Why Have you Become a Catholic?' In a Second Letter to a Friend*, 1842], p. 5.

38 G. E. Biber, *Catholicity v. Sibthorp or Some Help to Answer the Question whether the Rev R. W. Sibthorp is now or ever was a Catholic. In a Series of Letters Addressed to Him by the Rev. G. E. Biber, Presbyter of the Anglo-Catholic Church*, Rivington, London, 1842, Letter 2, p. 37.

39 *A Further Answer to the Enquiry*, p. 6.

40 [W. Palmer,] *A Supplement to an Examination* [*of Mr. Sibthorp's Pamphlet Comprising Observations on His 'Further Answer,' &c*, Parker, Oxford, 1842], p. 10.

41 Palmer, p. 23.

42 [W.] Dodsworth, [*Why are you Become a Romanist? A Letter to the Rev. Richard Waldo Sibthorp B.D. occasioned by his Letter Entitled, 'Some Answer to the Inquiry, Why are you Become a Catholic?'*, James Burns, London, 1842,] p. 12.

43 *Ibid.*, pp. 13, 14.

44 *Some Answer to the Enquiry 'Why are you Become a Catholic?'*, p. 10.

45 'he associated himself with dissenting teachers in teaching religion only one or two years before his thoughts were turned to Rome.' *Remarks on the Second Letter*, pp. 24–25.

46 Dodsworth, pp. 7, 9, 19, 20, 23, 24.

47 Drummond, p. 48–49.

48 *Remarks on the Second Letter*, pp. 28, 26.

49 Dodsworth, p. 15.

50 21 November 1841, Belcher p. 288.

51 On 19 December 1841, he wrote to Bloxam, 'Sibthorpe gives great edification here.' Belcher, p. 301.

52 *Statement and Depositions Relative to the Origin of the Fire at Springfield House, Southampton*, Dolman, London 1842, pp. 8, 9.

53 B. Holland, *Memoir of Kenelm Henry Digby*, Longmans Green, London 1919, p. 140.

54 *Serious Remonstrance*, p. 2.

55 16 February 1842, C.P. (Cholmeley's draft.)

56 Letter, 8 January 1842, Hole, Vol. II, p. 152.

57 8 November 1841.

58 December 1841, p. 657.

59 *Wesleyan Methodist Magazine*, LXIV (December 1841), pp. 1029, 1030.

60 C. P. Golightly, *Correspondence Illustrative of the Actual State of Oxford with Reference to Tractarianism and the Attempts of Mr. Newman and his Party to Unprotestantise the National Church*, MacPherson, Oxford, 1842,

pp. 1, 9. (Letter to the *Standard*, 12 November 1841.) Pugin told Bloxam, 'Sibthorpe utterly denies have (*sic*) used any such expression.' (19 December 1841, Belcher, p. 301.)

61 [W. Ward,] *William George Ward and the Oxford Movement*, [Macmillan, London, 1890,] pp. 199–200.

62 Letter to Henry Wilberforce, 19 February 1842; *The Letters and Diaries of John Henry Newman, Vol. VIII*, p. 469.

63 E. B. Pusey, *A Letter to his Grace the Archbishop of Canterbury on some Circumstances connected with Present Crisis in the English Church*, Parker, Oxford, 1842, pp. 35,23,8. 'If then, they who are in authority seem . . . to censure our teaching broadly, it comes to them like a rejection of themselves from our Church. They find their belief disavowed, themselves disowned; whither are they to turn?' *Ibid.*, p. 43.

64 31 October 1841, *The Letters and Diaries of John Henry Newman, Vol. VIII*, pp. 312, 313.

65 *Ibid.*, 8 November 1841, p. 321.

66 *Sermons Bearing on Subjects of the Day*, pp. 348–430. See E. A. Abbott, *The Anglican Career of Cardinal Newman*, Macmillan, London, 1892, Vol. II, p. 310.

67 *Sermons Bearing on Subjects of the Day, XXII (Outward and Inward Notes of the Church)*, pp. 379, 380–81, 383, 384.

68 *Apologia Pro Vita Sua*, pp. 156, 157.

69 Lathbury, Vol. 1, pp. 276, 277.

70 *The Foreign and Colonial Quarterly Review*, IV, (October 1843).

71 W. E. Gladstone, *Gleanings of Past Years*, 1879, Vol. V, pp. 24, 25, 35, 71, 57, 74.

72 M.C.A. Ms. 335.

73 3 November 1841, Belcher, p. 281.

74 2 November 1841; *William George Ward and the Oxford Movement*, pp. 197–99.

75 *Life and Letters of Ambrose Phillipps de Lisle*, Vol. II, p. 302.

76 Letter to Shrewsbury, Feast of St. Damasus, (11 December) 1841; *Ibid.*, p. 308.

77 *L.D.O.J.*, XIII, 333, p. 317.

78 Willson, brother of the architect friend of Pugin, was born in Lincoln on 11 December 1794. Ordained in 1824, Bishop Milner sent him to Nottingham where the flock was under the care of a 'venerable old French priest. . .' [T.] Kelsh, [*Personal Recollections of the Rt. Rev. Robert William Willson DD*, Davies Bros., Hobart, 1882,] pp. 1–5.

79 23 December 1841, Ushaw College, Wiseman Papers (W.P.) 849.

80 'the Revd Mr. Sibthorpe is full of zeal for the work . . . he is going to have splendid vestments made.' Pugin to Shrewsbury, 23 February 1842; Belcher, p. 326. A set donated by him is preserved at Douai Abbey, Upper Woolhampton, near Reading.

81 For example, in a letter to Mr. Masters, dated 23 July 1842, M.C.A. Ms. 492.

82 Letter to Bloxam (1 February 1842) OLL XIX.

83 Shortly after his conversion, Peter le Page Renouf wrote to reassure his parents about his temporal prospects, saying 'I have had offers made to me

on all sides. And at the present moment I can choose between Dr. Wiseman, Bp. Walsh, Mr. Spencer, Mr. Sibthorp and Lord Shrewsbury.' (24 March 1842; Cathcart, p. 95).

84 Feast of St. Stanislaus (7 May 1842) W.P. 856.

85 Letter Wiseman to Shrewsbury, 23 December 1841, W.P. 849.

86 On 11 November 1841, E. V. Utterson wrote to Coxe of the Bodleian Library, 'You have undoubtedly heard of the extraordinary change in Mr. Sibthorpe's religious principles. . . . I have always thought him crack-brained. It is said that he and Spoony Spencer are about to undertake a mission through the three kingdoms to convert the lieges to Romanism.' Macray, p. 165.

87 Of Hainton in Lincolnshire, a recusant family, although some of its members conformed.

88 Letter to Bloxam, 25 February 1865, Fowler, p. 171.

89 9 February; Wiseman wrote to Phillipps, 'Mr. A. B. is engaged in replying to Palmer and Dodsworth's flimsy pamphlets, which are really miserable – particularly the former. . .' *The Life and Times of Cardinal Wiseman*, Vol. I, p. 415. The letter is incorrectly dated 'December 8, 1842.'

90 He was ordained deacon on Passion Sunday, 13 March 1842, Fowler, p. 65.

91 OLL II.

92 R. W. Sibthorp, *Substance of a Sermon Preached in the Cathedral Church of St. Chad, Birmingham, on the Morning of St. Patrick's Day*, 1842, p. 24.

93 *L.D.O.J.* Vol. XIV, No. 354 (9 April 1842) p. 237 & No. 356, (23 April 1842) p. 269.

94 4 April 1842, OLL II.

95 *L.D.O.J.* XIV, 360 (21 May 1842) p. 335; 361 (28 May 1842) p. 349.

96 Letter to Fox, 4 April 1842, OLL II.

97 2 July 1842, OLL XIX.

98 Sibthorp wrote to Bloxam (2 July 1842) 'I am not going to Rome this summer with Bishop Wiseman, who set off on the 12th, being afraid of the heat of Italy at this time.' *Ibid.*

99 *Spiritual Memorandum*, 7 March 1847, W.P. 871. From misleading press reports, it was widely believed that Sibthorp was ordained within a few weeks of conversion. Newman wrote in 1865: '. . . as to time of preparation, it varies with the individual. I was myself ordained within two years – but Dr Manning, I think, in only a week or two. So, I *believe* was Mr Sibthorp.' Letter to H. Bedford, 4 August, C. S. Dessain, *The Letters and Diaries of John Henry Newman, Vol. XXII*, Nelson, London, 1972, p. 21.

100 Letter to W. D. Fox, 17 November 1841, OLL II (underlining in original italicised.) Sibthorp agreed to visit Delamere Rectory at the end of November, to show 'how much he valued his continual acquaintance.'

101 1 February 1842, OLL XIX.

102 1 April 1842, W. P. 851.

103 Sibthorp preached twice at the opening of St. Mary's, Stockton (7 July). M. Belcher, *A. W. N. Pugin – An Annotated Critical Bibliography*, Mansell, London, 1987, p. 207.

104 Letter to Bloxam, 2 July 1842, OLL XIX. The nun was Miss Clifford of St Benedict's Priory.

105 [R]. Chapman, [*Father Faber*, Burns & Oates, London, 1961,] p. 187. Sibthorp was a friend of Fr. Walker of Scarborough, see *Life & Letters of John Lingard*, p. 324.

106 Letter to Bowden, 5 August 1846, Chapman, p. 149. Sibthorp had little time for Faber: 'The Life of St. . . . (in the Lives of the Saints) is a disgusting volume. I cannot get through with it. Mr. F. . . is an extravagant of the first water.' Letter to Bloxam, 19 November 1847, Fowler, p. 87.

107 Letter to Fowler, 4 November 1864, Fowler, p. 158.

108 7 October 1845, OLL XIX.

109 Letter to Bloxam, 4 June 1849, Fowler, p. 104.

110 OLL XIX.

111 Just as in 1829, he was uncomfortable with Magdalen society.

112 1 March 1842, OLL II.

113 Letter to Joseph Oldknow, 22 November 1843, Add. Ms. 44360, fol. 325.

114 'Here in the Birmingham clergy house he was thrown amid coarse people. His companions were Irishmen from rough humble homes . . . They were ignorant and common, and he minded it.' Sykes, pp. 50, 51.

115 Bernard Smith was very impressed by Moore, see *The Life and Times of Cardinal Wiseman*, Vol. 1, p. 410.

116 For such Ryde was, in everything but name.

117 Letter to Dr. Newsham, 22 July 1842, Ushaw College, Newsham correspondence.

118 Letter to Mr. Masters, 23 July 1842, M.C.A. Ms. 492.

119 Letter to Bloxam, 2 July 1842, OLL XIX.

120 *Substance of a Sermon Delivered at the Opening of St. Oswald's Catholic Church, Old Swan, near Liverpool, on Thursday Aug. 4, 1842*, 1842, p. 2.

121 *L.R.S.M.*, 26 August 1842.

122 To George Dempster Johnstone, a Cholmeley connection.

123 Letter to Bloxam, 23 August 1842, OLL XIX.

124 Based on Fowler's informant ('He refused to live with the clergy, and took a small house. . .', p. 71). Sykes took Richard's move as evidencing a desire to distance himself from his colleagues. It probably had more to do with his love of gardening. He told Bloxam that the house was as far from the Church as Holmewood from Ryde and was 'quiet, retired, having a small, neat garden.' (Letter, 23 August 1842, OLL XIX).

125 *True Tablet*, 17 September 1842.

126 24 September 1842.

127 7 October 1843, W.P. 480.

128 2 November 1842, *Life and Letters of Ambrose Phillipps de Lisle*, Vol. 1, p. 274.

129 A. Wedgwood, *A. W. N. Pugin and the Pugin Family*, Victoria & Albert Museum, London, 1985, p. 53.

130 28 October 1842, W.D. 3/108.

131 *Life and Letters of Ambrose Phillipps de Lisle*, Vol. 1, p. 274.

132 James Mozley wrote to his sister, 'I heard rather an amusing account of a young lady's visit to Oxford last term. The young lady, who had come to Pusey in such deep distress and religious perplexity, it seems was flaunting about with young gentlemen a good deal of the time, shopping, going down the river, and amusing herself very pleasantly – dear, good Pusey all the time

being full of pity and concern for her painful state of doubt and anxiety.' 25 February (1842) [A. Mozley] *Letters of the Rev. J. B. Mozley DD*, [Rivingtons, London, 1885,] p. 111.

133 *Isaac Williams and His Circle*, p. 86.

134 24 November 1842, OLL XIX.

135 Fowler, p. 74.

136 Letter, 9 December 1842, Cholmeley, p. 78.

137 Letter to Quilter, 29 April 1843, Fowler, p. 73.

138 K. Mamelak, 'The Motor Vehicle Collision Injury Syndrome', *Neuropsychiatry, Neuropsychology & Behavioral Neurology*, 13, 2 (2000), pp. 125–35.

139 For example, on 28 October 1842, he wrote to Quilter, 'I now dare speak of nothing as fixed, but live only a day at a time.' Fowler, p. 74.

140 Letter, 9 December 1842, Cholmeley, p. 78.

141 *The Depredations of Churches*.

142 On 4 December 'he preached a most eloquent sermon . . . before a crowded congregation many of whom were Protestants. The Countess of Clare, a recent convert was present.' *True Tablet*, 10 December 1842.

143 24 November 1842, OLL XIX.

144 20 December 1842, *Letters of the Rev. J. B. Mozley, D.D.*, p. 136.

145 Letter to J. W. Bowden, 29 December 1842, Mozley, Vol. 2, pp. 405–6.

146 A forged letter from 'Bernard Smith' appeared the *Morning Herald*, 5 Jan 1843.

147 Letter to Bloxam, 3 January 1843, OLL XIX. *True Tablet* (31 December 1842) reported that Smith assisted Sibthorp in celebrating Mass on the feast of St Thomas. See R. D. Middleton, *Magdalen Studies*, S.P.C.K., London, 1936, pp. 251–52.

148 9 January 1843, OLL XIX.

149 *Morning Herald*, 25 January 1843.

150 Letter dated 24 January 1843, *The Tablet*, 28 January 1843.

151 The rumours even reached Rome, from where Mrs Massingberd wrote to her daughter (24 February 1843): 'There are strong reports that Mr. Sibthorp. . .is dissatisfied – that he has left Oscott, that he will not worship the Virgin, and that the matter is referred to the Pope, whether he may have special exemption.' Mass. 3/52.

152 Letter to Bloxam, 3 January 1843, OLL XIX.

153 26 December 1842, *ibid.*

154 3 January 1843, *ibid.*

155 Letter to Bloxam, 3rd d. in Oct. Epiph., *ibid.*

156 Fowler, p. 72.

157 *Nottingham Review*, 27 January 1843.

158 Letter to Lord Shrewsbury, 7 October 1843, W. P. 480.

159 In a letter to Norman dated 20 February 1843, he said that he was 'chiefly resident' at Edgbaston.

160 4 April 1843, OLL XIX.

161 29 April 1843, Fowler, p. 73.

162 In July, Walsh wrote to Willson, recently returned from Rome, 'The retirement of the Rev Mr Sibthorp has rather disconnected our plans, but not discouraged us.' Southerwood, p. 36.

163 OLL XIX. Sibthorp borrowed an altar stone and tabernacle from the priest at Newport, *Tablet*, 14 October 1843.

164 *Hampshire Telegraph*, 3 July 1843.

165 Letter to Bloxam, 27 March 1866, Fowler, p. 77.

166 Letter to Routh, 2 October 1843, Fowler, p. 75. Writing to Bickersteth he said had spent four months undertaking a 'calm, and deliberate and prayerful reconsideration of the great issues involved in the separation of the Anglican from the Catholic Church.' 5 October 1843, [Bickersteth papers,] Ms. Eng. c. 6398.

167 *Some Answer to the Enquiry 'Why are you Become a Catholic?'*, p. 33.

168 Letter to Bloxam, 21 July 1843, OLL XIX.

169 Letter, 29 December 1864, Mass. 4/42.

170 Letter, 30 December 1864, Mass. 4/44.

171 H. I. B. Dunton, *The Millerite Adventists and other Millenarian Groups in Great Britain*, 1830–60, 1984, unpublished PhD thesis, London University, 1984, Ch. 4 *passim*.

172 E. Bickersteth, *The Divine Warning to the Church at this Time of our Present Enemies, Dangers and Duties and our Future Prospects, A Sermon Preached before the Protestant Association at St. Dunstan's, Fleet Street on Saturday November 5, 1842*, Protestant Association, London, 1842, pp. 2, 40, 43.

173 E. Bickersteth, *The Restoration of the Jews*, Seeley, London, 1853, pp. 306–7.

174 Froom, p. 706. Brock was minister of Christ Church, Clifton; Dunton questions the basis of his figure (p. 48).

175 E. Bickersteth (ed.), *The Second Coming, The Judgement and the Kingdom of Christ. Lectures delivered during Lent 1843 at St. George's, Bloomsbury by 12 Clergyman of the Church of England, with a Preface by Rev. Edward Bickersteth, Rector of Watton*, James Nisbet, London, 1843, pp. 142, 444.

176 Letter to Bloxam, 17 May 1843, OLL XIX.

177 *Character of Papacy*, p. 23.

178 In a letter of 23 July 1843, OLL XIX.

179 Fowler, p. 77.

180 2 September 1843, OLL XIX.

181 Fowler, p. 75, the incident cannot be dated. One precious item was not destroyed: a Pugin chrismatory. Sibthorp later gave it to Bloxam, who in 1885 presented it to Newman. (Wedgewood, p. 53; *Newman and Bloxam*, p. 249).

182 OLL XIX.

183 Southerwood, p. 36.

184 *Wesleyan Chronicle*, 6 October 1843, 'J Y' was probably Isabella Young.

185 7 October 1843, Birmingham Diocesan Archives, B.692.

186 Southerwood, p. 37.

187 7 March 1847, W. P. 871.

188 14 October 1843.

189 *The Tablet*, 21 October 1843. Sykes attributes Lucas's restraint to Sibthorp's evident sincerity compared with that of Fr. Oxley, who had also recently defected (p. 57).

190 10 October 1843, M.C.A. Ms. 335.

191 Letter to Phillipps dated, 'St. John of Beverley' (25 October) 1843. *The Life*

and Times of Cardinal Wiseman, Vol. I, pp. 418–19. According to George Spencer, Sibthorp's return advanced Seager's conversion. Letter to Mrs. Canning, November 6, 1843, Passionist Archives, File 6, 'C'.

192   16 November 1843.
193   Lambeth Palace, Golightly Papers, Ms. 1805.
194   *Church and State Gazette*, 90, 2 (3 November 1843).
195   21 November 1843.
196   5 February 1849, *Life and Letters of Ambrose Phillipps de Lisle*, Vol. I, p. 181.

Chapter Six   *Struggling to Shore*

1   Letter, Lingard to Walker 14 November 1845, *Life & Letters of John Lingard*, p. 324.
2   10 October 1843, M.C.A. Ms. 335.
3   Charles 'had a very strong rather than very enlightened attachment to the Protestant Faith . . . When one of his brothers . . . joined the Church of Rome in 1841, he felt it a heavy blow, as indeed it was, to all his cherished and expressed sentiments respecting that Church. He wept bitterly; sought his brother out, and for hours with many tears implored him to recal his decision; but he never abated his kindness, nor withdrew his affection from him, and rejoiced when he resumed the ministry in the English Church.' *Gentleman's Magazine*, XLV, (January 1856), pp. 86–87.
4   OLL XIX.
5   *Ibid.*
6   6 November 1843, Passionist Archives, File 6, 'C'.
7   Ms. Eng. c. 6398.
8   J. Flavel, *England's Duty*, W. Baynes & Son, London, 1820 (first edition 1689), Sermon III, p. 51.
9   5 October 1843, Ms. Eng. c. 6398.
10   *The Times*, 28 November 1843.
11   *The Tablet*, 18 November 1843.
12   *Church and State Gazette*, 1 December 1843.
13   Letter, 7 December 1843, OLL XIX.
14   *Morning Herald*, 21 November 1843.
15   *English Churchman*, 30 November 1843.
16   Letter, 21 December 1843, OLL XIX.
17   2 October 1843, Fowler, p. 76.
18   M. Pattison, *Memoirs*, Centaur Press, Fontwell, 1969 (first edition 1885), pp. 195–96.
19   7 November 1843, *Letters of the Rev. J. B. Mozley DD*, p. 149.
20   B. W. Noel *et. al.*, *Lectures on the Points in Controversy between Romanists and Protestants*, Presbyterian Board of Publication, Philadelphia, 1840, pp. 111–12.
21   N. Wiseman, *Remarks on a Letter from the Rev. W. Palmer MA of Worcester College, Oxford*, Dolman, London, 1841, p. 16.
22   17 October 1843, OLL II.
23   22 November 1843, Add. Ms. 44360, fol. 325.
24   Letters to Bloxam, 7 & 21 December 1843, OLL XIX.
25   Letter to Bloxam, 2 October 1843, *ibid.*

26 22 November 1843, Add. Ms. 44360, fol. 325.

27 J. Oldknow, *The Duty of Promoting Christian Unity: A Sermon Preached in the Holy Trinity Chapel, Bordesley, Birmingham on the Morning of the Twenty-first Sunday after Trinity 1843, Being the Anniversary of the Gunpowder Treason*, James Burns, London, 1843, pp. 12–13.

28 Letter to J. Oldknow, 18 January 1844, Add. Ms. 44360, fols. 325, 326.

29 Letter to Bloxam (enclosing transcript of Sumner's), 7 December 1843, OLL XIX.

30 12 March 1844, *ibid.*

31 6 April 1844, *ibid.*

32 Letter to Bloxam, 25 April 1844, *ibid.*

33 Letter, 17 May 1844, *ibid.*

34 Letter to Bloxam, 25 July 1844, *ibid.*

35 Founded in 1843 by Vinzenz Pressnitz, a Silesian farmer.

36 21 August 1844, OLL XIX.

37 He added, 'I was shocked to observe it among such kind men as Mr. Dikes.' Later, Dykes wrote to Mrs. Hey: 'My friend S. recommended me to read the life of Xavier, a Romanist Missionary; and, as it was written by Dryden we procured the book; and it is well worth reading; for it does set forth, with the most unblushing effrontery, such lying miracles as must cause us to wonder at the attempt to impose upon the credulity of mankind.' King, pp. 221–22.

38 Letter to Bloxam 29 January 1845, *ibid.*

39 Letter to Bloxam, 30 June 1845, *ibid.* See Curnock, Vol. VI, pp. 54, 142.

40 Where Sibthorp always tried to stay when visiting London.

41 Letter to Bloxam, 25 July 1844, OLL XIX. Ward had presumably forgotten his resolve (p. 153, *vide supra*).

42 Elliott had begun the work in 1837; 'doubtless the most elaborate work ever produced on the Apocalypse'. Froom, p. 716.

43 22 November 1844, OLL XIX.

44 'so fixing 1865, or thereabouts, as the probable epoch of the consummation.' E. B. Elliott, *Horae Apocalypticae, or a Commentary on the Apocalypse, Critical and Historical*, R. B. Seeley and W. Burnside, London, 1844, Vol. III, p. 1421, Froom, p. 721. The events of 1848 however, reignited Sibthorp's perception of the imminence of the Last Times. The *Lincolnshire Chronicle* of 22 December 1848 reported that in a recent sermon he gave a 'masterly description of the state of Europe, religiously, socially and morally, as evidencing the probable approach of the Second Advent'.

45 Letter to Bloxam, 29 January 1845, OLL XIX.

46 Letter to Bloxam, 27 February 1845, *ibid.*

47 *The Celebration of the Blessed Sacrament of the Lord's Supper or Holy Eucharist anciently called the Mass; for all Days throughout the Year* – there were two editions, twenty copies of each were printed. In 1880, Gladstone wrote to thank Coningsby Sibthorp who had presented him with a copy. He said his uncle's work was 'a most touching exhibition of the real and very searching difficulties, which religious divisions and their consequences have strewn so thickly around the path of spirits, gifted as he was with the keenest Christian susceptibility'. 16 September 1880, 4 Sib/1.

48   Letter to Bloxam, 29 April 1876, pasted into Magdalen College's copy of the book.

49   31 March 1845, OLL XIX.

50   Although the first edition had no author's name, subsequently 'E.M' appeared, the pseudonym adopted by Sibthorp for both 1845 works. The 1850 edition of the *Dream* is the 'twenty-fourth thousand'.

51   Letter to Bloxam, 29 January 1845, OLL XIX.

52   Letter to Bloxam, 27 February 1845, *ibid.*

53   Letter 31 March 1845, *ibid.*

54   Letter to Bloxam, 8 August 1845, *ibid.*

55   Letter to Bloxam, 11 September 1845, *ibid.*

56   In December 1835, Aitken seceded and formed the 'Christian Society', a mixture of Methodism and Tractarianism, which by 1837 claimed 1,500 members in the Liverpool area. 'Known locally as Jumpers or Ranters, his supporters attracted attention mainly because of their frenzied revivalist activities . . .' (D. A. Gowland, *Methodist Secessions: The Origin of Free Methodism in three Lancashire Towns*, University Press, Manchester, 1979 pp. 106–7.) In 1838, he applied for re-instatement, and was re-admitted as an Anglican priest in April 1841. Advised by J. H. Newman, Hook appointed him curate of St. James's, telling Gladstone he was 'a most eloquent preacher, he propounds his notions with great force, though sometimes (as he preaches extemporaneously) with little judgement. I do not wish therefore to be committed to him, or to take the responsibility for his proceedings upon myself'. (January 1844, W. R. W. Stephens, *The Life and Letters of Walter Farquhar Hook*, Richard Bentley, London, 1878, Vol. II, p. 228).

57   Letter to Bloxam, 11 September 1845, OLL XIX.

58   7 October 1845, *ibid.*

59   'I withstood temptations occuring powerfully during those three years, especially at the time of secession to her of other clergymen, to return to the communion of Rome.' Letter to Routh, 12 May 1847, Bloxam, pp. 238–39.

60   7 October 1845, OLL XIX.

61   11 November 1845, *ibid.*

62   Letter to Bloxam, 15 December 1845, *ibid.*

63   *Ibid.*

64   C. S. Dessain, *Letters and Diaries of J. H. Newman, Vol. XI*, Nelson, London, 1961, pp. 52, 53.

65   J. H. Newman, *An Essay on the Development of Christian Doctrine*, James Toovey, London, 1845, p. 29.

66   He referred particularly to pages 404–6: 'The votaries of Mary do not exceed the true faith, unless the blasphemers of her Son came up to it. The Church of Rome is not idolatrous, unless Arianism is orthodoxy.' *Ibid.*, p. 406.

67   15 December 1845, OLL XIX.

68   Curate of Over and Nether Seale in Leicestershire.

69   Sibthorp added a footnote: 'I may say I scarcely doubt it.' Letter dated, 24 February 1846, Gresley Letters No. 164.

70   N. Yates, *Leeds and the Oxford Movement – A Study in 'High Church' Activity in the Rural Deaneries of Allerton, Armley, Headingley and Whitkirk in the Diocese of Ripon, 1836–1934*, Thoresby Society Publications, Leeds (Vol. LV, No. 121), 1975, p. 26.

71 Letter dated 3 February 1846. Substantial extracts appeared in the *Times* on 2 February 1892, appended to the Rev. O. W. W. Forester's letter regarding the death of Cardinal Manning. Edward Jackson may have been referring to it, when he informed Bloxam: 'Dr. Longley, the Bishop of Ripon wrote to Dr. Hook, whose senior curate at that time I was, stating that two ladies of rank in Ireland . . . were likely to go over to the Church of Rome. Every endeavour had been made to keep them in the Church of England, when at last they had said that having a deep reverence for Mr. Sibthorp, whose ministry they had greatly profited by, if anything would change their purpose it would be the reasons which have led Mr Sibthorp to return to the English Church. Bishop Longley added in his letter to Hook that as he was aware that I knew Sibthorp I might possibly obtain from him the information in question. On this I wrote to Sibthorp enclosing the bishop's letter and in reply, without expressing any unwillingness, Sibthorp wrote in full what had been requested of him. The letter was forwarded by me to Bishop Longley, but it failed of the purpose for which it had been obtained. It was lengthy and considered at the time a very important letter.' Letter, 18 March 1886, M.C.A. Ms. 492.
72 15 December 1845, OLL XIX.
73 *The Times*, 22 April 1846.
74 Letter to Rev. M. Amphlett, 17 March 1843; R. K. Pugh, *The Letter Books of Bishop Wilberforce*, Oxfordshire Record Society, Oxford, 1970, p. 18.
75 'I think myself bound to call upon you for such an explicit declaration . . . especially in regard to the principal points of difference between our own Church and that of Rome, as can alone justify me in my judgement in making myself a party to your re-admission to the post of teacher.' G. H. Sumner, *The Life of Charles Richard Sumner D.D., Bishop of Winchester*, John Murray, London, 1876, p. 303.
76 Adding, 'some of whom I know'; one was Aitken.
77 12 May 1847, Bloxam, pp. 235–39.
78 Letter to 'a friend' (Bloxam), 31 July 1876, Bloxam pp. 233, 234. Sabine Baring-Gould referred to the episode as an example of the bishop's 'narrow-minded evangelicalism.' *The Church Revival*, Methuen & Co., London, 1914, p. 172.
79 'I trust you will give me credit for having some valid reason. . . .' Letter to Routh, 2 November 1846, M.C.A. Ms. 465.
80 8 February 1847, Bloxam, p. 234.
81 13 May C. S. Dessain, *The Letters and Diaries of J. H. Newman, Vol. XII*, Nelson, London, 1962, p. 80
82 Letter, 5 May 1847, Fowler, p. 86. A denial of his return to Rome was published in the *Times*, 17 May 1847.
83 Letter to Routh, 8 February 1847, Bloxam, p. 234.
84 Letter, 7 May 1847, M.C.A. Ms. 465.
85 Letter dated 22 or 23 December, Fowler, pp. 89–90.
86 L.A.O. *Episcopal Act Book 1800–1858*, p. 516.
87 Letter to Bloxam, 11 September 1845, OLL XIX. The hospital was founded in 1676 by Sir William Turner, who 'endowed it with lands, said to be worth £1500 per annum'; T. Allen, *A New and Complete History of the County of York*, I. T. Hinton, London, 1831, Vol. VI, p. 375.

88   A.N., M.C.A. Ms. 492.

89   'a piece of land near Cottam's mill . . .', *Lincolnshire Press Cuttings*, Vol. IV, p. 37.

90   23 March 1847, Bloxam, pp. 234–35. Pugin, disturbed by Sibthorp's reversion to the Church of England had declined to supervise the building-work. See, P. Spencer-Silver, *Pugin's Builder – The Life and Work of George Myers*, The University of Hull Press, 1993, pp. 36–37.

91   7 May 1847, M.C.A. Ms. 465. The inscription reads, *Ad majorem Dei gloriam et in honorem Beatae Annae viduae Hierosol. has aedes eleemosynarias, anno sacro MDCCCXLVII structus et dotatos, memoriae matris suae amantissimae semper sibi deflendae dicavit Ricardus Waldo Sibthorp*.

92   11 January 1850, M.C.A. Ms. 528 (*A. W. N. Pugin*). The result of the architect not being involved in the construction was an 'unmodified Pugin conception in which all of the traits of informality, smallness of scale, and exaggerated medievalism may be seen in their most primitive form'. P. Stanton, *Pugin*, Thames & Hudson, London, 1971, p. 141.

93   [J.] Arram, [*St. Anne's Bede Houses*, unpublished thesis, University of Nottingham, 1994,] Appendix 1.

94   Letter to Bloxam, 3 November 1849, Fowler, p. 108.

95   Fowler p. 88.

96   Butterfield 'never exceeded his estimates by a shilling'. P. Thompson, *William Butterfield*, Routledge, Kegan, Paul, London, 1971, p. 62. In August 1876, Sir Arthur Elton noted in his diary that he talked 'a good deal' with Butterfield 'of the strange career of Waldo Sibthorp,' *ibid.*, p. 55.

97   Fowler, p. 367.

98   The total amount raised from the sale was £1597–18–2d; Arram, *Index to Minute Book*, Fowler p. 267.

99   The rector's application is dated 3 May 1848 (L.A.O. Cur. Lic. 327/12.) There is no record of it being granted.

100   Fowler, pp. 100–1.

101   *Lincolnshire Chronicle*, 22 December 1848.

102   Letter to Fowler, 29 August 1864, Fowler, p. 144.

103   *Things That Were*, p. 43.

104   In 1852 an American observed of Charles: 'He is a notorious libertine . . . upon the death of a favourite mistress an English bishop consoled him upon his loss.' D. V. G. Bartlett, *London by Day and Night*, 1852, quoted in J. W. Dodds, *The Age of Paradox – A Biography of England 1845–1851*, Victor Gollancz, London, 1953, p. 50.

105   Fowler, p. 94 n.1.

106   See Newman's letter to Pusey, 24 January 1842, *The Letters and Diaries of John Henry Newman*, Vol. VIII, p. 436.

107   Letter to Mrs. Allenby, 14 May 1845, OLL XIX. Harris's resignation at Alford was about the time of Sibthorp's conversion, which may account for a report in a 'provincial paper' reprinted in the *L.D.O.J.* (XIV, 340 [1 January 1842]) ' Mr. Harris of Aldford (*sic*) Lincolnshire, a talented dissenting preacher, was last week added as another convert to the Romish faith. He is reported to have lately corresponded with Mr. Sibthorp. His chapel is now closed.'

108   Letter to Mrs. Allenby, 12 Sept. 1845, OLL XIX; Harris converted in 1846.

109 *Dublin Review*, [XXVIII, LV,] (March 1850), p. 118.
110 Letter to Bloxam, 18 May 1850, Fowler, p. 112.
111 6 December 1864, Fowler, p. 160.
112 Letter to Bloxam, 23 May 1864, *ibid*., p. 140.
113 *Dublin Review*, (March 1850), p. 116.
114 'Willson helped Sibthorpe through a crisis of faith.' Southerwood, p. 147.
     Fr. Pius, *Life of Father Ignatius of St. Paul, Passionist (The Hon. & Rev.*
     George Spencer), James Duffy, Dublin 1866, p. 451.
115 6 October 1860, Fowler, p. 128.
116 Letter to Bloxam, 14 November 1863, *ibid*., p. 136.
117 *The Times*, 2 February 1892.
118 Vicar of Shoreham.
119 *The Times*, 2 February 1892.
120 Undated note, inscribed, 'Written in a copy of the Life of the Curé d'Ars,
     among the Rev. R. Waldo Sibthorp's books, now at Sudbrooke Holme,
     Lincoln,' in L.A.O.'s copy of Fowler.
121 Letter to Bloxam (May, 1864), Fowler, p. 141.
122 In the 5th edition of the *Horae* (1862) Elliott referred to 1866 as the likely
     end of the 'now existing dispensation.' (Vol. IV, pp. 224, 237.)
123 Letter to Bloxam, 27 April 1851, Fowler, p. 117.
124 Referring to Dean Stanley, Sibthorp wrote, 'One of the Bishops of the
     Church of England showed me some sentences of his quite as bad as anything
     in *Essays and Reviews*.' Fowler, p. 139.
125 J. Colenso, *The Pentateuch and the Book of Joshua Critically Examined*,
     Longmans Green, London, issued in parts, 1862–1879.
126 R. W. Sibthorp, *The Saviour's estimation of the writings of Moses shown in*
     His own use of them, 1862, p. 4.
127 November 1862, Fowler, p. 132.
128 Fowler was the Headmaster of Lincoln Grammar School and appointed
     Sibthorp's deputy in 1859. The year before he had married Martha Bodley,
     the daughter of Richard's old friend.
129 Arram, p. 55. He formally notified the bishop of his resignation on 21
     September 1864, and in November finally severed connections with Lincoln.
     Fowler, pp. 149, 150.
130 Letter to Francis Massingberd, 29 December 1864, Mass. 4/42.
131 Fowler, p. 143.
132 15 October 1864, *ibid*., p. 152.
133 29 December 1864, Mass. 4/42.
134 Fowler, p. 146.
135 *Ibid*., p. 145.
136 29 December 1864, Mass 4/42.
137 Undated letter, Fowler, pp. 146–47.
138 Letter, 4 January 1865, *ibid*., p. 161.
139 C. S. Dessain & E. E. Kelly, *The Letters and Diaries of John Henry Newman*,
     Vol. XXI, Nelson, London, 1971, pp. 563–64. Shane Leslie states that
     Sibthorp was received by Fr. Butler. *Henry Edward Manning, His Life and*
     Labours, Burns, Oates & Washbourne, London, 1921, p. 146.
140 To Bloxam, Fowler, pp. 161–62.
141 J. Morris, *The Last Illness of His Eminence Cardinal Wiseman*, Burns,

Lambert, Oates, London, 1865, p. 28. 'The Cardinal had been removed from his bedroom to the front drawing-room, an altar was erected each morning in the room between the front and back drawing-rooms, and it was here that one morning Mr. Sibthorp said Mass.' Fowler, p. 167. Heneage, was also present, having been bought, because of illness, from Hammersmith convent of which he was chaplain.

142 'To a remonstrant Anglican clergyman', 2 July 1866, *ibid.*, p. 185.
143 Letter to Bloxam, 25 February 1865, *ibid.*, pp. 169–70.
144 *Ibid.*, p. 168. His nephew commented, 'I did not expect to see you return to Rome, but I always perceived that you were not satisfied with the Church of England.' *Ibid.*, p. 162. In May 1865, Sibthorp re-visited Lincoln to inaugurate a devotion called the *Way of the Cross. Ibid.*, p. 172.
145 Letter to Bloxam, 25 February 1865, *ibid.*, p. 170.
146 Bloxam, p. 241. In June, he attended the consecration of Manning as Archbishop of Westminster, whom he described as 'like Lazarus come out of the tomb in cope and mitre. . .' Fowler, p. 173.
147 Fowler, p. 181. Roskell had been consecrated Bishop of Nothingham in 1853.
148 Southerwood, p. 371.
149 Fowler, p. 181.
150 Southerwood, p. 371.
151 Kelsh, pp. 139, 140.
152 'To an unnamed correspondent,' 22 July 1877, Fowler, p. 328.
153 *Leicester Chronicle*, 5 September 1873.
154 Meeting on 21 March; newspaper cutting in M.C.A. 492; for a less sympathetic account of Sibthorp's role, see *Nottingham & Midland Counties Daily Express*, 22 March 1876.
155 Letter to Bloxam, 15 March 1878, Fowler, p. 342.
156 Letter to Bloxam, 29 April 1876, *ibid.*, p. 303.
157 In June 1866, Sir Henry Thompson spoke in Convocation against the use of vestments, quoting at length from Sibthorp's letter to him '. . . a Protestant community cannot consistently draw near, even in externals to another, against which she was formed to protest'. Rev. Sir H. Thompson, Bart., *Ritualism: A Plea for Surplice. The Substance of a Speech Delivered in the Lower House of Convocation, June 28, 1866*, R. Pelton, Tunbridge Wells, 1866, p. 10.
158 Letter to Bloxam, 29 April 1876, Fowler, p. 303.
159 *Leicester Chronicle*, 5 September 1873.
160 *The Angelus*, 1, 9, (I am grateful to Fr. Dolan, Archivist of the Nottingham Diocese, for this reference).
161 Letter 'to W.', 3 November 1870, Fowler, p. 215.
162 Letter to Mrs. Bodley, 23 July 1872, *ibid.*, p. 235
163 Telling Bloxam, 'I have retired in time.' 19 June 1875, *ibid.*, p. 283. Writing to Ambrose Phillipps on 25 February, Newman was, 'truly sorry that poor Mr. Sibthorp has got into trouble'. Fr. Dessain comments, 'A dispute had arisen between him and the administrator of the Cathedral, Canon James Griffin.' C. S. Dessain & T. Gornall, *The Letters and Diaries of John Henry Newman, Vol. XXVII*, Clarendon Press, Oxford 1975, p. 234 n.2.
164 To 'Mr. C.', 6 September 1875, Fowler pp. 286–87.

165 Letter to Bloxam, 19 April 1875, *ibid.*, p. 281.

166 Letter to Bloxam, 9 April 1870, *ibid.*, p. 205.

167   Letter to Fowler, 13 June 1878, *ibid.*, p. 344.

168 Letter to Bloxam, 18 October 1875, *ibid.*, p. 290 (Romans 2: 18).

169 Letter 'to a Lincoln friend', August 1878, *ibid.*, p. 349.

170 Letter to Bloxam, 18 October 1875, *ibid.*, p. 290.

171 4 October 1879, *ibid.*, p. 177 n.1.

172 *Daily Bread*, No. 149, p. 300.

173 *Ibid.*, No. 60, p. 125. He told Bloxam that he refused to 'put His Blessed Mother in His place . . . My union with Him, if I have any union, is too close and intimate to make me question how my petition reaches her.' 19 June 1875, Fowler, p. 284.

174 On hearing of Quilter's death in 1871, Sibthorp commented: 'He has entered into *rest.*' *Ibid.* p. 223.

175 *Daily Bread*, No. 260, p. 529.

176 Letter 'to E.', 10 July 1876, Fowler p. 307.

177 *Ibid.*, p. 164.

178 *Daily Bread*, No. 324, p. 659.

179 *Ibid.*, No. 110, p. 221.

180 3 August 1878, Fowler, p. 348.

181 Letter to Maurice, 14 April 1877, *ibid.*, p. 334.

182 26 July 1878, *ibid.*, pp. 346–47.

183 *Ibid.*, p. 357; Orlando Forester's letter to the *Nottingham Guardian*, 13 January 1879.

184 Letter 'to Isle of Wight friend', 7 March 1879, Fowler, p. 361.

185 *Ibid.*, p. 365.

186 Letter to Fowler, 24 March 1879, *ibid.*, p. 364.

187 Letter to Fowler, 25 March 1879, *ibid.*, p. 364.

188 *Ibid.*, p. 365.

189 *Ibid.*, p. 369.

190 Diary entry, 25 April 1880; H. C. G. Matthew, *Letters and Diaries of W. E. Gladstone, Vol. IX, January 1875 – December 1880*, Clarendon Press, Oxford, 1986 p. 508.

191 11 May 1880, M.C.A. Ms. 492. The publishers wished to include extracts of this letter in the second edition of the biography, but Gladstone declined: '. . . it is rather too personal for the public eye: and at this moment, when there is a certain amount of jealousy about Lord Ripon's appointment, it would be grossly perverted by certain persons'. Letter to Fowler, 24 May 1880, Add. Ms. 44544, fols. 22–23.

192 R. W. Church, *Temper: An Address Delivered to the Junior Clergy Society in the Crypt of St. Paul's, October 12, 1880*, S.P.C.K., London 1880, p. 8.

193 'there always appears something defective in his Catholicism'. *Tablet*, 8 May 1880 (Ms. 492).

194 'the disillusion was – shall we not say it? – complete. That which he had sought, and fancied he had found, in Rome, fails him at the last.' Fowler, p. 362.

195 12 April 1881, C. S. Dessain & T. Gornall, *The Letters and Diaries of John Henry Newman, Vol. XXIX*, Clarendon Press, Oxford, 1976, p. 363.

196 16 April 1881, M.C.A. Ms. 492.

197 Fowler, p. 355.
198 Letter 'to C. O.', 19 December 1877, *ibid.*, p. 330.
199 Letter 'to E.', 10 July 1876, *ibid.*, p. 307.
200 'To another under bereavement,' 6 July 1877, *ibid.*, p. 326.
201 Scott wrote his memoirs in 1895, *Things That Were*, p. 43.

BIBLIOGRAPHY

This bibliography covers manuscript sources and lists the published works of Richard Sibthorp. Bibliographical details of other works cited are given in the chapter endnotes.

Manuscript Sources Consulted

Lincoln Archives, St. Rumbold Street, Lincoln

Sibthorp Family Papers

Documents from Dower House, Canwick deposited by Mrs Dudley Pelham in February 1961:
- Sib. 1, household and estate papers and maps
- Sib. 2, family papers, pedigrees, wills and correspondence

In June 1966, Sir Francis Hill on behalf of Mrs Dudley Pelham made a second deposit:
- 2 Sib./1, title deeds
- 2 Sib./2, wills and settlements
- 2 Sib./3, estate papers
- 2 Sib./4, correspondence, 1774–1822
- 2 Sib./5, miscellaneous
- 2 Sib./6, printed documents

Material purchased by Lincoln Archives Office in 1970:
- 3 Sib./1, correspondence, family and estate, 1782–1871
- 3 Sib./2, miscellaneous personal, property, 1692–1824
- 3 Sib./3, vouchers, 1815–57

Subsequent miscellaneous donations: (4 Sib.)

Papers relating to Sibthorp estates deposited by Messrs Burton & Co. (previously Burton Scorer): (B.S.)

Other Collections
- Massingberd family papers: (Mass.)
- Correspondence of Sir Charles Anderson: (And.)
- Correspondence of Bishop Kaye: (Cor./B.)
- Emeris family papers (Em.)

- The diary of John Rashdall (Misc. Don. 125.)
- Episcopal Acts Book
- Annual Archivist's Reports

Magdalen College, Oxford

In connection with his work on the *Magdalen College Register*, J. R. Bloxam assembled a considerable archive. Material relating to Richard Sibthorp consists of the following:

Ms. 465: 'The Sibthorp Correspondence' (letters addressed to Routh and Bloxam.)

Ms. 492: 'The Reverend Richard Waldo Sibthorp' (miscellaneous correspondence, printed matter and notes.)

The following include references to Sibthorp:

Ms. 459: 'Phillipps' (the letters of Ambrose Phillipps de Lisle.)

Ms. 335: 'Reunion.'

Ms. 528, 'Pugin Correspondence.'

Pusey House, Oxford

In March 1911, the widow of the Rev. Edward Hill, who in 1841 was one of Sibthorp's choir-boys at Ryde presented to R. W. Ollard a collection of Sibthorp letters:

OLL II: Letters from Sibthorp to W. Darwin Fox.

OLL XIX: Letters from Sibthorp to J. R. Bloxam.

Keble College, Oxford

Papers of the Rev. J. M. Gresley.

Bodleian Library, Oxford

Wilberforce papers: (Mss. Wilberforce c, d, e.)

Bloxam's correspondence with Gen. Rigaud (Ms. Add. B113–118.)

Diary of Rev. John Hill (Mss. St Edmund Hall 66–67).

Bickersteth correspondence (Ms. Eng. C. 6398).

British Library

Gladstone papers: Add. Ms. 44352, 44360, 44361.

Cornwall Record Office, County Hall, Truro

Hawkins family archive.

Hunt Institute for Botanical Documentation, Carnegie Mellon University, Pittsburgh, PA

Letters from Richard Sibthorp to Mr and Mrs Hawkins of Bignor

Archives of the Religious Societies

Birmingham University: archive of the Church Missionary Society.

Cambridge University: archive of the British and Foreign Bible Society.

School of Oriental & African Studies, London University: archive of the Religious Tract Society.

Lambeth Palace Library

Williams papers, deposit 3.
Letters of Bishop Wordsworth, Ms. 2146.
Golightly papers, Ms. 1804.

John Rylands Library, Deansgate, Manchester

Methodist archive.
Christian Brethren archive.

Ushaw College, Durham

Newsham correspondence.
Wiseman papers.

Birmingham Diocesan Archives, St Chad's Queensway, Birmingham

Correspondence of Bishop Walsh.
Oscott College Diary.

Other Archives

The Oratory, Edgbaston, Birmingham (Newman papers.)
Archive of the Trinitarian Bible Society, Kingston Road, London SW19.
Devon Record Office, Castle Street, Exeter (diary of Lord Fortescue.)
Norfolk Record Office, Martineau Lane, Norwich (Bishop Milner's journal, transcribed by F. C. Husenbeth.)
Passionist Archives of St. Joseph's Province, Retreat of the Immaculate Heart of Mary, Minsteracres, Co. Durham (Spencer papers.)
Isle of Wight Records Office, Newport, Isle of Wight (Oglander Papers, Poll books.)
Nottingham Diocesan Archives, Willson House, Derby Street, Nottingham.
Mercers' Company Archive, Mercers Hall, Ironmonger Lane, London EC2
Natwest Group Archives, Lothbury, London EC2 (papers of Abel Smith.)
Hull University Archives (papers of J. Scott, vicar of St. Mary, Lowgate.)
Letter from Richard Sibthorp to Mr Norman, in possession of the author.

Cholmeley Family Papers

Family papers assembled by Guy Hargeaves Cholmeley (consulted by kind permission of Miss Virginia Cholmeley of St. Breward, Cornwall.)
Family papers held by Sir Fred Cholmeley, Bt., Easton, Lincolnshire (copies of letters kindly provided.)

Published Works of R. W. Sibthorp

A Sermon Preached at St. John's Church Hull, on Tuesday Evening May 19, 1818. At the Close of a Temporary Residence in that Town, Topping & Dawson, Hull, 1818.
An Address to the Inhabitants of Tattershall, in Lincolnshire, On Entering the Living of the Parish, Topping & Dawson, Hull, 1818.
A Second Address to the Inhabitants of Tattershall, in Lincolnshire, Upon the Commencement of the New Year, W. Brooke, Lincoln, 1819.
A Sermon Preached at St. John's Church Hull, on Tuesday Evening, June 26,

1821, For the Benefit of the Church of England Sunday School Association, Topping & Dawson, Hull, 1821.

Farewell Sermon Preached in the Parish Church of Tattershall, Lincolnshire, on Sunday, May 15, 1825, L. B. Seeley & Son, London, 1825.

The Substance of a Sermon Preached at St. John's Chapel, Bedford-Row, London on the Sunday following the interment of Joseph Butterworth Esq. Late M.P. for Dover, printed for private circulation, n.d. (1826).

Sermon Preached at the Parish Church of St. Clement Danes, Strand, on Friday May 11, 1827 at the 33rd General Meeting of the London Missionary Society, Frederick Westley & A. H. Davies, London, 1827.

The Character and Tokens of the True Catholic Church, A Discourse Delivered at Tavistock Chapel, Drury Lane on Tuesday, Nov. 20, 1827, L. B. Seeley & Sons, London, 1829 (first edition, 1827).

The Character of the Papacy; As Predicted by St. Paul in 2 Thess. II, 4. Considered in a Discourse Preached at St John's Chapel Bedford Row, on Monday February 11, 1828 for the Benefit of the Auxiliary Reformation Society for St. Giles and the Neighbouring Districts, James Nisbet, London, 1828

Some Reflections on the Injurious Consequences of Withholding the Scriptures from the People. Being the Substance of a Discourse Preached at St Thomas's Church, Bristol, for the Benefit of the Ladies' Hibernian Female School Society, L. B. Seeley & Son, London, 1828.

A Sermon Preached before the Prayer Book and Homily Society at Christ Church Newgate Street on Wednesday May 7, 1828, printed for the Society by Ellerton & Henderson, London, 1828.

A Sermon Preached at St Paul's Church, Covent Garden on Tuesday Evening May 13th, 1828 before the Newfoundland School Society, Gunnell & Shearman, London, 1828.

Psalms and Hymns Selected and Adapted for Public Worship, P. T. Hellyer, Ryde, 1831.

Pulpit Recollections: Being Notes of Lectures on the Book of Jonah. Delivered at St James's Episcopal Chapel, Ryde, R. B. Seeley & W. Burnside, London, 1834.

The Book of Genesis, With Brief Explanatory and Practical Observations and Copious Marginal References, R. B. Seeley & W. Burnside, London, 1835.

The Family Liturgy, being a Course of Morning and Evening Prayers for a Family arranged and compiled on the Plan of a Liturgy, R. B. Seeley & W. Burnside, London, 1836.

The Claims of the Catholic Church. A Sermon Preached in the Chapel of St. Mary Magdalen College before the University of Oxford, on the Feast of St. Mark the Evangelist, A.D MDCCCXLI, J. H. Parker, Oxford, 1841.

The Commemoration of Founders and Benefactors. A Sermon Preached before the University of Oxford in the Chapel of St. Mary Magdalen College, on the Feast of the Nativity of St. John the Baptist, A.D MDCCCXLI, J. H. Parker, Oxford, 1841.

Some answer to the Enquiry; 'Why Are You Become a Catholic?' In a Letter to a Friend, Charles Dolman, London, 1842.

A Further Answer to the Enquiry; 'Why Have you Become a Catholic?' In a Second Letter to a Friend. Containing a Notice of the Strictures of the Rev. Messrs. Palmer and Dodsworth upon a Former Letter, Charles Dolman, London, 1842.

Substance of a Sermon Preached in the Cathedral Church of St. Chad Birmingham, on the Morning of St. Patrick's Day 1842, Charles Dolman, London, 1842.

Substance of a Second Sermon Preached in the Cathedral Church of St. Chad Birmingham, on the Evening of St. Patrick's Day 1842, Charles Dolman, London, 1842.

Substance of a Sermon Delivered at the Opening of St. Oswald's Catholic Church, Old Swan near Liverpool on Thursday August 4, 1842, Rockliff & Ellis, Liverpool, 1842.

The Office of the Holy Communion or the Celebration of the Blessed Sacrament of the Lord's Supper or Holy Eucharist anciently called the Mass; for all days throughout the Year, Hamilton & Bird, London, 1844.

A Summary of Christian Doctrine adapted for both Old and Young Christians by E. M., Robson, Levey & Franklin, London, 1845.

An Office of Family Devotion or a Catholic Domestic Liturgy. Consisting of Prayers for a Family for Morning and Evening. Selected from Various sources and arranged by E. M. a Presbyter of Christ's Holy Catholic Church, printed for private circulation, London, 1845.

The Dream that had a Great Deal of Truth in it. Or a Few Hints to Church-Goers, Edwards & Hughes, London, 1850 (first edition 1846.)

The Saviour's Estimation of the Writings of Moses Shewn in His Own use of them. A Sermon Preached at St Anne's Bedehouse Chapel, Lincoln on Sunday November 23, 1862, J. & F. H. Rivingtons, London, 1862.

A Catalogue of Porcelain & Pottery – Oriental, European and English. The Property of the Rev. R. Waldo Sibthorp of Nottingham, printed for private circulation, Nottingham, 1874.

Daily Bread: being a few Morning Meditations for the use of Catholic Christians, printed for private circulation, Nottingham, 1876.

Daily Bread: being Morning Meditations for the use of Catholic Christians, Bemrose & Sons, London, 1879.

INDEX

Aitken, Robert (1800–1873): high churchman and revivalist, incumbent of Pendeen, Cornwall (1847–73): 166, 168, 171, 230n.56, 231n.76

Allenby, Mrs of Kenwick House, Lincolnshire: 20, 24, 163, 178, 232n.107

Allies, Thomas William (1813–1903): author, clerical convert to Catholicism (1850): 186

Almondbury, West Yorkshire: 44, 202n.100

Anderson, Sir Charles (1804–1891): of Lea, Lincolnshire, landowner: 37, 200n.61

Antichrist: 14, 16, 62, 104, 135, 145, 146, 163, 170–71, 179 (see *Papacy*)

Arnold, Thomas (1795–1842): head master of Rugby School (1828–42): 164, 194n.89

Bagshawe, Edward Gilpin (1829–1915): R.C. bishop of Nottingham (1874–1901): ix, 176, 184, 185

Beaumont, Guillaume (d. 1822): émigré R.C. priest at Lincoln (1793–1818): 4–5, 10, 12, 13, 27, 28, 192n.61

Benson, Joseph (1748–1821): Wesleyan minister and bible commentator: 18

Beste, Henry Digby: (1768–1836): author, clerical convert to Catholicism (1798): 4, 10, 12, 13

Biber, George Edward (1801–74): controversialist, vicar of Roehampton (1842–72): 109, 112, 114

Bickersteth, Edward (1786–1850) clergyman, secretary of Church Missionary Society (1816–30): 7, 30, 31, 32, 35, 39, 41, 44, 45, 46, 47, 48, 76, 87, 202n.95, 206n.52, 207n.75;

advocate of pre-millennialism: 145–46, 154, 163, 227n.166

Biddulph, Zachary Henry (1792–1842): vicar of Shoreham (1828) and Backwell (1831) in Somerset: 11, 17, 193n.76

Bignor Park, West Sussex: residence of the Hawkins family: 55, 138, 189n.11

Bisse, Henry (1792–1859): Evangelical clergyman: 69, 70, 210n.124

Blakeney, Richard Paul (1820–84): clergyman, anti-Catholic polemicist: 109, 221n.15

Bloxam, John Rouse (1807–1891): vicar of Upper Beeding, Sussex (1862–1891): Sibthorp's biographer 20, 76, 186, 193n.76, 197n.154, 216n.111, 218n.142; assists in re-ordering of St. James's 90, 91, 92, 216n.110, n.114; Sibthorp's conversion (1841) 101–3, 106, 131, 135, 220n.185; Sibthorp's unsettlement and retraction (1843) 136–37, 140–44, 147, 153, 157, 227n.181; friendship with Sibthorp (1843–79): 155–56, 159, 161–69, 172–76, 179–81, 185.

Blumhardt Christian Gottlieb (1779–1838): director of Basle Missionary Institute: 65

Bodley, Mrs: 30, 185, 198n.20, 211n.157

Boston: new chapel-of-ease: 39, 40, 41, 201n.88

Brackenbury, Robert Carr (1752–1818): Methodist lay leader: 20, 22, 196n.134

Brackenbury, Mrs Sarah (d.1847): second wife of Robert Carr Brackenbury: 20, 196n.136

Brandram, Andrew (1791–1850): Bible Society Anglican Secretary (1811–50): 58